RHODESIA

Mapungubwe • Messina •

Lake Fundudzi •

KRUGER

Louis Trichardt •

NATIONAL

N1

Duiwelskloof •

PARK

Pietersburg •

Magoebaskloof •

Potgietersrus •

Phalaborwa •

• Makapansgat

MOÇAMBIQUE

Nylstroom •

• Naboomspruit

Blyde
River Canyon •

rmbaths

BUSHVELD

Pilgrim's Rest •

LOWVELD

N1

Lydenburg •

Skukuza •

• Nelspruit

PRETORIA •

HIGHVELD

N4

orp
rt •

JOHANNESBURG •

Barberton •

• Germiston

N1

• Heidelberg

SWAZILAND

N3

niging

• Standerton

Piet Retief •

S

Volksrust •

Pongola

NATAL

Transvaal

| 0 | 80 | 160 kms |
| 0 | 50 | 100 miles |

TRANSVAAL

Pongola

Ndumu
Game Reserve

Kosi Bay

Lake Sibayi

O.F.S

Newcastle

Bloodriver

Mkuze

Sordwana Bay
National Park

Mkuze
Game Reserve

Dundee

Isandhlwana

Rorke's Drift

Hluhluwe
Game Reserve

ZULULAND

Hluhluwe

Mont-aux-
Sources

Ladysmith

Umfolozi
Game
Reserve

St.Lucia

Royal
Natal Park

Tugela

D R A K E N S B E R G

N3

Estcourt

Eshowe

Richards Bay

Mtunzini

Giant's
Castle Park

Mooi River

LESOTHO

Orange

Valley of a
Thousand
Hills

Stanger

N O R T H   C O A S T

Pietermaritzburg

N3

Caledon

Ixopo

DURBAN

N2

S O U T H   C O A S T   R E S O R T S

Port Shepstone

Margate

TRANSKEI

Umtata

Port St.John's

Kei

INDIAN OCEAN

Natal

| 0 | 80 | 160kms |
| 0 | 50 | 100miles |

THE COMPANION GUIDE TO
South Africa

THE COMPANION GUIDES

GENERAL EDITOR: VINCENT CRONIN

*It is the aim of these Guides to provide a Companion
in the person of the author, who knows intimately
the places and people of whom he writes, and is able to
communicate this knowledge and affection to his readers.
It is hoped that the text and pictures will aid them
in their preparations and in their travels, and will
help them to remember on their return.*

SOUTHERN GREECE · THE GREEK ISLANDS
THE SOUTH OF FRANCE · SOUTH-WEST FRANCE
PARIS · ROME · VENICE · FLORENCE · LONDON
UMBRIA · SOUTHERN ITALY
TUSCANY · THE SOUTH OF SPAIN
MADRID AND CENTRAL SPAIN · JUGOSLAVIA
IRELAND · KENT AND SUSSEX
EAST ANGLIA · NORTH WALES · SOUTH WALES · BURGUNDY
DEVON AND CORNWALL · NORTHUMBRIA

In preparation
MAINLAND GREECE
THE ÎLE DE FRANCE · NORMANDY
EDINBURGH AND THE BORDER COUNTRY
THE WELSH MARCHES · TURKEY
THE LOIRE VALLEY

THE COMPANION GUIDE TO

SOUTH AFRICA

EVE PALMER
AND GEOFFREY JENKINS

COLLINS
LONDON—JOHANNESBURG

1978

William Collins Sons & Co Ltd
London · Glasgow · Sydney · Auckland
Toronto · Johannesburg

First published 1978
© Eve Palmer and Geoffrey Jenkins 1978
ISBN 0 00 211189 6

Printed by Cape & Transvaal Printers (Pty) Ltd, Cape Town

Contents

❧

5

Illustrations

❧

7

All photographs, except where otherwise indicated, by the authors.

Maps

❧

All measurements used are metric, except those used in an historical context.

Foreword

❧

This is a record of some of the joys and fascinations we have had as we have travelled through South Africa, sometimes by air or rail, sometimes on foot, occasionally on horseback, mostly by motor-car.

It is a personal record. We have written of those things that have entertained us or sometimes touched us—indeed, we found so many of these that in the end it was necessary to omit many even of them.

We know most of the main roads in South Africa and many of the byways. Everything we saw on them others can see as easily. Except for the short trip between Ndumu and Kosi Bay—when a four-wheel drive was necessary—we used an ordinary saloon motor-car, a Peugeot 404.

Many people stick to tarred roads, but sand and gravel have their own pleasures and these are sometimes the keenest of all. As for petrol prices and restrictions, we owe them a debt. They have polished our minds and appetites—if we can make only one journey instead of the three or four we yearn for, then we savour it down to the last delicious morsel: even a puncture among dubbeltjies and red sand becomes an Homeric adventure.

We owe a debt to many people, among others to Dr Edna Plumstead, and Dr James Kitching of the Bernard Price Institute for Palaeontological Research (it is not many people one can thank from the heart for algae and bones!); to Dr Anna Smith, Miss A Kennedy and all the staff of the Africana Museum and Library in Johannesburg for friendly, enthusiastic, highly efficient help; to our friends, Dr Inez Verdoorn and Miss Mary Gunn, and Dr R. A. Dyer and Dr L. E. W. Codd of the Botanical Research Institute—who always help in more ways than they imagine—to Dr 'Bob' Brain of the New Transvaal Museum; to Petrie Muller who rescued Lydenburg's historic gold scale; to A. R. Willcox; to Ian and Jean Garland of Zululand, and Jobe Mafuleka, with the three of whom we have shared many adventures; to Gwen and Len Skinner of Port Elizabeth; to Dr R. F. Lawrence and Dr Rex Jubb of Port Alfred; to Maurice and Sita Palmer; to David Rawdon and his staff, who introduced us to a new world of comforts and delights; to Phyl Hands and her wines; to Robbie Blake and his wife Yvonne who showed us how noble South African wines and sherries can be—the list could continue indefinitely.

Then there are all the nameless ones—the government officials, the parks rangers, the casual acquaintances who have helped with information and facts, friends, farmers, shop assistants, the staffs of publicity bureaux, librarians, railway officials. For photographs we thank the Africana Museum, SATOUR, the Communications Bureau, the Botanical Research Institute, and the Cape Archives.

We have, of course, drawn on many books for background information, and these are listed in the bibliography. Some deserve special mention, such as J. J. Oberholster's *The Historical Monuments of South Africa*, an immense tome of research and fact. For charm we rate Alys Fane Trotter's works on the Cape she knew so well; and for presenting history in a new light the *Autobiography of Sir Harry Smith*, that gay braggart who took over to a large extent our southern travels and who became our hero.

Lastly, our particular gratitude goes to Dr Anna Smith, not only for help during the writing of the book and her lively interest throughout, but for reading the manuscript and for many helpful suggestions.

CHAPTER ONE

Johannesburg

Gold to lay by and gold to lend,
Gold to give and gold to spend.

That was the Johannesburg of 1887—only months after the Witwatersrand gold-fields had been declared—as seen by *The Star* newspaper, which had hurriedly moved from its offices in the Eastern Cape to
share the new glittering wealth. It is still Johannesburg as seen by half
the world.

In a sense it is right. Johannesburg *is* gold. Igoli, it is called, the
City of Gold, names with a ring, and their touch of romance is
welcome for, although gold itself has immense glamour, Igoli as such
is not a romantic city. Yet it is THE city of South Africa, literally and
figuratively built on the gold beneath one's feet.

Before the age of air travel, Cape Town was the traditional port of
entry to South Africa. But it is a long time now since travellers coming
to South Africa were welcomed by Table Mountain in the dawn. They
would stand on the ship's deck gazing at it, at its foot Cape Town with
its ripeness and charm, a scene of immemorial beauty.

Today it is a different scene. Johannesburg has supplanted Cape
Town.

The traveller from abroad usually comes by air to Jan Smuts Airport
near the city and mostly from the north. The first hint of South Africa,
if one flies low enough to see it, is the thin line below of light and dark
cutting through the bush of Africa, the Limpopo River with its banks
lined with trees, South Africa's northern boundary. It is no Cape
scene, no beauty, but 'The Limpopo!' returning travellers exclaim on a
note of pleasure, 'there'll be the mine dumps soon—we're home'. And
indeed hardly have they left the river behind before there is the Igoli
world below them.

There it is, immense and spreading, ochre, green and white, with the
Witwatersrand—the famous Rocky Ridge of White Waters—running
through it from east to west in a half-moon 100 kilometres long, at its
heart Johannesburg. The Rand, as every South African calls it, is part

13

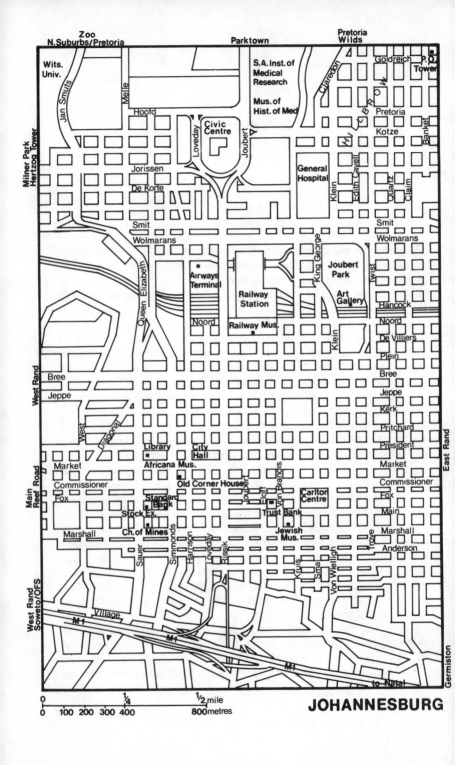

JOHANNESBURG

of the richest gold-fields ever known, and coming in from height above it, it is gold that welcomes the traveller today—the first suggestions of it—the ochre and white hills of sand flushed with green, the man-made hills that everyone knows as mine dumps and are the residue of the thousands of billions of tons of rock crushed for gold and then discarded. These great flat-topped pyramids on the city's outskirts, sometimes in the city itself, even more than the skyscraper skyline, spell Johannesburg. Less beautiful than Table Mountain 1 450 kilometres to the south, they are as evocative: only the story they tell is different.

Johannesburg is as alien to Cape Town as a city can be. Big business brings brashness and rush, sharpness, vitality and sparkle. Whether it is the altitude—it stands on a high bare plateau 1 750 metres (nearly 6 000 feet) above the sea—the bite in the air, or the traces of uranium in the water as some claim, Johannesburg has, not Cape Town's tranquillity, but fizz. No-one comes here to rest or drink the wine of its hinterland; they come to make and spend money, to gamble, shop, live it up, or sometimes in the winter just to have the fun of breathing champagne air.

Whatever people do here, it is not far removed from gold. Nearly two million live in Johannesburg. They live off gold or the life it generates—more than 400 000 work on the mines themselves. They dig gold, refine it, shape it, eat it, sleep it, buy and sell it; every business is linked, however indirectly, with it. It draws African labour from every corner, goldsmiths, film stars, adventurers, tourists, country cousins come to gape, crooks, the Salvation Army: the very pigeons bobbing and cooing in the Library Gardens might be termed golden birds.

It has built such things as the University of the Witwatersrand, the South African Institute for Medical Research, of international repute, and the sprawling African townships of Soweto to the south-west. Above all, it has built Johannesburg's skyline, which to the man in the street is Johannesburg, the tall lean silhouettes of the skyscrapers housing the banks, the mining houses and other giant concerns that have been built in the past 40 years on the soaring price of gold.

This city centre is the heart of Johannesburg. To the north lie the wealthy northern suburbs with Pretoria beyond; east, west and south other suburbs, less plush and sometimes incredibly shoddy that often thread in and out of the mine dumps, dreary, crowded, raffish and lively, adding their own particular tones to Southern Africa's biggest city.

It is a pleasure we sometimes give ourselves to rise up in a lift to the top of one of Johannesburg's high buildings, and see the city spread below, the wide Igoli world, with the mine dumps and mine works following the gold-bearing reef, east towards Springs, west towards Randfontein, southwards, to see how the gold mines have here contained the city, forcing it upwards to the sky; the suburbs like a huge sea, and central Johannesburg itself, surprisingly small and compact, in its wide landscape.

It is this small area of tall buildings and crowded streets that fascinates people most. Not only is it the most modern but paradoxically it is the oldest in Johannesburg. When the first public gold diggings were thrown open on portions of nine bare upland farms on the Witwatersrand in late 1886 (parts of them can be seen from the top of the Hillbrow Tower) the township to serve them was established in their centre on a piece of land called Randjeslaagte, the Dale of Little Ridges. It was an ill-shaped triangular remnant—*uitvalgrond*—left over which had not been included in the farms Doornfontein, Braamfontein and Turffontein when they were surveyed but was used only for casual grazing. The ugly duckling was state land and here the township, christened Johannesburg, was laid out: it was the heart of the mining area then and this is the skyscraper heart of the city of today.

Johannesburg now covers just over 500 square kilometres (about 200 square miles). The first village was the size of a postage stamp. It was bounded on the north by Bree Street, on the south by Commissioner Street, on the east by End Street, and by West Street on the west: the shorter side of it could be walked in a few minutes. Soon it was spreading to Fordsburg in the south-west, to Turffontein in the south where some of the richest mines developed, to Jeppestown in the east, to Doornfontein—Thorn Fountain—which had originally been bought for a trek chain and a span of oxen and which became Johannesburg's first fashionable area, to the farm Braamfontein in the north on which Parktown and other famous suburbs arose.

Looking down, one can see them all, and as well the suburbs which have now rolled beyond them. It is an exciting view, in its way phenomenal. The city below is unlike any other, not only because it is built on gold but because it sprang into life with a speed unknown anywhere else in the world. Whereas in 1886 'the soil did not produce sufficient of any life-giving thing to keep a respectable family of butterflies on the wing', a year later there was a city in the making with shops, bars, banks, hotels, churches, schools, social clubs, and a full-sized traffic problem.

Many of the main thoroughfares from those days that brought

people and goods to the town are still important streets and roads. There is Jan Smuts Avenue, seen from a height as a ribbon to the north, that was the original coach route to Pretoria, the Main Reef Road from east to west that was the wagon road of the 1890s bringing supplies to the mines, and in the central area—not easy to pick out from a distance—Commissioner Street that was made in 1886 by wagons loaded with stones that travelled up and down on a straight line for a week.

To be fully aware of the narrowness of some of the central streets, boiling with life, one must descend to their level. The congestion, it is said, was the fault of Paul Kruger, President of the South African Republic. He wanted smaller blocks and more streets, and got them. Now and again there are kinks and bends where the neat gridiron pattern planned originally by the surveyor was thrown out to fit in extra blocks. There is surprisingly little of the old days left in the central area, so that what remains is of rather disproportionate interest; these relics include the famous little bends in some of the parallel streets such as Eloff and Von Brandis that intersect Bree Street near the railway station.

These are a miscalculation from pioneer days. Some say that the streets of the expanding village had started at the far ends progressing inwards and that when they should have met at Bree Street they did not match. Others claim that both metric and Cape measures were used and this caused the irregularities, or that the surveyor mistook a vital peg, or—exuberantly—that the theodolite was faulty because it had been hit by an assegai on its journey to the Rand. Whatever the reason, they are amusing and solid reminders of free-and-easy days.

Street names are a constant link with the past and a study of them tells the history—the brave, rackety, raffish, scintillating early history—of Johannesburg. There are Banket, Quartz, Claim and Nugget Streets—golden names—but the majority honour prominent men of the time. In the centre of the city in what was the little township, are De Villiers Street, called after the first surveyor, Jeppe Street after the Jeppe family who became a famous part of the city, Pritchard after an early surveyor, President after Paul Kruger, Eloff after Jan Eloff who became mining commissioner early on. Dr Anna Smith in her *Johannesburg Street Names* describes how De Villiers came into Eloff's tent one day, laid his plan on the table—an empty whisky box—and said, 'Jan, I have put your name on this map so that I will not get mixed up with the stands'; and this is how, casually and by the way, the city's famous shopping thoroughfare got its name. Von Brandis Street honoured the much loved Captain Carl von Brandis who dispensed justice over the new goldfields, and who, it was said, sometimes paid the fines that he had imposed! It was he who proclaimed the goldfields, standing on a whisky case in front of his tent.

No street names, strangely enough, honour the first discoverers of gold. Harrison Street was named, not after George Harrison who found the Main Reef, but after a member of the Diggers' Committee who helped to run the village, J. S. Harrison.

Further afield is Ferreirastown, named after Colonel Ignatius Ferreira, colourful leader of the early gold-diggers, Bezuidenhout Valley after F. J. Bezuidenhout who had owned the farm Doornfontein, and names commemorating men who, with drive, money and know-how, helped to build the Rand. Among them were some of the greatest money-spinners South Africa has known.

There are Beit and Barnato streets, called after the financier Alfred Beit—who came from a wealthy Jewish commercial family and was known for vision, charm and generosity—and Barney Barnato, the irrepressible little Jewish actor from the East End of London, who ended up a millionaire. Phillips Street probably was named after the London-born financier, Sir Lionel Phillips, and Robinson Street honours the mining magnate, J. B. Robinson, relentless, hard and shrewd, who panned his first Rand gold in his sun helmet and who always wore one (even in London rain). Rhodes Avenue was named after Cecil Rhodes, and Rudd Road after C. D. Rudd, his partner. Eckstein Street was called after the Eckstein family—Hermann Eckstein not only brought men of science and talent to the mines but founded the company called Rand Mines Ltd., which erected the famous Corner House. Joel Road, Berea, commemorates the Joel brothers, nephews of Barney Barnato (Solly, the best-known, once won the Derby), and Albu Street the German, George Albu, who once worked in a draper's shop in Cape Town, finally becoming Sir George, the great financier.

There are names that should be there but are not. There is, for instance, no Amanda Street. Amanda Aquenza was Johannesburg's first barmaid, a buxom beauty who arrived by coach, was carried shoulder high into the Central Hotel, stood on the billiard table in corsets and voluminous drawers edged with lace, was plied with iced champagne, and auctioned for £150. 'Champagne', wrote E. C. Trelawney Ansell in *I Followed Gold*, 'flowed like water, while everybody was laughing and enjoying the fun.'

The name, Johannesburg, 'John's Town', the most important of all, clearly honours a Johannes, probably both Johann Rissik and C. Johannes Joubert, who chose the site for the township.

18

Two open spaces are pleasant links with the past, Joubert Park near the station, which was laid out when Randjeslaagte was surveyed, and the gardens officially known as the Harry Hofmeyr but most often called the Library Gardens, in the central area in front of the Library building. The lawns and the walk here make the only real open space remaining of what was once the great Market Square, the rendezvous of ox-wagons, farmers, traders, and prospectors: the pigeons are the last of the livestock.

As for the buildings, the oldest existing one in the city is thought to be the neo-Gothic Anglican Church, St-Mary-the-Less built in 1889, but this is in Park Street, Jeppe, away from the city centre. There is very little left in the central part dating from Kruger times: in many areas there is not much even 50 years old. In the square in front of the Library, for instance, every building has arisen since the mid-1930s, with the exception of two, a little furniture shop and the low white **Barclays Bank** branch in Market Street opposite the City Hall, which is one of the oldest buildings in the central area, dating from the 1890s. (People still remember that in the 1930s there were wagons in the streets of Johannesburg: and that sitting on their stoeps of an evening they could hear the rattles on the Africans' ankles as they swarmed along the streets to a dance.)

Victory House in Commissioner Street still stands. It was designed in 1897 by the architect W. H. Stucke, who was responsible for many of the early central buildings. On the corner of Eloff and Pritchard streets there are three more historic buildings, the little old **Starkees** built in 1893 with Markham's towering above it, topped with its amusing 'bird-cage', and **Cuthbert's** topped with its wide-brimmed-hat-tower—nobody can say these early creations lack character.

The old building that is probably best known is the **Rissik Street Post Office** facing the City Hall. It was built in 1897 and is the last of the public buildings from Kruger times in the city centre. Its wide, gaudy and incredibly ugly front, like a red and pale pea-green chessboard topped with a clock tower, is beloved by Johannesburgers who have fought tooth and nail to preserve it. It has a curiously jumbled look (which gives it its personality) as if different people had had a go at it—and indeed they had. A Dutch architect, Sytze Wierda, designed it with three storeys in the 1890s, on top of which Lord Milner had another built, together with the out-of-proportion clock tower. There isn't anything else like it in the city: but all the same it is no king. The modern skyscraper is this.

A little while ago a Johannesburg newspaper invited citizens to describe what they thought characterized the city, setting it apart from others. A mythical Aunt Agatha from England would be spending two hours in Johannesburg—what would they show her?

Letters of all kinds flowed in, suggesting sights from the tribal dances held in the mine compounds on Sunday mornings—a tremendous spectacle—to Hillbrow, a 'youth's mecca', and a discotheque. The writers chose to show Aunt Agatha power station cooling towers, the jewel-like saris of the Indian women, crowded pavements, crippled beggars, fish shops, shoe cleaners, black and white faces in Eloff Street, gardens, museums, fountains. But it was the tall buildings that most felt spelt today's Johannesburg. Many plumped for the **Carlton Centre.** Fifty-two storeys high, this great office, shopping and amusement complex—the biggest in Africa—with its piazzas and pools, a huge hotel, 140 shops, an ice rink, an exhibition centre and seven restaurants, has arisen on Commissioner Street, the street that was made by ox-wagons 90 years ago. For size, space, colour and movement the Carlton complex is unique. The very ground it stands on is today worth a fortune. Ninety years ago, at Johannesburg's first auction, the first stand in this area was sold for 55 cents and another for ten!

A block away to the left in Fox Street is the **Trust Bank Centre,** the new tall black office block dominating the streets, its exterior of glass and aluminium specially designed to repel heat. It was a stone's throw from here, in this same narrow street lined with tall buildings, that 'the siege of Fox Street' took place recently, when the staff of the Israeli Consulate, which has an office here, were held hostage by a psychopathic gunman, and the building was besieged by armed police. Although in the end the gunman gave himself up quietly, it was the most dramatic happening in the city centre for many years, and there are bullet marks on the buildings still to tell the story. People in the Carlton Centre shopping and drinking tea heard the noise of battle.

The **Standard Bank Centre** lies further along the street on the Simmonds Street corner. Aunt Agatha, it was felt, had to see this: it stands for all the new, lean, soaring towers of finance, industry and commerce that now govern the central city. Its construction plan, too, in which blocks of floors are suspended from great beams around a concrete core, is an exciting one, very modern in concept.

Between this and the Stock Exchange (see also p. 29) in the next block lies Hollard Street, with its fountain, pools and freedom from traffic Johannesburg's most tranquil central street. It is great fun to turn in to the **Stock Exchange** and to watch from the public gallery the brokers trading on the floor—sedate when we saw it but many times in the past the scene of frenzy. 'Between the chains,' people once called the street outside the old Stock Exchange which stood between Commissioner and Market Streets before the modern building was put up. Excited crowds playing the market used to congregate in the street outside the trading hall—too small to accommodate them—in such numbers that the Mining Commissioner closed part of the street in front to vehicles. Posts and chains were put up to demarcate the area and within this business was carried on. 'Between the chains' emerged as a name the whole world knew, one that is still used for the modern Stock Exchange and Hollard Street outside it.

Soon there will be a new Stock Exchange Building, the first to be built outside the central area.

Northwards along Simmonds Street, just across the intersection with Commissioner Street on the right hand side, is a solid, greyish, today rather uninspiring building which was the city's first skyscraper. It is worth standing on the far side and looking at it and the corner site—modern Johannesburg was born here.

This was where the **Corner House** arose. The famous group of mines, some of the richest in the world, known unofficially by this name, was founded by Hermann Eckstein with Wernher, Beit and Co.: the name was founded on Eckstein's, which in German means 'corner-stone' (and of course the building *was* on a corner). A corrugated iron shack stood here originally, which gave place in 1889 to a three-storey building—all balconies and railings it looks from the old photographs—in which Jameson and his friends are said to have planned the Jameson Raid. It was on this site that the third Corner House was built in 1903, which, as Barclays Building, stands today. It had nine storeys and was Africa's tallest building.

At the beginning of the century when Johannesburgers watched its construction, nobody knew how long the gold on the Rand would last or whether the city had any future. But when those astonishing nine storeys arose, it was clear that Corner House—the Rand Mines Group—*knew* the future was secure. So, then, did everyone else, who in their turn began to plan and build. 'Then and then only,' wrote Leyds in his Johannesburg history, 'was there a real forward march'.

The famous mining group moved from the building in the 1960s—the present Corner House is at the junction of Commissioner and Sauer streets.

Two minutes' walk further on, Simmonds and Harrison Streets divide the **Library buildings** and its gardens (see also p. 29) from the back of the City Hall (see p. 22). It is pleasant to stop here to look at the flower sellers on the corner—the flowers and pigeons always please—and at the **Library** designed by John Perry in the Italian style. Leyds thought it the city's finest central building, and it can still hold its own among the taller buildings.

Round the corner down President and Market streets is the **City Hall,** its classic columns facing the Rissik Street Post Office. The architecture would have been familiar to Aunt Agatha but not the life on the steps in front, the Africans on a winter's morning sitting in rows in the sun, gossiping and eating bread and icecream.

Behind the Post Office is the **Oppenheimer Fountain,** given to Johannesburg by Mr Harry Oppenheimer in memory of his father, Sir Ernest Oppenheimer: the line of bronze impala leaping across a pool in a cloud of spray is the work of Hermann Wald. The fountain and the little green open space surrounding it are charming. Some chose to show her the **Railway Station,** lying to the right of Rissik Street beyond De Villiers Street, the Visitors' Bureau at the entrance. Said to be nearly as big as the Grand Central in New York, it is a vast modern complex, stream-lined and cold.

One might wonder why the little open space of **Joubert Park**, a block away from the station, appears so important to the people of Johannesburg—it has no outstanding beauties—but it is a tranquil spot with trees and shade near both flatland and city, and it has been a park and picnic spot since early days. Today it is much used by old and young, nursemaids, Africans sprawling in the sun, sparrows, pigeons, and artists—this is the site of 'Art under the Sun', the regular exhibition that has become part of Johannesburg, where anyone may show their work.

On the south side of Joubert Park is the **Art Gallery** designed by the famous English architect, Sir Edwin Lutyens, facing—clearly enough—the wrong way with its classical face in shadow. It has a fine collection of English, Dutch and French works, and of South African painters and sculptors—Anton van Wouw's bronzes are famous. Just within the entrance is a Mancini portrait of a handsome woman in a big pink hat, crowned with grey ostrich feathers, a charming opulent portrait from another age. It is of Florence Phillips, wife of Sir Lionel Phillips—together they had helped to build the Rand—presiding over the collection that she had brought together.

Personally we go to the gallery first of all to see her, then Rodin's bust of Miss Fairfax, and the new Picasso. It pleases us out of all proportion to look at Florence Phillips, this early South African who in childhood had played in the holes in worked-out diamond claims, and who had seen her mother, carelessly sifting a pinch of sand between her fingers, find the first diamond near Kimberley's Big Hole—now in her jewels and ostrich feathers epitomizing so much of South Africa's story.

People often wonder how the beautiful, serene Miss Fairfax, one of Rodin's own favourite works, ever came to Johannesburg. Rodin presented Miss Fairfax herself with the bust after the friend who had commissioned it told him to stop work on it, when it was only half completed. He was Ernest Becket, later Lord Grimthorpe, Miss Fairfax disclosed on her 99th birthday, and she had just refused to marry him! (Miss Fairfax is alive and active, 106 years of age, and lives in New York). Later she sold the bust to Sir Lionel Phillips, whose gift to the city it was.

Picasso's *Tête d'Arlequin* a few years ago caused more controversy than any other work of art in Johannesburg's history. 'A mature post-cubist Picasso picture,' claimed the gallery staff. 'A joke, a clown, an obscenity,' retorted a good slice of the public. Nevertheless, in the first three weeks of its exhibition, 11 000 of them went to see it.

North of the station and of Joubert Park the land rises to a ridge. Rissik Street climbs this, with the station to the right, passes over the Johann Rissik Bridge, with its flower pots and flower boxes, and past the **Wesbank Building** on the right, which was originally the Schlesinger Organisation headquarters and one of the skyscrapers most generally admired, to the new **Civic Centre,** one of the city's most modern buildings.

What every visitor to Johannesburg goes to see is the **Albert Hertzog** or **Brixton Tower** on Brixton Ridge (see also p. 32), a few kilometres west of the Civic Centre. This lean modern pinnacle 220 metres high was built in 1962 as a transmission tower for the South African Broadcasting Corporation V.H.F. transmissions. Well out of the skyscraper area, it looks particularly dramatic on its bare hill. The view from the observation turret ensures this, a panorama of the Igoli world, with central Johannesburg a little to the east.

Below, near the foot of the tower, is a cemetery, a gash of red soil in the built-up landscape. It is almost the last hint of the red dust that every prospector, every Johannesburger, once knew. It was a force, and sometimes a potent one, in their lives (they ate and drank it, they breathed it and wore it, and finally were buried in it). Today Johannesburgers need to take a lift—213 m a minute—into the sky to see it amongst the concrete jungle.

We drove one morning a few blocks east of the Civic Centre to the corner of De Korte and Hospital streets to look at the building that has been described as the most beautiful in Johannesburg. It is the **South African Institute for Medical Research,** designed by the famous

23

architect Sir Herbert Baker, who also designed the Union Buildings in Pretoria: its domed tower, colonnades, courtyards and wings are reminiscent of the Pretoria Buildings. It has had a history of achievement. Designed originally to investigate the main diseases of the gold mines—silicosis, pneumonia and meningitis—its work now covers a huge field. What most men and women remember best are the Salk-type vaccine against polio and the oral vaccine developed here by a former director, Professor James Gear, in 1961. He became a national hero, and the splendid white-domed building a symbol of brilliant selfless work—work that has been described as South Africa's 'best and proudest export product'.

The little African herbalist's store in the grounds is built as an Ndebele house, and the cures are, not of science, but of Africa. It has a tradition older than the Institute's!

The Institute and the hospital next to it are on the edge of Hillbrow lying slightly to the north-east. This, no longer in the city centre but easily reached from it, is the most densely populated area in Africa and Johannesburg's most cosmopolitan suburb. It provides the site of the **Hillbrow Tower.** This, officially the J. G. Strijdom Tower, a Post Office tower used for high frequency radio-telephone communication, is taller than the Hertzog Tower: at 269 metres it is as high as an 88-storey building, making it the tallest in Africa. It is also newer than the Hertzog Tower, and, with the teeming streets about it and its fine revolving restaurant at the top, a good deal more sophisticated.

From the observation deck is another panoramic view, this time the central city spread out in greater detail than from the Brixton Ridge. There are diagrams and a coin-in-the-slot commentary to help identify the buildings below, and it is possible from here to pick out most of Johannesburg's landmarks. From this level it is an astonishing view: in the restaurant above, with the world apparently revolving about one, presenting a new moon landscape minute by minute, it is magic too.

We would choose to take a visitor to **Hillbrow** for a special reason—to taste traditional South African food in one of the few restaurants in the city which serve it. It is the Gramadoelas Restaurant, 44 Goldreich Street, a few steps from the entrance to the Hillbrow Tower. On a winter's day an old wood and iron stove, with a bright fire burning and black kettle upon it, stands in the entrance—the sight of it reduces some people to nostalgic tears. The restaurant is owned by Eduan Naude, who formerly helped to run The Casserole in Chelsea, London. It is a smallish, friendly, bright place with rough-plastered white walls, a yellow-wood cupboard, tables with red and black cloths, comfortable seats, and pleasant service. The bean soup, a traditional soup, is especially good; so is the Malay *denningvleis*, a fricassée of lamb spiced with nutmeg, mace and cloves. The *bobotie*, flavoured with almonds and lemon leaves, is delectable: everybody knows this traditional mincemeat dish and feels able to pronounce upon it.

West of Hillbrow Tower, well beyond the South African Institute for Medical Research, is the University of the Witwatersrand (see p. 38), and adjoining it the Milner Park Showgrounds, where the Rand Easter Show—the biggest agricultural and industrial show in Africa— is held every year in the two weeks near Easter. People also wished to show Aunt Agatha the northern suburbs which stretch beyond, with their lovely homes and gardens. Some of these homes are among the finest historic buildings in Johannesburg with an air and a verve that belong to the expansive, monied, adventurous days of the early magnates, who built many of them. Some of these have disappeared, others have been taken over by institutions, while a few are still privately owned.

Driving around the Parktown streets it is still possible to see old walled houses with the marks of age, with outbuildings that once were coach houses, perhaps with a loft above. When the gold magnates moved here from Doornfontein, many of them built homes on the Parktown Ridge, with a view northwards to the Magaliesberg as colossal as the times, and some of these still stand.

The first great house to be built, alas, does not. It was Hohenheim— Home on a Height—built by Sir Lionel and Lady Phillips in 1892 and 1893 on the ridge where Victoria Avenue and Jubilee Road meet, a long luxurious house in which the Phillips entertained the world, and in which later Sir Percy Fitzpatrick wrote South Africa's most famous animal story, *Jock of the Bushveld*. (A visitor listening to him of an evening telling Jock stories to his children in the nursery had per- suaded him to write them down—the visitor was Rudyard Kipling.) This home of great names, talk, plots, parties and champagne later became the Otto Beit Convalescent Home, and as such was well known in the city. It stood until recently when—as Johannesburgers slept—it was quietly demolished. After it had gone, they mourned it.

Another great house still stands not far from the site of Hohenheim. Driving along Oxford Road towards the city, a big house on the right hand side on top of the hill dominates Parktown Ridge. It is built of apricot-coloured stone and appears immense from the road below as it faces northwards to the Magaliesberg. **Northwards** it is called. This was where John Dale Lace and his wife, the beautiful queen of Johan- nesburg society, built their home at the beginning of the century.

Although much of the house was burnt down, a part remained to be incorporated in that built by Sir George Albu on the same site: it is thus linked with two of the famous names in early Johannesburg.

The Dale Laces were the city's most exotic couple. Dale Lace, who had made money in mining, was reputed to be 'the most handsome member of the Rand Club, and the best dressed' (in jail in Pretoria in the 1890s with the members of the Reform Committee, following the Jameson Raid, he carefully dressed in his brown suit, pink shirt and straw hat, while others walked round in pyjamas). The elegance, beauty and dash of his wife and her unconventional ways were even more famous. Joy Collier in her book, *The Purple and the Gold*, recalls her bath—the most original in Johannesburg—which, when a button was pressed, sped from the bathroom into the bedroom, and how one day her husband, when boasting of the bath to his friends, pressed the button and summoned the bath, with Mrs Dale Lace in it! Johannesburg knew her, driving her own team of spanking horses about the streets to the sound of a postilion's horn, sweeping about the veld with her pack of dogs, or superbly gowned, acting the part of hostess. There were rumours that in England she was King Edward VII's 'friend'.

All this prompted Denis Godfrey, writing about Northwards, to lament that whereas in England the summer home of Lily Langtrey, close friend of Edward VII, is now officially preserved, South Africa has no such sense of the niceties. Who has preserved Northwards? In a sense the Transvaal has. The building is now used by the Provincial Education Department and provides a most romantic setting for an official body.

When we saw its banquet room, with the marble fireplace, minstrels' gallery, high ceiling with its moulded ring of fruit and leaves, great gilded mirror and lamps, we thought it the most elegant room in Johannesburg. It is still, happily, used by the Provincial Education staff on special occasions, and they prize it.

Two other great houses in the neighbourhood are now institutions. **Pallinghurst,** home of R. S. Schumacher of Corner House fame, is the Hope Home, and **North Lodge,** built in 1905 by the brother of J. B. Taylor (a big name in the early days of gold) at the junction of Oxford Road and Victoria Avenue, is now a university residence.

Two of the greatest houses, fortunately easily seen and admired from the street, are still privately owned. One is **Stone House** in Rockridge Road a little beyond Northwards, a mellow old home with splendid stone- and woodwork, and open courtyard to the south, and to the north the view to the Magaliesberg that the magnates so loved.

This was the house that Sir Herbert Baker, South Africa's most famous architect, built for himself at the beginning of the century. Here Lord Milner and his 'Kindergarten' lived for a time, and then Sir Patrick Duncan, later Governor-General of South Africa. It is now a national monument.

The other privately-owned house lies opposite Northwards on the other side of Oxford Road, equally dominating its portion of the ridge, but whereas Northwards is stately, this house is exuberant— flamboyant some call it. It is **Dolobran,** the only one of the important houses which has been continuously owned by the same family: it was build by Sir Llewellyn Andersson, Rand pioneer, in 1906, and is still lived in by his descendants.

Driving up Oxford Road, it is on the left-hand side at the top of the hill, a big red and white house with a amusing green turret topped with a weather vane, and an entrance two storeys high. It is possible, looking at it, to imagine the interior, the gallery and sweeping staircase and fine old things. Among them are four Thomas Baines paintings given to C. J. Andersson, the explorer and father of Llewellyn, by the artist himself. A home housing four—to the general public unknown— Baines paintings is in itself a marvel. But it has more. Dr Anna Smith, formerly in charge of the Library and the Africana Museum and an authority on old Johannesburg, considers that this house, above all, has the old spirit. 'If anything in the future needs to be saved, I always say "Save Dolobran first".'

Motorists roaring up Oxford Road note out of the corners of their eyes the strip of iron railings painted bright green that are part of the outside wall. Even these have a dashing story. They are part of the ornate ironwork from the old Corner House, that was pulled down in the city centre to make room for Johannesburg's first skyscraper.

Another world, **Soweto,** lies away to the south-west of Johannesburg beyond the Main Reef Road with its mine houses and corrugated iron. This is the name given to the African townships here which together make the second largest city in Southern Africa—there are officially some 600 000 people but unofficially and probably more correctly, over a million. With its hundred thousand homes—in Dube, the rich township, very fine ones—and fifteen hundred shops, its beer halls and schools and crowded streets, it has life, colour, noise and excitement.

In spite of the Western-type homes, this is Africa with its richness and magic. Witchdoctors—hundreds of them—still practise here: their mark is the animals' horns above a doorway. People see these signs but not the magic, the special wand beneath the doorway of a store to ensure success, the *muti* that can protect or kill.

It was this teeming African Johannesburg life that gave rise to Africa's national anthem, *Nkosi Sikelel i Afrika*. Enoch Sontonga, who composed the first stanza in 1897, taught at a Methodist mission school on the Witwatersrand, and it was first sung in 1899 in a church in Nancefield near Johannesburg.

On the other side of Johannesburg, well to the east, is a house as different from anything in Soweto or Parktown as a house can be. It is possibly the original farmhouse in which lived F. J. Bezuidenhout, owner in 1886, when gold was discovered, of the farm Doornfontein (he had bought it, so the story goes, all six miles of it from End Street to Bedfordview, for a span of oxen and a trek chain). It stands now in **Bezuidenhout Park,** a part of the old Doornfontein, which the City Council bought in the 1920s.

The Bezuidenhouts made their money in gold and in property, selling parts of the farm for townships: so that instead of mine shafts and corrugated iron cottages, there are in the park wild thorn trees and grass, the big old farmhouse itself, and the well, now filled in. The clump of tall oak trees is all that remains of those that once—so it is said—marked the transport road to Heidelberg. There is the farm cemetery, with the graves of F. J. Bezuidenhout, who had been born in Beaufort West in 1825 and who died here in 1900, that of his wife, and of others. If anyone wonders how the Rand looked before gold was discovered, this is the place to tell him. It is perhaps the most astonishing thing about Johannesburg that it should still exist, innocent and aged, so near the city heart.

CHAPTER TWO

Treasure in the Rocks

⚜

The mine dumps suggest gold in the very pavements of Johannesburg, but it is a false premise as everybody knows who has walked the streets of this city built so solidly upon it. There is apparently not a trace of actual gold, not a mine, not a miner in action, no gold-bearing rock. Yet there *is* gold to be seen, and its story to be learned, if one knows where to search.

We ourselves began with the present and went back to the past. What we wanted as a start was a bird's-eye view of the fields as they are today, and we found it in the big model in the permanent exhibit of South Africa's mining and industrial wealth in the **Stock Exchange** in Hollard Street. It shows, better than anywhere else we know, the Witwatersrand gold-fields, the greatest the world has ever known, from which has come in a single century about one-third of all the gold ever mined by man, twenty billion rands' worth they say, a fortune so immense that it is impossible truly to grasp its size.

Here we looked at the famous golden arc, the half-moon of gold-rich ridges running east-west for 100 kilometres, with its 50 large modern mines, Johannesburg and the great mines of the Main Reef Group at its heart. This Witwatersrand field still yields 99 per cent of South Africa's gold—more than half that produced today by the rest of the entire world—and we stood there tracing its development in the past 30 years, east and west of the city, and south to the Orange Free State to the new gold-fields that in the 1940s roused the gold fever of the century.

The next stop was the **Library Buildings** on the corner of Sauer and Market Streets, a few minutes' walk away. Here we paid three visits—to the Geological Museum, to the Africana Museum (see also p. 48) and to the Africana Library (see also p. 49) on the floors above the public library—we say visit, but it took many visits to absorb something of their knowledge. There is no mining museum in the city; instead, much of the story of gold can be traced here, not as one whole but in a series of fascinating chapters.

The gold of the Rand lies in an enormous underground basin about ten kilometres deep with the Witwatersrand making the northern rim. Some of the gold-bearing rock is visible in outcrops on the surface of the ground; much is buried at depth. As time has passed, Witwatersrand gold has been discovered to reach farther and deeper than men ever dreamed: at more than three kilometres below the surface of the ground, some of the mines are now the deepest in the world.

In the **Geological Museum** we learned the nature of the rock in which lies the gold and of the Witwatersrand Geological System of which it forms part—a system that is composed of layers of water-deposited rock such as quartzite and shale, tilted at an angle. Interspersed with these are layers—reefs—of a special kind known as conglomerate, made up of water-fashioned pebbles laid in a fine cement containing iron pyrites. The conglomerate reminded old-timers of a pudding or Dutch sweetmeat made of sugar and almonds—banket it was called—and pudding-stone or banket they named this odd formation (banket is a name which has now passed into orthodox geology). The formation, however, is more than odd. It is fabulous. The sugar that binds the almonds—the fine cement—contains the minute, often invisible, grains of gold that are the treasure of the Rand.

The discovery of its value was possibly the greatest event in South African history.

Up to the 1880s, not even the most skilled and practised gold miners knew its worth. We are apt to think loosely of the momentous year, 1886, when the proclamation of the first gold-field on the Witwatersrand was signed on 8th September, as the year that gold was discovered on the Rand. In fact, gold had been known or rumoured here long before. That enterprising young traveller, John Barrow, for instance, had shown gold mines on his map of the country dated 1806 that could have been the Witwatersrand mines—whence this hint originated nobody knows and it remains a major mystery. From the 1850s onwards men were prospecting in the neighbourhood of the Rand and finding traces of gold, but nobody made a great find, because nobody knew where to look. The gold men found was alluvial or won from quartz. They knew the conglomerate well but believed that it could yield no gold, a blunder which lost them money and fame.

In the 1850s a Welshman, John Henry Davis, found alluvial gold near the present town of Krugersdorp (and was banished by the Government for this potentially dangerous knowledge), and in 1853 Pieter Jacob Marais, who had taken part in the gold rushes in California and Australia, found gold in the Jukskei River that rises on the Rand, a fine tail of gold in his prospecting pan that set the Transvaal talking.

A few years later in 1856 gold *was* found in conglomerate by a British ex-naval officer, Lieutenant Vincent Lys. He was travelling over the Rand when, near the Germiston of today, his wagon was bogged down in a marsh. He pushed several large 'pudding stones' under the wheels, and when later he crushed and panned these, they yielded gold. He let the matter drop and missed the great prize.

By the 1880s there were many men with experience of gold mining in the Eastern Transvaal prospecting the Witwatersrand. The first who clearly understood the possibilities of the conglomerate formation was a young geologist and prospector, Fred Struben, who—backed by his brother Harry—was by the mid-1880s describing the gold-bearing reefs of the northern and southern slopes of the Rand, panning conglomerate and talking of its promise. Yet it was someone else who had the luck to find the richest reef of all, the Main Reef. He was an Australian gold-miner and itinerant workman, George Harrison, who was building a cottage for the widow Oosthuizen on the farm Langlaagte, not very far from Wilgespruit, where the Strubens were working. This was the find that led directly to the proclamation of the gold-fields and the birth of Johannesburg—the reef itself was traced almost at once over a distance of 70 kilometres.

Who was then the discoverer of the gold-fields of the Main Reef? It is a question that has been debated—sometimes with ferocity—for 90 years. The Executive Council of the South African Republic at the time declared the Strubens the main discoverers. Others later plumped for Harrison, still others for his friend and associate, George Walker (who had been employed by the Strubens and who, it is said, panned his first banket in a frying-pan). Other names such as George Honeyball and Jan Bantjes continue as well to crop up. It is not, with many, a question so much of history as of flesh and blood. There are still people older than the gold-fields; and many Transvaalers heard the live story from their grandfathers and sometimes fathers.

What is certain is that, irrespective of who first found it, Johannesburg was born of gold. From then onwards the two stories march together.

There is little specific reminder beyond that in the Africana Museum and Library of that first gold rush, the frantic pegging of claims, the bawdy, bursting tent towns, the village leaping into life, the first pioneers, the coming of the magnates. Here photographs, books, cuttings, relics tell the early history and the great events that followed.

There are details in the museum of the cyanide extraction process which saved the gold-fields at their lowest ebb in the 1890s. Up to then gold had been recovered by the old method of utilizing mercury's affinity for it—the crushed ore was led over copper plates coated with mercury, with which the gold amalgamated. The amalgam was then heated until the mercury vaporized, leaving the gold behind.

It was a primitive method, as many found to their cost. Nevertheless, it was practicable, but only for the oxidized ore near the surface: deeper down the ore was of a different nature and it did not work. Easy gold near the surface, however, and the days of pick and shovel were now past. Only deep mining lay ahead. And if it was impossible to extract, easily and cheaply, the gold that lay at that depth, the mines were doomed.

It was at this moment that the cyanide process, based on the affinity of potassium cyanide for gold, was perfected. The MacArthur-Forrest Cyanide Extraction Process, it was called, and was the brainchild of a Glasgow chemist, John Stewart MacArthur, and two medical doctors, the Forrest brothers, working 9 650 km away in a small room behind their Glasgow surgery. Their experiments made cheap efficient production possible at depth and saved the Rand.

What held us longest was a pinch of yellow gold dust in a small basin in the **Africana Museum**. We knew that, rich though the fields were, the total amount of gold won from a mass of rock was little. Now we saw how little: this represented $4 \cdot 6$ penny-weight, the total amount of gold won from an average ton of conglomerate. Its very smallness was exciting. If this represented a ton of rock, what then was the measure of a gold bar! It lent to the total gold won over the 90 years a sort of magnificence of labour and adventure.

The city streets, too, tell their tales. In **Boundary Road,** near the modern Clarendon Place and the busy thoroughfare of Louis Botha Avenue, is a concrete beacon enclosing part of the original surveyor's beacon marking the northern corner of Randjeslaagte, the historic bit of land that nobody wanted, on which the village of Johannesburg was laid out. It is, in its way, a golden beacon.

We went from it to the centre of the city to see the next stage of the old mining village. We walked down Eloff Street from Commissioner Street to Bree, one side of the village in 1886. Exactly how small it was we were to find—it took us seven minutes to walk, stopping at the traffic lights. We looked at the kinks in the street where it reached Bree, then turned and walked back along Von Brandis Street. We trod with respect—we were walking on gold. The Main Reef runs below the city—a goldfield was proclaimed in the middle of the original village—and gold is supposed to lie under the New Law Courts in Von Brandis Square which we passed on our left.

We left the city centre and drove to the **Hertzog Tower** on the

A series of comparative skulls and busts from *Adventures with the Missing Link*. From left to right: a young male gorilla; a male *Australopithecus robustus* from Sterkfontein; a female *Australopithecus africanus* from Makapansgat; Neanderthal Man, *Homo neanderthalensis*; and modern man, *Homo sapiens*.

Johannesburg—Igoli—the City of Gold, seen from a mine dump

Smuts's library at Irene, now faithfully reconstructed at the University of the Witwatersrand

The most famous rock-painting in Southern Africa, the White Lady of the Brandberg

Die Weiße Dame vom Brandberg
Die Wit Vrou van die Brandberg
The White Lady of the Brandberg

Brixton Ridge with the gold-fields model in the Stock Exchange still fresh in our minds. From the top of the tower we saw it translated into actuality, the dumps and mine workings in the south stretching away left and right. We looked towards what was once the farm Turffontein, where great mines arose—the Ferreira Deep, one of the richest of all time, and the Robinson Mine and Robinson Deep, founded by Sir J. B. Robinson of the white pith helmet.

The Tower is staffed by retired railwaymen, genial and full of talk. One pointed to the south. 'Do you see that over there?' he asked, 'that's the first mine of all, the start of it all.' It was **Langlaagte,** where Harrison found the Main Reef. We looked down on it with passionate curiosity. He was granted a Discoverer's Claim here, number 19, which he sold for £10—no dream, no premonition warned him of what we were seeing that day. He walked off to the Eastern Transvaal and was, his friends thought, taken by a lion. Certainly nobody ever heard of him again. That claim down below survived him, to be declared a national monument, and the area around it was given his name, the George Harrison Park.

We descended to ground level and went in search of it.

On the way we passed John Vorster Square off Commissioner Street west. Just south of here engineers, excavating a new tunnel for a sewer, struck gold in February 1977. 'Jo'burg sewers flush with gold,' were the headlines in the evening paper.

The **George Harrison Park** lies a few kilometres from the centre of Johannesburg on the left-hand side of the Main Reef Road. Whereas Commissioner Street is grand and modern, the Main Reef Road, which is its continuation westwards, has a sort of timeless shoddiness—it must be Southern Africa's ugliest road. Past the burned-out buses, the empty beer cans and litter (all, indeed, another side of gold) we came to the Park and would have passed it by if we had not seen the old stamp battery inside the fence alongside the road. There was no notice when we saw it, no name, nothing to suggest the significance of the spot. We learned later that there are big plans for the park.

The old stamp battery, now a national monument, is of particular interest; with it and similar machines gold used to be crushed. It is the last one of which we know in the vicinity of the city. Most people today pass it by without knowing what it is. Without any explanation to illumine it, it is not a romantic link with the past, not part of the city's coat-of-arms but 'that bit of junk on the Main Reef Road'.

Farther along the road, less than half an hour's drive from Johannesburg, we turned northward to the **Discoverers' Way,** the Ontdekkersweg, running close to it and almost parallel. We passed Discovery noting the famous names—Struben Avenue, Walker Avenue, Lys Avenue—and into the town of Roodepoort (South Africa's thirteenth and newest city), the Red Pass of the early farmers.

Roodepoort, now rivalling Germiston for the place of third town of the Transvaal, is another centre built on gold. It was in the hills and valleys round here—less than 30 kilometres west of Johannesburg—that many of the early prospectors worked: today it is still a mining town.

We turned into Dieperink Street at the side of the town hall and stopped at the **Museum.** This is a municipal project, a charming little late Victorian period museum of the early prospecting days with a special exhibit on gold. There is also Miss Elizabeth Viljoen to show visitors the geological formations in diagram and specimen and to sketch the history from those early days to those of the surrounding gold mines of the present.

We knew, as we listened to her and looked round the tiny room with the gold exhibits, the gold scale so fine it can weigh a signature, the photographs and books, that if we were introducing anyone to Witwatersrand gold, this is where we would begin. It would be right in another way, too, for this was Struben country whence the promise of the Witwatersrand came, at a time when Johannesburg was still empty veld.

Outside the museum a young woman panned gold for us. She used conglomerate, given to the museum by one of the nearby mines and crushed in the museum grounds, and we watched with delight a process which had fired the gold fever from California to the Rand. Presently as she washed the ore, swirled the water and washed again with all a prospector's cunning, we saw gold, a few specks among the dross, glinting in the sun. It was a tremendous moment.

We left the museum to drive across Discoverers' Way to Allen's Nek on the Honeydew road. **Allen's Nek** is a cutting through the hills, and we turned left here on a road that led to Kloofendal and to the tract of land that is being developed as a municipal park. It is also the site of the old Confidence Reef where the Strubens dug for gold and where their five-stamp battery had been erected. Although buildings do impinge in places, it is still a sylvan valley of wooded hills and grassy slopes, with a stream at the bottom.

We talked about the Strubens as we climbed the path. These were no itinerant workmen—their father was Captain J. M. Struben who had been chief magistrate in northern Natal, had been nominated as President of the Orange Free State, and had settled on the farm, The Willows, just outside Pretoria in the 1850s. Both Harry and the younger Fred had a bent for geology—in Fred it was a great gift—and as they moved about the Transvaal, hunting, transport-riding and farming, they looked for metals. By the 1870s they knew 'that colour of gold' had been found in the creeks coming from the Witwatersrand. By 1884 they knew a great deal more. Fred was working a shaft at Sterkfontein near Krugersdorp and finding gold, and prospecting eastward to the farm Wilgespruit or Willow Stream—often known later as Cliffendale (Kloofendal) or Struben's Farm—and here he found the quartz outcrop which he and Harry called the Confidence Reef.

Any great find (and at the time it was great) must have in it something of a miracle. Fred's discovery did have something other-world about it. On 18th September 1884—he was 33 years old—he was, in his own words, fossicking about in the valley without finding anything of value when he looked upwards from the foot of a hill and from this position noted 'a disturbance' in the rocks of the southern range. The possibility of a reef here flashed into his mind. He raced up the slope and there was the reef cutting through the displaced strata. He broke off a piece of surface rock and took it to the stream nearby, crushed it on a large flat rock and panned it in the pan he always carried with him. Out of that little bit of rock came nearly a teaspoon of gold. The pan, he wrote afterwards, was covered with it. Even then, he was not sure it was gold so he hastened home to test it.

It *was* gold and nine months later, on 5th June 1885, Harry Struben made the first public announcement on the reef in the grounds of the Union Club in Pretoria. A table was spread with quartz from it—people were not asked to believe in the gold within it; they could *see* it. The gold assay was the richest known in the Transvaal and the republic, on the verge of bankruptcy, went mad with joy.

The Confidence Reef, however, belied its name. At its most dra-matic the very quartz on the surface of the ground was permeated with visible gold and it had seemed that it must go on forever. But it soon disappeared, and the most feverish prospecting failed to locate it again.

Nobody had time to be too disappointed, for the Strubens had filled the air with excitement. Fred was soon crushing quartz from the district in the five-stamp battery, tracing and mapping the reef for miles, and experimenting with conglomerates—by the winter of 1886 when Harrison and Walker stumbled on the Main Reef outcrop at Langlaagte, Fred knew that the strange formation contained gold.

Half-way up the hill to the Confidence Reef we ducked through a hole in the high wire fence, and we were at Fred Struben's workings. We climbed from one to another, past pits in the hill hidden by bush, from which he had hauled the golden quartz, into a quarry, a strange red secret place honeycombed with dark holes, the entrance to the old mine shafts that went back and down into the hill. One was lined with the long grey roots of a little *notsung* tree at the entrance. The excavations and caves in the Transvaal are often guarded by their own particular sorts of trees: here it was these little ones with the delicate leaves and long orange flowers, crowding across the face of every shaft. The soft red walls with a soapy touch reared above us; on their surface are still the hand and footholds that Fred Struben and his men had made 90 years before, and the mark of picks.

Out in the open, as we were tracing a quartz outcrop on the surface of the ground, Miss Viljoen said suddenly, 'There are signs of prehistoric goldmining in these hills, you know.' Now it is generally held that no ancient goldmining ever took place along the Witwatersrand, so we were enthralled. The museum, she said, had searched for the traces unsuccessfully, but she believed the first-hand reports to be reliable. It was a long way to John Barrow and the mystery of his 170-year-old map showing gold mines on the southern Transvaal highveld, but this, we thought, might be the answer. It was a fine idea to have, standing in the Strubens' valley close to the spot where the stamp battery had once crushed the gold ore of the pioneers.

The battery still exists. We found it not far away in Florida, on the corner of Goldman and Seventh Streets, opposite the park. It may one day—it *should*—be returned to the Strubens' valley.

We were happy, apart from its historic interest, to know that anything as beautiful as the valley could lie so close to the Main Reef Road. That it is now visited by a good many people is due largely to the enthusiasm of the Roodepoort Museum staff and to the Knowledge Seekers.

The Knowledge Seekers, with its headquarters in Johannesburg, is an enterprise run by two young people, Robin Graves and his wife Frances (a lecturer in history at the College of Education), to cater for people who want to know about South Africa. They run tours, always well organized, to places of interest often not covered by other organizations, with guidance and commentary by experts, which are very good value and great fun. Their Gold-Seekers' Tour, arranged sometimes on Saturday mornings, covers much of the ground we had and draws tourists from all over.

The Chamber of Mines, dealing with what it terms a modern dynamic industry, runs no historical tours. Instead, through it, it is possible to see a modern gold mine in action: it runs five tours a week of surface and underground workings throughout most of the year, excursions that are not for the faint-hearted, the claustrophobic or bronchial sufferers. They are among South Africa's showpieces and are always in demand.

When people have seen all that they can, both the old and the new, they are still left with a question unanswered. How did it all happen? Why are the gold-fields here at all?

Modern geologists know at least part of the answer. The fields, they say, were born when the world was young. The gold-bearing rocks are ancient, of Pre-Cambrian days—even in geological terms which deal in hundreds of millions of years, this is old. The rocks of what is known as the gold-rich Witwatersrand Triad vary from about 2 800 million to 2 300 million years in age. The great basin of the gold-fields was once an inland sea or lake into which swiftly-flowing rivers and streams carried silt and pebbles, and among other minerals gold and uranium in suspension. The basin filled up and solidified; great forces tilted, buckled and deformed the layers, dykes and faults separated one part from another, leaving the patterns geologists know today.

Why was the gold laid down, not at random, but in distinct zones, and how?

There have always been theories. One of the newest is as strange as we could wish. Mineral though it is, it was born of *life*, of some of the earliest living things of all.

This at least is the theory that some of the leading scientists now hold, the end of a long road that began more than half a century ago when geologists first noted that there was not only gold in the Witwatersrand conglomerate, but small specks of something else. The specks were carbon. Soon scientists were noting something of tremendous interest, that the gold and the carbon were definitely associated, and that the higher the carbon content was the higher also was the amount of gold (and of uranium as well).

So carbon, gold and uranium were bedfellows. But what did it mean? Scientists disagreed. They argued about the nature of the carbon. First they believed it was inorganic—it had to be, when the rocks which contained it were older than life. Modern scientists know better. Pushing back the accepted dates when life began to a time before the Witwatersrand rocks were laid down, they showed that these specks of carbon had come from living things, from the earliest plants of all, primitive algae.

Now scientists knew that gold and carbon were associated, and that the carbon was organic. These were bits of knowledge dovetailing neatly to give a new picture of the gold-fields' origin. One of the simplest and most exciting accounts is given by Dr Edna Plumstead,

Johannesburg geologist and palaeobotanist of world repute—it is worthwhile tracking down her Alex L. du Toit memorial lecture given in 1969, 'Three Thousand Million Years of Plant Life in Africa', an annexure to volume LXXLL of the Geological Society of South Africa, and reading it in detail.

Living plants, the algae of that ancient lake, made the Witwatersrand goldfields by trapping and depositing the minerals and metals in the water. The algae existed in what she termed a killer's world without free oxygen, in water shallow enough to allow sunlight to penetrate but deep enough to protect them from ultra-violet radiation, water not less than 10 metres deep. Thus the areas in which they could live were limited—platforms at a certain depth—and so, much as a gold-trapping corduroy table does in modern mining, the tiny submerged water-weeds trapped the grains of gold and other minerals, depositing them in their own narrow zones. And this is why, where the carbonized remains of the algae are, there is also gold, and why they occur in definite layers.

We talked to Dr Plumstead in front of her fire one winter's day, and she painted for us that far-off primeval scene when the humblest of plants were laying down a modern fortune. As we spoke with her, we began to comprehend the practical importance of geobotany, the study of the relationship of soil and plants, in modern mining; on it may rest the discovery and understanding of the gold-fields of the future.

One day we will be able to visualize better Dr Plumstead's ancient world, for a model of its geology and environment, as exact as men can make it, as being built by the Economic Geology Research Unit at the University of the Witwatersrand. How did it all begin? Soon we will be able to go and see.

Johannesburg is the centre not only of Rand gold but of many other things as different as fossils and jewels, art and steam engines: it is the heart of a web, strands from every corner of the country homing here, so that it is possible, without moving from Johannesburg, to learn the stories of distant things.

A great university is a place where many famous tales are told. **The University of the Witwatersrand,** spread out over 32 hectares (80 acres) at Milner Park a little way northwest of central Johannesburg, *is* great. Rightly enough for a Johannesburg establishment, its beginning was closely linked with mining—it was an offshoot of the South African School of Mines established in Kimberley in 1896—and progressed and changed until in 1922 it became officially the University of the Witwatersrand, or 'Wits' as it is familiarly known. Today

its facilities have grown far beyond the original mining and techno-
logy, there are ten and a half thousand students, and the whole
university is bursting at the seams.

Among the stories told here, not only of the gold-fields and such
fascinations, is that of evolution. South Africa is particularly suited to
be the centre of such a history. Whole chapters were written here,
telling of an ancient world, of antique plants, of the beginning of
mammals, of the beginning of man himself. In the **Geological
Museum** in the basement of the Department of Geology, in the
University of the Witwatersrand for instance, is a lump of rock worthy
of a pilgrimage—within it is embedded, as far as is known, the
beginning of life itself on earth.

It stands just on the left of the entrance door, a rock some 50
centimetres long and 10 centimetres deep, dark-coloured with lighter
markings, and is labelled 'Banded Chert Carbonate Sediment' from the
Komati River valley of the Eastern Transvaal. In that dark heart is
trapped the first clue to the beginning of life: minute specks that once
were living blue-green algae, the first and most primitive plants of all.
Three thousand, four hundred and fifty million years ago the algae
(older than the algae which trapped the gold) existed in a soft,
jelly-like material that hardened through the ages into rock. The
banded chert we looked at was a part of that ancient rock.

Ten minutes away from the Geological Museum is the **Bernard
Price Institute of Palaeontology** of the Witwatersrand University—
the B.P.I.—which deals with the study of ancient life in all its forms.
Although it has no sample of this famous rock, it was Dr Plumstead
working here who described to us something of its story, of the ancient
Pre-Cambrian period to which the rock belonged (a time until recently
thought to have been without life), and of how those first algae held
within it, were more than *first* life. They brought with them the gift of
future life. They lived in a killer world without free oxygen, on which
all life today depends, and they were its first source. Scientists know
because tests of the residues showed it—that the algae were green.
Green is the vital word. When a plant makes green colouring matter,
which is chlorophyll, it gives off free oxygen. Thus because they were
green, they gave the world the breath of life. After them came the
higher plants, the land plants, the animals, then man. The world as we
know it was on its way.

Such is the major excitement of the Pre-Cambrian in South Africa.

For the next 2 000 million years South African rocks show little
outstanding fossil life; not until the Devonian period, some 395 million
years ago, does the story resume in earnest—in the rocks of this

period, in the valleys of the western and southern mountains, are some of the early records of land plants. In the rocks of later days are still other fossil plants and they helped change the world.

They look ordinary enough to modern eyes, and that is why they are extraordinary—because modern they were. If Dr Plumstead is correct, they were the ancestors of modern plants, the flowering plants, that cover the earth today. Scientists know them as the Glossopteridae, and traces of them are widespread in what geologists term the Ecca and Beaufort series of the Karroo System, South Africa's major geological formation. They evolved in South Africa, probably in the Southern Transvaal, perhaps in part where the Bernard Price Institute stands today, to spread slowly from here across the world. At the Institute it is worthwhile making a point of looking at these bold leaves, outlined on rock in fine and precise detail, that 200 million years ago brought their own special gift of life to the world.

The rocks show more than the march of early plants. They show the onward march of animals as well, among them that of some of the strangest creatures ever known, reptiles in the evolutionary state of turning into mammals—mammal-like reptiles they are called. They make one of the most fascinating chapters of evolution, one that South Africa has largely contributed, for much of the rock of the Beaufort beds (of the Karroo System) is the richest storehouse known of the fossil remains of these creatures.

There were giant and small lizards, dragons, creatures appearing part hippo and part crocodile, half-reptiles with the teeth of dogs, and all of them, even from the oldest beds, had some hint of mammal. A palaeontologist as eminent as Dr Robert Broom thought them the most important fossil creatures ever discovered.

The Bernard Price Institute has one of the world's best collections. If one has the luck to be shown round (by appointment only) by the man who built up this collection, Dr James Kitching, a visit to the Institute becomes drama. Dr Kitching is judged today to be the world's greatest modern fossil-finder. Friends know him as 'James Hawk-Eye', the Americans as 'Eagle-Eye'. It is a long time now since as a boy he hunted fossils in the New Bethesda hills of the Karoo but his enthusiasm remains as ardent. No visitor to the Institute forgets him.

The Institute dates from only 1946. Linked in South Africa with famous people such as Professor Raymond Dart and visited by scientists from all over the world, it has become one of the few great such establishments in the world. A glimpse of Dart is a thrill that it can still sometimes give. 'The Reluctant Anthropologist,' he is sometimes called, the man who never planned to hunt a fossil but who over

50 years ago recognized a fossil skull as that of 'the Missing Link', a creature that was part man, part ape, so changing the whole course of the study of ancient man. Since the 19th century the world had talked of such a possibility. It took Dart to show that it was more than a joke or a dream.

Today the whole world knows that Dart's creature was *Australopithecus africanus*, the Southern Ape of Africa—the name was a misnomer, for he has proved to be more man than ape. He lived in five places of which we know in South Africa between about one million and three million years ago, and here he left his bones and teeth, and perhaps his tools and weapons. Around these scientists have built his story.

But when in 1924 the 32-year-old professor of anatomy looked at the first evidence, a small fossil skull from a limestone cave at Taung in the North-West Cape, this knowledge lay in the future. His was a flash of inspired recognition.

It is one of Johannesburg's greatest stories. It began with a student of the University of the Witwatersrand with a collecting mania and a sharp pair of eyes. Her name was Josephine Salmon, and one spring night in 1924 she went visiting friends in Johannesburg and saw, on a suburban mantlepiece, a fossil skull from a limeworks excavation at Taung, which she was sure was that of a baboon. Such a skull would have been a rare find, and she hastened to tell her lecturer in anatomy of it. He was Raymond Dart, who was interested and arranged for further fossil material to be sent from Taung.

It arrived in two big wooden cases as he was dressing to be best man at a wedding—he describes it all in *Adventures with the Missing Link*—struggling into a stiff-winged collar, urged by his anxious wife to hurry; tearing off his collar, wrestling with the wooden lids, frantically ransacking the contents and finding a mould of a brain, and below a stone showing marks of skull and bone, suggesting a face.

He guessed as he stood there holding the brain what it was going to show, and it did. For the next two months he spent every spare moment working with a hammer, a chisel and a knitting needle to expose the face, his excitement growing as the work progressed. On December 23rd the rock parted and he saw the face of a child on the way from ape to man, to Dart a face that looked out on the world 'after an age-long sleep of nearly a million years'. It fell, wrote Sir Arthur Keith in London, 'like a bombshell on anthropological Europe', and it rocked the world.

The Taung Baby, as it was soon called, had been found a long way from Johannesburg, the next excitement in the search for ancient man was almost on the city's doorstep. Forty-four kilometres from Johannesburg in the Krugersdorp direction—a drive of perhaps three-quarters of an hour today—lies the farm Sterkfontein, where gold was found in early prospecting days. Later, limestone quarries were opened here which yielded lime-preserved bones and skulls of various kinds. When quarrying ceased on Sundays, visitors were welcome. 'Come to Sterkfontein and find the missing link,' the invitation read. In 1936, 12 years after the discovery of the Taung Baby, somebody did.

This time it was Dr Robert Broom, the fighting Scot, medical doctor turned scientist, then on the staff of the Transvaal Museum in Pretoria, who had come to South Africa to throw further light on the origin of mammals and who was now turning with ardour to the origin of man. Hearing of fossil bones which had been found at Sterkfontein, he went hunting here (in a black suit and a silk tie, his famous traditional working clothes!) and in a matter of days found another *Australopithecus*, another ape-man, this time an adult.

It was no isolated find: many more followed, not only at Sterkfontein but at Swartkrans and Kromdraai a few kilometres away, and to the north in a limestone quarry at Makapansgat near Potgietersrus. These five sites are known today and hundreds of ape-man bones have come, and continue to come, from them. Many famous South Africans have helped to recover them—Dart and Broom and their assistants, among them Dr Kitching and his brothers Ben and Scheepers; Dr John Robinson, Broom's assistant and later successor at the Transvaal Museum; Dr C. K. (Bob) Brain, now the museum's director; and the team from Wits today headed by Professor Phillip Tobias and Mr Alun Hughes.

North of South Africa in Tanzania, Kenya and Ethiopia more sites have yielded the remains of early men or part-men, including those of *Australopithecus*, and it had become clear that the Southern Ape, whatever his affiliations, was once widespread over much of Africa. At the present time, he is known from no other continent.

Two species of *Australopithecus* lived in South Africa. One was a small, light creature, some 1,2 metres tall, a hunter and—his teeth showed—an eater of meat. He was the gracile ape-man, named *Australopithecus africanus*, and through the Taung Baby was the first known. Many scientists now consider that he has a strong claim to be the ancestor of modern man.

The other—the taller with the big molars and huge jaws—was a plant-eater, *Australopithecus robustus (Paranthropus)*. He disappeared perhaps a million years ago.

Gracile ape-man has come from three sites in South Africa, Taung,

Sterkfontein and Makapan, and from further north in Africa: the robust from Kromdraai and Swartkrans in the Transvaal, and from many places in East Africa—the famous 'Dear Boy', *Australopithecus boisei (Zinzanthropus)* was closely allied to *robustus* and came from Olduvai Gorge in Kenya.

They lived in South Africa longer ago than scientists dreamed. Modern dating makes Makapan the oldest site, more than three million years old, Sterkfontein just younger, Swartkrans and Kromdraai about two million years, and Taung, the youngest, less than a million years old.

When Broom went to Sterkfontein one Sunday in 1936 this knowledge, again, lay in the future. Yet he was hoping things would happen, and soon they did. The supervisor of the quarrying operations, Mr G. W. Barlow, who had been asked by Broom to look for fossils, a few days later handed him a brain cast which had been blasted out. It was that of an ape-man. Broom and his helpers set to and discovered in the quarry the first adult *Australopithecus* (it was *africanus,* then named *transvaalensis*) of the same line as the Taung Baby. Twelve years later, almost in the same place, another and more famous skull was blasted out: it was the nearly complete skull of a female of the same species, called at the time *Plesianthropus.* Soon to the world she was 'Mrs Ples' and her photograph decorated newspapers across the world.

Broom said later the sight of the skull and glittering rock was the most thrilling he had known. With him was John Robinson, then his young assistant. Years later, when he was Broom's successor at the museum, we asked him about it. 'What was Mrs Ples like? A hole lined with white crystals.'

In 1973 an African labourer at the Sterkfontein excavations, Stephaans Gasela, was eating his lunch when he looked down and saw at his feet a tooth in a lump of rock. It belonged, as further work was to show, to a complete face, a palate and teeth, identified by Professor Tobias as belonging to *Australopithecus africanus.* It was the most important find since Mrs Ples; and was discovered close the the spot where Broom and Robinson had found her skull some 25 years before. Tobias thought it could have been a relative.

Two years after Broom saw that first skull at Sterkfontein—long before Mrs Ples came on the scene—a schoolboy, Gert Terblanche, picked up part of a skull, palate and teeth in a block of breccia on the farm Kromdraai, just east of Sterkfontein. They belonged to the first robust ape-man known. The same Barlow who had given Broom the first Sterkfontein specimen showed him the palate and the tooth, and

Broom was off, in a rush of passionate exuberance, to Gert's school—Gert was carrying around in his pocket four of the ape-man's teeth, 'four of the most wonderful teeth ever seen in the world's history'. More of the skull and jaw were recovered, and Broom's cup was full: now he had Kromdraai ape-man as well.

It was largely Broom's work on these and other early finds that swung the world to the opinion that ape-man bones showed human kinship.

One can follow much of this history at the Bernard Price Institute. Yet it is possible to get even closer—to the bone, so to say. The **Sterkfontein caves,** where so much of the great adventure took place, are open to the public every day except Wednesday. They lie 11 kilometres northwest of Krugersdorp on a turn-off from the well-signposted Tarlton road, an easy 45 minutes from either Johannesburg or Pretoria.

We visited them one day, looked at the little museum on the site, and then descended with the guide into the bowels of the earth. They are marvellous caves, a series of six large rooms, now with electric lights that form great pools of light among the glowing rocks, dim stalagmites and stalactites and deepest shadow, slowly dropping water and doubtless antique ghosts. There is running water and a small still lake: in the light of a torch we saw tiny sightless freshwater shrimps—found only in underground water in the Transvaal. *Australopithecus* had neither fire nor artificial light. He and the shrimps might have lived here together for a million years, with blind eyes, never knowing one another's form.

Nearer the surface are still fossil bones—there is one on the rock wall close to the entrance—and hard by is the site where Mrs Ples lay in her breccia for two and a half million years. (Work continues here all the time under the auspices of Wits.) At the exit, there is a bust of Broom holding Mrs Ples, with Smut's words: 'Every South African feels prouder because of Robert Broom, every South African feels bigger because of him.'

This Sterkfontein valley was very much Broom's. It is a mild, gentle valley, the low grassy hills never suggesting the treasures they contain. Just across the valley from the Sterkfontein hill, crowned with its wild olive, is another rocky tree-girt hill, as undistinguished in appearance. This is Swartkrans, where Broom and Robinson found many remains of the robust ape-man: over 70 have come from here up to date, making this the richest fossil ape-man site of all. More: there was evidence that true man lived there contemporaneously, perhaps a race of early hunters who killed ape-men for their food.

The site is now being excavated by Dr Bob Brain. We looked across at it from the road. One spring day, with the white stinkwoods showing first green leaf, we had gone with him and his family and Dr John Robinson to see the cave. This had once been an open rock shelter, with a vertical shaft descending to a cavern below, where bones, debris and soil had accumulated over the millions of years and—preserved by the lime—had hardened into rock. We looked at the tender green cloud of foliage of the stinkwoods framing the mouth of the cave—they often grow like this at the entrace to dolomitic Highveld caves and perhaps did in ape-man's time as well—and it was then, with the ancient past and present meeting, that Bob Brain had suggested to us a fusion more dramatic.

What, he had said, if Swartkrans ape-man had not died a million and more years ago? What if he were still alive, South Africa's own 'Abominable Snowman'? What if he were living and breeding in those wild wooded valleys over there?—and he waved his hand. Bob and Laura, his wife, had done a cartoon series on ancient life which had been published in *The Star*, and in this they had suggested this possibility. Reports of red-haired ape-like creatures had been received from the Western Transvaal since the 1920s, they said soberly, and for years they had spent their weekends camping (hunting and hoping) in an isolated valley where such hints lingered. Bob Brain is not a romantic but a scientist—'a scientist's scientist' Robert Ardrey called him—so this was received with fascinated respect.

Bob Brain's must be the strangest story born of Johannesburg's environs. It is almost of the city itself, for when one day we went to find the valley, and mounted to the windswept heights above it, we saw from them, clear and substantial, the Hillbrow Tower almost in the city centre.

CHAPTER THREE

Rand Treasures

❧

From evolution to General Jan Christiaan Smuts might be judged a long flight, but it is not. General Smuts—no South African thinks of him as Field-Marshal—was one of its exponents and a friend and supporter of Broom's. So to walk from the Bernard Price Institute for Palaeontology over the bridge across the motorway and through the Wits campus to Smuts's library in the **South African Institute of International Affairs** is perfectly in order. Smuts would have approved.

Smuts's old house is outside Pretoria, yet the University is now the home of his library, which was removed *en bloc* and later set up in a room of the Institute, as like the original as possible.

It reflects Smuts himself—the Boer who became Prime Minister and more, a world statesman—full of learning, honours and simplicities. The two big desks are here, the sofa and easy chairs, the safe, the old brown and green patterned carpet worn thin by many feet, the historic photographs—the 1910 National Convention and others—the cartoons on the walls, and the huge wastepaper basket lined with thick bright cotton. Mrs Smuts lined it thus because Smuts would peel his naartjies and oranges here, the pips falling through the open weaving onto the floor.

In a drawer of a small desk is a letter headed 'Private and Confidential' from the British Government in 1938 enclosing their scheme for the partition of Palestine and asking Smuts's opinion.

On the big stinkwood desk given him by the Transvaal branch of the South African Party in 1934 is his address book—the first name is that of Princess Alice, the second that of Field-Marshal Viscount Allenby, followed by Lady Dawson of Penn and Professor Gilbert Murray, famous Greek scholar.

There are, above all, Smuts's books and there are thousands of them—history, philosophy and religion behind his desk within hand's reach, a Bible dated 1748, psychology, science—we noted Robert Broom's *The Mammal-like Reptiles of South Africa*. The most valuable book in the collection was a copy of *Das Kapital* with annotations in

46

Karl Marx's own handwriting. It had little connection with Smuts personally and was recently sold, fetching a great price.

Upstairs in a glass case was his copy of *Holism and Evolution* written by him in 1926—his proof copy with his own annotations was stolen recently by a thief who took as well the pen with which Smuts signed the Treaty of Versailles in 1919. Gone, too, was the picture Churchill had painted of the Pyramids and presented to him; it was cut from its frame one night.

Our guide and 'overseer' as we wandered was a young librarian called Jacky Kalley, a great-granddaughter of Dick King, the man who in 1842 had made South Africa's most famous ride over 600 miles from Durban to Grahamstown to get help for the British forces besieged in Durban by the Boers. We asked her if she knew what had become of Smuts's saddle that had stood in his old library. She did not, but her eyes flashed: as well they might—she must have saddles in her blood. (The saddle we found later was in the Cultural History Museum in Pretoria.)

The University of the Witwatersrand has another collection more famous than Smuts's, the **Gubbins Library**.

Many of South Africa's great collections of books and other Africana have been built up by private people. John Gaspard Gubbins, a farmer in the Zeerust district of the Western Transvaal, was one of these—his library is now a notable part of the University, his collection of Africana other than books was the basis of the Africana Museum.

Mr R. F. Kennedy, former City Librarian, called the farmer a prince among Africana collectors. 'We used to say of him, "He dines with the bishop and comes away with his cope." ' On his farm Malmani Oog near Ottoshoop he collected a magnificent library of Africana including many famous missionary items. His books, manuscripts and letters came from all over the world, and he built up the collection with passion, discernment and perseverance.

By 1930 his collection was overflowing and he decided to move his books to the University, partly for their safety—on the farm they were housed under thatch with all its fire hazards. Then came the great calamity, the great irony, in the history of Africana collecting in South Africa. The books—more than half had been transferred to the University—had been placed in an old building. In December 1931 a fire broke out and every single one of the books and manuscripts was destroyed. It was, in a way, a national disaster.

Gubbins was made of stern stuff. Far from being crushed, he set to to rebuild his collection—although much had gone for good he did (with help from all over the world) do just this, and this is the Gubbins Library today.

He did more than make the library. His was the idea behind the establishment of the **Africana Museum:** he and Humphrey Raikes, famous principal of the Witwatersrand University, 'formulated' it. The city council made it fact.

If one enjoys associations, the thing to do is to go from the Gubbins Library into the city and visit the Africana Museum housed in the same building as the Public Library on the old Market Square.

Pass by, for the moment, the Cape silver, the old maps, coins, costumes, stamps and paintings and other lovely and curious things for which the museum is famous, and go on to the Wilson tombstone near the Cape silver collection, the little soapstone tablet commemorating the death of a girl that was the starting-point of the Gubbins Library, and of the Africana Museum to which it now belongs.

It was this tombstone that startled Gubbins into an awareness and passion for history and all its richness, sending him out on that long laborious road collecting the things of Africa. The tablet was picked up by an African labourer in a load of stone needed for ballast for the railway near Ottoshoop; it had, miraculously, fallen face upwards, the man saw the lettering, took it to Gubbins whose farm was nearby, and Gubbins knew what it was. From the crude inscription he knew it was the tombstone of 22-year-old Jane Wilson, wife of the American missionary, Dr Alexander Erwin Wilson, who had established a mission at Mosega in the Western Transvaal in 1836.

Here, one terrifying day, when the men of the mission were away, Jane Wilson—who had been ill and was resting—was awakened by screams. They were those of a little Bushman whom the Matabele servants had captured and were torturing. She tried to help him but in spite of her commands and pleading, he was slowly killed before her eyes. When Dr Wilson returned he found his young wife alone and in a state of shock and collapse. Here at the mission she died. (She was the first white woman to be buried in the Transvaal). Her husband carved the inscription on the little tombstone with a penknife, placing it—no doubt because of the softness of the soapstone—*inside* the grave; and there it rested forgotten for 76 years. Its discovery, it is said, changed Gubbins's life.

Years later two American visitors, who had been stranded through a motor accident in the Western Transvaal, were rescued by Mr and Mrs Gubbins. They heard the story of Jane Wilson, of her husband, and their baby Martha, who had been taken back to America, and were deeply moved: so that when they returned to the United States, they remembered and talked of it. One of the men to whom they told the story was a newspaperman in Georgia, by the name of Stovall. Coincidences have always surrounded the Wilson stone—Stovall was the son of the baby, Martha, born at Kuruman, and grandson of Jane!

We do not know if any of Jane's descendants have seen the tablet. It would be worth travelling half across the world to do. As far as South Africans are concerned, it might today be taken as the symbol of the fascinations, the everlasting fascinations, of Africana.

Gubbins' book-buying had been financed largely by a fluorspar mine on his farm. The **Africana Library,** which is part of the Johannesburg City Library (on the floor below the Africana Museum) was built largely by gold. Its basis was the collection owned by Harold Strange, the English stockbroker who became general manager of the Johannesburg Investment Company and President of the Chamber of Mines. It has been built up through the years by marvellous librarians into one of the great Africana collections of the world.

This is the place to visit to see both old and new books on Africa. There is naturally a great deal of Johannesburgiana—a vast amount of reports and technical books and papers on gold—and histories and biographies of all kinds. There are no very early books on the gold of the Witwatersrand. What might be called the first detailed history of its discovery was that of James and Ethel Gray published in 1937.

There are, however, many popular books which are now Africana.

What is Africana? Anna Smith defines it as anything and everything relating to Africa; South African collectors usually restrict it to those things relating to Africa south of the Zambesi River. Many authorities specify the things must be rare.

In South Africa today it has become a booming business—Johannesburg has gradually ousted Cape Town as the centre—and items that 30 or more years ago were selling at a few pounds, now fetch astronomical prices. In 1912, for instance, the Johannesburg Public Library paid £1 800 (R3 086) for the whole of the Strange Collection. Among this was a set of six books that are now alone valued at R15 000-R20 000—Le Vaillant's *Histoire Naturelle des Oiseaux d'Afrique.* The Africana Museum has a famous collection of Thomas Baines's paintings—Baines was the prolific, leading 19th century artist of South Africa. In 1942 four of his paintings fetched just over R140 each at a Johannesburg sale: In 1973 his oil 'Table Mountain and Cape Town from the Sea' was sold for R18 500. Recently nine of his bird paintings, owned by the Museum, were published in sets at R60 a portfolio—who knows what these prints will fetch tomorrow!

49

The inexperienced (and sometimes the experienced) who wish to join the Africana game and to learn something about it cannot do better than haunt the Africana Library and Africana Museum, 'collections', wrote Kennedy, 'in the same building and having one head, and together forming an unsurpassed Africana Repository'.

For those who wish to buy books, there are very good Africana dealers in Johannesburg. Our favourite is Frank R. Thorold's—commonly known as Thorold's—at 103 Fox Street, run by Robin Fryde. Cornelius Struik, so well known in Cape Town, has opened an Africana bookshop in Norwich Union House, 91 Commissioner Street, and Gerrit Bakker at 84 Loveday Street.

They do, for the beginner, help answer the question, 'What to buy?' Otherwise there is little popular guidance. *The Enchanted Door* by the city's well-known writer on Africana, Denis Godfrey, gives advice and fact with the romance behind them. Africana itself now, and scarce, it may have to be consulted in a library. Until recently Godfrey wrote a regular article on Africana for a leading newspaper: wise people cut out the series to keep for reference. Kennedy's *Africana Repository* is wonderful background, and so is the chapter in *Africana Curiosities,* 'Collecting Johannesburgiana', by Mrs Nagelgast (E. B. Hughes).

The Africana bookshops themselves are splendid places to browse in, and the booksellers helpful and friendly. Some of the most exciting city days we have known have been in Johannesburg Africana shops, sitting on the floor when volumes filled the chairs, wedged between books, dizzy with old books, their feel and smells.

In 1969 the world-famous auctioneers of the old and precious, Sotheby and Co of London, opened an office in Johannesburg. Their important annual sales of Africana, held in the Carlton Hotel—Africana occasions causing great speculation and interest—are open to all.

It is at the Carlton Centre that the Bushman Exhibition of the Museum of Man and Science has always been held, an exhibition so popular that it has been presented several times. The Museum of Man and Science has recently been merged with the Africana Museum. Johannesburgers are hoping at the moment that this particular exhibition will continue—as of old—as part of the city's life.

This is a kaleidoscope of past and present that enchants Johannesburg. Relatively few people here (or anywhere) have seen a Bushman shelter with paintings on the rocky walls; still fewer have seen a Bushman. They stream in here to see what it is all about. It is the paintings that usually attract them most of all, the stylized paintings of men and realistic pictures of animals—the eland above all—the snakes with ears, the winged animals and other mythical creatures, painted in the colours of the earth.

One of the highlights of the exhibition is the work of Harald Pager, his original copies of Bushman paintings in the valley of the Natal Drakensberg known as Ndedema. A good many other people have lately been working on rock art—among them Townley Johnson, Paul Friede, Adrian Boshier and his wife; Patricia Vinnicombe, Ludwig Abel, Hjalmar and Ione Rudner and Gerhard and Dora Fick. But it is Pager's works with which we personally are best acquainted through this exhibition.

They are the outcome of a great adventure by this Johannesburg industrial designer, and his wife Shirley-Ann. For two and a half years they lived in a remote valley, Ndedema Gorge, where they studied 17 Bushman sites and copied nearly 4 000 paintings. They existed much as the Bushmen had, using the same shelters, sleeping on grass, taking their water from a stream. But their working methods were otherwise. They were based on the precise rules of an archaeological dig, and were unique in their sphere—they plotted and surveyed every inch, charted the paintings on the shelter walls, measured and described.

Pager describes the reproduction as neither colour photography nor orthodox tracing. First the painted rock surfaces were photographed and the life-size black and white prints taken back and compared with the originals. Any indistinct outlines were filled in and measurements checked; and thereafter, working next to the originals, he painted in the figures with oils. He made no selection whatsoever. All the paintings, in Pager's words, were copies 'right down to the last exfoliating fragment and paint smear'.

There they are, life-size and glowing with colour; and if one walks back to the Africana Library, they are there again, reproduced to a smaller scale in Pager's *Ndedema*, the book which Raymond Dart described as 'fabulous, unique'.

The other great books on Bushman art are there, too, among them those by George Stow, M. C. Burkitt, Dorothea Bleek, Maria Wilman, L. Frobenius, Walter Battiss, Van Riet Lowe, Bert Woodhouse and Neil Lee, and others, and those of Alex Willcox, full of superlative colour photography.

The greatest number of rock paintings, and often the best, are in the south-east of the country, concentrated in the Drakensberg, Lesotho, the eastern Orange Free State and the eastern Cape—described as the richest storehouse of prehistoric art in the world. Many of the illustrations in the books were copied from paintings in these areas.

If one wishes, too, to learn something of the controversy concerning the age of the paintings, one can do it at the Library. Because until recently it has been impossible to date the paintings themselves (although the litter at the sites has sometimes given a clue) ages ranging from a few centuries to 2 500 years have been assigned them. When, therefore, a new method of determining their age was brought to South Africa not long ago, it caused something of a stir. It is known as the paper chromatography method and was introduced by Dr E. Denninger of Stuttgart, who for years had been working on the effect of age on albuminous binding media in paints. In Europe he had used this to date whitewash on the walls of German cathedrals, and paintings on panels, sculptures and canvas: in South West and South Africa he used it to date rock paintings. It does not, however, cover all paintings, only those with 'binders' containing albuminous material, which are not more than 1800 years old.

Although his findings could not be proven, they are still of tremendous interest, and—where it has been possible to estimate age—correct. His tests showed that the oldest rock paintings were mainly those in the Limpopo valley of South Africa, with those in South West Africa even older. Some samples from South West showed no reaction —either they originally lacked amino acids, the basic constituents of albumen—or were over 1 800 years; others had a date of 1 500 years, while the majority were between 400 and 800 years of age.

The most famous and controversial rock painting in Southern Africa, the 'White Lady of the Brandberg', figuring in every representative rock art exhibition, was dated at between 1 200 and 1 800 years (an age which some experts for various technical reasons find difficult to accept).

In the Limpopo valley the ages of the paintings varied between 800 and 100 years, the majority being old, while those in the Orange Free State and Natal Drakensberg were mostly younger, the age varying from about 800 years to 60 plus-minus 20 years. In the South West Cape none was more than 500 years old.

All this and a great deal more can be learned between the Carlton Centre and the Library Building (the Africana Museum itself has famous Bushman exhibits) ten minutes' walk away: it makes a morning of particular charm and interest.

Bushman engravings of wild animals from the Western Transvaal, as apart from paintings, are on view at the **Open Air Museum of Rock Art**—a branch of the Africana Museum—in the grounds of the Zoological Gardens. It has been possible to move these individual engraved boulders to a place of safety whereas it has been impossible—even if desirable—to move a whole painted wall from a rock shelter. To see these original paintings in their wild setting is often difficult: it is also thrilling. The Rock Art Tour run by Johannesburg's Knowledge Seekers, therefore, is good news. It is usually held over a long weekend with Johannesburg as the starting-point, and is led by Bert Wodehouse, co-author of *Art on the Rocks of Southern Africa,* who takes visitors through Bushman shelters in the South-Eastern Orange Free State and North-Eastern Cape. It is the only tour, including such authoritative commentary, of which we know.

The Africana Museum has several other branch museums scattered through the city—the Bensusan Museum of Photography in Empire Road in Parktown, the Bernberg Costume Museum in Forest Town, and the **James Hall Museum of Transport** at Pioneer Park near Wemmer Pan to the south of the city, which is one of Johannesburg's very popular museums.

Among the amusements here are old cars, old trams, wagons, spiders, Cape carts (truly South African vehicles), governess carts, phaetons, bicycles, rickshaws—nearly every form of transport known in this country.

The oldest car at present in South Africa, which we had seen in the Africana Museum, is a 4 h.p. built by Clement of Paris in about 1894, a marvellous old veteran that had once taken part in a demonstration in England—it was to celebrate the removal of the red flag which by law had been required to be held by a man walking in front of any self-propelled vehicle!

What we wished to see was South Africa's first motor-car of all, but alas, it had been destroyed by fire. It was a 1½ h.p. Benz, and it was imported by John Hess of Pretoria who exhibited it at the Berea Park in Pretoria in 1897 and at the Wanderers Grounds in Johannesburg: it ran on benzine and the driving wheel, as in other early models, stood upright on the floor. It caused a sensation, crowds arriving from all over the countryside to look at it. Paul Kruger came to inspect it. He would not ride in it, and how odd this was, he who had dared to float above Paris in a balloon, but he presented Hess with a medal to commemorate his introducing the first motor-car into South Africa on Monday, 4th January 1897.

Another Benz, almost as famous, is an 1899 model, now housed in the private Kleinjukskei Motor Museum near Johannesburg. It is the oldest running car in the country.

There is still another transport museum, the **Railway Museum,** next to the railway station, near the centre of town. Even draughts cannot dispel the charm of this collection with its veterans—the first locomotive to go into service in the Transvaal, an 1884 Saxby and Farmer

(London) model which steamed nearly 193 000 km in its working life, the little model of the first locomotive of all in service, the famous little engine that ran in Durban from the harbour to Market Square.

There are scores and scores of model trains and all their rolling-stock, old-time signal machinery, lanterns, a tickey (three-penny bit) automatic platform-ticket dispensing machine dear to the sentimentalists, model aircraft, and ships and other marine exhibits, elegant crockery and glasses once used by the Railways, the crockery designed for the Royal Tour in 1947, and that in service in the Blue Train today, white with golden proteas. Nothing tells more eloquently of the passing of the years than the dinner menu of a December night in 1903 of the Cape Government Railways, the many courses ending with plum tart, cheese, biscuits, dessert, vanilla ices and black coffee. The price was three shillings.

Above all, there is Mr Frank Cage of the Museum staff, an enthusiast who welcomes train fans with advice and guidance. These stream into South Africa from Britain and the Continent, the United States, Canada, Australia and Japan, because alone among countries in today's energy-starved world, South Africa gives them full value—here there are 1 700 steam engines still in use. They all received a mass reprieve from being 'phased out' in favour of electric and diesel locomotives when the oil crisis overtook the West in 1973: and they are now a world attraction drawing not only individuals but whole tours from abroad.

The tourists are a special breed, talking in terms of boiler pressure, coupled and carrying wheel diameter, valve gear and locomotive types, who may be seen photographing, examining and debating the intricacies of steam in the principal locomotive sheds throughout the country. For them, steam trains in everyday use are worth crossing the ocean to see.

'It's like having a dinosaur in your backyard,' they say, 'and showing it off to the neighbours.'

'Train lunatics,' Mr Cage calls them. He will give up a Sunday happily to show them the full-sized cab-room of a steam engine in the museum, complete with platform, controls and sound effects, the hiss of the brakes and the steam, 'the whistle in the night', and then take them to Germiston to see steam engines in action. Finally, it is back to Wemmer Pan near the James Hall Museum where the Model Club has its own miniature locomotives and track. The models are strong enough to bear adults and every visitor wants to drive them, women as well as men.

At the back of the Railway Museum, on Hospital Hill, in the

grounds of the South African Institute for Medical Research, is another museum, at the moment surprisingly little known, the **Adler Museum of the History of Medicine.** This, the only one of its kind in South Africa, was founded by a husband-and-wife team, Dr Cyril and Dr Esther Adler, who in 1974 presented it to the University of the Witwatersrand.

Among the immense amount of solid information on the history of medicine, dentistry and pharmacy, there is a lot to amuse and fascinate. We passed from the Chris Barnard Medallion struck to commemorate the first heart transplant in 1967 to a witchdoctor's mat and basket, Chopi divining bones, and a Barbara Tyrrell picture of a pregnant woman of the Ngwane tribe, with a buckskin apron to impart strength and beauty to the foetus.

There is an African herb shop as well in which we spent a long time, looking at the *mutis* of Africa, the bark and roots and fruits, the jackals' teeth and animal skins, that bring health, luck, beauty and courage to those who use them well. We looked at the labels—'To forget—Invisible—Luck—To keep you awake—Not to have Twins—Sneezing—Lion skin to chase away evil spirits'—and thought how right it was that they, so African in spirit, should be lodged here in a building designed by Sir Herber Baker, the first great architect to use for preference the materials of Africa, its own rocks and woods.

This is an important stop to anyone interested in Africa and the way it thinks and feels, and something very much of the present. Eighty-five per cent of urban blacks, including such people as priests and lawyers, consult witchdoctors regularly, it was revealed at a symposium on the place of traditional medicine man and witchdoctor in African health care, held in Johannesburg recently.

Further afield, in the northern suburbs are two more museums, one of peace and one of war. The **Museum of Reza Shah the Great,** at 41 Young Avenue, Mountain View, is as much a monument as a museum of Persian art—here during World War II Reza Shah of Iran, father of the present Shah, lived in exile, and here he died in 1944. The home, now owned by the Iranian nation, has some of the finest Persian carpets and wall-hangings to be seen in Johannesburg.

Away to the west off Jan Smuts Avenue is the **Zoo.** It is pleasant to lunch here under the umbrellas in the sun, and then go on to the **South African National War Museum** in its grounds (not, however, reached from the zoo but from the streets outside).

It is not so much a war museum as a museum of courage. Here are gathered relics and momentoes of every kind from the battles and war fronts in which South Africans have served. The fighter plane from

World War I, suspended from the roof, is not much more substantial than an outsize dragon-fly; the German one-man midget submarine—the long, light, solitary iron coffin—was surely manned by someone with a special brand of nerves.

There are the immortals from World War II—Hurricane, Messerschmitt, Focke-Wulf—and the Supermarine Spitfire fighter similar to those used by South Africans in the Battle of Britain. One of the prize exhibits is a Messerschmitt 262 jet night fighter with radar—one of Hitler's secret weapons—believed to be one of the last two in existence. Another is a Hawker Hartbees biplane—it is the last of the military aircraft that were built by the South African Air Force in the years before 1939.

There is a picture of Sailor Malan who destroyed 35 enemy aircraft in the air above England and the Continent, a Union Jack with faded writing upon it—Somme, Delville Wood, Arras—that went with the South African Scottish Regiment through World War I, and a battle flag of the Boer Republics from the Elandslaagte battlefield of 1899, stained with the blood of Boers who had raised it again and again.

From the war-torn London of the Battle of Britain in which South Africa fought there are two relics which bring visitors up short. One is a railing from Buckingham Palace, the other part of the High Altar of St Paul's Cathedral.

Then there are the rich **Jewish Museum** and the new **Harry and Friedel Abt Museum** in Sheffield House in Kruis Street—at the moment the latter is displaying an Ullmann tapestry and we would go to see this alone. These tapestries are one of the loveliest things to come out of Johannesburg. Ernest Ullmann, the famous artist, and his wife Jo, who made them, lived on a farm on the city's outskirts together with a vast assemblage of guinea-fowl and other wild creatures that flocked round them. This talented and much-loved couple between them developed a type of wall-hanging which, in Ullmann's words, was not woven into a design by means of vertical and horizontal strands but, like the famous Bayeux Tapestry, was embroidered cloth. They used mosaics of different material, stitching these to the background, to make their stories, all with a colour, life and glow that have enchanted the world. No other artist-craftsman, Ullmann claimed, could match his wife's results—she had not only great skill and the desire for perfection but intuition: she always knew what was exactly right.

They made the first great tapestry for the Chamber of Mines Pavilion at the Rand Easter Show in 1955. It formed the background to an exhibit of gold bars. 'We used gold-embroidered figures, symboliz-

ing the history of gold and applied them to rich brocades and silks.'
They were fascinated by the result, and the Ullmann tapestries, the
hundreds that followed, were on their way.

They now hang in South African embassies throughout the world, in
government and provincial buildings and in private collections and
homes. Strangely, few are to be seen in public places in Johannesburg.
The great exceptions are those decorating the restaurants of the
Strijdom Tower. Patients who have been in the Brenthurst Clinic in
Parktown know more about them than most. Ernest Ullmann used to
tell how, after recovering here from a heart attack, Dr Jack Penn,
famous plastic surgeon and his good friend, brought him a pad and
pencil and asked him to design a tapestry for each of the new wards,
something that 'would make the patients chuckle', nonsense if he
wished it. He set to work at once on his designs and soon the whole
ward was laughing.

Ullmann thought that the charm of any fabric wall-hanging 'lay in
the warmth of the material, bringing memories of the earliest experi-
ences of life, producing some kind of "bird's nest atmosphere."'
Perhaps it is a bird's nest pleasure the patients feel as they lie in
hospital and look at the tapestries. Dr Penn is his *The Right to Look
Human* says that it is remarkable to see the comfort they bring, and
how the patients talk continuously of their humour and craftsmanship.

Ernest Ullmann died in 1975, so that this tapestry work—this
unique Johannesburg form of art—has come to an end. Ullmann's
brilliance and joy in living can, however, still be seen in other forms in
the streets and open places. There is his bronze group of young buck
and fountain in Jan Smuts Avenue opposite the Witwatersrand University; everybody speeding up Jan Smuts Avenue, every student, knows
it. In Mutual Square, Rosebank, are his terrazzo figures of a young
man and girl embracing—'Young Love' he called it—and at the
S.P.C.A. his exquisite asbestos and fibreglass figures of a girl and
horse. 'The Playmakers,' the famous bronze group of three revellers,
stands appropriately enough in front of the Civic Theatre making, with
the water, the gayest, most spectacular fountain in the city. The bronze
family group in front of the Library is our favourite: the rather solemn,
dignified trio is given unexpected frivolity by the busy pigeons—
Ernest Ullmann would have welcomed them.

In spring there is one place we always visit, **The Wilds,** in
Houghton just off Louis Botha Avenue, Johannesburg's famous garden
of South African wild flowers. There are other open spaces in the
northern suburbs—the Zoo and the Zoo Lake adjoining it, the Melrose
Bird Sanctuary, and Melville Koppies to the north-west where Stone

Age men left their hand axes, and the men of the Iron Age their forges and smelting sites; but on a sunny Sunday in September it is here that people come in droves to see the flowers in bloom and the pink-coloured *keurbooms* (the pick-of-trees, the early colonists called them) drenching the air with perfume.

The Wilds is not an old garden. In 1936 when the Empire Exhibition was held in Johannesburg an exhibit of indigenous flowers and shrubs was presented which delighted the public: and thus the idea of an indigenous garden in the city was born. It has so established, so familiar an air, that Johannesburgers today forget it has not been there for ever.

If we were showing spring-time Johannesburg to a visitor from abroad, The Wilds would top the list. Then, after a day of sight-seeing we would end with something as indigenous and splendid—the night sky of Southern Africa.

Driving north up Jan Smuts Avenue, the **Planetarium** stands on the left, in the grounds of the University of the Witwatersrand. Here by night, and sometimes by day, a show is staged, the dome within becoming Johannesburg's night skyline with the starry heavens above. To sit here quietly looking at an African sky, picking out the familiar stars and constellations and moving with the lecturer into a new remote adventure, is an enchanting way to spend an hour. To visitors from the Northern Hemisphere, this is a brand-new night sky. To most South Africans it brings back memories of starlit nights in the bush and the veld with night winds and wild things, and can be a moving thing in a city where the stars are seldom noted.

CHAPTER FOUR

Pretoria

❦

When the gold barons looked northwards from their Johannesburg ridges they were looking towards Pretoria and a countryside filled with history, and a prehistory they certainly never guessed. Across the Highveld sea of grass, almost 64 kilometres away, rose the Magaliesberg range running east and west with Pretoria at its foot, and beyond it the bushveld stretching away to the Limpopo and the heart of Africa.

The country around the Magaliesberg is near Johannesburg and yet completely different: the lower altitude, the warmth, the valleys, the streams and the trees made here a different, an individual story. Who, before the days of gold, would have chosen the bare Highveld when a day's journey away he could have had a warm watered valley in the hills?

This what the Trekkers must have felt, when they first saw the gentle wooded valley where they settled and where Pretoria arose, and perhaps this is what the people also thought who had lived here before them—1 500 years before, archaeologists now reckon. If Ape-man ever flourished here, no records have been found, but early modern men enjoyed the valleys and the streams, and about the time the Roman legions were leaving Britain, they were here in this Magaliesberg countryside, and built a village near the Hartebeestpoort Dam of today. Whence they came, nobody knows, but they were of a Negroid race, and their bones which show it are probably the earliest hint of Black men south of the Sahara.

When we travel northward from Johannesburg along the Ben Schoeman Highway, the Magaliesberg slowly take on form before us. Straight ahead is Pretoria in its sylvan setting, the series of green valleys between the hills, and over to the west is the Hartebeestpoort Dam. It is a scene not only of prehistory but of history, where the written story of much of the Transvaal began.

It was not only Africans of 16 centuries ago who found this country good but those, as well, who came later. When the first Whites pushed into the western and southern Transvaal in the early 19th century, they found a people who had happily made this their own. John Campbell,

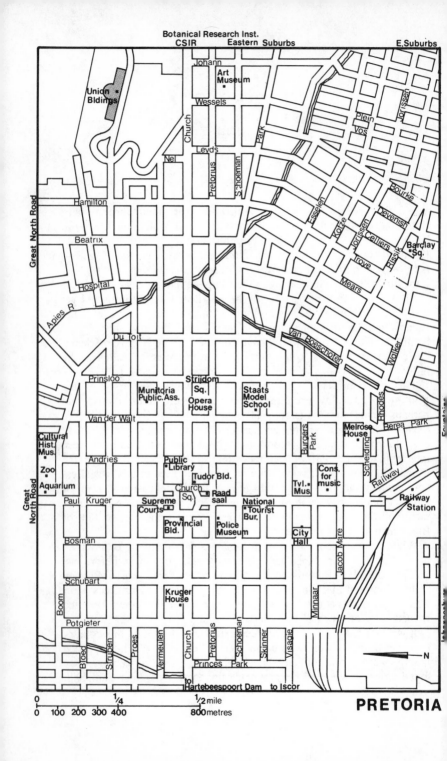

PRETORIA

0	¼	½ mile
0 100 200 300 400		800 metres

the missionary, in 1812-13 described the country to Pretoria's west, near Zeerust, as one of milk and honey, contented people, fine painted houses protected with stone walls, fat cattle, and grain. And Robert Moffat, a missionary even better known, who followed him in 1829, stopped just short of the site of Pretoria, and left a different story.

In those intervening years a catastrophe had taken place unequalled in the story of the Transvaal. Mzilikazi, one of the generals of the great Zulu king, Shaka, had broken away and with his soldiers moved west and north. Years later he was to reach Rhodesia and there to build a new people, but on his wanderings he passed through this fat country of the Magaliesberg and found it to his taste. He stayed, building his capitals from near Pretoria westwards to Zeerust, and from end to end he ravaged the land: as a tale of carnage there is nothing in Southern Africa to match it, save Shaka's own story.

Moffat passed the ruins of innumerable towns, recording the dilapidated walls, the stones and skulls, the serpents, that were all that now remained: the hunter, Cornwallis Harris, who came later in 1835, confirmed the destruction, and so did others.

At the time they did not know it, but they were seeing the end of a civilization, an Iron Age civilization, in the Southern Transvaal, and at the same time the setting for a new one. It was the coming of the Whites, and Mzilikazi had made it easy for them. There was almost nobody left, save his men, to meet them.

Mzilikazi did not have it all his own way. From the east and south the Zulus came to defeat him, and from the south the Voortrekkers: it was they under General Hendrik Potgieter who finally routed him and in 1837 sent him on his journey to Rhodesia. The last of the Matabele in the Magaliesberg, it is said, passed northwards over Mzilikazi's—or Silkaat's Nek—west of Pretoria.

So that when in the 1840s the first little band of Trekkers entered the valley of the Apies River near where Pretoria was later to arise, it was a deserted place. They came into a wild valley of great loveliness, the **Fountains Valley,** which is today the main southern entrance to Pretoria. It still has traces of woodland, despite wholesale destruction to accommodate modern highways and road and rail bridges, but then its glory was its trees, alive with the little monkeys that gave the river its name, Apies—Monkeys'—River. The Voortrekkers camped under the trees, were married and had the children christened beneath them, and feasted in their shade.

Today the remnants of the Fountains they knew which have been saved from the roadmaker's bulldozer are used for holiday and weekend 'braais' or barbecues; a caravan park occupies a site near where the pioneers outspanned; thousands of cars rush by every rush-hour and on holidays. The Fountains Circle is a well-known landmark and the city's biggest traffic bottleneck, for into it debouch vehicles from two major four-carriage freeways, the Ben Schoeman Highway to Johannesburg, and the throughway to Jan Smuts Airport, as well as the main road to the city's eastern suburbs.

Elandspoort road (a modern concrete flyover) is all that is left here to commemorate the farm Elandspoort—or Eland's Pass, a name which in itself tells a story—on which Pretoria grew up.

Johannesburg was born of gold, Pretoria of the church (with trade hard on its heels). It was first a *kerkplaas*, a church-place, which the minister from Potchefstroom 160 kilometres away sometimes visited, and by 1854 the first Dutch Reformed Church on Church Square was on its way. Six years later the village became the seat of government of the South African Republic—and in 1910, 50 years later, the administrative capital of South Africa.

Johannesburg may have sprung into life in one hectic year but not Pretoria. It was a village that, like so many South African *dorps*, spread slowly. The people who made it were of the Cape and they built in many ways a Cape village: there was the typical grid pattern, the church at its heart, the open furrows in the streets, and also hedges of willows and billows of pale pink single roses that sometimes grew to the tops of the trees, and big leafy gardens of yellow peaches and vegetables.

The village was named after the great Voortrekker leader, General Andries Pretorius, and Pretorius Street after his son, Marthinus, President of the South African Republic. Street names in the city centre, as in Johannesburg, tell a story. Du Toit Street was named after Andries du Toit, a wandering trader, who laid the village out—his equipment, says Dr Gustav Preller in *Old Pretoria*, was a surveyor's chain bought in Cape Town, a ship's telescope with spirit level mounted on a tripod to serve the purpose of a theodolite, and a dozen metal pegs. (He was later proved to have been fantastically accurate.) He, incidentally, bought a part of the present suburb of Arcadia and the price was a Basuto pony!

All the names have a curiously innocent and rural ring: so did Pretoria itself for most of its life. Today, it is true, it is losing a good deal of its village air. Creeping outwards (and in the centre upwards), it today is the biggest municipal area—570 square kilometres—in South Africa, while Pretorians boast that Church Street is the longest street in the world! It may be only the fourth biggest city in terms of population, but it has more civil servants to the square kilometre than any other town in South Africa, a superabundance of scientists, students, industrialists, diplomats—indigenous and exotic—and police-men: on the east the ultra-modern complex of the C.S.I.R., the Council for Scientific and Industrial Research, and the Botanical Research Institute with its fine gardens: to the south the Bureau of Standards and UNISA, the University of South Africa, raised dramatically over the Fountains road; slightly west is Voortrekkerhoogte, the largest military base in the country, and Waterkloof, the biggest supersonic jet fighter base in Africa: on the west Iscor, the South African Iron and Steel Corporation, one of the highlights of South African industry, and beyond it the atomic power research station at Pelindaba (Mzilikazi country); to the north Onderstepoort, the greatest veterinary research institute in the Southern Hemisphere.

So that Pretoria is not only the administrative capital but in a very real sense the seat of planning and action for the whole country.

Curiously, when people visit the city for pleasure it is not to see the administrative capital with all its adjuncts. It is for a village reason—the wheel has turned full circle—they come to see the trees.

They are not the trees of early Pretoria, the wild trees that made the enchanting setting. They are not indigenous at all but tropical South American, the jacarandas which botanists know as *Jacaranda mimosi-folia* and which have given Pretoria the name of Jacaranda City. For more than 70 years they have been used to line Pretoria's wide streets—wide enough to pass a wagon and the famous long wagon whip—so that today tens of thousands of them give, not only summer shade, but one of the astonishing city sights of the world.

In October and November when they bloom, their violet-mauve bells clothe Pretoria: from the hills about they appear like a deep mauve mist, with roofs and ribbons of tarmac between them; and on street level they are not only violet above but below-foot as well where the fallen flowers lie in sheets, slippery sheets as broken bones have shown. This is the time to go up to Meintjes Kop or to the Muckleneuk Ridge south of Sunnyside, or onto the Johann Rissik Drive, for a long unhurried view of the wide valley between and the steep flowery streets climbing the hills.

Pretoria still has its first two jacaranda trees, which were planted in 1888 or 1889 in the garden of Mr J. D. Celliers at Myrtle Lodge, now the grounds of the Sunnyside School. These were the parents of many of Pretoria's jacarandas. Still more grew from seed imported by James Clark, famous nurseryman in Pretoria in the old days, from, strangely enough, Australia. Perhaps some had grown from slips given to the Voortrekkers by the great tree-grower of the Cape, Baron von Ludwig. Other old trees which are still living are those in Arcadia Park near the

Art Centre, and in Bosman Street, and these latter have a special aura about them: they started the jacaranda boom.

In 1906 Bosman, then Koch Street, towards the centre of the town, was planted with sapling oaks. In November of that year Paul Roos's very successful Rugby team touring Britain was defeated—for the first time in an international match—at Glasgow. British troops which were stationed at Voortrekkerhoogte, then Roberts Heights, went mad with jubilation and uprooted the oak saplings as they roistered in the streets. James Clark suggested, and provided, jacarandas to replace the oaks, and this was how Pretoria officially began to plant the trees. Some of these Bosman Street trees were cut down some years ago when the street was widened, and the wood was used to make furniture for the City Council's reception room, the Hilmar Rode Hall, in Munitoria.

There is little in Pretoria today as old as the Sunnyside jacarandas. **Church Square** is older by some 30 years, although the buildings that ring it—old as they are for the Transvaal—are younger: most of them were built in the 1890s in Kruger days. The mud-walled thatched Voortrekker church that once stood in its centre was struck by lightning in 1882 and burnt down—it was here that Sir Theophilus Shepstone was sworn in as Administrator in 1877 after he had formally annexed the South African Republic in Britain's name.

The **Raadsaal,** the 'Houses of Parliament' of the South African Republic, was built in 1891 on the south-western corner of the square. Designed by Sytze Wierda, who did the Rissik Street Post Office in Johannesburg, and built by John Kirkness, its sturdiness, its columns and tower and other extravagances, were built on gold. Five years after the Witwatersrand goldfields had been declared, there was money in the Transvaal for all these things, for the doors and windows made in the Orkney Islands, even for the helmeted Amazon that tops the central tower and whose identity has been lost in time.

On the opposite, the northern side, of the square is the **Palace of Justice,** now the Supreme Court, again designed by Wierda and begun a few years after the Raadsaal was completed. With it and the Raadsaal, Italian Renaissance came firmly to Church Square. Its grandeur did not deter the British from commandeering it in the Anglo-Boer War in 1900 and turning it into a hospital, and this was the start of its life. Embedded in the brickwork still are sawn-off bottle openers which were let into the walls for sick Tommies to open soda-water bottles—no fresh water was provided because of an epidemic of enteric fever and dysentery. The advocates' robing room of today was the mortuary!

The Gilbert Reynolds Memorial Gate at the visitors' entrance to the Pretoria National Botanic Gardens

Melrose House in Pretoria, a Victorian extravaganza

An Ndebele village

The Dutch oven at Boekenhoutfontein

To the south-east across the square on the corner of Church Street is **Tudor Buildings,** built by George Heys. It is one of the oldest buildings left in the centre of the city, but it is not so much this that we enjoy as the Heys touch within—we associate it with highwaymen, gold and glamour.

Heys made his money in coaching and here he left his tribute to transport in various forms in the stained-glass windows on the half landings of the old staircase: we remember most clearly the railway engine on the first landing and on the second the sailing ship with red pennons flying. Heys commissioned these at the beginning of the century, and they were made by Douglas Strachan, who later made the stained glass for the Scottish National War Memorial in Edinburgh and the Palace of Justice at The Hague.

The highwayman himself (the last of them all) could be seen until a couple of decades ago in an office block at the back of Tudor Buildings in Pretorius Street. He was a liftman called Tommy Dennison, who as a young man had robbed the Pilgrim's Rest coach, thereafter paying his debts and celebrating in the village, where he was arrested. He was old when we knew him in his green beret, still full of his exploit, still grumbling at the lies men wrote about him, still on St Patrick's Day with a shamrock in his lapel. He added tone to the entire block.

The square itself is a sad thing today, a bus terminus and short cut for people hurrying to and from work. In its early days it was the heart of the town, an outspan, a church centre, a market place, full of people and dogs, tents, wagons, bargaining, eating, drinking, fighting, praying. Even after the market was moved to the old market place on the site of the present new Opera House, it was still a lively centre.

Part of it died, of course, when it was left without a church. Yet as an open place in the centre of the city it should have made a new life. Many people did their best for it, including Mr V. S. Rees-Poole, the architect, who helped to reshape the square early this century. It was planned as a bit of Europe with fine paving, fountains, formal trees and masses of lively people enjoying it all. It never came off—there was no money for it.

The **Kruger Statue** that now dominates the square was a gift of Sammy Marks, the Lithuanian hawker who became industrial magnate and general benefactor. In the 1890s he commissioned the sculptor, Anton van Wouw, to make it. At the end of the Anglo-Boer War the British refused to have it erected in Church Square for which it had been planned, and it was only in 1913 that it was taken out of storage and set up in Pretoria, in Prince's Park and not in the square at all.

Twelve years later it was moved to the garden in front of the station, and only in 1954 was it transferred to the square where it now is. Pretoria is eighty per cent Afrikaans-speaking and the vicissitudes of the statue of this great Afrikaner have stirred many people.

So now Paul Kruger, with two of his burghers on either side, presides over the square, heavy and sombre, his back to Paul Kruger Street, which as Rees-Poole said, could and should have been a magnificent boulevard, such as no self-respecting statue would wish to turn his back on. The statue is the cold hand of death to that once-envisaged lively heart of the city—who could drink a cinzano or dance in the rain in that austere and tragic shadow!

Once upon a time Pretorians did look at the statue with something of amusement and curiosity. The story went that Paul Kruger's wife, Tant Sina, had asked that his top hat be made hollow to hold water for the birds—it was one of those homely touches that the Krugers both excelled in—but the hat in fact is solid.

The only really lively sight on the square today is the pigeons and their benefactress. At about six o'clock of a summer evening, and earlier in winter, when traffic has stilled, a small blue panel van draws up on the north side of the square, and the pigeons, which have been waiting on the grass in the square, rise in a body and fly to meet it. An old woman eases herself out: she is much bent with arthritis and laden with bags, and her coming is not made easier by the birds that perch on her parcels. This is Mrs E. de Kock, who for ten years has been feeding the pigeons here.

She stands near the birdbath (erected, through her pleas, in the north-east corner) throwing crushed mealies and lettuce leaves, and the birds jostle, crowd, whirr and peck around her. She had come during the Christmas holidays, she told us, not in the evening but at five o'clock in the morning when the pigeons had not been expecting her, but somehow they had known of her coming and had flown from everywhere, over the Provincial Buildings and the other roof tops in a grey cloud, and mobbed her.

She is a highly practical St Francis, armed with surgical scissors and tweezers, picking out the sick and wounded birds, and dealing with them. We watched her cutting nylon threads out of a pigeon's deformed feet—it had been caught in a pigeon-snare people still sometimes set—her glasses falling down her nose, muttering. 'Be still, my dear, it's got to be done,' and then critically watching it fly away. 'It's lop-sided and it will lose some toes, but perhaps it will do.'

Close to the square, in Church Street West, is one of the entrances to the new **Transvaal Provincial Building,** which has its main entrance in Pretorius Street to the south. This is the entrance to the Transvaal Division of Nature Conservation. Outside the door is Hennie Potgieter's statue of a man and super-bull called 'Curbed Freedom'. It helps to set the tone for Pretoria's street statues—sturdy horses and enormous animals, all muscle and brawn, top hats and frock coats, slouch hats and spurs. Not for Pretoria are Johannesburg's slender leaping antelope or cavorting revellers. Pretoria's statues tell a different story in a different key. Every time we pass Hennie Potgieter's bull, Pretoria's choice—and something we too admire—we think of the statue 'Man and Woman' executed by the great Moses Kottler for the Population and Registration Building (then in Van der Walt Street). It showed the nude figures of a man and woman, with the man's hand resting lightly on the woman's breast—and Pretoria cast it out as indecent. (Kimberley received it with joy!)

The Provincial Building is famous for its works of art, which are a true treasure trove most unexpectedly buried in this enormous modern building. The Nature Conservation entrance has two fine mosaic panels by Ernst de Jong representing day and night in the animal world, and within, Louis Steyn's marvellous batiks of birds, mammals and fish—he is sometimes called 'the father of batiks' because it was he who introduced this art of painting with wax to South Africa. Beyond is an Ullmann tapestry, a riotous medley of Ullmann-African animals—we would walk all the way down Church Street to see the Charlie Chaplin lion with outward-turning paws.

The other works in the main building can be seen by appointment, including the painting 'Discovery' by the well-known artist, Alexis Preller. It took over three years to complete and its colour and imagery delight. Fellow artists talk about Preller's design, draftsmanship, tonal values, and so on, and how he was influenced by the old murals he saw in Europe. To us, this is Africa as Preller saw it—perhaps as the early Portuguese saw it as well as they sailed under the Southern Cross—with astrologers and navigators, the symbolic sailing ship and flight of birds, tall turbans in bright colours, green and emerald fishes in a green, green sea, and the big blue globe, the astralobe, like a dream of night.

The **Odendaal Rooms** are worth a visit in themselves. The Provincial Buildings are new: but this complex of three rooms has a special link with early Pretoria, for the beautiful carved walnut door and panelling, the chandeliers and other things, were once part of Hollard House, one of Pretoria's great houses, which stood, until demolished recently, on the corner of Andries and Jacob Mare streets. William Hollard, an Austrian by birth, was one of the colourful characters of

Kruger times, an advocate and friend of Kruger, and the man after whom Johannesburg's Hollard (Stock Exchange) Street was named. Mr F. H. Odendaal, the Administrator, rescued some of his fine things for the Provincial Building when Hollard House was torn down.

These rooms, in a quiet way, are history. They are also Hollard himself. He must have had an eye for good material and workmanship, but beyond this we could remember little of him excepting the fact that—friend of Kruger though he was—he had never mastered Afrikaans, so that his eloquent pleadings at the bar were in mixed German, Afrikaans and English. 'Hollard's taal,' it was called with amusement, and people still remember the term.

A few paces from Church Square to the north is the Post Office Museum, soon to be removed, and to the south in Compol Building in Pretorius Street is the **Police Museum.** This, with its exhibits—macabre mostly—is very well done, old and young revelling in unlawful gold, the bank notes forged in the motor-car garage, the door-knob that was the hiding place of 18 diamonds, the murder weapons. There is a great deal more to it than this, of course, all of it extraordinarily interesting.

To the west of Church Square and only five minutes' walk away, is a far more poignant reminder of Paul Kruger than his statue. It is **Kruger's house,** the old home built for him in 1884 in which he lived as President until 1900 when he left Pretoria during the Anglo-Boer War to journey into exile. It is one of the few houses remaining that is older than the Sunnyside jacarandas. It was also pre-gold, a long, low, simple home with a stoep running its length in front, the stoep on which the President drank early coffee with his visitors and settled the affairs of state. Now a museum, the house has been restored as nearly as possible to the original Kruger home.

Many of today's visitors still find the place charged with atmosphere and are much moved by it. We ourselves always pause to look at the lions outside. Barney Barnato of diamond fame gave them to Kruger. Perhaps we only imagined that they have Kruger features.

To the north-west of the city is a small humble sight that bird lovers sometimes go to see. It is an undistinguished reed forest near the market in **Von Weilligh Street,** which is the traditional home of half a million swallows that fly here in our spring at the approach of the European winter. They are welcome travellers. The Transvaal Division of Nature Conservation a few years ago requested the management committee of the city council to spare this little forest as the area round developed, and the committee agreed!

Further east in Boom Street are the zoo—the National Zoological Garden which includes the beautiful little Aquarium—and the National Cultural History and Open-Air Museum, all full of interest. The pavement outside is crowded with Ndebele women sitting chatting and displaying their beadwork, a bright lively sight that tourists love.

Our favourite place of interest and amusement is to the south of Church Square. It is the **New Transvaal Museum** which stands opposite the City Hall in Paul Kruger Street, the skeleton of a 24-metre Fin Whale suspended before it. It took a structural engineer to arrange the hanging of its great white bones—now the city's most dramatic wall hanging.

This is an important museum. On its collections many of the standard works of South African natural history have been based, including Dr Austin Roberts' *The Birds of South Africa* and *The Mammals of South Africa*, and Dr V. Fitzsimons's *The Snakes of Southern Africa*. This is where Dr Robert Broom worked on early man—people used to greet him sometimes in his silk tie and stiff collar hurrying down the long dark passages in the basement where most of the work is done and feel as if they had saluted a king: and here Dr 'Bob' Brain, the present director, continues the work.

In 1910 Austin Roberts—a 27-year-old amateur ornithologist with one year's formal schooling—joined the museum staff: he was to serve for 38 years and pioneer the systematic study of birds and mammals in South Africa. His bird book, that gentle best-seller (now revised by Dr G. R. McLachlan and Dr R. Liversidge) has introduced countless South Africans to birds. People today go to the Transvaal Museum to see in particular the exhibits on palaeontology and the Bird Hall named after Austin Roberts.

There are good collections of birds in most South African museums, but the Hall is something special, not only presenting the country's phenomenally rich bird life (eventually all 875 species will be covered) but telling their story as well—the greatest attraction of all is the case of birds, which are illuminated and identified one by one as their calls ring out. Soon the museum's newest venture will be open to the public, halls which tell the story of life from the first algae to man himself, and tell it as an adventure story—which of course it is.

In the same building, connected by a door, is the **Museum of the Geological Survey.** Although this is a marvellous place to browse in, there are for us three major sights to which we always gravitate—a boulder, a mural, and a set of tapestries.

The boulder is a relic of the very early days of gold in the Transvaal. In 1871, 15 years before the Witwatersrand goldfields were declared, gold was discovered on the farm Eersteling, slightly off the Great North Road between Potgietersrust and Pietersburg, by a man called Edward Button. While Button was making arrangements to exploit the gold, his partner, William Pigg, developed the gold-bearing quartz reef, a laborious job in which Africans crushed the quartz by hand. Pigg, driven to desperation by its awkwardness and slowness, developed a new method of crushing the ore with this big round boulder.

He placed it in a slight hollow in a rocky outcrop, bolting across it a beam—a tree from the veld: on either end of this he put an African to play see-saw and rock the boulder, while he fed pieces of quartz under the side of the rock that was tilted up, and swept out the crushed fragments.

Next to the boulder in the museum is a photograph of a painting by Thomas Baines, who visited Eersteling and left this record of the oddest piece of gold machinery to come out of the Transvaal.

In another room is the mural, taking up an entire wall, which illustrates the fauna and flora of the Karoo between 250 and 150 million years ago. It is the work of the Pretoria artist, Dick Findlay, a careful, detailed picture of the strange plants, the swamps and desert, the reptiles—including those on the evolutionary way to mammals—and the dinosaurs of that ancient era. It was done in close consultation with the Bernard Price Institute for Palaeontology in Johannesburg, so that this is as true a picture as artist and scientist can make it, and the impact is tremendous.

The third highlight here is the Ullmann series of tapestries, the very spirit of a South African geological museum, depicting gold, diamonds, uranium, iron and coal, but as nobody else has ever seen these things. 'Diamonds' is a languid beauty, built up bit by bit with consummate skill and obviously too with laughter, gold a golden king with a wicked eye and a boxer's nose, holding the world in his hands—oblivious of the bird of prey above his head, spreading its claws about his crown.

Back in Church Street and three blocks east of the square is the new **Opera House**—which it is claimed will rival Sydney's famous one—and the Strijdom Monument next to it with Danie de Jager's statue of a horse group. Van der Walt Street runs southwards at the side of it, and three blocks up is the large, rather ugly brick-and-sandstone **Staats Model School** which today houses the library of the Transvaal Education Department. It is famous as the building in which Winston Churchill was imprisoned in 1899 during the Anglo-Boer War.

Churchill, then a young war correspondent for the London 'Morning

Post', was taken prisoner near Estcourt in Natal and brought to Pretoria. From this building he escaped on December 12, 1899, by climbing over the high iron fence—he was wearing civilian clothes he had bought—and hiding in the bush on the banks of the Apies River: an electricity sub-station on the spot is today called Winston! The story that he swam the Apies River (in dry weather a trickle of water only) has caused laughter in Pretoria down the years. It was a piece of reporter's imagination, Churchill told South Africa's first President, Mr C. R. Swart, many years later. He could not swim!

Further on, Van der Walt Street cuts Jacob Maré Street at right angles. This is one of the old thoroughfares—Burgers Park on the northern side was a lion's lair when the first Trekkers arrived; and later two of Pretoria's oldest houses were built next to it.

Travelling from the western end of Jacob Maré Street towards the east, there is, on the left hand side, an extraordinary mock-medieval creation with a candlesnuffer tower, that is today used by the **Pretoria Conservatoire of Music.** Pretoria was largely built by shopkeepers who were its early aristocracy, and this was the moment of just such a merchant prince, Eddie Bourke, in 1888, who imported the builders from Holland. There is still a Bourke there, the charming ghost of Mrs Eddie who has been seen in her favourite gown, with her basket on her arm, on her way to feed the birds. It was her daily task for many years.

A little beyond on the right hand side is **Melrose House,** two years older than Pretoria's famous jacarandas. It is also a good deal older than any of Johannesburg's great houses, for it was built in 1886, the year the Witwatersrand goldfields were proclaimed.

It was not gold that built it but coaching and trade. George Heys, whose home it was, was not only a merchant, but in Pretoria he ran a coaching service, 'Express Saloon Coaches', that was part of the life of Kruger days, and which carried the mail for years. His house was a family home until recently; now, as a museum, it is open to the public. It is also a national monument.

It is pleasant to stop in the busy street and pass between the eagles, wings outstretched, topping the pillars, and the little fountain beyond, and look. This is a Victorian mansion, plush, solid, costly, slightly ridiculous, to many immensely nostalgic—built by a London architect, the materials English, transported here by ship and ox-wagon almost 100 years ago, the very name based on a Scottish ruin, Melrose Abbey. There is a turret, a conservatory, a billiard room, stained glass windows, an organ from America, a verandah with imported ironwork, the entrance guarded by two proud lions.

71

In the Anglo-Boer War first Lord Roberts and then Kitchener occupied the house—Kitchener introduced his turbaned Sikhs as servants. Vivien Allen, who wrote *Kruger's Pretoria* recently and is the great-granddaughter of George Heys, says it was a family legend that the hole in the carpet in the room on the left of the front door—which Kitchener had made his office—was caused by his sub-ordinates turning smartly on their heels to salute him as he sat at his desk.

What everyone goes to see in particular is the table in the dining-room. On this, the Treaty of Vereeniging ending the Anglo-Boer War was signed in 1902.

A family retainer still cares for Melrose House. He is Andries Letsaola, head-cleaner, who went to work for the Heys well over 60 years ago at the age of six, and has been there ever since.

Still further along the road is the big modern business complex of **Barclay Square,** with shops set around an open square. Tucked away under the steps on the eastern side is a little shop, Klaus Wasserthal's, with a window full of candles, gorgeous ones in all shapes, sizes and colours, which are made by Klaus Wasserthal himself in his candle factory outside Pretoria: from here they go to shops in all the cities. This is more than a candle shop, however, for some of the best indigenous craft work, both African and European, is offered here for sale. There is no permanent exhibition of South African crafts in Pretoria (or anywhere else in the country, for that matter), so that a shop like this, with friendly knowledgeable staff, takes on something of the function of a craft centre.

Devenish Street, which runs past Barclay Square, leads into **Esselen Street,** the busiest thoroughfare of the suburb, Sunnyside. We have a favourite place here, too, the little shop of Erich Frey, master goldsmith. His work, internationally famous, is a joy: just as good is his talk of the oldest worked gold ever known, from a queen's tomb in Mesopotamia, of the gold dust that bearers carried in porcupine quills through Africa.

Du Toit Street at the end of Esselen leads back again into Church Street, and to the right, heading east, are the **Union Building Gardens,** and at their top, half way up Meintjeskop, the Buildings themselves.

Most of the old houses that are a landmark in Pretoria were 'foreign', built with materials brought across an ocean. How much stranger still that the man who looked at South Africa's soils and rocks and forest trees and saw them as the bones and the bloom of South Africa's own great buildings, should have been an Englishman from Kent.

He was Sir Herbert Baker, the architect who left his mark through-out the country, who built his own home on a Johannesburg ridge facing towards Pretoria, who, as Cecil Rhodes's choice, rebuilt Groote Schuur in Cape Town, and renovated—bringing back to beauty—so many of the Cape Dutch houses of the Cape.

His greatest work was this one, the Union Buildings, overlooking the city. If Rhodes gave a lift to Herbert Baker, it was Smuts and Botha—Louis Botha was South Africa's first prime minister—who made him internationally famous. He was their choice to design the Buildings, the buildings of government in Pretoria for a united South Africa. They had found someone with a vision who dreamed in terms of a high acropolis, classically designed and fitted to a hot country, its shapes and colours to be seen in bright light against blue skies, with colonnades, towers, court yards, amphitheatre, sculptures, fountains and gardens, set upon the high hill overlooking the city. He designed it and the gardens on different levels, in great sweeps and formal terraces, using for his material local stone, Pretoria bricks and Vereeniging tiles, stinkwood from the Cape forests and Rhodesian teak. He did not only make a fine government building of a new kind for South Africa: this was the prototype of others he built in hot countries through the world, in Rhodesia and Kenya, in Australia, and at New Delhi. This, in fact, was the beginning of 'the new Imperial Architecture''.

The Buildings are the grandest in South Africa and we take our visitors to see them and walk up through the gardens Sir Herbert planned. An unusual pleasure comes from their smallest part—if we may call a nestling pigeon a part. The clock in the tower, which has been there as long as the Buildings themselves—is a good one, as reliable as Big Ben itself. Except in nestling time. Sometimes, then, the chimes ring out a moment late—for the young pigeons are learning to fly. Their take-off platforms are the hands of the clock and here they crowd in rows, their combined weight just too much for the minute hand on its upward journey. It lags infinitesimally.

The Union Buildings are in the suburb of **Bryntirion**. Here is also a famous official home built by Sir Herbert Baker in the Cape Dutch style, that of the State President, once Government House, with its splendid gardens—all are sometimes open to the public. The entrance in Church Street is guarded by two sentries in green and gold uniforms. South Africa has few such decorations, and they are enjoyed by everyone speeding up Church Street east. Libertas, the official home of the Prime Minister in Pretoria, is in Bryntirion not far from the Union Buildings, and so are many other official homes. This is an exclusive suburb, much shown off to visitors, who are taken to see it, often on a leisurely Sunday drive, ending up with the Union Buildings and its panoramic view.

The view is a grand one, a city panorama of valley and hillsides of streets and homes, and to the west of skyscrapers and the smoke of Iscor and other industries. Church Square is to the right, with the Railway Station beyond it, Sunnyside and Arcadia, Pretoria's oldest suburbs, with Burgers Park a green square, ahead, Brooklyn and Waterkloof suburbs slightly to the left.

There is the **Station** with its Herbert Baker tower. It was in front of this that a bandstand, erected in 1893 when an important official was visiting the town, collapsed, Paul Kruger in the fall landing on top of and squashing the wife of General Joubert, who never forgave him— a small-town story of fine calibre that in its way made history.

The line running north-south is the Apies River. Its concreted banks give little to the city today: but we remember an old lady, still exquisitely gay and pretty, who told us how she used to dance on its grassy banks under the trees on New Year's Day in company with all the village of Pretoria.

The green patch with the glint of water slightly to the right is the **Bird Sanctuary,** named after Dr Austin Roberts, in Boshoff Street, New Muckleneuk, in the heart of the eastern suburbs. It is a place of city and country birds alike, and one of the wetlands that brings to it even the pink-backed pelican from Lake St Lucia in Natal. Over to the east, just short of the broad band of Crown Avenue running up the hill, is Rupert Street in Brooklyn suburb. In Kruger days this was wild country—koppies, bush and grass—and here in a cottage lived the young Eugene Marais, later to be famous as naturalist and writer. Somewhere here, where a plush house is today, he would make a fire in the veld, put down a pot of rice, and sit by it in the lantern light with a group of little boys, watching the field mice visiting, and telling ghost stories.

Across the valley from Meintjeskop is a line of hills with the **Voortrekker Monument** built upon them, dominating the country to the south. As its name suggests, it honours the Voortrekkers, that band of Afrikaner men, women and children who in the 1830s broke away from British rule in the Cape and with their wagons and oxen, their Bibles and guns, pushed into the almost unknown north to find a new home. They were a courageous people, and their very name is still immensely evocative to every Afrikaner; so that when this monument was opened on 16th December 1949, there was a great upsurge of sentiment, which has never entirely died away. Afrikaners visit the

Monument rather as they do a church; the rest of the world to see the country's grandest monument and a chapter of history well displayed.

Gerard Moerdyk, the well-known architect who specialized in Dutch Reformed churches, designed the Monument, using the ancient building forms and patterns of Africa—he borrowed from Zimbabwe, from the African veld with its tawny lights, from the wild animals. The long frieze around the wall depicts some of the events of Voortrekker history—the frieze, although modelled in South Africa, was made in Italy in marble, identical, it is said, to that used by Michael Angelo. The story goes that one of the faces looking out at visitors is that of the Duke of Windsor. It is regularly denied, and as regularly crops up again, because the likeness is there. English visitors can often pick out 'the Duke' among all the other figures.

The Monument contains a touch of drama reminiscent of high altars in ancient histories. The roof has been so constructed that on 16th December at 11 a.m. a ray of sunlight shines through, lighting up the portion of the frieze showing the Voortrekkers making a solemn vow before the Battle of Blood River, and an hour later illuminating the sarcophagus in the middle of the crypt, with its words *Ons vir jou, Suid-Afrika*—we for you, South Africa. Blood River was the great battle in which the Voortrekkers, on 16th December 1838, defeated the Zulus under Dingaan near Vryheid in Natal. Andries Pretorius, the man after whom Pretoria was named, was the Voortrekker Commandant-General; and the frieze, lit by the shaft of sunlight, shows him and his men vowing that if they won the battle they would build a church and observe the day of victory as one of thanksgiving.

Far away to the east, is the **C.S.I.R.**, a goodlooking group of modern, stream-lined buildings housing the country's single biggest scientific complex, and beyond it, across the road, the **National Botanic Gardens,** with the National Herbarium of the Botanical Research Institute in the centre standing on a hill. At the main entrance stand fine wrought-iron gates, the work of Swiss-born Hans Brugger. The northern is known as the Reynolds Gate, and is a memorial to Gilbert Reynolds, the man who first made aloes familiar to South Africans in his book, *The Aloes of South Africa*. They are big—two together are nearly seven metres in length—and in their design Brugger has used as the theme, not only aloes but grasses, and the leaves, flowers and fruits of other South African plants done in flowing lines and exquisite detail.

The huge gardens beyond are a good place for a botanist to glimpse the flora of South Africa and a fine one for anyone to ramble in. The koppies are covered with the trees and plants indigenous to the area, and although none matches the showiness of the Cape plants, they have their own beauties and interest.

The **Botanical Research Institute** is the government institution dealing with the flora of South Africa as a whole. It was only a few years ago that it moved into this new building from an old home not far from the Union Buildings on Meintjeskop, a rackety ancient affair full of rotting wood and holes and draughts, where some of the finest botanists matured and some of the great work on South African plants was done.

What the new building has is room for display and work, and everyone interested in plants finds it a Mecca. We personally go to see four people whose combined years of work total two centuries, all retired, all still working, with a knowledge of South African plants and botanists—and a generosity—that are unbeatable. On the first floor are two ex-Directors of the Institute, Dr R. Allen Dyer, and Dr L. E. W. Codd. Next to them is Miss Mary Gunn, after whom the Mary Gunn Library in the Institute is named, who started here as a teenage typist in 1916, taught herself what she knows of books, made here one of the best botanical libraries in the southern hemisphere, and ended up as supreme authority on botanical Africana.

On the floor above is Dr Inez Verdoorn, again self-taught, without a formal lesson in botany, who has become one of South Africa's great systematic botanists: for well over 60 years almost every researcher here has depended in some way on her knowledge and generosity. When we are in luck, there is also Cythna Letty (Mrs Forssman), the artist, now retired, who sometimes visits the Institute: she was its official artist for a very long time, and is South Africa's best-known botanical artist, and internationally famous. Most of her original paintings are here.

When we have seen all this, or even a part of it, we are ready to dine at leisure. Far over to the east on the Lynnwood Road, well beyond the Institute, is a row of Lombardy poplars on the left of the road, and a sign which says simply, **Lombardy Restaurant.** This small restaurant is not only Pretoria's best restaurant but one of the finest in the country. Owned and run by an Italian couple, Mario and Maria Moggia, it is exquisite in its setting, furnishing, service and food: the flowery garden with its trees and grass sets the tone, while every vegetable, every strawberry, egg and jug of cream is 'home-done'. They and their family cook the food. The unforgettable array of sweets, for instance—the pears mahogany-red with wine, the light-as-air creation topped with tiny golden eclairs, the liqueur-flavoured cream and toasted almonds—all this delectable froth is theirs, each member of the family making his and her own contribution. Sometimes we drink a glass of wine with Mario, and he shows us his cellar with the 10 000 and more bottles of fine wine. A cellar is a place of promise: and we number this among Pretoria's sights and are happy to have an end so mellow to our day.

CHAPTER FIVE

Smuts, the Cullinan, Kruger

❧

There is plenty to be seen as well on a day's excursion into the country round Pretoria. Once a week, for instance, at 10 a.m. on a Monday morning, the **Blue Train** leaves Pretoria station in its journey to Cape Town. This is one of the famous trains of the world—and its charges are in proportion to its excellence: but for R3, a ticket bought at Pretoria takes one as far as Johannesburg, and for an hour one may ride over the Highveld feeling like champagne and cream. This little-known trip is only possible when there is sufficient room on the train: on this first leg of the journey there usually is, for most people board the Blue Train in Johannesburg. The return trip, Johannesburg to Pretoria, is made on a Thursday.

The present Blue Train was put into service in 1972 with the principal object of providing passengers with every luxury. Its name originates from a luxury dining car built in 1933 for the Blue Train's forerunner, the Union Limited: it was known as the 'Protea' (it is still in service with other trains), and was painted blue and cream. The 'Protea' was famous for a generation, and its colour scheme so popular that eventually the whole train became blue and cream, and the Blue Train was born.

The Union Limited itself was carrying on a famous train tradition— its own forebears had the names Imperial Mail and Diamond Express, and were distinguished in their own ways, too.

We climbed aboard one Monday morning, over the red carpet spread on the station platform, and settled into our standard compartment. This, the lowest in status, gave us luxury we had never seen in a train before; it was a compact, five-star, blue-decorated hotel bedroom and lounge combined, with a radio, a push-button controlling the venetian blinds, iced drinking water, shaving points, a locker for shoes (shoes put there at night are always collected in the corridor through a special opening, cleaned and returned, without disturbance). The glass in the windows was faintly golden from the thin layer of gold diffused onto one's face to deflect the heat and glare.

There are 16 coaches in the train, which can accommodate 108 passengers. When the train was moving—we only knew it was, because the country was flowing smoothly past our windows—the train manager took us on a tour to see the deluxe and semi-deluxe carriages and the kitchen, and afterwards we sat in the lounge car drinking coffee and talking to the staff. We were too early for lunch—crème reine margot, crayfish cocktail, fried sole and sauce rémoulade, asparagus princess, roast duckling with orange sauce, monkey-gland steak, roast leg of mutton with apple jelly, bavaroise moscovite, vanilla icecream with raspberry sauce, cheese and biscuits, fruit and coffee—but we heard about it. The friendliness and manners of the staff were as splendid as the meal.

Presently a tourist, camera in hand, leapt up from the table beside us. Would we all—train manager, stewards, passengers—remain still so that he could record this moment. This was his second visit to South Africa from Germany. And why? he cried, gesticulating and waving his camera. Just to travel in the Blue Train!

A little way out of Pretoria, the train slipped through the station of Irene. Near here, just out of the village of Irene and well-signposted, is another Pretoria sight, as different from the luxury and sophistication of the Blue Train as anything can be. It is **Doornkloof,** once the farm and home of General Smuts.

It is one of the most astonishing 'great houses' in the world—a great house where history was made many times over—a large, ramshackle, wood-and-iron building, standing on stilts, wind in the rooms, bees in the walls, and below the floor the open space used to store apples, pears and quinces (where snakes lurked), the happy playground of the Smuts children. Built in India for the British Army, it is said, the house was shipped to South Africa, and reassembled in Middelburg, Transvaal, where it was a British officers' mess in the Anglo-Boer War. Smuts bought it in 1908 for R600: it was once more taken to pieces and set up here again on Doornkloof, and 'The Big House' it has remained ever since.

It is surrounded by trees, wild trees predominantly, the white stinkwoods the birds planted, much loved by Mrs Smuts, and the *blinkblaars*. A veranda encircles the house. Within is the kitchen with the wood and iron stove where there was always a great pot of boiling water to make tea for visitors, and some 18 rooms. Nobody ever knew for sure how many. The walls are of wood, and when the family wanted another room, up went an extra wooden partition, or when a particularly big room was needed, a wall was removed.

Today the house is a national monument and is being restored, as far as possible, to what it was in Smuts's day. Then all the women slept at the back of the house, Mrs Smuts in a narrow slip of a room. It is kept as she had it, with the washstand, basin and jug and yellow-wood cupboard, and the narrow iron bedstead, on it the tiny suitcase in which she stored the papers and letters she always took to bed with her. (Her family used to laugh at her—surely the bed was narrow enough without housing a suitcase as well.)

The General's room on the other side of the house was not used by him as a bedroom except when he was dying: he slept, summer and winter, on an iron bed on the stoep outside, with a kitchen chair next to him to hold his coffee cup. Near him was the room known to the family as the *donkerkamer*—the dark room—reputedly haunted although the family never saw a ghost. Nevertheless, children sent to the General with a message, used to hurry on tiptoe past the room, and none would sleep there.

This was the room of the King and Queen of Greece during the last war, when Greece was overrun by the Germans and Smuts offered the royal family sanctuary in South Africa. It was as austere as Smuts's own room. Queen Frederika, who always slept in the nude, used to warm herself by propping the heater up level with the bed. 'What she needs is a good pair of nice woollen pyjamas,' Mrs Smuts—thinking of the wooden walls—lamented, but the Queen never bought them.

When Mrs Sylma Coaton, Smuts's daughter, told us the story, it brought back her mother almost in the flesh. We never knew her as the lovely young woman Smuts had courted, but we remembered her as 'Ouma' during World War II, small, downright, with her celebrated shock of grey hair in a fuzz round her head, organizing comforts for 'the boys up North'. Libertas, the official home of the Prime Minister in Pretoria, had just been given to the Greek royal family as their wartime home. (They were no doubt revelling in the warmth.) 'But why don't *you* live there yourself?' someone asked Mrs Smuts, and she answered, 'Can you see me washing the Oubaas' socks in a pink marble basin?'

Today inside the front door stands an ancient telephone, a model of the standard telephone used by Glasgow municipality late in the last century—it was Smuts's Hot Line to his chief-of-staff during World War II. Everybody stops to look at it. Some of the fine old furniture, like the big old stinkwood cupboard in the diningroom, is back, and the morning we went to see the house Mrs Coaton and her daughter, Mrs Lilian Dreyer, were there, sorting letters and labelling.

We knew by heart Smuts's reputation, his aloofness, sternness, ruthlessness, courage, wisdom, austerity, the great cold qualities—ice-cold some called them—that had helped to set him among the gods. We knew, too, the story of someone entering Smuts's room to find his grandchildren clustered around him, shining a torch into his mouth to see his false teeth.

His daughter—and granddaughter who grew up in the house and was married from it—remembered other homely and to the world surprising things. On the sideboard in the diningroom is a big pink and green cheese dish. It was there in the same place in family days and held big hunks of cheese. There were two bowls of sweets and two tins, one with rusks and one with biscuits, and masses of fruit, and everybody passing through the room helped themselves as they liked. Sometimes the General's face would fall, his daughter recalled, when he took the cover off the cheese dish to find that the children had taken the lot.

It was 'a marvellous, happy, wild childhood'. The children would go with their father into the veld, throw down a blanket on the ground at night and sleep without thought of snakes or germs. Smuts's feeling for the wild world of plants was a mixture of love and reverence. 'Don't pick,' he would admonish his children, 'worship and pass on.'

He himself did gather plants sparingly for a scientific purpose: he was a devoted botanist and had his own herbarium within the house at Doornkloof. Botany was one of the pleasures never far from him, even in war. Many of his specimens were identified and named for him by our old friend, Dr Inez Verdoorn. They corresponded on and off through the years, even during the North African Campaign of World War II, which might so easily have absorbed all his energies. The year 1942 was Tobruk and El Alamein to South Africans but Smuts still had time to write to her, 'We see little of each other in these stormy times when one finds little leisure for Botany. But what a consolation it is for those who can afford the time'. He had, he said, found many plants in the Western Desert of Libya, 'all bristly and thorny and forbidding', and he was looking forward to reading botany 'as soon as the work is over'.

The books that once filled Doornkloof are gone. Besides the General's there were those of Mrs Smuts: she had, among others, a collection of poetry and many books in German. Thinking of her as Ouma in her later days, we sometimes forget another side; during their courtship Smuts taught her Greek! We looked round the Doornkloof library: the only familiar thing was a small square white box decorated with an orange tree in green and gold. We also had had one: it contained a slice of Smuts's 80th birthday cake, given us when we danced at his birthday ball 25 years before. When last we had seen the room, on a September day in 1950, the day after Smuts had died—

quietly, pulling off his shoes as he sat on his bed—it had been massed with books and the big table with papers: his Boer War saddle stood on the floor against the wall together with his saddle bags. In one, when they opened it, they had found a Greek Testament, in the other, a copy of the sayings of Marcus Aurelius.

Kyalami, one of the big international motor-racing circuits, lies in this country between Pretoria and Johannesburg, and close to it is the **South African National Equestrian Centre,** where its former well-known director was Major George Iwanowski, a Polish officer who was once with the Polish cavalry, and assistant-director of the Polish National Horse Stud.

At 11 a.m. every Sunday morning a show is held at the Centre that is unique in South Africa, when the Sentrachem National Lipizzaner team performs to a wildly excited audience.

Most people know of the Lipizzaner horses, the white horses of Vienna, and many have seen the film, *The Miracle of the White Stallions*, showing the escape (somewhat romanticized) of the official Austrian stud from the Russian army during World War II. It was not from Austria but from Hungary that a famous stud came to reach, at length, Natal.

The original Lipizzaners were bred in Andalusia in Spain, and from here travelled to Austria more than 400 years ago, where a stud was established at Lipizza in 1580—the names of those first stud stallions, Maestoso, Conversano, Neapolitano, Favory, Pluto and Siglavy, are still part of the name of every Lipizzaner. They belong to the oldest human-bred race of horses in the world, and in Vienna, where they are the glory of the Spanish Riding School, they and their riders are part of an ancient but living art, evoking as much sentiment as the Vienna Woods themselves.

Soon after their arrival in Natal, the stallion, Maestoso Erdem, was being ridden by Major Iwanowski, and from the partnership of stallion and noted horseman came an exhibition of classical riding such as South Africa had seldom seen. With it also came the idea of a second Spanish Riding School—but in South Africa—and around this ambition the Major built up a Lipizzaner team. The stud is now owned by the organization, National Chemical Products. Breeding is carried on at its farm, Waterkloof, near Newcastle in the Natal Midlands. So here the Lipizzaner line continues—white stallions and mares, black foals, growing into dappled youth, and finally into the milk white colour of maturity—in South Africa with a dark fleck here and there.

Although the stallions do give performances in other parts—they were at Cape Town's Festival recently—the permanent show is always near Kyalami. Here Major Iwanowski trained the horses to provide the only show of its kind outside Austria, a team of Lipizzaner stallions drilled as in the Spanish Riding School, performing—with a team of specially trained riders—the same age-old movements.

The traditions of the Spanish Riding School are preserved as strictly as in Vienna. 'Not,' says Mrs Jill Meyer, who took over the team from Major Iwanowski when he retired early in 1978, 'that we are anywhere near as good as in the Spanish Riding School.' But they are good, good enough to be visited by the Director of the Spanish Riding School and to be invited to Vienna to train. The standard of this now all-woman team was reached by dedication, discipline and hard work: riders give part of every day to training. What a sight they are in their own right, white breeches, black boots, tricorns, top hats, and hunting scarlet.

We had seen the white horses in Vienna. We went one winter morning to watch them on the Transvaal Highveld, to see the art of dressage, the Ballet of the White Stallions, something between ballet and gymnastics—it was enchanting: Major Iwanowski, tremendous on Neopolitano Cypriora 11, doing the half-pass-in-passage, one of the most complicated and beautiful movements of all (mastered by only one horse in 40 years at the Spanish Riding School itself): the Pas de Deux, two riders and horses moving in unison, one the mirror of the other; the pirouette, volte, pesade, levade, 'the airs above and on the ground'.

Even the setting was splendid. It was not the old baroque hall of the horses of Vienna, but a big *manège*, roofed, with the sides partly open to the Highveld, and behind it—as the doors opened at the end—a glimpse of a great courtyard with a white tower and a round water trough like a fountain in the centre, all flooded with sunlight. Against this backdrop, the stallions and riders, in silhouette against the sun, moved through the doors.

To the east of Pretoria, not an hour's drive away from the city, is the **Premier Diamond Mine,** to which regular tours are run.

Kimberley has always been the centre of diamond mining in South Africa, yet it is from here, not Kimberley, that the king of diamonds, the Cullinan—the largest and purest diamond known in the world— was taken on a January day in 1905. The story of how it was found, and cut, to become the glory of the British Crown Jewels, is an extraordinary one: the mystery still surrounding it is one of the strangest of all.

At the end of a day's work in that summer of 1905, Fred Wells, the surface manager of the Premier Mine, saw what he thought was a piece of broken bottle sticking out of an open-cast face. He dug it out with his penknife. It was so big that even a fellow mine official doubted whether it could possibly be a diamond. But it was. It weighed 1 lb 6 oz (3 106 carats) and was fit for kings and queens. To kings and queens it went.

The Transvaal presented the diamond to King Edward VII on his birthday in 1907. It yielded nine major stones, the largest of which is the Cullinan I, which is The Star of Africa, weighs 530 carats, and is mounted in the Royal Sceptre. The Cullinan II, somewhat smaller, graces the Imperial State Crown alongside jewels which *are* British history, like the Black Prince's ruby, drop-like in form, which was given to the warrior-prince by Pedro the Cruel in 1387 after the battle of Nagara, and which was worn on a coronet about his battle helmet by Henry V at Agincourt. Apart from the Cullinan, the crown has 2 700 other diamonds in it. Queen Mary's Crown of blue-white diamonds contains two other Cullinan stones—this crown is considered more impressive than the Queen's. The bits of 'broken bottle' from Premier Mine remain the brightest and best of them all.

The King of England himself had handed the original rough diamond to the man who cut it, Joseph Asscher of Amsterdam. As the guest of John and Mary Mackenzie (he was the manager of Consolidated Diamond Mines) we heard the story one night over dinner at Oranjemund, heart of the world's richest diamond fields at the mouth of the Orange River. Here, too, was Laurent Duizend, great-grand-nephew of Joseph Asscher, who cut the stone.

'You won't believe it,' he said, 'but the King gave my great grand-uncle the diamond and he simply put it in his pocket and carried it across the Channel to Amsterdam like that!'

He went on, 'Cleaving a gem, especially one as unique and valuable as the Cullinan, is a nerve-shattering business. Uncle Asscher studied the lines of the cleavage planes of the great stone for months before attempting it. To any other eye but his they were invisible. He didn't even know whether he was right. When he struck the decisive blow, either he would be proved right or the Cullinan would be reduced to a heap of white powder, like a car's broken windscreen.

'He used a short metal rod as a striker and a blade made of hardened steel. The stone was set in a "dop" of solder to keep it firm. Security was tight. Everyone was cleared out of the factory and armed police were on guard. Uncle Asscher had a doctor and nurse present to attend him—just in case he needed attention.

'When he struck the cleaving knife with the metal rod the first time, the blade snapped; the Cullinan stayed intact. At his second blow, the diamond fell in four into a tin tray which had been placed beneath. Uncle Asscher fell too—on to the floor in a dead faint. The doctor and nurse were certainly required to revive him.'

This is where the mystery began to tantalize again. When Fred Wells scraped the Cullinan diamond out of the earth, it had, even in the rough, a distinct cleavage face: he thought he had only half a diamond. Others bore this out. In the words of a De Beers Mines official report, 'it was only part of a much larger stone'. Wells thought the other part had gone through the crushers. Engineers at the mine, however, say the crushers had a special trip mechanism which prevented any big diamond being smashed: so it did not end like this.

Others had a different tale. Four years later the story was circulating that the finer and larger portion of the stone had been discovered by African workers and removed to a safe-hiding in the fastnesses of the Soutpansberg, the last northern range of mountains in the Transvaal. Now Laurent Duizend said that he, too, believed in 'the other half'— would that it could be found in his lifetime.

A good many people visit Premier Mine; even more stop at a shop 52 kilometres from Pretoria on the old Warmbaths road. It is **Papatso** (barter), a great tourist attraction, where a wide selection of African handwork from all over the country can be seen and bought.

The centre, originally in Pretoria, was moved here some years ago, and what has been lost in accessibility is made up by its new attractions. The shop is the centre of a small complex, which has been built as a Tswana village, a group of round earth-coloured huts, the shop with its *lapa* or courtyard outside where African women come to sell bead- and other work, and wait in the shade of the little thorn trees. We played a game of chess here, with a chess set from the shop, fit for a chief (or a king). The pieces had been designed by a North Sotho and carved in Swaziland out of Rhodesian soapstone: the knights were warriors' shields, and the castle was a Zulu beehive hut.

Tourists in search of other African sights usually try to see the **Ndebele Village** 45 kilometres north-west of Pretoria in the direction of Hebron. It is necessary to get a permit in Pretoria from the Commissioner at the corner of Von Wielligh and Struben streets first, and thereafter to follow the signs on the road with care.

The Ndebele people, and their homes, are the most distinctive in the Transvaal. The African women we see in the streets of Pretoria and on the country roads around with shaven heads, bright blankets and big neck, arm, waist and leg rings of beads and copper, are Ndebele women. Their beadwork is famous, and so are the designs they paint upon the walls of their homes—other African peoples decorate their walls but no work is as magnificent as theirs. Both beads and murals can be seen in the Ndebele village.

To be frank, the village is not a sight that we personally much enjoy, being now highly commercialized. But, lacking the opportunity to see the charming Ndebele homes that are built on private farms, it is to the village that people come to view this individual art.

The homes of Africans south of the Sahara are traditionally round, often of pole and dagga and thatched—they are rondavels to most people—and are arranged in a particular pattern, but within this broad generalization are different concepts and styles. The Southern Ndebele, of which the Pretoria Ndebele are part, site their cattle kraal in front of their home (the cattle kraal being the focal point of all African tribal life), a witch-doctor treats the site with protective medicine, and building then begins.

Firstly the Ndebele men make the latticework and roof of thatch and then the women make the walls of clay and cowdung—in the words of Professor A. L. Meiring, flicking it on 'in small handfuls, very much in the way a swallow builds its nest'. There are also storage rooms and a walled *lapa* or courtyard, both front and back, where the life of the home goes on; and there are the mural decorations done by the women that are the outstanding feature. This is an art handed on from mother to daughter, and is one of the most delightful things to be seen in the country round Pretoria. The best decorations are usually on the walls of the front *lapa* and main hut. The colours are traditionally those of the earth, Pretoria's soils yielding the browns, yellows, reds and greys, chalk giving the white and soot the black; the blue is washing blue. They are all ephemeral colours, washing away in the rainy season, so that redecoration is as regular as the rains. Only now are these natural colours beginning to give way to the more permanent commercial paints, and the result is not always so pleasing.

The patterning is largely geometric, and is based on that of the beadwork. What delights onlookers most today, however, are the city sights that the women have incorporated in the designs—the motorcar, the train, the lampshade, the razor blade, the vehicle number plate TP seen again and again.

With the owner's permission, says the official permit, one may enter a house in the Ndebele village. We laughed about this as a dozen voices *pleaded* with us to enter here and there. Even if commercially inspired, however, the invitation is a good one. Most white people who know African homes, know those which are West-orientated, rectangular brick buildings with windows and furniture within, so that the simplicity and lack of clutter of a traditional African home astonishes. We stood for a few moments in the round thatched room—it was lit only through the doorway—until our eyes grew accustomed to the dimness. This was the main hut: it was quite bare except for a clay shelf, on which sat an old woman, bowing and exclaiming, and a grass mat rolled up. As in traditional homes we had seen in other parts, it was neat as a pin.

It reminded us of the African homes that Moffat described 150 years ago to the west of Pretoria. The Ndebele of Pretoria, however, predated Moffat by some 350 years. Originally of the Nguni stock—which includes the Zulu and the Xhosa peoples—they moved from Zululand into the Transvaal about 400 years ago, splitting at length into two main sections, one of which moved to the north, becoming almost indistinguishable from the Tswana people around them. The southern people, preserving language and customs, live from west of Pretoria eastwards to Belfast on the Highveld, with extensions, writes Mrs H. J. Bruce of the Africana Library, up to Lydenburg and south to Carolina. (Their painted houses can be seen from the main road, N4, as one travels east to the Lowveld.)

Of the two tribes which today make up the Southern Ndebele, the Pretoria tribe—that of the Ndebele village—is called Manala and the more eastern Ndzundza, names which were borne by the first and second sons of the chief who led the Ndebele people out of Zululand. Of these three, Mrs Bruce tells a story straight from the Old Testament.

The old chief, overtaken by blindness and fearing that on his death his six sons would dispute the chieftainship, called Manala, the eldest and bade him go out and kill a zebra for his meal. The mother of Ndzundza, the second son (shades of Rebecca and Jacob) overheard, and sent him to kill a goat which she hastily cooked for the chief. Ndzundza imitated his brother's voice and the biblical deception was complete, the father presenting him with the royal symbols, the club of rhino horn, the medicine horn. After the chief's death, the Ndebele say, the sons and their supporters fought each other, and thus was the Ndebele people broken up into its six parts.

In the last century, the Southern Ndebele were much harassed by Mzilikazi, and we thought of this as we travelled westward from Pretoria into Mzilikazi country towards Rustenburg, Groot Marico, and beyond it to Zeerust, where he had built his last capital in South Africa.

This was Moffat country too, and it was probably at a spot beyond the Hartebeestpoort Dam that Moffat's African attendant told him the tale of the chief of the blue coloured cattle, which epitomized the tragedy of the countryside. There, he said, pointing to the ruins of a town that Mzilikazi had devastated, there had lived this great chief, this king, with his multitudes of cattle. In the distance he and his people had seen the clouds rising from the plains. It was the smoke of burning towns fired by Mzilikazi's Matabele. The onset on the chief's place was 'as the voice of lightning and the Matabele spears as the shaking of a forest in the autumn storm'. They raised the shout of death and flew upon their victims—their hissing and hollow groans told their progress among the dead. A few moments laid hundreds on the ground. Then they entered the town with a roar, pillaged and fired the houses, speared the mothers and cast the infants to the flames. They slaughtered cattle; they danced and sang till the dawn of day; they ascended the hill where the men had grouped and killed until their hands were weary of the spear.

Stooping to the ground where he and Moffat stood, the man took up a little dust in his hand: blowing it off and holding out his naked palm, he said, 'That is all that remains of the great chief of the blue-coloured cattle'.

Today the ruins of these stone-walled African towns can still be seen, and their number can be gauged from aerial photographs. Professor Revil Mason recently counted over 90 separate groups of ruins on photographs covering 102 square kilometres immediately south of Rustenburg.

It was near the site of the Hartebeestpoort Dam that Moffat met Mzilikazi face to face. The wheel was not known to Southern Africa until the white man brought it. Mzilikazi had never before seen one or a 'moving house'. So terrible in slaughter, he was a child now, retreating before Moffat's moving wagons as if they were live things, one hand within Moffat's, the other over his mouth. It is a strange little cameo in this turbulent history, and Moffat told the story well.

Blood-soaked this country may once have been, but today it is a pleasant place, with the Hartebeestpoort Dam, a popular holiday resort, 40 kilometres from Pretoria, the lovely low woodland that is called the bushveld beyond, and the Magaliesberg like a backbone through the country.

This mountain range and the neighbouring country, easily accessible from both Pretoria and Johannesburg, knows a different menace today from Mzilikazi's. Some see it as the site of the townships, the resorts, the roads, and all the services that will be needed to nourish the Pretoria-Witwatersrand-Vereeniging complex of the future—

Kommandonek, the path by which Moffat probably crossed the mountains, already has a disfiguring silica mine. Others think of this wild lovely range that divides the Highveld from the bushveld to the north as a place of beauty and distinction, containing—according to a report of the Mountain Club—more species of plants, insects and animals than the whole of the British Isles (there are more birds of prey than in the whole of Europe). For them its preservation is almost a matter of life and death: now at least part of the range has been proclaimed a nature reserve.

We took, not the northern road to Rustenburg, but the longer one south of and parallel to the mountains. Soon we passed **Broederstroom** near the dam. It was here that, some time in the 5th century A.D. the Negroid people from the north settled and built a village. The remains of this 'relatively intact Iron Age village' is the oldest known south of the Sahara, filling archaeologists with joy. The Knowledge Seekers, the same organization that runs the gold tour on the Rand, has an 'Iron Age Seekers' tour as well to Broederstroom, and further west along the mountains, to Olifantspoort where the remains of whole villages have been unearthed.

Some 12 kilometres beyond Skeerpoort we slowed up to look at the range. There is a nek over the mountains here, on the farm **Hartebeestfontein,** and at the top the remains of a big tree, together with a heap of stones. It is the most fascinating pile in the Transvaal, not only because it is an *isiVivane*—in itself of interest—but because it is possibly the very one Cornwallis Harris, the hunter, saw in 1836 when he was hunting elephant near here, and when the country was almost unknown.

isiVivanes are the heaps of stones—the lucky heaps—sometimes still seen at crossroads, on steep passes or on dangerous spots, that mark African routes from Somaliland to Southern Africa: they have been made through the centuries by African travellers who have added their own stone to the heaps, asking at the same time for strength and luck upon their errands. They are the oldest roadway signs in Africa.

Harris described such a heap on the top of a Magaliesberg pass, and although some historians deny that this is his heap, even a distant association is exciting. It was not far from here that he saw and shot the first sable antelope known to science, which gives the locality an added interest.

We were not done with Moffat yet. Through Rustenburg and its countryside, beloved of holiday-makers—warm and lush, rich with fruit trees and flowers—we turned north-west towards **Boshoek.** What we hoped to see was the famous 'inhabited tree' that Moffat had visited in 1829. It was, he wrote, a gigantic wild fig, supporting in its branches 20 houses, in which several families lived, to escape the lions that then abounded. Moffat climbed up the notched trunk to the top hut some 10 m. above the ground, and was served powdered locusts by his hostess: and while he was eating them, other women from neighbouring roosts came stepping from branch to branch to see him.

Everybody must have a Swiss Family Robinson streak for this often-repeated story has become a classic: while for nearly 140 years men have sought the tree. In 1967, largely through the efforts of the Africana expert, Professor P. R. Kirby, a tree, believed to be Moffat's, was tracked down on the farm, **Bultfontein,** in the Boshoek district, owned by Mr Arnold Fuls. So, winding along the hot, sandy, bush road, we came to the farm and were escorted to the tree by Mrs Fuls.

If it was big in Moffat's day, it is enormous now, a wild fig as he thought, *Ficus ingens*, which has layered itself, spreading over some 37 metres. How did they know this was the inhabited tree? The locality was right, and when the first Fuls had come here 100 years before, the Africans still knew this as the tree Moffat had climbed. And then there were the wagon ruts, the faint old scorings on the rocks. We looked at them and accepted it all: it had to be true.

The tree, we learned, has a later history as a place of refuge. In the Anglo-Boer War the little German community around here fled into its branches at the approach of troops, whether Boer or British, remaining in safety behind the heavy curtain of leaves.

Talk of this war sent us on to see another sight close by, the farm **Boekenhoutfontein,** owed by Paul Kruger, where he lived from the early 1870s until he became President of the South African Republic in 1883.

Moffat seems far away, while Kruger is almost modern history: yet not 45 years separated Moffat's tree from this farmhouse. In style, it would certainly have been familiar to Moffat: he would have seen such a solid, flat-roofed home with a raised stoep in front over and over in Cape towns and villages. Only he would not have recognized the coach house with the often-described smooth iron roof. When Kruger was building this, he found that he had just too little corrugated iron (which he had imported) to complete the roof; so he hammered out the corrugations to give the extra size. It is a famous little Kruger story.

Behind the farmhouse is a koppie and here, among the *bergboegoes* with their narrow aromatic leaves, is the spot where Kruger used to kneel and pray. His prayers, we imagine, were as sombre and trouble-laden as his thoughts. But perhaps we are wrong: there was the lighter side too. He galloped from the Transvaal to the Orange Free State, 20 hours in the saddle, to court a girl: and later, in Paris, he chose to float in a balloon.

Perhaps he valued flowers. At the side of the homestead is an old rose bush with small, double, creamy-yellow, scented flowers, *Rosa fortuneana*. (Graham Thomas, the world's greatest 'old rose' expert, identified it for us from England.) Kruger himself may have planted it—nobody remembers, but the old vine behind the house is his—so that perhaps it gives a glimpse of him that does not belong to history books.

CHAPTER SIX

The Road North

❧

The national road N1, the Great North Road to the Limpopo and Rhodesia, pushes through the Magaliesberg; the high grassy plains are gone for good and the bushveld lies ahead.

Bushveld it is called, but tree veld it really is, lower and drier than forest, denser than park land. Here are a great number of species, thorn trees which are foreign to the N1 that swoops southwards through the Orange Free State to the Cape, trees like umbrellas or round like thunder clouds, with thick furry pods glinting in the sun, with silver leaves and swathes of pink paper fruits, with flowers smelling of violets and poisonous roots that kill, so frail they hardly cast a shadow, wild figs so dense that travellers stopping in their shade can hardly see light filtering through their leaves. On the koppies among the boulders are the angled tree euphorbias with the poisonous sap that men call *naboom*—to many their very shape means Africa. It is a wild fascinating assembly that even cultivation has not banished; and in one form or another this bushveld stretches in a band across Southern Africa.

Eugene Marais, the writer, suggested that the biggest trees in the world were in the Transvaal. In terms of height this is not so, but in spread or girth he may be right, for there are trees reaching over 60 metres or with boles into which a room can fit. The tallest wild tree known in the Transvaal is not far from Pretoria, on the farm Zandri-vierpoort, near Warmbaths, the first stop on the road north. It is a monkey thorn or apiesdoorn, *Acacia galpinii*, 36,6 metres (120 feet) tall, and although it sets no world records it is a beautiful giant with exquisite airy foliage.

Some people stop at Warmbaths to enjoy the hot springs. Others continue past the hill, Buyskop, to Nylstroom and the north. There are hardly five kilometres of this road that are not redolent of history and adventure, and this red hill bears the name of one of the greatest adventurers of all, Coenraad de Buys, the first white man to settle in the Transvaal. A free burgher of the Cape and a bold, black-bearded giant, he could endure no authority, but turned his back on Dutch and

English, and—about the year 1819, long before the Great Trek—journeyed with his white, black and coloured family through the Orange Free State and across the Vaal, daring hostile tribes and wild animals. His family settled finally in a southern kloof of the Soutpansberg west of Louis Trichardt where they lived as a family clan.

Following Buys were the Voortrekkers. North of Warmbaths they came upon a river: that long, long wagon trek from the Cape had taken them, they thought, the length of Africa, so that this was the Nile, and Nile, or Nylstroom, they called it.

It does not take much imagination to think of this grass and tree land as lion country. All the early accounts were full of wild animals. So it should come as no surprise to know that even today lions do sometimes roam here. They come over the border from Botswana and occasionally from the Lowveld to the east and make headlines as they hunt.

This is not only bush—but bird veld. At Naboomspruit, 41 kilometres from Nylstroom, is the turn eastwards to one of the famous bird spots of the Transvaal, the farm Mosdene, now a private nature reserve, owned by Mr E. A. Galpin, and before that by his father, Ernest E. Galpin, after whom the giant thorn tree, *Acacia galpinii*, was named. Ernest Galpin was a banker and botanical collector—a prince among collectors, he was called—and he bought Mosdene, not because it was first-rate cattle ranching country, but because it wasn't! It has a variety of veld types, and a part is seasonally under water, so that here come bushveld birds of many species and water birds, birds of west and east whose areas of distribution overlap here—in all over 420 species, roughly half the number of species in South Africa, have been recorded.

It is a beautiful tree-studded farm abounding in life—we watched Richard, Mr Galpin's son, pick up an errant leguaan on the verandah of the house with expertise, as his Africans roared with horror, and put the frightened dragon carefully in the grass. The University of the Witwatersrand has put up a small laboratory here: students and scientists are perennially welcome, and so are most ordinary visitors.

Naboomspruit and the road immediately north and south are in Waterberg country. Even people who have never seen this lovely little-known range and its foothills know of them, because Eugene Marais lived here for a time and described them in his books.

When he was living in the Waterberg towards the beginning of the century, he was observing *and living with* baboons, and this Waterberg adventure was not only the first systematic investigation into these animals but the first detailed study of animal behaviour in South

Africa. The articles he wrote have been collected into a small slim volume, *My Friends the Baboons*, that has become a wild life classic, though some scientists now dispute his methods and conclusions.

We usually talk of Eugene Marais' Waterberg as we motor through the foothills of the range on the way to Potgietersrus—of the leopards, and the baboons (that are still there in great numbers); of winged death, the deadly mamba that he knew as a lightning-fast movement of attack through the branches of trees, a snake 'more full of menace than a wounded lion', that also still inhabits the Waterberg in numbers.

Forty kilometres from Naboomspruit, on the right-hand side of the road, stand two old camelthorn trees with a story more deadly than any mamba's. Here in 1854, and in two other places nearby, parties of Voortrekkers were massacred by the local chief, Makapan, and his men, the children of one party being dashed to death against the trees and the leader, Hermanus Potgieter, flayed alive. The place is known as **Moordrif**—Murder Ford.

It was an act that everywhere roused the Voortrekkers who, banding together, rode against Makapan to avenge the murder. Makapan and his followers fled before them up a valley slightly north and east of Potgietersrus, and here they took refuge in a gigantic dolomitic cavern known ever afterwards as **Makapansgat**—Makapan's Cave. With its main entrance fronted by a rocky precipice, it was an impregnable fastness, impregnable that is to arms but not to hunger and to thirst. Here 2 000 of Makapan's followers were starved by the blockading commando on the hill below: and when the commando finally rushed the cave, there were few active defenders left to fight. It was a scene of death. The skeletons and bones lay in the cave for a long time, and from here witchdoctors for many years drew their supply of bones to make strong *muti*—six of the defenders' skulls landed up eventually in the Royal College of Surgeons' Museum in London. This is the cave called today Historic Cave.

This has not always been a place of death, but of a busy and perhaps of a good life. The cave faces up a lovely upward-sloping valley green with trees—its head is as high as Johannesburg—and through it runs a clear stream. The valley is malaria-free, the water without bilharzia, a home of richness, health and beauty. Many people must have found it this. In the huge complex of caves—of which Historic Cave is but a part—men lived continuously over a period of three million years, from Ape-Man to Iron Age Man of almost the present day, and here they left their bones and tools, the ash of their fires and the remains of the creatures that they ate.

The first hint that this was a fossil-rich valley came to Professor

Dart away in Johannesburg in the 1920's from a local mathematics teacher, Mr W. I. Eitzman, who had collected fossilized bones from the limeworks here. Dart was too busy shaping the Medical School at Wits to attend to distant bones, and it was Professor C. van Riet Lowe, well-known director of the Bureau of Archaeology, who first investigated the valley in 1936. In a limestone quarry on a steep slope near the Historic Cave, in a deposit exposed by the workmen, he found Early Stone Age tools and animal bones, together with ash. They were the ashes of a hearth—the earliest evidence that man used fire in Africa south of the Sahara—and Van Riet Lowe named the site the Cave of Hearths. The lower ash is now dated at 120 000 years. In this cave a number of cultural levels from Stone Age to almost modern times were later found.

In 1936 the site was proclaimed a national monument. Then came the war and interest in Makapan languished. It revived with a flourish nine years later when Professor Tobias, then a student, and a party brought back from a site lower down the valley the fossil skull of a baboon. Such baboon fossils had been found at Australopithecine sites—could this skull point to a new one here? Dart remembered the baboon skull that had led to the Taung Baby. This one was not to be resisted, and he was off to Makapansgat himself.

He and his students, and many more scientists as well, worked here. Considering their names, it seems as if all those well-known in palaeontology and archaeology in South Africa—men such as Broom, Dart, Van Riet Lowe, the Abbé Breuil, James Kitching, B. D. Malan, Philip Tobias, Captain G. A. Gardner, Alun Hughes, Bob Brain, Revil Mason and many more, beat a path to this fascinating valley. Here, in those early days of excavation after the war, came James Kitching and his brothers, Ben and Scheepers. It was Ben who found an Early Stone Age jaw bone—the first human bone of this age definitely known in South Africa; James who found the first Australopithecine in the waste heaps at the limeworks—he and Alun Hughes, Ben and Scheepers, were to find many more. These Dart named at the time *Australopithecus prometheus*.

This was the place where James Kitching began his astonishing knowledge of bone.

Makapansgat is closed to casual visitors. Nevertheless, it is possible sometimes to see it by arrangement (the Knowledge Seekers have tours here). We went by invitation of James Kitching. Turning off the main road some 14 kilometres beyond Potgietersrus, we reached, at last, the dumps where the Makapansgat lime workers had cast their waste material. Here was James Kitching and with him his son,

Matthew, and Brian Maguire, all of the Bernard Price Institute for Palaeontology. They were searching the breccia waste, for many fossil finds had been made here, including the first fossil centipede found in South Africa, spotted by a seven-year-old girl with sharp eyes. As James showed us, the mass of material is rodent, the little fossilized bones, teeth and jaws (sometimes the complete skeletons) found in owl regurgitations. These, which Bob Brain calls 'the gift from the owls', have often been a boon to fossil hunters, and we looked at them with attention.

James took us on to the limeworkers' drive. They had driven a narrow rocky cutting through the hillside, and we passed through to find a low cliff with a dark cavern, a white stinkwood guarding the entrance, and above a kirkia tree making a soft feathery landmark. James pointed; in that rock above he had found an almost complete ape-man skull.

The cave had been formed aeons before as a pocket of the dolomite had been dissolved by water, gradually becoming lime-encrusted, in time opening to the hillside, drawing to its comparative shelter and protection the small and later the larger creatures of the outside world. Here at Makapansgat, while the floors of the caves had built up, the roofs had often fallen in, so that fossil bones had been exposed on what is now the surface of the ground. James had picked them up on the hillside above.

We passed into the cavern. On its low sloping roof we could still see innumerable fossil bones in the dim light, among them those of *Makapania broomi*, a buffalo long extinct, now linked for ever with a modern scientist. 'Its brain case is still sitting there,' said James.

We looked around at the bones of the animals that had retreated here, that had been eaten here, that had fallen in through the sinkholes and been buried in the mud—one was a sabre-toothed cat, another a buck: their bones were clearly outlined.

Water was dripping from the dolomitic roof. This had been a good cave for *Australopithecus*, James thought: he must have lived in the part where there was light. There was safety and there was water too. He picked up an owl pellet, an oval of hair and feathers some three centimetres long, regurgitated not by an antique but by a living owl. He broke it open; and inside we saw the tiny delicate skull of a field mouse, the minute teeth still intact. We found others with bird skulls, and, 'This owl took a locust's hind leg', he said. We looked at them with delight. Had *Australopithecus*, we wondered, considered them at all?

There were the other sites, the Cave of Hearths, with the famous

A giraffe in the Kruger National Park—shape, pattern and stance unequalled

A sight to remember

Letaba Rest Camp in the Kruger National Park

The rolling hills and grass beehive huts of Zululand

hearth now enclosed in a small building, Rainbow Cave, Hyena Cave. But it was Historic Cave that held us. The great cavern, where Makapan and his men faced the Voortrekker commando, is still haunted. We were sure of it. The skeletons are now gone, but we were glad to move from the black interior to the light and the tumbled rocks. We hauled ourselves across them, over a rocky path with a dull shine—an historic way oiled and shone by human skin, by the thousands of Iron Age hands and feet that once had passed here.

We had our own personal bushveld excitement on the hillside among ancient man. In a deep rocky cutting we noted that James was carrying a big dead branch. 'For the ringhals,' he said in an offhand way. 'Many?' we asked (we hoped nonchalantly too). They usually lay, James told us, all one and a half metres of deadly basking spitting snake, along the rocks at shoulder level. 'But they don't trouble me,' said James. 'Sometimes I find I'm *wet* and then I know that they've been spitting.'

It was near here that James had had the worst moment of his life. He had come face to face with a mamba, rearing in the narrow path, and they had faced one another for 20 frightful minutes, the mamba swaying to and fro, its fangs a metre from his face, James absolutely still, knowing that only immobility could save his life. The mamba eventually slid away, and James stumbled back to wring the perspiration like water from his clothes.

We did not see any snakes that day, not even the puffadder that always warms its back beneath the metal turnstile near the cocopans on the hillside. 'Don't disturb it,' James said tranquilly, 'it's enjoying its hotwater-bottle'—and we did not.

The only wild creatures we met that day were the owls. Apeman had done a lot better. In his millions of years of life—from Makapansgat to Taung—he knew scores of animals now extinct, many small ones and the larger, the sabre-toothed cats with dagger teeth, the Makapan breed with daggers 15 cm long (we had seen the bones); an hyena with great long hunting legs, jackals, four species of baboon, one the size of a gorilla, pigs, giant dassies, *Chalicothere* of the rhino order with split hoofs and an elongated neck; many antelope including a giant hartebeest, zebras, horses.

Later we sat under the trees in front of the little house that James had built in the valley and picnicked with the three men, talking about these things and the bushveld around us. James was telling us of a half-blind African who had once worked for them, and whom they had heard screaming in the bush. When they found him he was in agony—a ringhals had spat into his eyes—and they had rolled him over and over in the stream to wash the poison out. When he recovered a miracle had happened—he could see. What were probably cataracts had been burned away by the venom.

It was at this point that Brian began to shiver. This was an old legacy from the days when he and James had collected deep in the caves and contracted cave disease. Six thousand kilometres to the north, Egyptologists working 50 years ago on the tomb of Tutankhamen died unexpectedly and mysteriously—they had called upon themselves, the current legend ran, the Curse of the Pharaohs, and perished. Cave disease is an infection caused by a fungus from bat droppings: so, doctors think today, was Tutankhamen's Curse. Tutankhamen's tomb and Makapansgat—what strange companions Africa breeds.

A little to the east of Makanpansgat is a spot where history of a different sort was made. In 1836 the man who initiated the Great Trek, Louis Trichardt—he had set off from the Cape the year before—passed northwards to the Soutpansberg in a gap, Strydpoort, between Makapan's and Strydpoort mountains. It was a pass through which later the main road from Schoemansdal to Pretoria was to run, and it predated the present pass, Chuniespoort.

Voortrekker names and associations lie thick from here to the Limpopo. Louis Trichardt is met again and again. Potgietersrus bears the name of Piet Potgieter, son of the famous Hendrik Potgieter, who was killed while attacking Makapan in Historic Cave. Yet this is also, strangely enough, a gold road. At a point 27 kilometres north of Potgietersrus on the main highway a road branches off. The sign shows **Eersteling** (First-born), an extraordinarily appropriate name for the spot where the first gold was mined in the Transvaal—but one that was given to the farm in Voortrekker days before gold was dreamed of.

Here, perhaps in 1869 although the date is uncertain, the prospector, Edward Button, found gold, and in 1871 the Eersteling goldfield was proclaimed. We had read something of the story of Button and his partner, William Pigg, in the Geological Museum in Pretoria, when we had seen the boulder Pigg has used to crush the quartz. The boulder is safe in the museum, and the outcrop of rock on which it stood is a national monument. So is the chimney which, together with a steam engine, Button had imported from Britain and transported here by ox-wagon from the coast.

Ahead lies **Pietersburg.** This busy, modern small town, named after Commandant-General Pieter Joubert, contemporary of Paul Kruger, is generally known as the capital of the north. It is not this, however, but the roads leading from it that offer most attractions. Almost due east is the road via Haenertsburg and Tzaneen to Phalaborwa and the eastern Lowveld, ahead the road N1 to Messina and the northern border, to the north-west the road to Alldays (still sometimes lion and cheetah country), and well beyond it to Botswana.

The first section of the eastern road offers one of the scenic drives of the Transvaal, mountain, forest—indigenous and exotic—water, and with the drop in altitude, tropical flowers and fruits, the hot blue hazes and the great pawpaw leaves that usher in the Lowveld.

We have our personal memories as well, of Sheila Thompson who owns and runs a wild flower nursery near **Haenertsburg,** whose Cape bulbs, flowering cherries and rhododendrons in bloom draw gardeners from far and near, and of **Magoebaskloof** with its world view. It was immediately beyond the site of the Magoebaskloof hotel that John Buchan lived for a while in a cottage and wrote *A Lodge in the Wilderness*. Sheila Thompson remembers that her father, seeking refuge here in a storm, found him at work.

Buchan wrote of the trees and flowers he knew here, arum lillies and agapanthus, of the clear grey-blue water swirling in pools and rapids (which are trout streams today), the winds blowing as clean as in mid-ocean, 'a place enchanted and consecrate', where he promised himself he would build a dwelling in his old age and leave his bones. Although he never did, others have: this is a favourite spot for retiring Johannesburgers and others, and for weekenders from the cities.

The mountain sides are largely pine-clad now, but past the De Hoek sawmill and on the right is a plantation of our favourite tea, Sapekoe, and a tea factory, and we salute the Middelkop Tea Estates as we ride by.

Tzaneen is a hot little town overflowing with tropical flowers and fruits, a good stop-over spot, and the road east continues to **Phalaborwa** with its mines—phosphate, vermiculite and copper—and the Kruger Park beyond. Phalaborwa's is an interesting countryside, which was inhabited once by an African tribe who smelted iron and copper, and whose iron work was famous far and near. Alliances were built around it and marriages too, for brides were paid for not in cattle but in hoes—the people and their prehistoric workings make a story in themselves.

A little to the north-east is the **Hans Merensky Nature Reserve** which has one of the country's newest museums, the Tsonga Kraal. The site, excavated by the Department of Archaeology at the University of the Witwatersrand, was found to be an ancient one, the potsherds dating it about A.D. 300: there were remains, as well, of occupations such as smelting and salt working. Around these themes, the Provincial Administration has had a village built, that of a chief and eight wives, in the traditional Tsonga pattern, which attracts many people interested in tribal life and African culture.

Sometimes instead of motoring directly up the Great North Road we branch off at Pietersburg and make a triangle—Haenertsburg, Tzaneen, Duivelskloof, Mooketsi—and so back to the main road south of Bandolierskop. Once, armed with a permit from the Department of Bantu Administration and Development, we visited the kraal of Modjadje, the Rain Queen, near **Duivelskloof.**

The further north one travels in the Transvaal, and the further away from the main roads, the deeper one falls into Rider Haggard myth. Rider Haggard as a young man in the 1870's spent some time in Pretoria, where he was registrar of the High Court during the Sir Theophilus Shepstone régime. He listened to the splendid after-dinner stories told at Government House: and he travelled officially as well, soaking up atmosphere with every breath. (Some half a dozen caves, from Potchefstroom to the eastern Lowveld, are claimed to have been the prototype of those in *King Solomon's Mines*.) Certainly Modjadje, Queen of the Lovedu tribe, is the original of *She*.

Modjadje, the Rain Queen, was in Haggard's day—and is today—a real person, traditionally with the power of making rain. She *is* immortal in that she is supposed to hand on her powers to a new queen, a new Modjadje, who is versed in tribal customs, after she herself, aware of failing powers, has taken poison. She is said to have white blood—the tale that sometimes goes that the original queen was a Portuguese woman with the power of making rain—but the story is so interwoven with mystery and magic that it is difficult to separate fact from fiction. All Rider Haggard had to do was to add beauty and romantic drama; the rest was there for the taking.

A forest of sacred cycad trees has a part in the queen's rites. We went to see them, climbing past the village up the red path to the trees on the crown. What significance these have now is not clear, but they are still greatly prized and the forest is a beautiful strange one, unique in Southern Africa.

Cycads are known popularly as living fossils because they are the descendants of a flora that once flourished in South Africa over 150 million years ago—they and dinosaurs lived side by side—but whereas dinosaurs passed away and the form of almost every kind of life has changed since then, the basic character of the cycad race continues as before. If an artist today wishes to paint a dinosaur's cycad, he goes out and paints a living one—and is not far wrong!

Cycads are not rare—there are almost 30 different species in the eastern parts of South Africa—but they do not grow in numbers together, with the exception of Modjadje's cycads in this forest. They are all strange plants, their appearance befitting their lineage, with a crown of enormous divided spiky leaves, and with seeds in big often bright cones.

Botanists call the Modjadje cycad *Encephalartos transvenosus* and many visit the forest. We were escorted by a councillor's son to see them covering two hills, and were attended as well by a crowd of solemn, incredibly polite children who watched us with enormous attentive eyes. The trees made a wonderful sight, both near at hand and stretching away over the hills—some were up to 12 metres tall and all had the outline of tall tree ferns: it was only when we touched the leaves we felt the spikes. Several bore cones in their hearts like gigantic orange-red pineapples 80 centimetres long. Although their race is ancient, no single tree among them was probably more than 500 years old, yet dinosaurs' food they looked, prehistoric and full of magic.

If magic is on a tourist's programme the next stop should be **Fundudzi,** the sacred lake of the Bavenda, that lies in a remote valley of the Soutpansberg east of Louis Trichardt.

The quickest way is to travel straight from Pietersburg to Louis Trichardt along the national road N1. Most people stop briefly at the spot six kilometres outside Pietersburg to see the monument marking a spot on Louis Trichardt's route to Mozambique. This is not magic but history. After Trichardt had passed through Strydpoort, he and his party went north to the Soutpansberg, and in 1837 they set off again on their trek to the sea, first turning southward and crossing the bare plateau near this spot: a bronze map at the monument points the route. It was an epic journey on which nearly all the party were to die, and is still remembered with emotion by Afrikaners.

Soon the line of the Soutpansberg—the Salt Pan Mountains—rises ahead, with Louis Trichardt, the town that bears the Voortrekker leader's name, at the foot. Westwards from here is the road to Schoemansdal, the Voortrekker town of which only ruins remain today, and eastwards the road to Punda Milia in the Kruger National Park skirting the foot of the mountains. The road to the village of Sibasa turns northwards from this, and it is from Sibasa—the administrative centre of the area—that most people approach Lake Fundudzi.

A good deal of African territory can be visited today only by permit and this includes the lake: yet it is often possible to obtain permission and officials can be very helpful. Moreover the Knowledge Seekers, always enterprising, sometimes run a tour to the Venda homeland, including both Fundudzi and the Rain Queen's village. We ourselves saw the lake with a fishery official and two members of the South African police, riding on the back of their lorry on the red track from Sibasa that twisted through the green hills, and higher up the mountain, through the wild forest, crossing stream after stream of clear running water and smelling the fresh strong mountain world.

We stopped on a grassy shoulder of the mountain high above the lake with a path falling away before us to the valley below, and down this we scrambled: it was to be a long pull back and up, we were to find. Soon Fundudzi lay before us. It is a big stretch of water about four kilometres long, enclosed by steep hillsides and cliffs, and fed by the Motale River. It is both remote and inaccessible, and has always been associated with the religious rites of the Venda people who believe that the lake is inhabited by spirits of their ancestors, to whom they make offerings of grain and beer. Stories about the lake are innumerable—of human sacrifices, of sheep that graze beneath the water, of trees and shrubs that rise up and return again to the deeps, of how it is death to drink here. When we saw the water glittering far below us we were enthralled, but near at hand it was all ordinary enough. We stood on the rocks looking into the water but could see no sign of life, no ghostly sheep, no movement, no flesh-and-blood fish or bird or fly, no sign even of the crocodiles that leave their wicked imprints in the orange sand. Yet there are crocodiles, said to be sacred. One story goes that they never molest the Africans who wade into the water with offerings to the spirits.

A good many of the beliefs about the lake are fading. Yet when we asked our guide if anything lived in the lake, he answered in a perfectly matter-of-fact way, 'The Spirits of our Fathers'.

One strange lake dweller was vouched for by Mr R. Hewitt Ivy, Native Affairs Agriculture Officer, who had a famous knowledge of the area. It was an old hippo bull that lived here for several winters, in summer disappearing down the Motale River. Mr Ivy had heard the hippo and seen its tracks but had never glimpsed it. He was to do so, however. The high priest of the lake, Netshiavha, called a group of African girls, who were fetching water from a stream, and told them to sing and call the hippo, and as they stood on the banks trilling in Venda style, the old bull rose out of the water and approached them. When they left, so did he: when they returned and recommenced their song, he reappeared as well.

When we came down the hill track later, we saw the Venda villages on the slopes and heard the drums. The Venda people, who came originally from Rhodesia, settled in these mountains about 200 years ago. They are a race with individual culture, traditions, dress and ceremonies; and are generally best known for their initiation ceremonies, and the great fertility rite, the *domba*, in which girls and boys (but today mainly girls) are prepared for marriage. These strange, and to Westerners often savage rites, have received much publicity so that most people at least know of a great ritual like the Python Dance, done at the *domba* and danced by the girls. Close together, gripping one another, hands on elbows, the girls move slowly, rocking and rippling in a long 'python' line—the python snake is linked in Venda thought with fertility and rain. There are the drums too, part of Venda life, the big *ngoma* beaten with a stick, and the small *murumbu*, which the women grip between their legs and beat with their hands, the music of flutes and of the *mbila*, the resonated xylophone.

We heard no flute or xylophone, but the sound of the drums followed us as we travelled: on the main road we heard them no more.

North of the mountains are other Venda sights of great interest, the ruins of the settlements of the early people, hilltop, stone-walled, with walled meeting places, complete with stone monoliths and patterns in the walls like those of the famous Zimbabwe across the Limpopo River. Some of them are national monuments. Machemma is, the settlement on the farm, Solvent, north-west of Wyllie's Poort, which has a link with Zimbabwe that fascinates all, a conical tower the remains of which still stand. The ruins at Verdun to the north have also been proclaimed a monument, and so have those at Dzata to the east.

There is no hotel in all the Sibasa countryside, and we were glad to reach the Mountain Inn on the slopes above Louis Trichardt, an iced drink and a cool wind.

Next day we followed the western road to the ruins of **Schoemansdal,** or Soutpansbergdorp as it was first known: they are a reminder of the days when elephants roamed the countryside and Schoemansdal existed by virtue of its ivory trade. Today there is a cemetery only among the wild thorn trees, with the lizards flickering over the sand, and the grave of the Voortrekker leader, Hendrik Potgieter, who defeated Mzilikazi and who founded the town.

It is said that the mud fort with its stockade of elephant tusks, erected by João Albasini, that most flamboyant adventurer, was near here. Albasini was an official in the Portuguese service in the early 19th century who, finding official life tame, crossed into what is the Kruger Park of today, as hunter, trader and explorer, in the end settling in the Soutpansberg where he became a man of wealth and power, and a chief among the Africans.

The road continues westward joining at length the road to Alldays, and rounding the western extremities of the Soutpansberg; and there is a route back to road N1 slightly north of the mountains, via the salt pan from which the mountains take their name. But if time is limited, the national road to the north is the one to take. Nothing diverts us from Wyllie's Poort—Wyllie's Pass—through which the national road bursts on the northern side of the Soutpansberg.

The road over the mountains is a scenic one, through pleasant high places, but it is this pass at the end that is famous, famous at any rate among botanists, for here meet forest trees and plants and those of sun-baked rocks, of south and north, so that botanists, incoherent with joy, are known to take a day to traverse a kilometre. A modern road now runs parallel to the old one, and this passes through two tunnels through the mountain named after Prime Minister Hendrik Verwoerd.

The original passage was discovered towards the beginning of the century by Lieutenant C. H. Wyllie, and was named after him. We always loiter through the lieutenant's passage, admiring the reds and yellows of the cliffs and the marvellous vegetation, and listening to the baboons "hoching" in the rocks. There are plants hereabouts that most people see for the first time, like the 'euphorbia of the Soutpansberg', named by Dr Dyer in Pretoria, trees which grow on the slopes near the southern entrance to the poort and nowhere else: they can be seen, with their many slender branches from the road.

A little way north of the poort, the dry Lowveld bush appears. Many people streak through it to Messina and Beit Bridge as fast as the law allows, but there are turn-offs of interest. Just north of the mountains is the eastern road to Venda country.

Past the turn-off to the Njelele Dam is the road to **Tshipise** on the right. The mineral baths here bring people from all over the northern Transvaal and it has become a favourite camping and recreation centre. We, who remember it as an empty place where we could rest in the shade of the big nyala trees in quietness, never linger now. The country round is a harsh low bushveld, with mopane trees that fold their leaflets together in the hot sun, so that the only shadow they throw is a thin line. Many travellers in mopane veld, including Livingstone, have denounced them, and so have we, stopping in the sand on those north-western tracks, boiling a kettle every 40 minutes and drinking tea with our heads under a mopane bush at 100 degrees Fahrenheit in its shade, and our feet at 130 degrees in the sun.

This arid northern landscape is dominated by the strangest tree that grows in Africa, the baobab. This is remarkable, not for its height— although tall ones are known—but for its girth and shape: the bole can reach almost 40 metres in circumference, and this is round, grey-brown to almost purple in colour, and bears a crown of comparatively slender branches and thin branchlets. In winter, when it is bare of leaves, its shape is distinctive. Africans often claim that the branches are roots and that it is growing upside-down, or that the maternal ancestor of the tree was an elephant.

The tree, which grows in dry hot places from the northern Transvaal to Ethiopia, has always been thought a curiosity, and has figured in botanical literature for nearly 400 years—there was an account of it from Egypt in 1592. The Frenchman, Michel Adanson, after whom it was named (*Adansonia digitata*), wrote of it in the 1750s: and in the 1970's people are still describing it. Many early travellers in Southern Africa who camped beneath one noted it and a number of these historic trees have been located in fine fettle. Indeed, a baobab can go on for 3 000 years and more—carbon dating has given the age of a smallish specimen as 1 000!

The biggest baobab known in South Africa is one on the farm **Nonsiang** near Messina, not far from the national road. It is 26 metres tall with a girth of just over 19 metres.

Messina is the site of prehistoric copper workings. Interesting though it is, it does not hold us, for it is to the west that there lies the most exciting thing in the northern Transvaal, a hill called Mapungupwe.

Mapungupwe, the Hill of Jackals, is a small flat-topped sandstone koppie some 300 metres long and 65 high on the farm Greefswald in the valley of the Limpopo River about 65 kilometres west of Messina. The valley is a hot blistering world of scrub, baobabs, and koppies with the Limpopo beyond, its banks lined with fever trees with yellow trunks that overhang crocodile-filled pools. The hill lies a little south of the main stream where it is joined by the Shashi River, athwart an almost forgotten migration route from the north, its cliffs rising sheer from the valley below.

Although this has not the stone-walling, the Temple nor the Acropolis of Zimbabwe to the north, the hill—and a spot in the valley adjacent to it, dubbed K2—have proved two of the most important archaeological sites in South Africa.

On the hill once lived a people—or through the ages peoples—who used it as a fort; who prized it so dearly that they covered its bare surface with soil, thousands of tons dragged up the perpendicular walls from the valley below; who had gold ornaments of fine workmanship and made pottery and sophisticated arrow heads: who left here the remains of their fortifications, of their homes, layer upon layer, and of their bones—bones that showed no Negro kinship but rather that of robust Bush-Boskop (Hottentot) people; and who had buried their dead with ceremony.

There were succeeding peoples, it is clear. Perhaps there was once a slave people in the valley, a working group who toiled up the cliff face with their loads of soil, while the master race lived on the hill top above.

The hill has always been taboo to local Africans who hold it in awe, so that until the 1930s it was no more than a rumour to the outside world. In 1933, however, a farmer in the neighbourhood, Mr E. S. J. van Graan, and a small party, located the hill, which appeared inaccessible for no path was visible up the precipice-like walls. A local African gave them the clue, a cleft in the rock hidden by a wild fig tree that grew against the face, and up this they scrambled. They must have seen with excitement the tiny holes along the sides of this narrow path, into which had been fixed the cross-bars which served as a ladder for the people who once lived here.

When they reached the top they were transfixed. A storm which had passed over the hill shortly before had washed away the surface soil and laid bare a skeleton with gold necklace and bangles, skulls, beads, bowls and golden ornaments. It was a burial mound on which they had stumbled, and the treasure-seekers got down on their hands and knees and started to fossick with hunting knives, unearthing pieces of plate gold as they worked. It was archaeology's good luck that among the party was young van Graan, a student at the Pretoria University, who recognized the value of the site and took the story straight away to Pretoria. Soon there was a train of scientists to the hill: they have worked there intermittently ever since.

Archaeologists know a good deal now, although there are still mysteries. There is the gold, for instance. This was the biggest hoard of *wrought* gold found in Africa since that in Tutankhamen's tomb in Egypt. There were such things as a gold-plated sceptre or staff of office, found with a skeleton that had been ceremoniously buried knees-to-chin; a golden rhinoceros with solid gold tail and ears; a bowl of gold plate. Moreover the quality of the goldsmithing and purity of the metal raised questions that have never been satisfactorily answered. The gold was hand-beaten to an almost uniform thinness of approximately one-tenth of a millimetre, a feat which few modern craftsmen can achieve. Two pieces of gold plate were nearly 94 per cent pure, bangles were over 91 per cent—a staggering figure of refinement.

There were, also, the thousands of golden beads which adorned the limbs of perhaps royal corpses or which were part of shrouds—10 000 were found with the skeleton of one young woman. Every bead, beautifully shaped, was barely a millimetre across, and yet it had been pierced by a hole for stringing. What sort of drill, what technique, had been used to accomplish such a thing? (Away in Pretoria, Erich Frey was called upon to solve the riddle, and he did. After various experiments, he made beads which were the replicas of Mapungupwe's—using a goldsmithing technique employed in ancient Assyria!)

It had been easy for us to get our permit from the Archaeological Department of Pretoria University, to visit the site. Now, bumping over an incredibly bad farm road, we approached the hill through baobabs and *Commiphora* trees. It was drought. Sand blew, the birds and game had gone: only the commiphoras were in good heart. These little spiky trees pleased us enormously at the time. The sap of species from the far north-east of Africa and from Arabia was the fragrant myrrh of the ancients, and every now and then we broke a twig to smell the pungent scent of these southern brothers: they set the scene for antiquity, the hill and its old secrets.

We found the cleft in the rock face behind the fig tree, and pulled ourselves to the summit: then, as so many had done in recent times, we walked up and down the flat top, filled with speculation and wonder. The golden ornaments had gone—they are hidden now in the strongroom of the University of Pretoria—but the story was still a live one, and the valley below us filled with that same hot purple haze that the first people must have known.

There happened only recently in this northern Transvaal a thing as new as the wind off the Soutpansberg. Its background was this.

In 1976 by an act of Parliament (the Forest Amendment Act which had been passed the year before) a **National Hiking Way** was proclaimed, a scheme by which South Africa is to be spanned by continuous hiking trails from north to south, from the Soutpansberg in the Transvaal to the South-Western Cape. The trails follow the mountains that ring the big inland plateau to the east, dropping down in places to the sea—they are for hikers with a pack, carrying their own food, sleeping at camps along the trails, leaving no mark of their passing, their heads in the clouds—for this Hiking Way offers heady joys. There are high places with their views of rock and clouds, tracks through forest, water, fynbos, ocean and salt winds, all the things that grow, live and fly, remoteness, and the pleasure of matching muscles against mountains.

James Clarke, the well-known conservation writer, compares the trail with America's Appalachian, the most famous in the world. Why not? he asks. Whereas South Africa's trail is shorter, it is also a great deal richer—with 25 per cent more natural plant species, and infinitely more mammals, birds and other 'natural curiosities' than the Appalachian Trail plus all the other trails in America combined.

Some parts of the Hiking Way have already been proclaimed: there is a trail in the eastern Transvaal, the Fanie Botha trail, one in the north starting at Hanglip in the Soutpansberg, and several in the Cape.

When the scheme was broached, it touched imaginations everywhere. But would it work? Was it feasible? *The Star*, Johannesburg's evening newspaper, thought it would, and to prove it, it sent out a relay of its journalists, men and women, young and not so young, and a few students and schoolboys, to walk the length of the country along a route that the final National Hiking Way might take. It called the venture Trail Blaze, and people everywhere found it thrilling.

Trail Blaze was blessed by the man who had dreamed up the National Hiking Way, the Minister of Forestry, Mr Fanie Botha (it was his department that organized and set the Hiking Way in motion). These people were pioneers, he said, and they were. They walked, often in company with forest officers, from the Limpopo to Cape Point, across the hot dry bushveld to the Soutpansberg, through little known forest and bush and over less known mountain tops to the Drakensberg and along the mountain spine, down to the sea at Port Edward and on along the coast. In the north-eastern Transvaal white men travelling 'by legs' set the Africans agog—'Go by bus', 'Take a taxi'—but the relays made it, with endless adventures and misadventures, on foot the whole way. The journey took about 16 walking weeks, but because one hiking team did not always take over immediately from the one before, journalist Christopher Prophet ended at Cape Point in August 1975, a year after news editor Ron Anderson had set out from the Limpopo.

The starting point of Trail Blaze was Mapungupwe, with two ancient *isiVivanes*, the Africans' good luck heaps of stones, guarding the approaches. They mark a route, taken by travellers centuries ago, northwards probably to Zimbabwe and to Sofala, southwards to—who knows where? Not if one had searched the Transvaal could a better, a more classic, spot been found for the start of high adventure on a modern trail.

CHAPTER SEVEN

Eastern Trails

✣

The Trail Blazers, when they left the Soutpansberg, walked south and east into the northern Drakensberg—'the wildest, the most mountainous and impassable country in the whole Eastern Transvaal'—and along the spine of the mountains southwards.

They were travelling along the great divide that splits the Eastern Transvaal in two, with the high plateau on their right, and on their left beyond the mountains, the drop to low ground—the Lowveld—stretching north and south for almost 500 kilometres, and away to the Lebombo Mountains in the east for another 100. Through forest, bush, kloofs and mist they walked, still down the backbone of the mountains, past the Abel Erasmus Pass, the Blyde River Canyon, God's Window, and on to Sabie, the Highveld with its grass and plantations still to one side, on the other the Lowveld haze.

What the Trail Blazers were doing was a fashionable thing in a very unfashionable way, exploring the delights of the Eastern Transvaal 'by legs' instead of by motor-car. The thing they did the hard way and the long way from north to south, motor-cars do, often from west to east and in a few hours, slipping along the tarmac roads to the escarpment and over, to what have become some of the tourist draws of the country.

There is the main road to the Lowveld, the N4, starting at Pretoria and running eastwards to Nelspruit and Komatipoort on the eastern border, and the northern road from Pietersburg to Phalaborwa. Once tourists thought of these mainly as roads to the Kruger Park, the great fascinating chunk of Lowveld country on the far eastern side: today there is so much to see between the escarpment and the Park that some people never get there at all.

First there is **the escarpment** itself, wild, rugged, beautiful, healthy and *cool*, with its incomparable mountain scenery, its trout streams and waterfalls, forest and pools; and a thousand metres below, the bush and plantations, the fruit and tropical flowers, the wild animals and the crocodile-filled streams of the Lowveld—it is the land of languor, malaria and heat, and although science has done a great deal

109

to mitigate these, they still remain—in an inverted sort of way, they are part of the Lowveld's mystique.

Standing on the edge of the escarpment, Johannesburg and Pretoria at one's back, the low land below still appears a place of mystery. Yet the history of the Transvaal began, not in the cities, but here. The main road N4, dropping down the escarpment, passes through Nelspruit, terminating at Komatipoort on the eastern border. Through here, in the year 1725, came a party of Dutchmen under Frans de Kuiper who had set out from Delagoa Bay—Lourenço Marques and now Maputo—to explore the interior. They journeyed through the country between the Crocodile and Sabie Rivers, now part of the Kruger Park, but were forced by hostile tribes to return. They were the first white group—the first history makers—known in the Transvaal, and a plaque at the customs house at Komatipoort commemorates their visit.

This had not been one of idle curiosity. The fabled kingdom of Monomotapa still burned in men's minds, and the aim of this official party was to find its gold-fields. They did not, but what they did was fascinating enough—they made the beginning of the Transvaal's story of gold.

In actual fact, they were not very far from what they sought, not Monomotapa's gold but gold that a century and a half later was to be famous across the world.

In that time between the Dutch expedition and the finding of gold, the Lowveld was seldom a permanent home for white men; malaria, tsetse fly and heat saw to this. But it was a hunter's paradise and fortunes in ivory were made here. Standing on the escarpment edge, it is possible to see—or imagine one sees which is almost as good—the country where João Albasini lived on the Sabie River (the same Albasini of the Soutpansberg), the first white man to live here who, the story goes, built an army of fighting men of which he was leader and amassed a great fortune in elephant tusks—the remains of the house he lived in before he moved to the Soutpansberg still stand, and Africans still know the name by which their great-grandfathers called him—Juwawa.

But he found no gold. This was to be discovered after his day, not in his lowlands but first to the west in the high country of the grand views that draw visitors today.

The first gold was found near the present villages of Sabie and Pilgrim's Rest, north of the national road N4, in 1873, and next year, with the country bursting with prospectors and fortune-hunters, strikes were made at Barberton to the south-east. Barberton was Lowveld proper, malaria country, at the head of De Kaap Valley, or the Valley of Death as prospectors called it.

Sabie can be reached from Nelspruit, but it is always from **Lyden-burg,** the little high-lying town north-east of Belfast on road N4, that we choose to approach it. It is not only for the views east of Lydenburg we go, but for ten minutes in the Standard Bank where we pick up our first gold thread. There stands in a glass case in the foyer an old pair of scales almost a metre across and as tall, on which were probably weighed some of the famous Eastern Transvaal nuggets.

The banks, naturally enough, were early on the scene after gold had been found. The Standard took a long cool look at Pilgrim's, at Spitzkop near Sabie where one of the earliest strikes had been made, and at other diggings, and decided to concentrate its activities at Lydenburg, where it opened in 1877. Here came those magnificent old scales, which were rescued from oblivion many years ago by the manager of the bank, Mr Petrie Muller, recently retired manager of the main Church Square branch of the Standard Bank in Pretoria.

Another banker, Mr A. G. A. Melville, recalled how, long before Petrie Muller's day, the diggers used to come into the Lydenburg bank with their finds, and how one had taken a handful of nuggets out of a bag and offered them to him 'to buy sweets'.

From Lydenburg we always head east over the highway that rides Mount Anderson, the second highest peak in the Transvaal—over 2 000 metres at the summit of the road—and at this point we like to remember the astonishing gold rush to the top of the mountain. It was started by a traveller who, resting his horse, saw a nugget in the grass: it spoke true, that nugget—there was gold on the top of the world, and probably still is. From here, we drive down the Long Tom Pass to Sabie. Long Tom has a fine name and an historic one, for during the Anglo-Boer War the Boers mounted their Long Tom guns on these heights: how they dragged them up the mountain remains a wonder. Near the summit is a spot where the last of these was fired in the Anglo-Boer War, and the mark of one of its shells can be seen across the valley at Bomgat (Shell Hole). We have travelled this road more often than not in mist, but on clear days the views are superlative and we take our time.

Sabie, in the foothills of the mountains, is a pleasant village in the heart of the largest tree plantation in the world. It is also in the heart of waterfall country, for there are some dozen close at hand with names like Horseshoe and Lone Creek. One day, passing the little Anglican Church built long ago by Sir Herbert Baker, we heard children singing carols, 'Once in Royal David's City' rising clear and sharp in the mountain air, so that to us Sabie always means Christmas songs as well as waterfalls and gold.

It was from close by that the first gold came, from Hendriksdal, a little to the south, and from the slopes of Spitzkop near the village.

The remains of the work of the early miners can still be seen scattered over the countryside, telling something of the urgency of that gold boom, now just over a century away. There are, in particular, the furrows—the water races—they made to lead water from the streams to their claims to wash the gold-bearing gravel. Near Sabie is 'Swan's Race' telling the saddest little story possible.

John Swan was an old digger who had found rich gold on Hendriksdal but too far away from water to be worked. So he decided to bring the water to the gold 17 kilometres away: and he set to work—digging a furrow. Six and a half years later, he had completed 13 kilometres of the furrow and had lined it with stone in a workmanlike way. Then his funds ran out. Five kilometres away lay the gold—but he died before his furrow ever got there. Parts of it are still to be seen just south of the village.

From the spate of names, telling of this golden country—Whisky Spruit, Baker's Bliss, Pilgrim's Rest and dozens more—Mac Mac north of Sabie has the most telling name of all. In the early spring of 1873 Thomas Burgers, then president of the South African Republic, set off to see the diggings for himself. Besides gold, he found at one camp Scots and Irish licensed diggers, dozens of them with names beginning with Mac or Mc. 'I shall call this Mac Mac', he said, enjoying his joke as much as did the diggers. Mac Mac it remained.

We drove one day from Sabie northwards past the **Mac Mac Falls,** the lovely Mount Sheba Nature Reserve upon our left, past the Jock of the Bushveld plaque to the junction of the roads leading to Graskop and Pilgrim's Rest, taking the road to the left to the Pilgrim's village. It was here, in that same year 1873, in a creek in this steep valley in the foothills of the mountains, that still more gold strikes were made. These are closer to us today than the first ones near Sabie because the village of **Pilgrim's Rest** that grew up around the gold-rich creek is preserved as it was in its days of glory: even lacking working gold, it is still a mining village and this can be sensed in every metre of it.

The first gold here was found by an eccentric, Alec Patterson, nicknamed Wheelbarrow Alec because he wheeled a wheelbarrow everywhere he went. Doing his thing, he came to The Creek—and struck it rich. He did not name the place but the next man to come, almost on his heels, did. His name was William Trafford, and he too saw with joy that tail of gold in his prospecting pan. A. P. Cartwright in his *Valley of Gold* says that the men of one of the first parties to reach Mac Mac called themselves 'the Pilgrims', and that at one time everybody there took up the name. So that when Trafford saw his first gold he yelled in a great booming voice which the mountains echoed, 'And so the pilgrim is at rest'. Pilgrim's Rest!

So a new gold rush began. The diggers were a rough, goodnatured, rowdy, lively bunch of men who were at the same time surprisingly well-behaved and law-abiding, and they came from everywhere. A whip around for a cricket eleven in those early years brought a remarkable tally of the Old School Tie: three Wykehamists, four Etonians, four Harrovians, two Cheltonians, one Uppingham boy, and two Cliftonians!

What the diggers had first looked for was the alluvial gold of river beds and banks, poor man's gold because there was generally only enough to keep them going, and they needed little equipment with which to find it beyond their picks and iron prospecting pans. In these they washed the gravel, swilling it round and round, adding more water gradually, sluicing it finally away and leaving behind it (it was their prayer) a tail of gold. It was gold they could *see*, maybe a particle, maybe a fortune, and it was (and is) the most romantic way possible of finding it: the shallow pans are still the most glamorous basins ever made.

Soon diggers found there were nuggets as well as gold dust in the streams. At Pilgrim's Rest these were sometimes big—one (that disappeared) was said to have been as big as a rock and have weighed 25 lb; another, the Lilley nugget, weighed 119 oz and came—according to Cartwright—from a spot where the village stands today. There was gold everywhere, it seemed. What was more, it was no flash in the pan—some R80 million in nuggets and gold dust was won from these fields in their lifetime.

Today the Transvaal Provincial Administration has taken over the whole village of Pilgrim's Rest on the steep slope above the famous creek; many of the original old houses have been restored and there are plans to re-start some of the old workings in the stream below—there *is* still gold there, as there is in most of the streams of the countryside. It is already a tourist draw, and with gold being won from the creek again, it will be irresistible.

We drove into the village one morning. Away to one side, fading into the blue of the mountains, we could make out the line of the hell-run that wagons had had to take to the village in early days, culminating in a dreadful descent. From here the wagon drivers could see a village of tents clinging to the hillside like washing on a line. The tents were replaced by pioneer homes, small, corrugated iron cottages set on patches scooped out of the hill, and it was these we saw as we stopped in the main street, on our left hand raised above the street, on our right one step down towards the creek, all now spick and span and carefully preserved, looking like a full-scale film set stuck on a hill.

The Royal Hotel, a truly historic building, is the heart of the village. We breakfasted there, not very well (a pioneer hotel in a mining town, we told ourselves!) before we explored the bar. This most famous bar in the Transvaal began life as a Roman Catholic chapel in Lourenço Marques, as one of the much-worn seats testifies—it was originally a pew. The chapel was dismantled, brought piece by piece by ox-wagon to Pilgrim's Rest in 1882, and reassembled: and here visitors, unfailingly intrigued, sip a drink today surrounded by shovels, lanterns, boots, prospectors' pans and chunks of 'fool's gold'.

We walked up to the old graveyard and looked down on the village. Some of the long Welsh inscriptions on the headstones in memory of children were particularly touching; the mountains must once have echoed 'Land of My Fathers'. Athwart the general east-west direction of all the other graves was Robber's Grave, north-south, and unnamed. His 'different' grave was a punishment until doomsday of a man who was said to have robbed a claim and to have been summarily executed by a foursome of diggers. The execution was an act of rough justice, probably condoned by all. Everybody who visits Pilgrim's Rest goes to see the heap of stones that is the grave today.

We drove back again from Pilgrim's Rest along the steep road to **Graskop**—Grassy Head—not far away. The little village perches on the very top of the escarpment, and from it a road falls away through forest and plantations to meet the Lowveld road running northwards near the edge of the Kruger Park. The steep road down is Kowyns Pass and a good scenic drive.

There is a tarred road now from Graskop northwards along the edge of the escarpment to the **Blyde River Canyon** that is called the Panorama Route: this somewhat trite name does little to suggest its magnificence, for the views from here and from the turn-offs along it, such as at God's Window, are unforgettable.

The Canyon is a huge cleft in the Drakensberg through which the Blyde River flows northwards to join the Olifants—the Elephants' River—on its way to the Lowveld. It is the most spectacular valley in South Africa, and until recently one of the least known as well: now thousands of tourists drive the roads to what is planned as a giant play-ground, and many stay at the rest-camps here to explore its delights.

Nearly 50 kilometres long and at its widest six-and-half kilometres across, it lies within the Blyde River Nature Reserve and stretches from Bourke's Luck at the head to the mountain of Mariepskop. Just before it plunges into the gorge, it is joined by the Treur River: below their junction are the famous potholes (shaped like giant pots, thought the early comers), some almost seven metres deep, that were gouged, shaped and polished by swirling stones and water. It is an historic scene. In those northern mountains Louis Trichardt and his followers struggled for over two months to find a passage to the Lowveld.

Flat-topped **Mariepskop,** jutting out into the valley, tells a later tale. On a slope of the mountain the ashes of Deneys Reitz were buried in 1944, Reitz who as a 17-year-old Boer boy rode off to fight the British in the Anglo-Boer War and whose story, *Commando*, later became a classic. Mariepskop was his love and here his ashes were returned. Fixed into a rock is a bronze plaque with the words:

> Vir strenuus et fortis
> Cui ne erat timor mortis

(A man active and brave in whom was no fear of death.) The spot can be reached from near Acornhoek on the eastern side.

We stood among the rocks on the Canyon's western edge and looked out past the three peaks—the Three Rondavels they are prosaically called—to Mariepskop beyond, a scene of many shapes and colours, peaks, table-tops and precipices, red and yellow streaked with darker shades, with purple shadows and blue distances, in a vast, still, empty world, and hoped that it would always be as good as this, that people would never dim its wildness and beauty.

From the Blyde Canyon we turned west to join the Lydenburg-Ohrigstad road, but before we went south on this we turned north to see the Abel Erasmus Pass and the **Strijdom Tunnel,** the longest road tunnel in South Africa, and beyond them the superb road winding away to the Lowveld. Then we went south through Lydenburg, turning back a few kilometres on N4 to take the Waterval Boven loop through the Elands River valley.

This stretch is once more history, gold and scenery mingled. Here, at 'Above the Waterfall', the railway built from Lourenço Marques emerged from its steep climb from the lowlands up the escarpment to the Highveld. It may not sound much today but in the 1890s it was a great feat: yet in spite of its excellence, the ordinary engines could not get to the top. But the little mountain engines of Europe could, and for them some four kilometres of rack railway were built, part of the way through a tunnel, between Waterval Onder and Waterval Boven, up which the little engines pushed the trains at the pace of a brisk walk—they were the only 'rack' engines in South Africa and were used well into this century until a railway line was built on the opposite side of the valley. The old tunnel is now a national monument.

The railway line was an achievement in engineering terms, and at the same time a tragic chapter in Transvaal history. For every sleeper laid, they used to say in the 1890s, malaria killed a man.

Waterval Onder, at the head of the Elands River Valley, was the place where President Kruger lived after the approach of the British had forced him to leave Pretoria in 1900, and so the village was an unofficial seat of government until the President moved to Nelspruit before leaving for Lourenço Marques. Krugerhof, the square house he lived in, is still there, much as it was in his day, and this, too, is now a national monument.

The President was at Waterval Onder indirectly because of gold: it shaped the Transvaal's history and brought the Anglo-Boer War in its train. 'Pray to God', Kruger had said when gold had been found near Barberton, 'that the curse connected with its coming may not overshadow our dear land.' Kruger must have thought of this continually in his days at Krugerhof. He had left the gold of the Witwatersrand far behind him, but the gold that he feared was now very close. It was there in the village stream, in the fields to the immediate north, and to the south and east—the gold of De Kaap Valley that had drawn from him those anguished words.

De Kaap is the great Lowveld valley south of Nelspruit and east of Waterval Onder, the valley known to old-timers as the Valley of Death because of the malaria and tsetse fly that killed off both men and animals. On a slope of this valley, in the foothills of the Drakensberg, lies **Barberton,** malaria-free now, the pretty quaint little town with its narrow winding streets filled both with history and with colour.

The colour is there in a very real sense, in the sub-tropical vegetation and the bright tumbles of flowers. It is a pleasure to walk slowly through the streets looking both at them and at the old buildings, some of them still with an authentic gold-rush air. So they should have, for gold made Barberton as it did Pilgrim's Rest.

The story, though different, has that same ring of adventure and life. After the finds near Sabie and Pilgrim's Rest—the Lydenburg Fields they were called—prospectors moved south and east, finding traces of alluvial gold as they went. Then on a winter's day in 1884 a hunter turned prospector named Graham Barber and his two cousins, Fred and Harry Barber, from the Eastern Cape, together with their friends Edward White and Holden Bowker, found gold that started one of the great gold rushes of South Africa. They were fossicking about in a narrow ravine near the town of today when they noticed a streak in the wall of the valley. Graham fetched a piece of quartz from it and the party crushed and panned it right away in the stream nearby. There was gold in it all right, but not the type of gold of the northern fields—that gold was alluvial and this was reef gold. So this was Barber's Reef and a new era had begun.

The excitement was tremendous. Away in the bush, as they were, there was no champagne to be had, but they used the next best thing. It was a bottle of gin; the mining commissioner broke it in state over the piece of gold-bearing quartz, and named the camp Barberton—Barber's Town.

Soon it was a village and then a town of 20 000 people, of bars, canteens, hotels, banks and brothels, even of a Stock Exchange working day and night. Men rushed in from every corner of the world: not even malaria that killed thousands of them where they worked could stop others coming. There was the Sheba Reef—the Sheba Mine was in its time the most famous gold mine in the world; its name and that of Bray's Golden Quarry rang on the bourses in London, New York and Paris. In 30-odd years of life Sheba yielded nearly a million ounces of fine gold. When John X. Merriman, once prime minister of the Cape Colony, saw Sheba in 1887 he noted that even the antheaps round about had been broken down and panned—and had yielded gold. The famous Eureka City blossomed in the mountains well above malaria level: today it is a ghost city full of memories.

It was still largely poor man's land, the miners breaking up the quartz with hammers and then grinding it up fine—their favourite 'machines' were natives' discarded grinding stones, the big flat stones with the rubbed hollows in the centre, and they stripped the entire Sheba area of these in no time.

There are plenty of signs of these old days. The facade of the **Stock Exchange**—the first in the Transvaal, the second in South Africa—still stands, and is one of the sights of Barberton. The little **Museum** is another. Among its fascinating relics is one that takes us straight back to tragic old Paul Kruger, watching the gold finds with fear and apprehension. It is his personal rifle, a German Mauser dated 1896, which he gave to a woman, Mrs Florence Gould of Komatipoort, who sang for him in Lourenço Marques on his birthday in October 1900. He was then awaiting a ship to take him to the Netherlands, and although he did not know it, to permanent exile.

There is something else we always go to see, the bronze of Jock of the Bushveld in Fitzpatrick Park. Jock is South Africa's most famous dog. He belonged to Sir Percy Fitzpatrick, financier and politician, who wrote his well-loved story about him that most South Africans read from childhood into age. Fitzpatrick as a young man in the gold boom days was a transport rider from the diggings to Delagoa Bay—Pilgrim's Rest, Lydenburg and Barberton knew him well—and with him went Jock, his golden part-Staffordshire bull terrier. The route they followed, the old transport road to the sea, is now known as the Jock of the Bushveld Road, and has commemorative plaques along its length. There is one near Lydenburg and one near Sabie, and they march across the Lowveld and into the Kruger Park—the route was traced and marked in the 1950s by Sir Percy's daughter, Mrs Cecily Mackie-Niven, an ornithologist of note. The Barberton bronze was done by Ivan Mitford-Barberton, the well-known sculptor, who belonged to a branch of the Barber family that changed its name to Barberton, so that a modern Barber also left his mark on Barber's Town.

Barberton still ranks as South Africa's third biggest gold producer. Now, however, it is company business, big business, and the days of the individual diggers are almost—but not quite—gone. It is a fascinating game, picking up bits and pieces of gold boom days, either by oneself or with the Knowledge Seekers—under their aegis visitors can sample, crush and pan for gold using a sluice box and a cradle; they can also see an old-timer in the flesh and hear his stories.

When we heard this we thought again of the Trail Blazers who had walked south and east over these mountains. At Sabie a woman reporter, Muffy Turbeville, together with Robin Graves of Knowledge Seekers, and a forest officer, started on a trail which ended in the mountains above De Kaap Valley and Barberton. They passed by Battery Creek, finding 70-year-old prospector, 'Old Sparg', who had been prospecting for half his life, who lived in a wattle and daub hut on the back of an old truck, and who existed on his gold finds. He showed them his latest pickings, gold dust and nuggets in an old jam tin. They sat on the grass, wrote Muffy, listening to his life story, and were enthralled.

CHAPTER EIGHT

Kruger National Park

❦

North-east of Barberton, an hour's drive away, is the Lowveld's greatest attraction of all, the **Kruger National Park.**

It is not only the Lowveld's showpiece but South Africa's number one tourist draw, for foreign visitors and for many South Africans the essence of Africa, an untamed country of wild beautiful animals living as they did 10 000 years ago—that it *is* (somewhat) tamed, that vegetation and animals are scientifically managed with knowledge and skill, is not immediately apparent to many visitors. What they long for is wildness (combined with comfort!) and the Kruger Park gives superb value.

So, incidentally, do some of the private reserves on the Park's western border—Timbavati, Mala-Mala, Rondalia-Letaba, Sabi-Sand, Sharalumi and Sohebele—which are mostly open to visitors who here can have private views of wild life, plus luxury accommodation, for a price. It is to the Kruger Park, however, that most people go.

In size it is a whole country in itself, 19 000 square kilometres—roughly the size of Belgium—running in a 380-kilometre band north-south in the Lowveld, bounded on the north by the Limpopo River, on the east by the Lebombo Mountains, on the south by the Crocodile River; on the west by the tract of low country reaching to the Drakensberg escarpment. (All its boundaries are now fenced.) Like the rest of the Lowveld, it is a bit of the great low tropical plain of south-east Africa down which have travelled all manner of trees and plants, and the creatures as well associated with them, populating now this far hot corner of South Africa.

It is bush or scrub country and sometimes savannah and parkland, well-grassed with stony outcrops, lone koppies rising out of the plains and huge granite boulders, and rivers—the Crocodile, the Sabie, the Letaba, the Olifants and the Limpopo—falling through gorges or flowing tranquilly, with pools and sand banks, trees and creatures associated with them.

Here lives the greatest concentration of wild animals in the world.

There are lions, the animals that everybody most wants to see—

1 500 of them—in the grass or on the roads, resting in the shade, warming their bellies, stalking, killing, eating, sleeping, smelling the motor-car tyres, flicking the car radiators with their tails, red with the blood of a kill or playing, entrancingly, touchingly, with their great golden spotted kittens in the sun. There are leopards (if one is lucky) lying lazily along a branch, the dark rosettes dappling the tawny skin an almost perfect camouflage; and 200 or more cheetah, seen surprisingly often in the Park; and—especially in mopane country in the north and among the tall trees, or in river beds—7 500 elephants, great grey mountains of flesh moving as quietly as mice on their enormous padded feet.

There are 24 000 buffalo (more than any other species of animal with the exception of impala), with those solid sweeping horns and mean little eyes—the most dangerous wounded animal of all, hunters used to say; black and white rhino, sable, the noblest antelope of all, and roan, once fast disappearing from South Africa but now numbering nearly 300 here; 4 000 giraffes, the tallest animals in the world; zebra, kudu, and smaller antelope by the many thousand.

In the rivers are 2 000 hippos, and crocodiles—nobody knows how many of them there are; and all the myriads of smaller things everywhere, jackals and hyenas, wild dogs and honey-badgers (the bravest animals of all), antbears and pangolins, porcupines and hedgehogs, squirrels and mongooses, rats and mice, warthogs running with their tails erect, baboons, monkeys and nagapies, well over 400 different kinds of birds; lizards, snakes and tortoises, spiders and insects. It is the richest treasure house on earth.

There are 13 rest camps strung from south to north, that are comfortable, superbly clean, and protected against malaria; some are air-conditioned, with private shower and refrigerator (that fridge is a touch of luxury that not even the diehards care to forego). There are restaurants as well as facilities for cooking outside, and shops at the rest camps; all is extremely carefully planned for the visitors' comfort.

These are bare facts. They do little to indicate the charm of the rest-camps, this 'other-world' inhabited by tourists so briefly and with such delight. Within the last few years the camps have been much modernized, a development that regular visitors to the Park looked on with suspicion. Could the charm survive? Those hot little huts were part of the excitement of it all, the first ones without windows and with peepholes in the doors through which people gazed to see if it was safe to venture out: fighting with the paraffin lamps was part of the fun, and so in rush-time was the bed under a tarpaulin on the ground, with the stars above and the jackals calling. There is still charm, and if we personally remember the old days with nostalgia, most visitors today do not: they probably find it all as beautiful and exciting as we did then.

The night sounds are still there as of old (if one remembers to turn off the air-conditioning); and it is possible to listen in the dark to a party of lions calling, or even a lion roaring, the most elemental and shattering sound ever to be heard from the embrace of a luxury mattress. There are the jackals, and sometimes an hyena laughing, if that high witch's cackle can really be termed a laugh at all; frogs and bats and crickets, and an owl hooting in the night.

The southern-most camps are Malelane and Crocodile Bridge, connected by 2 000 kilometres of main roads and by-ways with the others, Lower Sabie in the east, Pretorius Kop, and Skukuza, the biggest and the administrative and research centre, to the west, and northwards on the main road Tshokwane, Satara (with Orpen away to the west and Nwanedzi to the east), Balule, Olifants, Letaba, Shing-widzi and Punda Milia. When booking accommodation beforehand people often take into account the fact that certain species of animals are likely to be seen near certain camps, although this tends to be seasonal and is affected by such things as rain, availability of water, and the state of the grazing.

The two main draws, lion and elephant, can usually be seen throughout the Park, although the Lower Sabie Road and the country to Satara are traditionally among the best lion areas. The north was once the elephants' stronghold, yet they are seen today in the far south: they are still at their best at a spot like Pafuri in the extreme north, against the noble backdrop of the Limpopo River and its great trees. Kipling fans will remember that it was on the Limpopo that the Elephant Child got its trunk. In autumn animals such as zebra and blue wildebeest migrate southwards from their summer homes in the central areas east and west of Tshokwane to roughly the Sabie River, returning northwards with the early summer rains.

The dry seasons of winter and early spring are traditionally the best times to see animals. Because the grass is low and many of the trees bare, this is a good time to spot them: moreover, they congregate round water holes, and visitors often spend hours, most profitably, at a single dam or windmill—there are now well over 300 artificial drinking places and a great many natural pools. Where the game is, so also are the lions: so these are good 'lion' months as well. Even elephants are more often seen then, for in summer when they are breeding they tend to shun the roads.

After the first rains in late spring, the Park bursts into green leaf,

121

and the streams and pools fill up: the animals then disperse and are no longer so easily seen. Summer is the time, nevertheless, when the Park is full of young animals, and migratory birds as well, and the countryside is lush and beautiful. April and May are months of ripe autumnal beauty before the winter's cold: they are our own favourites.

There is often a lot to be seen on the roads themselves. Lions hunt along them, and so do cheetah: giraffe walk down them in magnificent single file, baboons and monkeys beg along them (and, it is said, warthogs as well). Elephant love them: they always have great skill in finding the best paths, and these are ready-made for them. There are great piles of their droppings to mark their passing, and the pips in these provide a feast for squirrels and birds. Then there are the game birds, the little warm-coloured francolins and quail and guineafowl: everybody knows them scurrying along and nipping neatly into the grass on the roadside—and there are also starlings, doves, larks, and others, feeding on the open road. There is a maximum speed limit of 50 kilometres an hour, and it is easy to see why.

That this fabulous animal world still exists is something of a modern miracle, for into it there came the early 19th century hunters, above all João Albasini.

It was his army of trained elephant hunters armed with guns that almost wiped out the Lowveld elephants, so that at the beginning of this century only 25 were left. By the 1890's the number of the larger animals had so dwindled that conservationists—even then there were some—were talking of the end of an era, visualizing a Transvaal empty of them. Among them was Paul Kruger who, only two years before he left the Transvaal permanently, proclaimed the Sabie Nature Reserve between the Sabie and Crocodile Rivers. 'If we do not close this small portion of the Lowveld,' he told the Volksraad, 'our grandchildren will not even know what a kudu or a lion or an elephant looked like.' He won this battle: and it is now part of history that on this Kruger victory both British and Afrikaner built—Lord Milner who reproclaimed the areas as a nature reserve after the end of the Anglo-Boer War; Colonel James Stevenson-Hamilton, who in 1902 was placed in charge of the reserve, who was the first warden of the Kruger Park and the greatest man in its story; Colonel Deneys Reitz (whose ashes lie buried on the slopes of Mariepskop not far distant) who as Minister of Lands under the Smuts Government fought for the concept of a national park; and Piet Grobler, grand-nephew of Paul Kruger, who followed him as minister. By virtue of these last three men, in particular, the National Parks Act was passed in 1926, an enlarged Sabie Nature Reserve becoming the Kruger National Park. It was an important event, for in one go the Park was lifted above the continual bickerings that had bedevilled it, and its status ensured by Parliament.

Today the Kruger, and all other national parks, are governed by a body known as the National Parks Board of Trustees, a non-profit-making organization, appointed in terms of the Act. Their purpose is clear, first the conservation of wild life and the research necessary for it, and only *secondly* the enjoyment of visitors. It is an order that most people accept gladly.

In the years following the National Parks Act, it was Stevenson-Hamilton who fought to extend the Kruger Park's boundaries and to protect its animals; at the time of his retirement in 1946 his was one of the best-known names in conservation in the world. He died in December 1957.

The Park has come a long way since the early Stevenson-Hamilton days. In 1927, the year it was thrown open to the public, the revenue from tourists amounted to R6, paid by the occupants of three cars. Today it is R6 000 000 annually paid by more than 400 000 people.

We ourselves usually come to the Park through the Numbi Gate, which is the Pretorius Kop entrance. We have never, in our many visits to **Pretorius Kop,** seen any dramatic sights there, but the lonely hills, the vegetation, and the long blue distances are beautiful; even the lights seem to us to have special values. The camp is not only the second biggest but the oldest, with several historic spots, including— near the Gate—the grave of Willem Pretorius, after whom the camp was possibly named, who trekked through the bush here with Karel Trichardt in the 1830s, contracted malaria, and died. He was buried by João Albasini.

About 24 kilometres from the camp near the Hippo Pool are the ruins of Albasini's own house, once the centre of his thriving ivory trade, now only a pile of rubble, and quite close to the camp, near one of the western loops, is the hill called Manungu after one of his black lieutenants.

Pretorius Kop was the home chosen by Harry Wolhuter, the Park's most famous ranger. In 1902 when he arrived, there were no wildebeest or impala and few kudu: today they are the most common animals, and the kudu bulls with their great twisted horns one of the sights. There are as well sable, rhino, giraffe and zebra, and sometimes lions and leopards.

The road between Pretorius Kop and the Malelane-Skukuza road, now marked Voortrekker on many maps, was once the old transport road to Delagoa Bay, and before that probably one of the trade routes

123

along which men travelled to the interior in search of tin and perhaps of gold. Most people know it best as the **Jock of the Bushveld Road:** there is a Jock cairn and plaque next to it close to the camp.

Malelane is a pretty little camp close to the main road to Komatipoort. From here a winding road leads to **Crocodile Bridge,** and the point, just east of the rest camp, where the first whites entered the Transvaal in July 1725. They camped at Gomondwane between this camp and Lower Sabie.

Enormous herds of buffalo, many hundred strong, now live between Crocodile Bridge and Lower Sabie: they represent another triumph—at the beginning of the century there were no more than 100 in all the park. Now these great dark moving masses are one of the most stirring things the Park has to show, in a fearful, rather sinister sort of way.

Skukuza to the north-east of Pretorius Kop on the Sabie River is more a village than camp today. The buildings are the same thatched rondavels seen throughout the Park, but there are in addition a big restaurant, a supermarket, a library, a church, a golf course, a football field and air-strip. (Tourists leaving Rand Airport at Germiston at 7 a.m. reach Skukuza at 9.30 on the first leg of a high-powered one-day trip: here they can hire a car or mini-bus to sightsee, and catch the plane back at 3 p.m.) The headquarters of the information service is here, where visitors can learn, among other things, about the current distribution of animals.

Skukuza, meaning 'to sweep clean' or 'to turn everything upside-down', was named after Colonel Stevenson-Hamilton. It has always been a camp of many adventures, with splendid sights along the roads near it.

South-east of Skukuza is the smaller **Lower Sabie Camp,** also on the Sabie River, the southern road along the river connecting the two being known as the Lower Sabie Road. This is one of the most famous stretches in the whole Park, a wonderful lion road, which also teems with all sorts of lesser creatures as well. Small turnouts overlooking the river abound. They are usually in the shade of big trees and here we love to sit quietly, sometimes for hours, waiting to see what will come. Last time there was a lion chasing a baboon into the bush in front of us, and a giraffe delicately eating the big wild gardenia blooms on the top of a tree—we watched its elastic lips pulling off the white flowers and wondered if it was enjoying the perfume.

Another time there was a leopard eating its impala kill up a sausage tree not four metres away, playing with the dangling head like a kitten with a swinging thread. We could hear the crunching of the bones from where we sat. On yet another trip we saw a pangolin. James

Clarke calls this a cross between an antbear and a plastic fir cone, and this is exactly how it looks, a sturdy 100 cm high creature—a reptile-like mammal in Austin Roberts' words—with a broad flat tail covered with gold-brown scales and a long sticky tongue with which it scoops up ants. It is very rare, and nocturnal as well, so it is one of the Park's least-known characters.

North and north-east of Skukuza the road goes on through Tshokwane to Satara and the north. It is a good road for many people, and here, we, too, have seen many things, including cheetah: there are said to be only about 500 left in South Africa, and the majority are here.

It was on this road that Lourens Fourie, the radio-announcer, and some companions saw one of the battles of the world, porcupines versus lions. Lourens, who was in the Park collecting material for a new radio programme, was returning by starlight from Tshokwane when he saw two porcupines in the road, and 13 lions as well.

Some of the lions, intent on a succulent titbit, were following the porcupines, other blocking their way, and between them marched the porcupines—'march' was the word Lourens used when he told us the story—in perfect step together, their quills fanned out, their heads well down, swinging round those formidable banded quills as a lion advanced. One used the ground below the car as an escape route, the other with a series of sideway manoeuvres finally reached the grass as well, and into this they disappeared. Their victory was complete.

Were the lions noisy? we asked Lourens. No, they had worked in complete silence. It was the porcupines that had growled!

There are always ground hornbills along the road, gigantic with scarlet wattles and huge bills, grey louries shouting 'Go away, go away', vultures, secretary birds, and at Tshokwane, our favourite picnic place, hornbills and starlings that try to share our breakfast with us. We enjoy them as much as the red flowers of the overhanging sausage tree that fall into our tea.

On a turn-off to the right are the Lindanda flats, where we never fail to see a steenbok, the solitary little antelope with the big eyes and ears veined like a leaf. Last time there were vultures as well.

Lindanda, meaning 'loin cloth', was the African nickname given to Wolhuter, for this is Wolhuter's country where, over 70 years ago, he had his remarkable adventure with a lion that is now a Lowveld legend. A memorial stone recalls it, together with the stump of what was clearly not a large tree.

Wolhuter told the story himself in his *Memories of a Game Ranger*, a book that remains a perennial thriller. Returning at dusk from a patrol, his horse was attacked by a lion which knocked him out of the saddle and on to the top of a second lion. This seized his right shoulder in its jaws and dragged him for 60 metres; when his spurs caught on the ground, the lion shook its head, its teeth lacerating his shoulder still further. He was conscious enough to wonder if the lion would eat him before it killed him, and to listen to it *purring*!

Then he remembered his knife. Working his left hand round his back as he was dragged along, he found it still in its sheath, and eased it out. Feeling for the lion's left shoulder—his head was pressed against its mane—he lunged with two back-handed strokes behind the shoulder, reaching the heart, and with a third severed the jugular vein. The lion dropped him and slunk off (to die). Wolhuter then remembered the second lion and, with a wounded shoulder and useless right arm, dragged himself into a forked tree nearby—it is its stump that is preserved and marked today. Soon the second lion, following the blood spoor, found him and reared against the tree trunk straining to reach him. But there was also Bull, his dog, who had suddenly appeared, to dash at the lion and retreat, and so through the dreadful night to draw him off repeatedly.

In the end there was help from Wolhuter's Africans, but—until they found the lion—none of them could believe that he had killed it with a knife, for no man had done such a thing before.

Both knife and lion's skin are exhibited today in the library at Skukuza.

Fifty years after the adventure we went to see Wolhuter's tree and on the way back, on what was then a narrow dirt road out of Pretorius Kop, we met a small, dark, ancient car with a gaunt hatchet-faced old driver. He deviated not a centimetre as he approached us, until—as he was upon us—we swung frantically still further to the left and fell into a ditch. We sat there laughing. If Wolhuter felt he owned the roads of the Kruger Park, we were certain we would not dispute it with him.

Besides Wolhuter's, there have been very few cases of lions attacking people in the Park. The number one rule—stay in the car—is responsible for this: it is a rule so simple and so obvious that it is usually obeyed.

Satara lies up the road, a big place now and streamlined. In spite of its all-African flavour it bears a name derived from an Indian word, 'satrah', meaning 'seventeen'—the surveyor who named it had a Hindu servant, or so the story goes.

From here a road leads to **Orpen,** the little camp on the western boundary, where tourists still find the old paraffin lamps and open braais. At the Rabelais Dam not far from Orpen a group of lions took up residence recently, so that tourists saw them every day stretched out under the trees near the water: they were so obvious that it was hardly fun to see them.

Near the camp two Pretoria visitors, Mr and Mrs Bill Wainwright, were attacked by an elephant some years ago. Elephant attacks are very rare—there have been only five incidents in which they have seriously damaged cars in the Park—and in this case the car was unwittingly driven between a cow elephant and her calf on the other side of the road. The elephant knelt on the car—a Peugeot—rocking it backwards and forwards, ripping up the bonnet and ramming it against the windscreen, finally spearing the radiator with a tusk. Mr Wainwright, somehow through the horror dredging from his memory an old warning, 'If an elephant charges your car, bang on the roof', leaned out and banged. The elephant stopped and calmly walked away. Mrs Wainwright partially blacked out during the incident—and so can bear to retell the story; but her husband, who had been keenly alert all the time, cannot. When she told it to us, he excused himself and went away: if he had listened, he said, he would not have slept that night.

About 25 kilometres from Orpen is an interesting and lovely north-south road, the southern part, via Hlangulene—a particularly good road in winter to see zebra and wildebeest—connecting with Tshokwane, and the northern via Timbavati, striking the main road near **Olifants Camp** to the north. This camp is a fine modern complex perched on the edge of a cliff overlooking the Olifants River: it offers a combination that visitors find irresistible. They can lie on their luxury mattresses drinking coffee of an early morning and listening to the sounds of the hippos rising up from the river below: and they can look out of their front doors on to one of the great views, the river in the broad valley, silver in the early light, with its reeds and trees, the whole landscape studded with the tiny, far-off black spots that are elephant, buffalo and other animals drinking in the dawn.

Letaba further on is a dramatic camp set among big old trees, where elephants can often be seen immediately beyond the fence. It has attractions, also, like the new tarred road to Phalaborwa with dams along it and sights of sable and roan, and the new Engelhard Dam to the east, the biggest dam in the Park, which attracts great numbers of animals and water birds. Buffalo are common round the camp, sometimes in big herds.

Nevertheless, it is **Shingwidzi Camp** that we always make for, with its wattle and daub huts among the tall mopane trees—it has a lightness and grace that is quite individual, and in July when the pink and white impala lilies bloom, distinctive colour as well. We have had wonderful times here, picnicking with the starlings—they fill the camp at times—and hunting for eland, nyala and sable along the river roads outside; and it was on one of these roads that we once had an elephant adventure.

The road was a winding up-and-down track with a path across leading to the river below. We could see a herd of elephant at the side of the water, across which a small dark spot was moving steadily. As we watched a form took shape and an elephant emerged—he had been walking below the surface of the pool, his feet on the river bed, the tip of his trunk above the water. We had heard of this incredible thing, this living snorkel, but had thought it a fairy tale: now we saw it was true.

So entranced were we that we hardly noticed that our car was blocking the path, but as the animals began to scramble up the pathway, we pulled the self-starter—it was clearly time to move. We pulled in vain, again and again, but nothing happened. The heat, 35 degrees Celsius in the shade, had vaporized the petrol in the fuel lead. We almost completely blocked the narrow path, which had been beaten—we realized in a flash—by innumerable great feet. What would the elephant think of us? What would they do to the beetle in their path? We turned up the windows and waited. What happened was the most ordinary thing in the world. They never even noticed us, but parted on either side—craning our necks upward we could hardly see the 22 great heads as they passed, only the gigantic moving limbs about us—several scraped us as they passed, and then they vanished into the trees beyond.

There are endless stories about elephants, their sagacity, their memories, their vengeance, their docility. A passing motorist near Shingwidzi had the chance to prove the often-told story that baby elephants, deprived of their mothers, adopt the nearest thing as parent. A baby elephant he came on standing in the middle of the road by itself adopted his car as mother, seizing the door handle in its trunk and accompanying it into the rest camp.

The camp that is our favourite in all the Park is **Pafuri,** now a picnic site only. We do not linger at **Punda Milia,** attractive as this wonderful old camp is, but are off to the north-east along one of those Transvaal bush roads through baobabs, mopane and thorns, and nyala trees filled with monkeys, to the old Pafuri camp on the banks of the Luvubu River. This is a subtropical world of palms, fever trees and crocodiles, dim in the deep shade of the big mahoganies, and when we first saw it, moving with elephant and striped nyala.

There is a lookout point where the river joins the Limpopo, and near it a spot under the trees where once there was a rest camp of tents. We

The statue of Dick King and 'Somerset' on the Esplanade in Durban

The round homes of Africa—the Transkei

A Transkei beach

slept one night in a tent under a leadwood tree, only next morning remarking the heaps of elephant dung lying about. 'Oh yes,' said the African attendant who was not much taller than a broomstick, and as skinny, 'oh yes, the elephants come in sometimes. But then I bang on my pan'—he banged his frying pan to show us, 'and they go away.' As a send-off, it was first-class, and we enjoyed it all the way back to Pretoria.

CHAPTER NINE

Zululand and Tongaland

❧

When we want, within the space of a few hours, to reach a new country, we take the road to Natal.

It *does* have a new look to Transvaalers, this great strip of country lying between the Drakensberg mountains and the sea, with green rolling hills that are clearly and indefinably Natal hills, mountains that wear a different air to Transvaal ones, the rivers and streams, and above all, the blue sea, the lagoons and beaches, the wild banana trees and all the other subtropical plants along the coast that belong to an exotic, warm, languorous world of holiday-making and swimming and lying in the sun. Transvaalers sometimes find it hard to believe that people *live* and *work* along the Natal coast: it is so obviously holiday land.

They come to it from the landlocked interior by the tens of thousands to all the resorts from Durban southward to Port Edward—Natal's famous South Coast—and northwards as well for a shorter distance. Or after they drop down the escarpment into Natal from the Transvaal and the Orange Free State, they spread out along the foothills of the mountains, to the hotels and camps, to rest, climb, explore the forested kloofs, swim in the mountains pools and fish for trout in the clear streams.

Sometimes they take the roads to the country north of the Tugela River to the famous Natal game reserves, all open to the public, or to Lake St Lucia with its fish and crocodiles and birds, or Sordwana Bay still further north. Beyond in the extreme northeast is Kosi Bay with sea, lakes and forests, where seedlings grow on trees in mangrove swamps and palms have leaves nine metres long. It is as remote from Johannesburg as any place can be; as fascinating as anything Africa has to show.

When we can, we go there. We take the road south-east through Ermelo and Piet Retief, passing over the Pongola River into Natal, and at the village of Jozini near the J. G. Strijdom Dam, six hours' drive away, we are there, clocking into the motel above the water with the anticipation this country always brings.

We are, as people, history-minded, finding things are usually the richer when their story is known, yet here we never give a thought to all those things that helped to make Natal, to its discoverers, to the bitter, bloody, tragic and heroic wars—Black against Black, Black against White, and Whites between themselves. For this is a world of present delights. We take a look at the vast plain stretching eastwards towards the sea, have a shower and a long cool drink, and wait impatiently for our friend, Ian Garland, and Jobe his man, to arrive and join us. Before us stretch the joys of mountains, rivers, pans, forest, crocodiles, birds, snakes, frogs, lilies on the pools, tailor ants spinning their webs from umdoni leaf to umdoni leaf; and Ian Garland and Jobe are our interpreters who tell us where the frog is croaking, what butterfly swoops about the palms, what bird sings.

They run into one another, the memories of the marvellous days. There were those at **Mkuze,** the Natal Parks Board game reserve a little to the south-east of Jozini, one of our favourite places, where we stayed in a little rest camp in the heart of a park-land of wild thorns. When we think of the Kruger National Park we think first of animals but when we think of Mkuze we remember Africa.

The immense sycamore fig trees under which even by day the light was dim, the fever trees with their ghostly trunks, the flat-topped thorn trees in the dusk, the sun going down behind the Lebombo Mountains, were a mood of Africa. In the darkness we heard a nightjar: like the jackal's cry, it was the sound of African night. And in the early morning there was the pan overlooked by the Bube Hide where we watched the animals drinking, an immemorial scene, quiet and without drama, a silver pool, waterlilies, an nyala, and presently a warthog rolling in the mud.

Close to the reserve gates we found two other things of Africa, an **isiVivane** in the grass on which we ceremoniously placed our stone, and a little bush not 20 centimetres high that is known—at least second hand—all over the African bushveld because it gives off an all-pervading smell of cooking potatoes. The smell is often, particularly in spring when the tiny flowers are in bloom, THE smell of the hot dry lowveld from South Africa northwards to the tropics. The bush is called *Phyllanthus reticulatus* by botanists, but to everyone else who knows it, it is the potato plant, and a great amusement.

Ndumu Game Reserve to the north is some four hours' drive away through Tongaland, the stretch of country northwards of Zululand that is now under the control of the Zulu homeland of KwaZulu. It is mostly a flat, low flood-plain country, once the bed of the sea, that we met at Jozini and followed northward to the border, the Lebombos on the west and eastward flats with lakes and pans, open sand forest, swamps, and sea. It is a wonderful area for all who study plants, birds, insects and fish, for here is the southernmost limit of many tropical species; yet it is an area that has yielded up its secrets slowly and mostly in the last few decades—many still remain to be learnt.

Once we took the western road through the village of Ingwavuma in the Lebombos. We knew these mountains from the western side in the Kruger National Park, always looking like a range of smoky hills; here among them they were heights with immense views, with strange trees and shrubs, kraals hidden among foliage and neat little living fences made of poles that had sent out roots and grown. It all had a simple ancient look, and an ancient world in human terms it was, for—if scientists are right—this was where the earliest known 'modern' man, *Homo sapiens*, lived, probably more than 80 000 years ago.

In a cave here, known as **Border Cave,** close to Ingwavuma village, the skeleton of a child and fragments of an adult skull were excavated that clearly belonged to *Homo sapiens*: as scientific dating made the picture clearer it was found that they were more than 80 000 years old. It was a date that rocked, not only South African scientists, but those everywhere.

Southern Africa, palaeontologists had admitted, had their ape-men, but as far as modern man was concerned, he had appeared not in Africa but in the Middle East and Europe about 35 000 B.C. The Border Cave discoveries blew this theory sky high.

It had already been questioned in Swaziland across the border from the Ingwavuma cave. *Homo sapiens* is 'thinking man'. In the 1960s discoveries had been made in Swaziland—not very far from Border Cave—which showed that men at least 40 000 years B.C. had been actively and purposefully engaged in mining—he had clearly shown himself thinking man. This had motivated two Johannesburg researchers, Adrian Boshier of the Museum of Man and Science, and Peter Beaumont of the Bernard Price Institute for Palaeontology, to begin work again—under the direction of Professor Dart—in Border Cave where the child's skeleton and the skull of Ingwavuma Man had been found in the 1940s.

The child had been buried, and moreover ceremoniously buried, and next to its body had been placed a perforated sea shell, a pendant or perhaps a toy. Burial in itself is a ritual of later human development; and someone here, 80 000 years ago—in burying the child, and in doing it in this way—had shown not only tenderness but, it was implied, the hope of life after death.

What Boschier and Beaumont had done in the 1970s was, among

other things, to obtain material with which it was possible to date the burial, and it was this that was the incredible sequel. So tens of thousands of years before *Homo sapiens* was known in Europe, a thinking man or woman had here been aware of the spirit as apart from the flesh and left a record of his belief—it was the earliest evidence of such belief in all the world, and it was found here in these ancient hot hills with their euphorbias and stony crests.

The eastern road to Ndumu is the shorter. In the country here we once passed a kraal under a mahogany tree, its great branches with their dark shiny evergreen leaves throwing the deepest shade in Africa, and under them the little thatched homes—it was the only cool spot in the open burning forest—a pan with waterlilies where a woman was setting up a fish trap; a woman on her knees cracking the kernels of the marula fruits with a stone to feed her family; a little tree with thick succulent leaves at which Jobe shouted with dismay. It was a member of the euphorbia family, notorious for its poisonous sap, which is called *Synadenium cupulare* by the pundits and by Jobe the Crying Tree—it cried like the plumed viper, umDlondlo, he said, luring creatures to it which it then slew. Even birds that flew past it dropped dead. Why then, we asked were we—who had touched it—still alive? Why were there no bleaching bones about its stem? Jobe considered. No, he said, this *could not* be the Crying Tree: it was self-evident that it was not. It was, instead, its little brother.

And so, as we went north, we spoke of the magic beliefs of this countryside, where the people were still deeply attuned to all the natural things about them. There was a group of women under a wide-spreading marula tree sitting with their pots and baskets—the marula that is the tree of Africa, venerated for its abundant fruits. When a Zulu woman had a baby girl, said Ian, the family would make a fire of marula twigs, and on this boil a pot of water in which mother and child were washed—and thereafter the little girl would be tender, soft and fertile like the tree. Boys were washed in water boiled on a fire made of umFomothi sticks, the big lusty straight-stemmed trees, *Newtonia hildebrandtii*, with the rough bark, the emerald foliage and the bright red pods that we had stopped to wonder at, for this magic bath conferred upon the boys the toughness and hardness of the tree—and perhaps, we thought, its magnificence and glamour too.

It was evening when we reached **Ndumu,** the little camp with a few thatched cottages upon a rise above the rivers and the plain, and we sat in the hot dusk with Moçambique across the Usutu River from us, listening to the Fishing Owl—the ghost owl—booming and moaning in the blackness.

133

The sound we came to think of most vividly as Ndumu was the scream of the Fish-eagle, the wild scream that is heard down the coast to the Cape where there are rivers and lakes with fish and wooded banks, to many the most African of coastal sounds: it was the wildest and freest cry we had ever heard matching the wild mysterious tropical jungle along the rivers, the flood plain with the pans ringed with dense vegetation, the hippos and the crocodiles. There were also jacanas, the lily trotters, running on the waterlily leaves—we could see their long toes as they ran—and other excitements among the 400 species of birds here, but above all there were the crocodiles, these most sinister, most African of creatures—and African they are for the crocodiles we watched were the same Nile reptiles of Egyptian waters.

It was at Ndumu that the Natal Parks Board originally made its famous Crocodile Farm, where the creatures were studied and reared, which was later moved to Lake St Lucia in the south, and it was here that the Crocodile Specialist Group of IUCN (the International Union for the Conservation of Nature and Natural Resources) had their second meeting a few years ago. Everyone was thrilled with what they saw, from the conservation point of view and from the sheer spectacle of it—a crocodile at close quarters is always massive drama, and Ndumu offered the perfect setting.

It was here that the Natal Parks Board ranger, A. C. Pooley, South Africa's crocodile man, saw a sight that made the wild animal story of the year, at the same time solving the mystery of how crocodile babies, hatched in the sand far from water, reached the water in the end. He told the story in *African Wildlife*, the summer number of 1974, making this the most attractive number ever of this fascinating magazine.

The mystery was hitherto unsolved because crocodile eggs hatch out with the dawn, and nobody up to Pooley's day had been on the spot in the half light to see exactly what happened. He not only saw it, but took some of the most extraordinary pictures known.

The crocodile carried the new hatchlings to the water *in her mouth*. Pooley watched her seizing the tiny creatures in her teeth, manipulating and gulping—when she opened her jaws to secure more he could see the first lying across her tongue, others asleep in her pouch. And he listened to the excited squeaks of the new arrivals greeting the old, and the welcome of those already in her jaws. When he offered the mother a baby through the fence, holding it by the tail, she accepted it, he said, 'as a Labrador retriever would handle a baby sparrow'. With all 19 hatchlings safely installed in her pouch and mouth, she moved down to the pool, and he listened to the splashing sounds as the babies made their first acquaintance with the water. There was a photograph of the crocodile manoeuvring a baby into her mouth—Pooley certainly saw a crocodile smile!

From Ndumu we turned east, armed with twin necessities, an official permit and a four-wheel drive. We crossed the Pongola River on a pontoon operated by a gay, inebriated old ferryman known as iNkunzi bomfu, the Red Bull. Then it was a long sandy haul to **Kosi Bay,** packed with fascinations: we ate *mkwakwa* fruits on the way, the big round cricket ball fruits with seeds covered with orange flesh, collected in the forest by a band of small black girls; and drank *busulu* in the swamps, the fermented sap of the ilala palm, that decorates the land with its large handsome leaves. Then we were in forest near the coast, in front of us the huge sand dunes bordering the sea, and soon we were setting up camp in the Kosi Bay Park on the shores of Lake Hlangwe where the wild banana leaves flapped in the wind like pistol shots, and the wild hibiscus flowers changed colour from hour to hour.

The Kosi Bay system is made up of four lakes, joined to one another and connected to the sea by an estuary and is a place that every naturalist longs to see. Fishermen know it well, and so do botanists and ornithologists because—in particular—of two kindred wonders, the raphia palms, *Raphia australis*, and the huge birds whose lives are bound up with them, the palm nut vultures.

We came to the palms along a path through forest, fern and mud and found them—these great handsome trees—soaring, unbranched, 24 metres to the sky, with their nine-metre long leaves, blue-green with midribs that were glowing red. Out of the heart of one there rose a three-metre high brown plume, the inflorescence, and we craned our necks to look; at our feet lay a fruit, as big as a goose-egg, covered with bright, shiny, chestnut-brown scales.

The tree was scientifically undescribed when we saw it, one of the curious trees of Africa, indigenous only to a stretch of coast from Kosi to southern Moçambique, and as we gazed up we saw as well one of the continent's most curious birds perched high up in it, many metres above our heads. It was the bird that is something between a vulture and an eagle, the palm nut vulture, *Gypohierax angolensis*, that eats the thin fleshy layer around the kernel within the fruit and on this depends for its very life. Where the tree grows, there lives the vulture. At Mtunzini far to the south, said Ian, a local magistrate had once planted a grove of the palms, and years later when they were fruiting, out of the blue had come the palm nut vulture to begin here as well this strange bird and plant association.

There were pelicans and flamingoes, avocets with their entrancing slender curved bills, spoonbills and kingfishers in bright colours, and many more, and in the water a multitude of fishes. They were being trapped in the estuary, which was seamed with wooden palisades, part of a workmanlike plan for directing the fish into large wicker traps. We watched this typical Kosi scene with pleasure; it looked as old as pelicans, to us the most ancient-looking birds alive.

The Tongaland coast is precious to naturalists for two reasons in particular, its coral reefs offshore, which are unique, and its beaches where breed the loggerhead turtles, and the leatherback which are the rarest marine turtles, and the biggest, in the world. In South Africa they breed only along a small strip of beach in the extreme north-east, mostly just south of Kosi Bay, and these breeding grounds, dis-covered—with a burst of publicity—only in the 1960s, have now become of international importance.

Turtles—slow, unaggressive, unprotected creatures—come up onto beaches to dig their nests and lay their eggs in the sand above the high-water mark, returning thereafter to the ocean; while the newly hatched young must also in their turn make their way to the sea. In the old days in Tongaland, when the turtles were protected by supersitious belief and not harmed by men, this age-old cycle and ancient journey through the sand was one of comparative safety. But supersitions die, and so did this one; and then the turtles' lives were forfeit and their massacre began: when some 15 years ago the alarm was sounded and an official survey was made, there was hardly a leatherback left. The Natal Parks Board through the years since has reversed the position: it not only started the turtle research but its men still patrol and safeguard the beaches where the turtles breed. That year of the first survey five leatherbacks were seen: in the season from 1975 to 1976 there were 65 leatherbacks and 351 female loggerheads, a triumph that set turtle men everywhere talking. The first survey team learned a lot; now tagging and carapace notching is teaching still more.

It has been a programme followed by the public step by step. Not many people, it is true, have ever seen that night scene with the great turtles emerging from the surf, hauling themselves up onto the lonely beaches on the hot breathless nights, making their nests, laying their eggs—all within hours—and plodding their laborious way back to the sea. Or the tiny hatchlings, beset by enemy crabs and birds and small quick flesh-eating mammals, making their first enormous hazar-dous journey to the ocean. But the press, and *African Wildlife* in particular, told them about it, and for many it was a brave and romantic story.

We sat around our camp fire talking of Tongaland and the sights we had seen. Some two decades ago a Natal Parks Board ranger, the young blond giant, Ken Tinley—noted ecologist today—who knew much of Tongaland by heart, proposed a national park for the territory; and even before him conservationists had been clamouring for it, to include in particular Kosi Bay. Then in 1969 Dr Allan Heydorn, Director of the Oceanographic Research Institute in Durban, urged the necessity for a maritime park to save turtles and coral reefs. A buzz of interest had sounded, but nothing eventuated. Then KwaZulu, with its Conservation Department, of vital importance to any future plan, appeared on the scene. They favoured such a park, and that is all the public knows at the moment. But if it materializes—and there is good reason why it should—then this will be the richest, most exciting park of Southern Africa.

It is possible at the moment for the determined to reach Kosi Bay by getting a booking from the ranger in charge of the Kosi Bay Nature Reserve, and a permit from the Secretary for Agriculture and Forestry, KwaZulu Government, Ulundi, to travel there. Not many go at present, but a maritime park or reserve would be a great draw. We ourselves cannot think of Tongaland as anything but lonely and remote, and we hope—park or no park—that this it will always be.

South of Kosi Bay a line of big lakes stretches down the coast as far as Richards Bay, marvellous lakes, each with their own beauty and particular interest and importance.

The sandy track connecting Kosi Bay with **Lake Sibayi** was not negotiable even by Landrover and we reached the lake by a rough road branching from the main road at Ubombo south of Jozini. We arrived in the rain, putting up a tent in a dripping forest, drinking whisky under a tarpaulin, listening to the Samango monkeys screaming in the trees and the hippos grunting in the water. Later a research station was set up here by Rhodes University, but there was nothing when we saw it but forest and water and the things that inhabited both, a tranquil place where—standing on the edge of the clear fresh water of the lake—we could smell the salt across the narrow forested dune between us and the sea.

There was one road running through the forest under an arch of tall trees with the lake to one side—the lake without an outlet, blue and calm, engirdled with green, breath-takingly beautiful. The forest we explored was tropical with wild figs so immense that they could shelter a village, wild mulberries, trees with fire-bright new leaves, one—with fruits that split to show crimson and black—had young leaves that were salmon-pink and more beautiful than flowers. It was *Blighia unijugata*, bearing a generic name given in honour of Captain William

137

Bligh. So Bligh of the *Bounty* was here in our Zululand forest! It was something more to relish along the forest paths.

It was a plant- and bird-lover's paradise, and Ian Garland knew everything from the dune shrubs to the forest giants, and everything that flew and roosted in them. An interpreter in these little known places is important, and as we followed in Ian's footsteps, the richness and joys of Sibayi closed about us. Back in the city, we remember in particular the early mornings—the hippo in the shining lake, the monkeys overhead, and the fish eagles calling, followed by Reichenow's lourie, the Narina trogans, the broadbills and the emerald cuckoos—and the mealiemeal porridge with a Sibayi flavour of wood smoke and—we like to think—of crocodiles.

To the south of Sibayi lies the **Sordwana Bay National Park** beloved of fishermen, a place of forest, mangroves, water and coral reefs, and still further south Zululand's largest and best known lake of all, **Lake St Lucia,** a great shallow stretch of water that is linked at its southern end with the sea, which because of its unique dual nature has given rise to animals and plants associated with both fresh and saline water. It is generally regarded as South Africa's bird paradise, where in a weekend 'you can probably see more birds than anywhere else in the world', which—because it is geared to visitors and is accessible (reached from Durban within a few hours) has given bird-lovers greater excitements than any other spot in South Africa.

Our first introduction years ago to the lake was a Satour film called *Lake Wilderness*, made by Sven Persson, which we remember as a classic: so do people all over the world for it was widely distributed, proving the finest advertisement South African wild life ever had.

What the film showed was a great water in a low green jungle, its crocodiles (we heard them squeaking in their eggs), its hippo, and its birds filling the air, the reeds, the mangroves, the mud flats, a picture of an innocent, wild, abundant world that enraptured people and brought some across the world to see it.

Then in the late 1960s wild life experts began to note a change. There was severe drought, and for various other reasons as well the fresh water that flowed down the rivers that fed the lake dwindled or stopped, while at the same time the age-long seepage into the lake grew less. The nature of the water began to change. The salinity began to rise, and it rose fast. First the experts noticed that it was a little more saline than the sea. Then it was three times as salty, and by 1971 the salinity was 116 parts per 1 000: in the Dead Sea itself—dead because of its salt—it was only four parts higher.

The reeds died and so did the crocodiles, encrusted with salt. Some, the fortunate few, were air-lifted by helicopter to a place of safety. The hippos could not submerge because of their new buoyancy. Barnacles appeared. The birds went. The lake appeared completely dead, and people wondered if it had gone for always.

But it had not. In 1972 the summer rains were heavy and fresh water started to reach the lake. It was a miraculous reprieve, and although things did not return absolutely to normal, the crocodiles came back and so did the birds and other life. The experts, frightened and alerted now, set to find out exactly what had happened and why, and to devise means of saving St Lucia from a similar future horror.

This time to work with age-old elements they brought the most modern and sophisticated of techniques, and electronic computer fed with data assembled by a range of experts, a team from Johannesburg's Witwatersrand University collaborating with Natal authorities.

After five years assembling the data, the computer 'spoke'. What it 'said' was that St Lucia could be saved from similar disasters in various ways, such as by bringing water to the lake from the Umfolozi or Pongola River; that the lake had, through the ages, had its salinity problems but only half as severe as in 1970, and that if no action was taken catastrophes such as the last would occur about six times every century. At the moment everyone is looking to the future with hope. In the meantime the hippos submerge again in the water, there are crocodiles on the mudbanks, and the birds are back.

The **St Lucia Game Reserve** and Park that surrounds the lake in a narrow band is a great attraction once again to those who long to experience the wild first hand, because of its Wilderness Trails on which small parties of people are taken by a ranger by boat and on foot, walking through the bush and sleeping under the stars.

The lake is shaped rather like a tree with a knobbly trunk and two-forked crown, with the estuary at its foot—the lake's southern end. This part is an angler's Mecca, and full of other sights as well—we remember a hippo here long ago that used to come out of the water and walk delicately among the hotel visitors. Then there is Charters Creek on the left half way up the 'tree-trunk', with a fine hutted camp, and north of this Fanie's Island with another; Bird Island is ahead, named for its pelicans, spoonbills, and other species, and False Bay upon the left.

We sailed across the lake once with Paul Dutton, the ranger, and—unbelievingly—watched him as he slipped into the water to give the boat a shove off a mudbank on which a number of monster crocodiles were lying. 'Oh, they're my friends,' he said casually. 'They'd never harm me,' and indeed it was not until they heard our alien voices that they moved at all and slid into the water. We noted, with a shudder, that they were extraordinarily quick.

The **Hluhluwe Game Reserve** lies a little to the west with a bigger and more sophisticated camp than in the other reserves—with good accommodation, a store and electricity. It is a place of typical Zululand scenery, of hills and valleys, famous in particular for its rhino, both black and white: with plenty of other game as well including the occasional lion. It was all the sadder, therefore, that what left the deepest impression on us were the ticks. It is these blood-sucking, insect-like creatures that are the curse of those who walk through cattle and game country in South Africa, not snakes or spiders or such seeming hazards—those one seldom sees. But the ticks are everywhere, sometimes, at their most evil, no bigger than a pin's head, swarming up shoes and socks with astonishing speed, settling into their blood meal over every unprotected centimetre of skin, leaving at the best a maddeningly itchy lump and at the worst a boil and tick-bite fever. At Hluhluwe we were able, as in the other Natal reserves, to get out of the car and to walk about in the company of an African ranger. Here as we stood looking at a white rhino, we were too interested to notice the dark tide rising above our ankles and brushing off against us at waist level—it was made up of ticks individually almost too small to see and they had reached the hair of our heads before we realized what had happened. There was only one thing to do. At the store we bought bottles of paraffin in which we bathed, generously and for a long time.

Everybody used to the bush takes their own tick measures, but one is universal—the long bath well-dosed at the end of the day, and always the careful going over of their clothes.

Umfolozi Game Reserve to the south-west, with its rolling hills and long Zululand views, is not only one of the loveliest spots in Southern Africa, but famous as the place where the white rhino was saved from extinction, and where the first Wilderness Trails—along with those at Lake St Lucia—pointed the way to today's greater country-wide wilderness venture. It was in May 1973 that the first national wilderness area was proclaimed in the Natal Drakensberg, but years before this Natal Parks Board rangers were taking groups of people on hiking trails of several days through their own wilderness area here. It might have had no legal status, but to people it was almost always a wonderful experience, and thousands walked the trails and walk them still. What these trails did show as well was what the public response to the wilderness idea would be—they more or less guaranteed its success.

The first trail in 1963 was led by Ian Player, who was to found the Wilderness Leadership School, the independent organization dedicated to teaching young people conservation based on environment.

The white rhino's is a rare success story. After the terrible extermination of game of the past—in an official attempt to eliminate tsetse fly—the numbers of the rhino here were reduced to 30, and it seemed that these ponderous docile creatures were on their way to extinction. Care, knowledge and dedication saved them and they flourished, so much so that a population explosion in time posed a question in itself. Drug darting to immobilize animals briefly was developed at Umfolozi, and through it the transfer of white rhino to other areas was made possible—well over 800 have been moved to populate the countrysides they once inhabited, while a number have been shipped abroad.

Next to the elephant, the white rhino is the largest of all land mammals, an enormous, slow, inoffensive creature with a square mouth, in contrast to the black rhino, which is smaller and long-lipped, and reputedly evil-tempered. There was a white rhino in an enclosure at Umfolozi the day we were there, and we watched his dog friend licking his eyes; then we knuckled his forehead through the fence with all our strength while he leaned against it ecstatically, begging for more.

The next wonder was a man-made one on the southward road to Mtunzini. **Richards Bay,** roughly half way between Durban and Lake Sibayi, was until recently a holiday village at the mouth of a big lagoon, a little place surrounded by marshes, attracting anglers and bird watchers to its abundant fish and bird life. Few people a decade ago knew it; still fewer had ever heard of Admiral Sir F. W. Richards, who was in command of the naval units during the Zulu wars and who gave his name to the bay. Yet it has become the scene of something unusually interesting, the first big South African harbour and city to have been planned and programmed on every level from the very start. All South Africa's other harbours and cities have had small and often random beginnings, gales, currents, streams of fresh water, adventurers, soldiers and traders taking a hand. But the plan to build a new harbour at Richards Bay to divert traffic from Durban harbour was a deliberate one, handled at top level.

The site in the first place was carefully chosen. There was a natural harbour, fresh water, plentiful labour close by, and it was nearer the Transvaal's coal mines and maize lands and Witwatersrand industries than any other port, nearer even than Durban. A great new railway line in no time, it seemed, was on the way to connect them with the Bay.

The Bay itself is cited as a model of planning; everything—it is promised—is cared for, from the coal in great coal berths to the super-tankers in the dredged-out harbour and the wild life on the shores around. There will be room for expanding industries, and suburbs as modern as planning can make them, and if we sigh a little for the mangrove swamps—the dark secret places—now reclaimed, it is, we know, a sentiment not of the times: for the Bay is a complex, modern adventure promising (and perhaps providing) the best of two worlds.

When we reached Mtunzini not an hour's drive down the road, there was the best also of the old and new. Ian Garland's farm, Twinstreams, lies along the coast, part sugar cane fields, part of the coastal forest he guards with passion, still a pocket of the old wild Zululand. Here is happening one of the newest of the new things in South Africa. KwaZulu as an independent homeland is new, and so are its responsibilities to its soil, plants and animals: new, too, are the plans to train the Zulu people in ecology and conservation, to fire them with the wish to care for their astonishing wild world.

It is not yet a comprehensive plan, but it is a start. At Kosi Bay, young Zulus from KwaZulu's Conservation Department are working with Natal Parks Board rangers; at a place like the Cwaka Agricultural College at Empangeni, conservation is taught: and in the last few years the Wild Life Society of Southern Africa has taken a hand by introducing courses in conservation and ecology for teachers supplied by the KwaZulu Government. Twinstreams is used as a base for these courses, with Ian Garland as the Project Leader and a versatile, enthusiastic Zulu, Simeon Gcumisa, to run the courses. They are a great hit.

The farm itself, an hour and a half's drive from Durban, is known to a great many other people as well for it is the unofficial rendezvous of many—Black and White—who are interested in the wild life of Zululand. We have our particular memories of good talk and plant presses, barringtonia flowers lying undisturbed, like white powder-puffs, on the surface of the streams, a lagoon, the smell of mud and the salt of the sea, and forest paths full of butterflies, the Mother of Pearl and the Golden Banded Forester that flits in the shadows and is gone.

CHAPTER TEN

Natal

❦

By comparison with Zululand roads, the main road from Johannesburg to Durban has little glamour. It runs south-eastwards through Standerton, Volksrust and Newcastle: at Ladysmith it is joined by the Free State road from Harrismith, and then it is on to Pietermaritzburg and Durban beyond it. It is known as N3 and is one of the busiest in the country, for several times a year it is *the* holiday route, with motor-cars almost bumper to bumper, rushing from the Transvaal to the sea, a horrible road at such times without a moment to savour its possibilities.

This is one route where it is necessary to loiter to enjoy the journey, and to branch both east and west, east to the rolling grasslands, the valleys and hills where so much of Natal's early history was made—and where the signs of history still linger—west to the Drakensberg, that incomparable range of mountains that is today the most popular mountain holiday region in South Africa.

At **Volksrust** the mealielands of the Transvaal's Highveld are left behind, for this is the border town, with the drop down the escarpment by way of Laing's Nek Pass only a little way ahead. It is a place where we sometimes pause and consider Natal before us with its rich and war-like past and its present prosperity and pleasures.

Almost exactly a hundred years ago a party which had laboured by ox-wagon along the road from Durban and up the track had camped near the mountain top. It was that of the first Anglican Bishop of Pretoria, the Right Reverend Henry Brougham Bousfield, formerly of Andover, Hampshire, with his wife, Charlotte Elizabeth, their eight children, and entourage, and we think of them here somewhat wryly.

It had been a frightful journey over roads that were no more than tracks with choking dust and torrential rain, yet they had had that priceless commodity, time. At seven o'clock on Christmas morning the Bishop held Holy Communion here, 'with the sky, earth and stones for our church', wrote his wife in her journal, 'and the little table often used in Andover . . . was our altar'. They cooked their Christmas dinner in a hole in the ground at the side of a bank, a hole at the top for the chimney, and a stone for the door, and they ate loaves of bread freshly baked, a couple of ducks and a beefsteak pie, and then the Bishop and his wife had a little walk to a waterfall where the Bishop picked ferns for her!

Rushing over the tarmac road, we have little of either their discomfort or fun. Yet we think about the same things as they did: in 1878 the Bousfields were meeting rumours of war on every side and seeing the preparations for it, and here on the mountains we think of those same wars.

The country to the far left of the national road, east of the Buffalo River and north of the Tugela, is traditionally the Zulu stronghold—the Tugela is the mighty river of Natal that rises in the Drakensberg, meets the national road at Ladysmith, and runs eastwards into the Indian Ocean some 90 kilometres north of Durban, bending and winding and twisting on its way. Here centuries ago came the Nguni people from the far north, and of these the Zulus—numbering four million today—were but an insignificant branch until the coming, and the proving, of a young Zulu warrior, who was to change the history of Natal.

His name was Shaka. He was to become the warrior-king of the Zulus, the man who, with ruthlessness and military genius, welded the tribes of Natal into a terrible, efficient army of 50 000 men such as Southern Africa had never seen—the Black Napoleon, historians called him—whose rise to power, and whose acts as king, caused the greatest upheaval and terror that Natal has ever known. With his army he laid waste the country and the territories adjoining, in a reign of blood and horror, but when he died in 1828, assassinated by his brother Dingaan, he left a Zulu people, united, strong and proud.

He was no enemy to the Whites—in 1824 there were only a handful of them centred on Port Natal. It was Dingaan, his successor, who warred with them, above all the Voortrekkers who, with their wagons, guns and cattle, had pushed northward from the Cape and in the late 1830s were descending the Drakensberg into Natal in search of a new home. When they reached their promised land below the mountains they found it empty as far as Port Natal. Just as the Voortrekkers reaching the Transvaal found a land devastated by Mzilikazi and without people, so here Shaka's impis had cleared the country, killing—it is reckoned—a million people. Dingaan's warriors came loping across the empty land from the north-east to annihilate the Voortrekkers, and the places where they fought were spread out before us as far south as Estcourt on the national road, and east beyond Dundee.

There are the great names also where the British later battled with the Zulus—among them Isandhlwana and Rorke's Drift—and away beyond the Umfolozi River, the great kraal of the Zulu king, Cetshwayo, near which he was finally defeated by the British and Zulu power broken. It was the preparations for these wars that the Bousfields had seen in 1878.

Even here in the north-west where we prepare to drop down the pass, there are the marks of war, this time of the first Anglo-Boer War of 1880-81. About five kilometres south of Charlestown, just across the border, a path leads from Majuba station to Majuba Mountain where the Boers defeated the British—a defeat that rocked South Africa and Britain—and a few kilometres further on on the right hand side of the road is the stone building, O'Neil's Cottage, built in the form of a cross, where the peace terms were drawn up: it is now a national monument. Long before we first saw it, we had a concept of that meeting between Boer and Briton—given us by Anton van Wouw, who had sculpted the scene on one of the panels at the base of the Kruger Statue in Pretoria.

Twenty years later, after the outbreak of the second Anglo-Boer War in 1899, the Boers invaded Natal. Many of the battles were fought further down the road in the neighbourhood of Ladysmith; and this town itself was the site of a siege of the British by the Boers from November 1899 to February 1900. It was a famous siege and a famous name that people still remember.

It is strange what a fascination these old battlegrounds still exert: people visit them in numbers, re-fighting the battles, re-planning the manoeuvres, and even for many non-historians they have a melancholy interest and sometimes glory.

Newcastle today means thriving industries, steel and electricity, but it was the Boer stronghold in the Anglo-Boer War; and the district of Dundee to the south-east—now the centre of the Natal coalfields—was a battleground of all races. It is through the town of Dundee that people turn from the national road to reach three of the greatest battlegrounds of all, Blood River, Isandhlwana and Rorke's Drift.

Nineteen kilometres from Dundee on the Vryheid road is a turn-off to the east to the site of **Blood River,** the greatest battle in Afrikaner history, and one of the bloodiest in Africa's story. It was here on 16th December 1838, that a Voortrekker commando under Andries Pretorius defeated Dingaan's Zulu army on the banks of the river, known ever afterwards as Blood River because the bodies choked it and the water ran red.

Pretorius had drawn up his commando in the angle made between a deep donga and the marshy river: the laager was in the traditional form of wagons tied to one another with the spaces filled in with 'fighting-gates', and here Pretorius's 470 men faced 10 000 Zulus. It was a story of incredible courage on both sides, the Zulus attacking in waves, to be mown down by gun and cannon fire, until at the end of the battle 3 000 Zulus lay dead. In Pietermaritzburg still further down the national road is the Church of the Vow, which the Voortrekkers had built after their victory and according to their vow, and on the battlefield itself is a monument in the form of a laager of wagons. It is a peaceful landscape, still seamed with the great gullies that the Voortrekkers had used to guard a flank, and which the Zulus later used to full advantage as cover against the British.

A little to the east near **Nqutu** among the hills is the spot where Louis Napoleon, the Prince Imperial of France and only child of Napoleon II, was killed in a surprise Zulu attack in 1879. The marble cross was erected by Queen Victoria, and it marks the spot where a dynasty ended.

Blood River joins the Buffalo a little south of the battlefield, and it was below the confluence that the battle of **Isandhlwana** was fought. iSandhlwana is the name of the hill where a Zulu army defeated Queen and Empire, a catastrophe that for a while shattered British prestige in South Africa. In the summer of 1879 the British forces under the commander-in-chief, Lord Chelmsford, camped on this bare hill and here—while he was away on reconnaissance—the Zulu army, making use of the country seamed with dongas, crept up and surprised the camp, annihilating the defenders.

It is a lonely place today, peopled, if one is fanciful, by white stones and by ghosts. At the small field museum is a relief model of the mountain and the battlefield, with Mr Elford Zulu, the African keeper, to explain the dispositions.

To the north-west some 16 kilometres away is the old ford across the Buffalo River known as **Rorke's Drift** because of the store belonging to James Rorke that once stood here, where at the time of Isandhlwana a small British garrison was stationed. The store had been taken over by a Swedish Mission; and it was the mission buildings that were the scene of the action that followed Isandhlwana when 4 000 Zulus attacked and were beaten off by some 100 men under Lieutenant John Chard. The British had thrown up a hasty barricade of stones, bags of mealies, biscuit tins and cases of tinned meat, and here they fought through the night by the light of the burning thatch, retreating from room to room, their rifles too hot to hold, often fighting man to man, Briton against Zulu, bayonet against spear.

Every one of the defenders was wounded, and 11 gained Victoria

Crosses, more than in any other battle ever fought: later it was claimed that every man deserved one.

Today the name, Rorke's Drift, does not signify battle: for here the **KwaZulu Art and Craft Centre** of the Evangelical Lutheran Church has grown up to become world famous. It was begun only in 1962 with the object of developing the creative talents of the Africans in a purely African idiom, and its rise has been fast and spectacular. From here has come a stream of spirited tapestries, printed fabrics, ceramics, graphic art and sculpture that has made it the most famous African art centre in South Africa—where African art of all kinds is burgeoning.

The tapestries, in particular—a Rorke's Drift speciality—have travelled widely. They mostly tell a story, a Biblical one, of folklore and legend, or scenes from everyday life, translated into decorative and beautifully finished hangings of rich colours, all with a simplicity, verve and freedom—pigs alongside priests, huts and giraffes and shields together with geometric designs and mythical figures that enchant people everywhere.

It was the Queen of England who gave the centre its first world publicity just over a decade ago, when she admired a huge Rorke's Drift tapestry at the Royal Society in London. Today a good many African artists owe their training to the centre; and at Rorke's Drift itself there is an exhibition hall where visitors can view and buy.

All interested in Zulu culture find this Isandhlwana-Rorke's Drift complex fascinating. At the tiny Isandhlwana museum, for instance, they can see the Zulu warriors' shields—the great fighting shields of oxhide, judged the most precious of all materials, that to the Zulu people were flag and protector, and to the warriors the badge of honour and of courage without which they dared not return from battle. At the Art Centre they can see the shields again, woven into a tapestry depicting some ancient tale of glory.

Incidentally, whenever they look at the KwaZulu coat-of-arms they see a shield as well, which is its basis, the white shield of the royal regiment, which symbolizes the protection of the people—so, also, do the spears of Shaka held by the leopard and the lion, royal creatures, which support the shield: it was Shaka who designed this short stabbing spear that proved so terrible an instrument of victory and death.

It is only a step, figuratively speaking, to Nongoma across the country to the north-east where in December 1971 the young Zulu prince, Zwelithini Goodwill ka Cyprian Bhekuzulu, was installed with Zulu pomp and ceremony as paramount chief.

Nongoma was then the seat of the KwaZulu Legislative Assembly, but this has now been moved to Ulundi, further south, the KwaZulu capital, and if one is seeking the Zulu story, it is worth driving into this countryside and down the road to Melmoth. Travellers can reach Durban eventually by this roundabout, meandering, fascinating route of the east, or make it a purely Zulu trip, striking from the national road east and south, and looping back through Vryheid and Piet Retief to Johannesburg and Pretoria. Whichever way they take, the road from Ulundi south to Melmoth, branching on its way towards the village of Babanango, is the route to see, not so much for its scenery as its associations—if a modern motor-car rides the gravel road uneasily, it is nevertheless a royal road, heavy and rich with history.

To begin with, at **Ulundi** there is the KwaZulu mace. When the Assembly is in session, this stands in an honoured position in the Assembly Hall, every part of it a symbol of Zulu history and the life of the countryside today. It is made of the inner heart of the red bush willow: on top is a beehive hut, representing the honoured family unit, the basis of Zulu life. It stands upon the coil that according to Zulu tradition is made of grass—plucked from the doorways of all the huts of all the Zulu chiefs—representing national unity. Below it are a beer pot bearing a bull's head, and a grain basket, the basket adorned with shields, with a knopkierie and lions' heads; below this again the headring worn by Zulu indunas and the ostrich feathers worn by warriors of old, based in their turn by a square bearing Shaka's stabbing spears, and the spear that is described as 'the historical everlasting spear of the Zulus that is kept by the Paramount Chief'.

As in the other homelands, mace and crest are the work of a South African expert in heraldry, Mr W. J. Wijenberg, and his team, in consultation with the African homeland leaders. It is interesting to travel the roads and see these symbols as they are in everyday life, if not the lions and ostrich feathers, then the beehive huts on the hills, the pots and baskets, the grass and the cattle.

Some 30 kilometres south of Nongoma near Mahlabatini on the eastern side of the White Umfolozi River is the place where a former chief and king, Dingaan's easy-going peace-loving brother, Mpande, had his kraal, and close to it in a great basin was that of his son, Cetshwayo, who—with a little of Shaka's genius—was not peaceful at all: it was his army that defeated the British at Isandhlwana. In this place, at the battle of Ulundi, he in his turn was defeated by the British, and near here he build a second kraal, the site of which is a national monument to day. The hut floors and the hearths can still be seen, including Cetshwayo's own floor, nine metres wide.

Cetshwayo after his defeat was sent as prisoner to Cape Town and from here sailed to Britain where—most improbably to us today—he was granted an audience with Queen Victoria, and, more improbably still, the Queen presented him with a silver mug with the inscription 'Presented to Cetywayo by Queen Victoria'. He returned to Zululand in 1883 and died the year after, at which time his mug disappeared. Fifty-four years later a Zulu crossing a stream near Ulundi saw a handle sticking out of the bank and hauled it out. It was the the royal mug.

On the turn-off to Babanango lies the **Emakhosini Valley,** the Valley of the Kings. This wide grassy place, with its frieze of thorn trees and euphorbias, its hills and kraals, is sacred to the Zulus, for it is traditionally the birthplace of the people, where not only the first chief, Zulu, had his kraal some 300 years ago and where he was buried, but the place where most of the later royal kraals stood, and where graves of the early rulers lie. Shaka's father was buried here; here in 1787 Shaka was born, and here was the kraal Dingaan built for himself after he had murdered Shaka.

If Dingaan was afraid to use Shaka's site, he nevertheless used his design. His kraal was on top of a hill overlooking the valley, a city built as a huge oval with cattle kraals, 1 500 huts in two great horns meeting at the main gate, with the royal quarters at the head, with Dingaan's big hut, those of his women folk, and a great mound of earth—still to be seen—on which Dingaan used to stand to survey his kraal. He called it Mgungundhlovu, meaning either 'the place of the large elephant' (in praise of himself), or 'the secret meeting of the elephant' (in reference to his successful assassination plot): today it is more often known as Dingaanstat or Dingaan's Town.

It was here that the tragedy took place that led to Blood River—the murder of the Voortrekker Piet Retief and his men, who had journeyed to this kraal to seek from Dingaan a grant of land. They were killed, as everyone remembers, at the great farewell entertainment organized for them by Dingaan, and it was only after Blood River nearly a year later that Pretorius, having avenged them in that battle, found their remains and buried them in a common grave. He found the treaty as well in a leather bag near the bodies. He did not burn the kraal. Dingaan had had this done himself as he fled from it: king, assassin and fugitive, he had sat far off watching the flames. Soon he was to be dead, killed by the Swazis. Now the site of the kraal and Retief's grave some 1 000 metres from it are national monuments, as are the graves of the Zulu kings who lived here before.

Zulu, or Nkosinkulu, was buried in a spot near where Dingaan had the entrance to his kraal, and Senzangakona, the father of Shaka and

Dingaan, at the side of the road a little further towards Babanango. Pass it and its bronze plaque with respect. On this spot once stood the kraal where the first Royal Ring was made, the thick ring made of special plants and covered with a python skin, the 'most sacred object of the royal regalia'. The ground is held in respect even today.

One must know something of history to find one's way in and out of the kings and chiefs, the intrigues and battles and sacred places, yet southward on the road, over the hills and valleys and forested kloofs, at **Nkwaleni** about 20 kilometres from Eshowe, is a show Zulu kraal which is easy to appreciate. It is still possible to see the grass beehive huts on the hills, built of the plants of the countryside, without wire, string or nails, but they become rarer by the year, so this one is here to show a Zulu way of living and a Zulu art—it is a replica of such a hut that tops the mace.

Eshowe, the traditional capital of Zululand, is built on a hilltop, still with the forest near it that gave it its onomatopoeic name based on the sound of the wind in the trees. It was 27 kilometres from here that Shaka, after he had come to power, built his great kraal, the site of which is now marked by a monument beside the road. He called it by the name, Bulawayo, the meaning of which is controversial: it was a name borrowed by his renegade lieutenant, Mzilikazi, who—after he had ravaged the southern Transvaal—went north into Rhodesia and built there his kraal which he in turn named Bulawayo. Here the city of Bulawayo later arose.

The Eshowe road meets the main coastal road at Gingindlovu—the 'Gin Gin I Love You' of the British soldiers—and the next stop is **Stanger,** largely an Indian business centre, and not a town we care to linger in except to see the monument to Shaka in Couper Street. Here Shaka built his last kraal called Dukuza and here he was murdered, not by Dingaan alone but by his second half-brother and his trusted bodyguard as well. And it was here as he was stabbed that he faced Dingaan; 'Do you think you will rule the land? No, you will not—for the swallows have come.' The swallows—the White men—had indeed arrived; and how right it was that a dying Zulu king should make his last prophecy in words of poetry and symbolism.

Time fashions many journeys, and so it is here, and it is usually by the national, more direct road that people come to Durban. At **Ladysmith,** now third largest town in Natal, we personally pause a moment, not to think of sieges and cemeteries but of that most romantic of campaigners, Juana, wife of Sir Harry Smith, after whom the town was named, and whom we meet again every time we travel south.

To the west of the road running from Ladysmith southwards, and roughly parallel to it for a distance, lie the **Drakensberg,** with roads branching to it at intervals from the national road.

This is the range of mountains a thousand kilometres long that stretches from the north-eastern Cape to the north-eastern Transvaal, dividing Natal from the Orange Free State and Lesotho and providing the great escarpment over which drops the Tugela River, in its infancy here high up towards the heavens, no more than a thread of white.

It was also the last stronghold in South Africa of the Bushman people.

It is a range of breath-taking beauty—peaks, domes, precipices, crags, needles—that reminded the Voortrekkers of a dragon, perhaps because of its outline like a dragon's back, or because of the legend of a dragon inhabiting its heights. Whichever it was, they called it the Mountains of the Dragon: to the Zulus it was Quathlamba, the Barrier of Spears, and it would be hard to find wilder, fiercer or better names.

Most of the famous peaks and buttresses are along the border with Lesotho, where the range has an average height of 3 000 metres for a long way. There is Mont-aux-Sources in the north, Cathedral Peak further south, followed by Cathkin Peak, Champagne Castle and Giant's Castle, and still further to the south Sani Pass, through which a rough road leads to Lesotho.

This is the great inland holiday region of South Africa, with an all-the-year-round season, with national parks and nature reserves, and dozens of hotels, resorts, guest farms and camps where flock thousands of people in search of out-of-doors holidays. They climb—this is one of the most famous of mountaineering areas—walk, ride, swim, bird-watch, paint, and enjoy the wild flowers, all in comparatively cool summer weather, or sunny, crisp winter days with the peaks about snow-capped. Most of the streams are stocked with brown or rainbow trout, with the best angling in the south towards Himeville and Underberg.

West of Ladysmith at the little town of Bergville, the road to the mountains forks, one branch going to the Royal Natal National Park and the other south-west to Cathedral Peak. In late autumn, a superlative time to visit the Drakensberg, the traveller passes through a golden world with the far mountains gradually becoming nearer and clearer, until at last there ahead is the Amphitheatre, the shallow half-moon of mountain wall, flanked by the Sentinel and the Eastern Buttress, blue and purple, immense and startling beyond expectation, and the greatest and most famous view of all the mountains of South Africa, save Table Mountain.

This is the **Royal Natal National Park** with the Rugged Glen Nature Reserve beside it—which take in the Amphitheatre and the peak of Mont-aux-Sources high above and the few kilometres from the escarpment edge—a stretch of country with precipices and spectacular rock shapes, grassy protea-studded slopes, bridle paths, and sparkling streams with wooded banks. It is possible to climb that sheer frontal face of the Amphitheatre wall to the summit: it has been done but this is a rope climb for the few—the expert few. Most go up the bridle path on foot or horseback, scaling the rock face by the Chain Ladder, reaching the great plateau upon the top, Pofung, the Place of the Eland.

We ourselves had come to it years before on horseback from Lesotho, picking our way over the high, bare, mountains with the snow only hours behind us as we rode, until we reached the plateau and Mont-aux-Sources. That plateau was one of the highest and certainly the loneliest place we had ever known, without another living soul save us, with the air biting and the wind keening. We looked out from it across Natal, the Tugela a thread to one side plunging down the precipice and far below winding its way through the vast plains. Nobody can stand there, so close to the clouds, gazing at this world's view, without a sense of wonder, and adventure too, so that this is a climb for all who can manage it, to be remembered for always.

Two French missionaries, Arbausset and Daumas, who had come from the Lesotho side, were probably the first white people to stand here. On an April day in 1836 they looked over the escarpment into Natal, and on this day gave the peak its name, Mont-aux-Sources, Mountain of the Sources, because they found it was the source of four rivers—and this is why one of the most famous names in the Drakensberg is a French one. The missionaries thought the Orange River, the greatest river in South Africa, rose here. They were wrong, for it rises a little to the south, but this is nevertheless the birthplace of the Tugela and three other rivers which flow different ways—it is the continental divide.

Down in the foothills, still in the Park, is a contrast as great as possible, a luxury hotel. We remember that we had the room where, a notice told us, Queen Elizabeth of England had slept 25 years before.

Many people have wonderful times in this park, and we have fragmentary memories of special things, small astonishing beauties, mostly of water—pools with pebbles showing clear and overhung with wild trees, and dashing streams with boulders and islands in them and flowers like white shells.

Visitors find the geography of this section of the Drakensberg confusing. In 1973 a mountaineer and retired headmaster, R. O. Pearse, wrote a book on the Drakensberg called *A Barrier of Spears*, with maps and pictures that make this clear, and personally we would never go to these mountains again without it. Apart from being factual, it is also a superb adventure story endowing these giant peaks and rock masses with human story and endeavour.

Looking at the Amphitheatre from below, there is the ,Sentinel, which the Zulus call the Black One, to one side, a noble peak and in 1910 the first major one to be climbed. Pearse talks of that day of 5th October 1910, when it was scaled as one to remember, the beginning of the long story of man's conquest of the Drakensberg. 'On this day man first set his face to the high peaks.' There is Beacon Buttress with the beacon on its summit from where in fine weather Natal, the Transvaal, the Free State and Lesotho can be seen, the great rocky blocks of the Inner Tower; Devil's Tooth, the thin, terrible spear of rock with almost perpendicular sides which was finally climbed in 1950, and the Eastern Buttress, every one with its own drama.

Cathedral Peak, the landmark to the south-east, stands in a country of magnificent mountain views which draws its own share of mountaineers and holiday-makers—for every mountaineer there are probably at least 200 people who hike and climb in an unexacting way. South of this and not far away lies the Ndedema Gorge through which runs the Ndedema river, 'the reverberating one', until recently a valley beautiful but almost unknown. A few years ago it suddenly sprang to fame through the work of Harald Pager who came here with his wife, Shirley, to copy the Bushman paintings in the valley, and in the time he did so, lived in the Bushman caves and in the manner that the Bushmen once had.

The lower slopes of the Drakensberg are made up of a layer of Cave Sandstone which is famous for its weathered caves and shelters, and in these the Bushman artists left some of the finest rock paintings in South Africa. In **Ndedema Gorge,** where some of the last of the Bushmen had lived, Pager found a treasure house of Bushman art on the walls of the sandstone shelters. His work, the reproductions of animals, hunters, dancers, fighters, and strange mythological creatures he had found in the Gorge, is well-known now, and we—in company with a great many other people—had found it at the Bushman Exhibition in Johannesburg.

At the time of our last visit the north-south interleading gravel roads along the foothills of the mountains were in poor condition, and we found it easier to return to the main road, travel down it, and at Estcourt branch again to the mountains.

Estcourt to many means industries—sausages, bacon and chocolate in particular—but to historians it is important as one point of a rough triangle made with Chieveley up the road, and Weenen to the north-east, which was the scene of the massacre of the Voortrekkers by Dingaan's impis immediately after the murder of Piet Retief. Weenen means weeping, and this was a place of horror: the mass grave of the slaughtered is marked today by the Bloukrans Monument, reached by a farm road opposite Chieveley railway station.

We were glad to turn away to the mountains, this time to **Cathkin Peak,** the huge solid block of mountain, as Pearse describes it, on which generations of mountaineers have struggled and where one at least died. It was named after the Cathkin farm close by. As for Champagne Castle south-west of it, there are several stories as to how this dome got its somewhat frivolous name, one being that the bottle of champagne, which was being lugged to the top for celebration, was broken on the climb, thus christening the mountain itself.

Although 3 373 metres high, it is a comparatively easy climb: not so Cathkin, or Monk's Cowl between the two, Cathkin classified as an E class climb and Monk's Cowl F. Pearse talks of how this cruel difficult peak, 'sharp and pointed, like an up-thrust fang', has touched people's imagination; and how few mountaineers can resist its challenge.

There are the attractions besides climbing like the hotels, some of which are very good indeed, and the farm Dragon Peaks, which is the home of the Drakensberg Boys' Choir School, internationally famous now, which gives weekly performances, and **Giant's Castle Game Reserve,** which was proclaimed in 1903 mainly to preserve the eland and now is one of the Natal Parks Board's most popular reserves. The peak, 3 316 metres and one of the highest in the mountains, was climbed early on in the 1860s; it is still a popular climb, and there are other well-known routes in the nearby mountains.

We remember the camp for its charm, its thatched huts with the green slopes rising up on either side, the cheerful African who cooked our food, and for Mr K. B. Tinley, lean kindly giant, who was camp superintendent—the Tinley family have made their name in wild life and ecology from Natal westward to South West Africa. Then there was Bill Trauseld showing us slides of the wild flowers on which his book, *Wild Flowers of the Drakensberg*, was based, and Bill Barnes, the warden, who could tell us tales of the very dust and stones.

It was he who dreamed up one of the great attractions of the reserve, the **Bushman Cave Museum,** a big cave close to the camp with old paintings on the walls and models of Bushmen grouped within, incredibly realistic and well done. Besides, there are other sights, a variety of wild animals including the eland, birds of some 150 species, among them the lammergeyer, brown trout in the streams, and all the flower life that Bill Trauseld had captured in his slides.

In 1973, part of Giant's Castle Reserve became the heart of South Africa's first proclaimed wilderness area, an area of well over 100 000 hectares of mountain land. What this means is that a great section of the Drakensberg north and south of Giant's Castle will remain inviolate, safe from the marks of men and progress, without railway or road, building or telephone, where visitors will come by foot or on horseback, *by permit only* (from the Regional Director of Forestry, Private Bag 9029, Pietermaritzburg).

Officially, the wilderness areas have to be wild and uninhabited, and big enough to give people the feeling that they are cut off entirely from the outside world. The officials of the Department of Forestry, including the Secretary, 'Manie' Malherbe, who thought the scheme out, are men who once as forest officers worked in the lonely places and slept under the stars, so that they knew what they wanted and the value of it. For a lot of people the wilderness scheme they evolved is one of the most exciting concepts of modern times, making tolerable those motor-cars chasing bumper to bumper down the national roads.

From Mooi River—beautiful river—further down the main road another branch road as well leads to Giant's Castle, and to the **Kamberg Nature Reserve** south of it, famous for trout and cattle. For the romantic-historian the cattle are not to be missed, white animals with dark noses and spreading horns, that are the Zulu Royal Cattle. Once the pride of Shaka and other kings, they lived by the thousand in the hills of Zululand: 'the birds that have no rest', the Zulus called them because they were so many that they gave no rest to the birds that accompanied them picking at their ticks—from their hides and from no others the white shields of the royal regiments were made.

Lung sickness decimated them and their glory faded; then in 1952 the Natal Parks Board bought animals in northern Zululand, and from these a 'royal' herd has been bred.

From both Mooi River and from Nottingham Road south of it, roads branch to Himeville and Underberg, scenic roads through farming country with mountains on two sides, and the rivers and streams to which in September come trout fishermen from far and wide. Northwest of them on the Lesotho border is the **Sani Pass,** a name still synonymous with adventure. There is a luxury hotel there now, and beyond it a road up the face of the Drakensberg into Lesotho, a track of hairpin bends going upwards, it seems to travellers, to the sky—it climbs 1 500 metres in about eight kilometres. The trip, almost excruciatingly thrilling, can be arranged at the hotel below.

It is hard to leave all this beauty and adventure to return to the national road, and yet beyond Mooi River, in particular, N3 and the roads near it have their own interests. On the loop from Mooi River running almost parallel to N3 are the villages of Rosetta and Nottingham Road—named after the Nottinghamshire Regiment which was stationed here in the 1850s—then Rawdon's Hotel known to many travellers, Balgowan with the famous school, Michaelhouse, and so to the junction with N3.

We think of another traveller here, the *umfundisi*, the black priest, of *Cry, the Beloved Country*, Alan Paton's classic, who journeyed to Johannesburg to find his erring sister and son, and took the great train at Pietermaritzburg, climbing up through Lion's River and Balgowan to Mooi River, 'through hills lovely beyond any singing of it'. The hills are lovely still, and so are the rivers and streams, tumbling down rock and precipice to make the famous waterfalls of the area. Twenty-three kilometres from Pietermaritzburg and close to the national road is the best known of all, the Howick Falls, not high as waterfalls go, but a sight as the river plunges down the warm-coloured cliffs into the valley below.

There is the Midmar Dam on the Umgeni River on the right, Cedara Agricultural College, and the turn-off to World's View, the natural platform on the peak, Swartkop, overlooking Pietermaritzburg, where the old wagon road from Durban to the Drakensberg once passed.

Then there is **Pietermaritzburg** itself, the most charming of provincial capitals, lying in a basin with green slopes around it and a river in its heart.

It is an historic little city, named after two great Voortrekker leaders, Piet Retief and Gerrit Maritz: it was planned as the capital of the Voortrekker Republic of Natal but its life as this was brief for by 1843 there were British troops in charge, the British Fort Napier built overlooking it, and thereafter it was the seat of British administration.

It is English as English today, even to its Victorian buildings of bright red brick—it has more of them than has any other town in South Africa, and they give it atmosphere—and such is the swing in fashion that after a period in the doldrums, they are again much valued and admired.

The Voortrekkers laid the town out in a grid pattern with, as in Pretoria and other towns, their favourite Market Square in the centre and Church Street leading to it. Half an hour's walk about the centre tells a good deal of the story of the city (and of Natal). On the square the Vootrekkers built their gabled, thatched raadsaal or council chamber: it was here that after the British had annexed Natal the Supreme Court sessions were held, and where in time the present red brick City Hall arose—the municipal offices built later were also, in keeping, in red brick.

Facing the square, the Voortrekkers built the city's most famous building, the **Church of the Vow**—this, it may be remembered, the Voortrekker commando had vowed before Blood River to build should success be theirs. It was a simple little place with thick walls and a flat wooden roof that leaked, which was later put to more prosaic uses—it was among other things a wagon shop, a school, a smithy, a wool shed, and finally a museum, and the Voortrekker Museum it is today, now with a pitched roof and a porch, and a fine collection of Voortrekker relics. The original pulpit is one of the exhibits, and is a national monument. To Afrikaners, it is still a place both of solemnity and sentiment. Next to it is now a modern Memorial Church.

There is **St Peter's Church,** as well, at the corner of Church and Chapel Streets close by, once Bishop Colenso's Cathedral and consecrated in 1857. How many today, we wonder, remember Bishop John Colenso, the first Bishop of Natal? Yet in his day his name was famous—or perhaps notorious—for his unorthodox thinking tore Natal, metaphorically speaking, in two: he was charged with heresy, excommunicated, and later confirmed in his office by the British Privy Council. His tomb lies in front of the altar.

Then there is the Legislative Council Building in Longmarket Street which is now the **Provincial Council Chamber.** When Natal received responsible government in 1893, parliament sat here, and its splendid copper dome reflects its former status. It is cheek by jowl now with Shepstone House, completely modern, but with a name old in Natal history for Theophilus Shepstone, native administrator, was an illustrious name in the early days. In the same street between Fleming and Pine Streets is **Old Government House,** the amusing old building which is prized as one of the few surviving examples of early Natal architecture. It is now part of the Natal Training College. Behind the station is **Fort Napier,** the old military headquarters in Natal, and the little St George's Garrison Church.

The street names tell their own story as they do in other cities. Besides the Voortrekkers' Market Square, Church Street and others such, there are those like Prince Alfred and Bulwer Streets, Winston, Sherwood, Kitchener and Roberts, and of course Victoria and Alexandra Roads—it is a true South African hotch potch of history and story.

In Loop Street is an old home filled with beautiful Victoriana now known as the **Macrorie House Museum.** Perhaps it should be visited immediately after Bishop Colenso's Cathedral for it takes the Colenso story further. This is the house which was once the home of William Macrorie, 'opposing bishop' perhaps he might be called, who was bishop of the Church of the Province and Bishop of 'Maritzburg', at the same time that Colenso was Bishop of 'Natal'. Two rival bishops and two rival congregations in that small community were lethal: that wealthy Macrorie drove a carriage and poverty-stricken Colenso rode a mule did not help!

Feuds die, and there is left today only the buildings that saw them, and the story of the extraordinary schism that lasted generations. The **Natal Museum**—a national museum—is in Pietermaritzburg, and the University of Natàl has one of its two branches in the city. It is easy to feel that this is a university and museum town. Not so apparent is the industrial side, which is there, however, in good health—one region, Allandale, is given over to Indian industries entirely. All in all, what most visitors remember, apart from the red brick and the Victorian air of the centre of the town, are the gardens, the masses of green, the brilliance of the bougainvilleas, and above all the azaleas, in bloom from August to October, for this is the azalea city, where streets and public and private gardens burst with these fragile, butterfly flowers, so massed they often do not look fragile at all but solid walls and mounds of colour.

This is a good time to see the city: the **Botanic Gardens** have their azalea collection—they are worth a visit at any time to see their magnificent trees—and so has Wyllie Park. There is Alexandra Park, and Queen Elizabeth Park eight kilometres from the centre of the city where are the headquarters of the Natal Parks Board.

Personally we remember the city in spring as a flower dream, and especially the garden of Dr and Mrs Conrad Akerman, that marvellous place known to so many, with azaleas under trees, in borders and in pots, and a great pergola dripping pink Gladys Hepburn bougainvillea.

So that it was all the odder to us to find that the emblem of the city was an elephant, as far removed from flowers as could be. There it is today, in the heart of the city's coat-of-arms, reminding the world that this was once the Zulu's Place of the Elephant. A good coat-of-arms can touch off many things, and this one does. Above the elephant are five stars, four of them representing the great symbol of the southern world, the Southern Cross, and the central one the Star of Bethlehem, the Christmas Star; for it was on Christmas Day in 1497 that Vasco da Gama, sailing up the shores of Natal, saw this land and named it.

Thinking of these things, we set our faces on a spring day towards the coast.

On our left the road to Greytown branched north-eastwards through sugar cane and tree plantations, and on to Muden with its citrus orchards and unique citrus wine, and there was Kranskop to the east of it with long blue views of the Tugela Valley, with the silver river winding through it.

On our right the road to Richmond and Ixopo stretched away. We knew it as a road of great beauty, running through lush green farming country and green hills with Leonotis—lion's tail—flowering in orange patches. It was from Ixopo that Alan Paton's *umfundisi* had started out on his journey to Johannesburg, and when *Cry, the Beloved Country* was published in 1948, Paton made Ixopo's grass-covered rolling hills the best-known in South Africa. The name Ixopo is Zulu and onomatopoeic, describing the sound of cattle hooves sucking and squelching in mud, so that the name of the hills has a wild country sound which touched the imagination of many, who knew them then for the first time.

But now we were bent on other hills, those between Pietermaritzburg and Durban, which are not seen from the main road N3 but from the loop road beside it, branching from it at Cato Ridge—the **Valley of a Thousand Hills.** It is a fine name for this great valley of the Umgeni River with its hills upon hills, its small valleys and clefts, its mists, and on clear days its tremendous views. Just past the junction of the two roads, the loop road is joined by that coming from the Nagle Dam. This is the big dam on the Umgeni River that provides much of Durban's water, and it stands at the foot of a big flat-topped mountain known as Table Mountain, and to the Zulus as emKhambathini, the place of the flat-topped thorn trees. At the bottom of the valley are a picnic site and tearoom and much-photographed grass huts—this is the home of the Debe tribe.

Further on, overlooking the valley, is the Valley View Restaurant and Curio Shop; and beyond is the pheZulu Tourist Boutique at Botha's Hill. After the eastern junction of this loop road with N3, there is Kloof to the left with its gorgeous homes and gardens, and Pinetown, which was not named after trees at all but after a one-time governor, Sir Benjamin Pine. From the one original inn here, it has grown into a busy town, higher, cooler and less humid than Durban only 24 kilometres away, where it is sometimes possible for travellers to find a bed when Durban itself is overflowing.

It is a road a good deal more sophisticated than that to the north, one that to upcountry eyes has a crowded, lush, prodigal appearance with Durban at its end, itself unlike any other city. No other province has the contrasts of Natal, not even the Transvaal with its

Highveld and Lowveld; certainly none other has lonely snowy mountains where the lammergeyer flies and less than 180 kilometres distant, Durban, third largest city, with a golden mile of luxury hotels and the biggest harbour in Africa, with brilliant sun and sea, heat and a tropical opulence that visitors adore. It is the premier holiday city of South Africa, and a good many of those bumper-to-bumper motor-cars on N3 stop here for all the holiday weeks.

The Otter Trail—the path along the shore

The ultimate land point of Africa, Cape Agulhas, where a spar from a wreck washes among the needle-like rocks

The Drostdy, Swellendam

CHAPTER ELEVEN

Durban

❧

In 1976 more than half a million people visited Durban and they spent more than 250 million rand. They came by road, by rail—spilling out of the big station right into the city heart—and by air, a great many from Johannesburg less than an hour's flight away. Durban, like a great warm sponge, mopped them up gently, swelling as it did so. By 1980, it is said, the city will have more tourists than residents—at the moment close to 800 000—and what, visitors ask themselves, happens to Durban then? As it is, everything in season overflows and people have been known to sleep gratefully in baths!

Of course a good part of Durban loves all this, and so do the visitors. They are a definite breed, these people who choose the city for their holidays: they enjoy other people—rubbing skin to skin so to say—crowds, noise, laughter, all the special sort of liveliness that crowds engender, night clubs and dancing, trips in crowded boats, soda fountains and bodies on the beach. In 1975 when the Council for the Habitat conference was held in Durban, delegates felt that the city, from its very nature, played a special role. What do people most want? They want other people. Not 'nature', not the wild places, but other people. And in Durban they get them. So that the city is what one termed a lightning conductor, drawing to it those who want recreation and human masses, thus saving most of the rest of the Natal coast from ecological destruction.

Poor proud holiday Durban—a lightning conductor!

Yet in a way this is what it is, a very favoured one, hot and clean and welcoming, spilling over with colour, hibiscus and oleander, with palm trees, first-class hotels and boarding houses. Sooner or later, and usually it is the first thing of all, visitors stand on the Marine Parade on the Golden Mile of hotels and restaurants, holiday flats, lidos and pools and amusement parks, overlooking the blue of the Indian Ocean and the gold of its beaches.

As they stand with their backs to West Street, the best-known city thoroughfare, a block away on their left is the five-star Hotel Edward with its fine food, including its famous oriental cuisine in the Manda-

DURBAN

rin Room: and there are hotels and nightclubs left and right, like the Cascades at the Blue Waters Hotel, for those who want Moorish arches and sophistication. In front, on the ocean side, are the paddling pools, the amusement parks, the tent theatre and trampoline, the beaches, the sun-worshippers, the deck chairs and umbrellas, the popcorn and icecream, and the sea and the breakers, of stunning beauty and brightness. It is an Indian Ocean scene of intense light and colour, heavily speckled with human forms, that makes most visitors hum: the wilderness-lovers either do not view it or go away quietly and fast.

Personally we have memories of the amusement park, as crammed with every childish delight and pleasure, from great turning wheels and merry-go-rounds to coconut shies, as a fair, old, old in tradition but here brought up to date. Holiday crowds are usually good-tempered, and at night the air of fun and gaiety catches the old as well as the young.

Two things between the Marine Parade and the beach are amusements of a first-class order. The first, at the foot of West Street, is the **Aquarium and Dolphinarium** run by the Oceanographic Research Institute. It is a place of clear water, strange shapes and sea colours, round sea eyes, sharks, fingerlings, and shells, all representing the rich sea life of the eastern coast. Close on seven million people have streamed into the Aquarium to see these things, and in doing so have financed the South African Association for Marine Biological Research.

The **FitzSimons Snake Park** lies further to the left on the Lower Marine Parade, and is one of the fascinating shows of Africa. Everybody, if in complete safety, loves to see a snake, particularly a poisonous one; and here they can see them, mamba and cobra, Gaboon viper and puffadder, 60 species of them, poisonous and non-poisonous, with—glory be—an attendant nonchalantly mowing the grass between them! Those long sinuous serpents of death are not only deadly but beautiful, with a frightful fluidity and grace—it is an unbeatable combination, as one look at the visitors' faces shows. This is not only, however, a place of show and amusement; it is a producer of snakebite serum used in the treatment of snakebite, so that it is one of the life-savers of Africa.

Well over to the right, again facing the sea, is the famous **Addington Hospital** with a big stretch of sand opposite it, known as Addington Beach, and just beyond it on the way to North Pier is **Vetch's Pier,** the headquarters of the Durban Ski-boat Club. Ski-boats are Durban's own invention. They are quite young, post-World War II, and they were the brain child of an angler, Hayden Gray, who was too short to cast as well as he wished, so got round the difficulty by furnishing a paddle ski with an outboard motor and fishing offshore with this. The idea caught on. The modern ski-boat, which is still a fishing boat but smaller than the deep sea craft, is updated and modernized but 'still basically a power-driven hull', and Durban is proud of its 200 or so that operate from Vetch's Pier.

This is the Indian Ocean side of Durban on the coast stretching northward to Zululand, but there is another seashore even more famous. Natal Bay—Durban harbour—is the big scoop of sea south and south-west of the Marine Parade and the Golden Mile, North Pier making one arm almost enclosing the bay, with South Pier opposite it across the narrow entrance channel. On the far side is the wooded neck of land known as the Bluff and on the near side—the northern one—is the city centre stretching north, and east to the Marine Parade.

This is the bay that makes Africa's most important harbour.

Like all harbours, it is filled with fascinations, and although much of it is, for security reasons, not open to the public, there are still fine sea sights.

There is the **Ocean Terminal Building** taking up the whole of T Jetty, which sticks prominently out into the bay, where ocean travellers are received and from where they leave: from a glass-walled tearoom, perhaps Durban's most exciting, visitors can watch the shipping world.

The Point Docks lie one side and on the other is the Maydon Wharf stretching half around the bay; the Fishing Jetty where the deep sea fishing boats are berthed, the jetty from where the pleasure cruises start, beyond it the Small Craft Harbour (with yachting clubs near by) and still further on the Prince Edward graving dock and the floating dock, which some visitors find especially interesting. Over the other side of the bay are the Bluff and Salisbury Island, where people used to have the fun of seeing whalers moored—there was a whaling station in the harbour for 60 years which only stopped operations in the 1970s. Salisbury Island has now been taken over by the Navy, and there has been talk of preserving one whale catcher, to be moored in the harbour, as a floating museum.

It is a highly organized, sophisticated ocean drama, complete with kilometres of wharves and all the necessities of modern trade and industry, like handling appliances and cooling sheds, huge silos and terminals, that have put the harbour way out in front of any other on the continent. Durban harbour handles more cargo every year, incidentally, than all the other South African ports put together.

Silos and cooling chambers are not romantic, but every ship and every tiny boat has its own glamour—the **Small Boat Harbour** is pure adventure—so that with them, with flags fluttering, salt and the sea gulls crying, there are plenty of the traditional attractions left.

The best place from which to view it is probably the View Site on the Bluff, for from here are spread out the bay and the docks, the ships at berth, and beyond the harbour the city. Every ship, in essence, is almost as old as time, every skyscraper as new as new, a symbol of modernity, and the two seen together are always a marvellous thing.

This harbour is not only the heart of the modern port, but the place where Durban history began. Can one say it began with the Portuguese, with Vasco da Gama? Da Gama's crew probably, the experts say, fished in the harbour, setting a fashion to last down the years. The bay is still a perennial goal to anglers, the deep sea fishermen, after such things as shark and barracuda, fishing from North and South Pier, and others from all the jetties and wharves strung around the bay's edge.

Like all the water along the Natal coast, that in the bay is warm, thanks to the Agulhas current, and this brings a wonderful fish life, as much enjoyed 300 years ago as now. It is probable that Da Gama's men had the same fun with the skipjacks, the fighting fish, leaping and skipping in the water of the bay, as anglers do today. Durban bay is the place for them; and fishermen would certainly be happy to believe that they and others were the beginning of the story of Natal.

Shipwreck survivors came after Da Gama, and there were sailors that called and like Da Gama, left no definite record. In 1689 a Dutch sea party came to buy the harbour, a deal never implemented, and in 1824, well over 300 years after the Portuguese, the first settlers arrived. They were British, an assembly of young adventurers come to make their fortunes by ivory and other trading.

That the bay at Port Natal—as the little settlement was called—was found at all had been a stroke of luck. The year before, Lieutenant James King and Lieutenant Francis Farewell, ex-British naval officers, took a boat up the east coast to explore the trading possibilities and to find, if possible, a harbour. Near the entrance to the bay, guarded at the time by a high and dangerous sand bar, a storm arose. King took a chance and sailed the boat across it to find the prize beyond, a superb, sheltered, almost land-locked natural harbour.

Both men were tremendously excited. King rushed off to England to tell the Admiralty all about the harbour (nobody believed him); and Farewell set to to organize a band of settlers. By 1824 he had his party, including Henry Francis Fynn whose name was to become a great one in Natal, and more than a score of others. In due course they arrived, cleared a patch in the bush and pitched their tents near where the Post Office stands today. King, a disappointed man, followed later, only to quarrel with his friend, Farewell, to part in anger, and set up his home on the Bluff across the harbour. In 1828 he died here, and a bronze plaque marks his grave.

They were violent days full of quarrel, battle, malaria, dysentery and death. When Farewell and Fynn attended Shaka's court at Bulawayo, Shaka arranged a great spectacle for them of cattle parading, warriors, dancing and song, at which—for their benefit—he had, it is said, the necks of onlookers broken at random here and there. It was odd entertainment to British eyes, and more than some could take, one of the party deciding forthwith that life at the Cape was quieter. Soon no more than six of the original party at Port Natal were left, and of these Farewell was murdered in 1829, one died of fever, and two were killed by the Zulus: one, Henry Ogle, survived to farm near Durban. Fynn later became a famous magistrate.

Farewell and Fynn had received from Shaka a grant of land 160 kilometres by 50 kilometres around Port Natal, and here at the port a rough and tumble settlement continued, on sufferance of Shaka and later Dingaan. Eleven years after the first patch in the bush had been cleared, the traders decided to lay out a proper township which they named after the governor of the Cape, the much loved Sir Benjamin D'Urban.

After the murder of Piet Retief at Dingaan's Kraal and the bloody battles following it, the settlers for a while joined forces with the Voortrekkers. The British, however, who had vacillated for some time as to the importance of Durban, in 1842 decided that British it should be. This was not accomplished without a tussle, and the military force under Captain Thomas Smith, which had been sent as an intimidating gesture, was besieged with gusto by the Trekkers on a spot now known as the Old Fort. It was during this five-weeks' siege that the story of Dick King was told, to become the heroic legend of Natal.

On the **Esplanade** overlooking Durban harbour at the foot of Gardiner Street, is a statue of a man and horse, Dick King and Somerset, his golden bay, South Africa's most famous horse. Dick was a young man—transport-driver, trader and hunter—who had come to South Africa as a child with the 1820 Settlers. In 1842 he was already known to the Voortrekkers, for four years before he had made an heroic march into the midlands of Natal, through Zulu forces, to warn the Voortrekkers of the impending Zulu massacre. Now, as Andries Pretorius and his Trekkers were besieging Smith, Dick escaped from Durban by night, together with his faithful boy servant, Ndongeni, crossing the bay in a rowing boat, with their horses swimming behind them, and thereafter rode hell for leather for the south and for military help.

Ndongeni did not go the whole way, but Dick rode 600 miles of unknown forest, bush and hills to Grahamstown, crossing, it is claimed, 122 rivers in 10 days, and five weeks after the beginning of the siege, the reinforcements that Dick had raised were at Durban. The Trekkers retired to Pietermaritzburg, peace was made, and by the next year Natal was officially British.

It was not only Dick King but Somerset that made history that May and June of 1842, for Dick rode him most of the way.

Where he was raised is not known for sure. What is certain is that he was named after Lord Charles Somerset and first belonged to a British officer, who trained him well, but who after his retirement sold him to a farmer, Jan Hofmeyr, who was about to trek to Natal. Hofmeyr lent him to Andries Pretorius who admired his training: he did not flinch at the noise of battle, and his rider could fire from his back—one of the great virtues of a good Cape horse. Pretorius, it is said, rode him at the Battle of Blood River, and later when he attacked Durban: he was stolen by an African and sold to the British, and this was how he came to be in British hands at the time of the siege.

Legend has it that he died at Grahamstown of exhaustion at the end of the epic ride. Truth is kinder. Whoever he had once belonged to, he was a King horse after the ride; he lived, and came back to Dick King's home at Isipingo where he remained with all honour until his death. This is correct, says King's granddaughter, Mrs Doris Camp of Durban: her father, Dick's eldest son, and his brothers used to ride him there.

Dick King's statue is a reminder that Durban does have an old and storied past: there is extraordinarily little else, besides the **Da Gama Clock** on the harbour front to remind one of it. The clock, also on the Esplanade on the Ocean Terminal side of the Dick King statue, is a fine ornate creation, presented to the city by the Portuguese Government in 1897 to commemorate Da Gama's discovery of Natal 400 years before.

Nor has the city itself, apart from its street names, much harking back to the early days. Gardiner Street, leading from the harbour front to the city, was named after Captain Allen Gardiner, another ex-Royal Navy officer and Durban's first missionary; and Smith Street, an important thoroughfare, was named after the Smith who commanded the little garrison during the Trekkers' siege—it must be one of the few 'Smiths' in South Africa *not* honouring Sir Harry Smith. But

Harry found a place in Durban all the same: Aliwal Street, like every other Aliwal in towns and dorps throughout the country, honours Harry's victory at the Battle of Aliwal in India.

In the city centre, the **Old Fort,** where the British garrison was besieged by the Trekkers, is the nub of history. It faces the Old Fort Road, well behind the Railway Station, and is today a garden, and the Magazine a chapel.

The Durban Publicity Association has recently introduced an historical walking tour of the city centre. The research has been carefully done by Mrs Rita Kinnear, and it is no fault of hers that—in comparison to that in Cape Town, for example—it seems singularly poverty-stricken: perhaps it serves to highlight the fact that Durban is essentially a city of the moment.

The tour takes visitors to the **Town Gardens,** now called Farewell Square, in West Street opposite the Post Office, round about where Farewell's shack was built in 1824: then on to the **Memorial Stone** at the corner of Church and West Streets commemorating the fact that Winston Churchill, on the steps of the Post Office, then the City Hall, made the first speech of his career on 23rd December 1899. After he had escaped from prison in Pretoria and reached Delagoa Bay, he sailed to Durban. In the town he had been a hero, and here he made this historic speech. Thinking of the later ones of World War II, those grand, sonorous, rolling, fighting words that helped to win freedom for the Western world, this scene of his first speech has a special place in memory as well as history. For us, and probably for many more, it is one of Durban's highlights.

The tour goes on to the **Railway Station.** The first railway in South Africa was in Durban, beginning its life on 26th June 1860, and it ran from the centre of the town to the Point. Then it is on to **St Paul's Anglican Church** on the corner of Church and Pine Street, where the marble used in the apse is a gift from London's St Paul's, and further on to the **City Hall** which is—and it rings strangely today—a replica of the Belfast City Hall.

This is a specially important building for it houses the art gallery, a museum and the municipal library, including the Don Memorial Library, which has one of the finest Africana collections in the country. David Don was a Scot who came to South Africa in the late 19th century in the service of the Oriental Bank and ended up as a wealthy and influential sugar planter: he was a great and famous collector of books, manuscripts, maps and pamphlets on South Africa, which were presented to the Durban Library by his widow. We, personally, have a special memory of it, of its *Periplus of the*

Erythraean Sea, a little old book—a 1912 translation of the most famous of the ancient pilot books—written by a Greek of Alexandria, who sailed across the Indian Ocean from Africa to India and back, published 60 years after the birth of Christ, a book of old adventures and old mysteries, of incense, myrrh, tortoise shell and ivory.

The library is full of such pleasures for those who want them.

At the back of the City Hall is the **Local History Museum** in Aliwal Street, the first public building to go up in Durban in 1866, overflowing now with treasures. There are plenty of other pleasures: arcades, shops, restaurants, 30-storey blocks like 320 West Street, which—in the city heart—has its famous Bird-World of tropical plants and birds, or the **African Art Centre** at 8 Guildhall Arcade off Gardiner Street. This, sponsored by the South African Institute of Race Relations, sells the beautiful and authentic things of Africa, rugs and tapestries, beadwork, traditional grass work of a very high standard, pots, and carvings in three of the loveliest woods of Africa, wild olive, tamboti and red ivory. There is also the work of artists such as Azaria Mbatha, well known for his linocuts, particularly those with early biblical themes, Dan Rakgoathe, John Muafanjego, Wiseman Mabambo, and Tito Zungu, a quite remarkable ball-point pen artist. Miss Jo Thorpe is there to talk and give background, for she is in touch with almost everyone who produces anything.

In the block a little beyond, flanked by Broad and St Andrew's Streets, is another museum of character, the **Old House Museum.** This little old place, standing originally close to the mangrove swamps (that are no more) was built by John Goodricke with mangrove poles, wattle and daub and thatch, and it was one of Natal's true old verandah houses with a verandah encircling it. Brick and yellowwood followed, and it was a solid house when George Robinson bought it in 1858 and his son grew up in it, John, later to be Sir John and Natal's first prime minister. The house, a replica of the original, typifies now the home of an early settler: the pieces of furniture are heirlooms, or locally made, or fashioned from the timbers from wrecks. There is a clock from the wrecked *Minerva* that floated ashore in a barrel, and many treasures of all kinds contributed by old families.

One of the publicity brochures suggests that Durban is not a cosmopolitan town. Perhaps it is not in the sense that Johannesburg and Cape Town are: yet what most visitors enjoy is the feeling of variety that white, black, brown and golden skins give, with all the glamour of rickshas and the 'uniform' of the men who pull them, the feathers, beads, skins and dancing rattles. A good deal of the city's colour is provided by the Indian community, whose ancestors came to

Natal from the 1860s onwards to work on the sugar estates: most of them live round Durban and the majority are Hindus, and it is the Hindu women in their traditional saris who bring brilliance to the city. The saris, most ancient of ancient styles, are beautiful and elegant, and so often are the women, with their calm faces and dark eyes and shining straight black hair.

It is the men, however, who make the close contact with visitors, for they play a unique part in the serious business of enjoying food—they are the finest waiters South Africa has known. Their quickness, deftness, knowledge and memory set them apart: an Indian waiter will often remember the tastes of a regular diner—even a holiday diner—and those of his children for 50 years, and will look after and please them for this time and longer.

The Hindus bring as well strange things to the city, like fire-walking, hot curries to make one weep, and *samoosas*, the little pastry triangles filled with aromatic mince. T. C. Robertson, conservationist-epicure, who lives at Scottburgh down the coast, calls them 'little cookies like dimunitive atom bombs charged with curry instead of uranium 238'. His Hindu friends bring him these as an early morning offering when they have Deepvali, the Festival of Lights. This festival, falling on the New Moon night of Kartik in October-November, is a happy celebration in the Hindu world when lights, figuratively and practically, drive out the darkness, and hundreds of little clay lamps are lit in Durban's Hindu homes.

Grey Street near the city centre is now an Indian business area. The new **Indian Market,** on the site of the old one off Cathedral Road not far away, is not nearly as big as the old nor is there the same bustle and excitement, but these will come, and in the meantime its exotic goods and general air give pleasure to many tourists. The Hindu Temple, alien and exciting to Western eyes, is further off in Umgeni Road: it is **Sri Vaithianatha Easvarar Alayam,** and is the oldest and largest in the country.

Everybody knows, at least by hearsay, of the **Greyville Race Course** where South Africa's most glamorous racing event, the July Handicap, takes place on the first Saturday of July every year. It lies to the north of the city centre, with the long hill behind it which Gardiner, the missionary, in 1835 christened Berea after the Berea in the Acts of the Apostles, and where he had his first mission. It is a lush residential area now, with great trees and gardens bright with bougainvillea. This was the last stronghold of elephant near Durban, where one chased the city's first mayor, George Cato. If elephants have long disappeared, there are still wild beauties like the purple-banded sunbird, and the purple-crested lourie—violet, green and crimson—flying from tree to tree.

On the top of the hill is Muckleneuk—a big, white, gabled, pillared house standing among palms and bougainvilleas, designed by Sir Herbert Baker—which was the home of the late Dr Killie Campbell and is now the **William Campbell Museum** and Killie Campbell Africana Library, bequeathed by her to the University of Natal.

Margaret, better known as Killie, Campbell, was the daughter of sugar baron Sir Marshall Campbell and granddaughter of William Campbell who bought the estate and after whom the museum was named. In this home she accumulated one of the finest private Africana collections in the country. It makes it extraordinarily human to know that she started it from scratch with little knowledge or money, using her dress allowance to buy books, and falling into collectors' pitfalls like lesser mortals.

There are three collections, the library, the museum of history and antiques, and the Mashu museum, which is an ethnological collection, and which includes the paintings of Barbara Tyrrell depicting African tribal costumes, that have won for her world acclaim and two honorary doctorates.

Barbara Tyrrell was the Natal girl who some 35 years ago painted a picture of an enchanting little African maid in her tribal dress whom she saw in the streets of Richmond. What the little African told her of her dress and adornments gave her life a new direction. It led to a detailed study of tribal dress, and to the exact and beautiful paintings of tribal and ceremonial costumes that stand now as a record of a fast-vanishing culture. At the time she began few people realized that such a thing as tribal dress existed or that various styles had special meanings. She was to show South Africa and the world otherwise.

She posted her first paintings to Killie Campbell, and this was the start of a long friendship—together they planned her journeys, and it was to Killie Campbell Barbara rushed at the end of a trip to show her work.

We all know the reproductions of her paintings in magazine and newspaper, and in her two books, *Tribal Peoples of Southern Africa* and *Suspicion is My Name* which give the background to the African dress and fashions we see in tribal areas as we travel, and to the homes we often glimpse. Many of the original water colours on which the books were based are those in Killie Campbell's collection.

Only the library is freely open to the public, although the museum can be visited by arrangement.

Along most ways that visitors enter or leave Durban there are the signs of industries, with the greatest of all, the sugar industry, impinging everywhere, from the bulk terminal on the harbour to the monotonous rolling green cane fields north and south of the city.

Not so very long ago the North Coast road was relatively unsophisticated, with the little resorts along the coast all family holiday centres facing a blue uncrowded sea and backed by the green sea of sugar-cane. The national road along the coast is this no longer. **Umhlanga Rocks,** 15 minutes' drive from Durban, is no longer the fishing village many people remember, but a new and expensive national playground with the five-star Beverley Hills Hotel and places like the astonishing Mediterranean style complex, Cabana Beach, towering over everything, boutiques, flood-lit tennis courts, an enormous outdoor chessboard, riding, a fine golf course, restaurants, nightclubs, French cuisine. There is La Lucia as well, prestige township, dubbed not Golden but Millionaire's Mile, where the houses have a story-book magnificence.

The old North Coast road lying slightly to the west is by no means up-to-date and monied in appearance, but in actual fact the rolling cane lands it runs through are the backbone of Natal wealth—they reach along the coast from Zululand to southern Natal for more than 400 kilometres in a great band up to 24 kilometres deep, and inland in parts as well. What they produce are 2-million metric tons of sugar earning roughly one tenth of the total gross value of all crops in South Africa. This makes them a money-spinner with foreign exchange earnings worth, in the 1975-76 season, R206-million, a sweet prize in which a huge number of people shared in a large or a small way.

The first sugar point of note is the **Mount Edgecombe Experimental Station** of the South African Sugar Association about 19 kilometres from Durban. It is the most important cane research station in Africa, and in its 50 years of life has played an honourable part in raising the 200 000 tons annual output to the present 2 000 000 tons, while its plant breeding has won world respect.

Close by are the estates of the Hulett Group, a famous name in sugar, where the sugar mill can, by arrangement, be visited. Mount Edgecombe is naturally a 'sugar' township. Verulam up the road was started by early British settlers and named after their patron earl: it, too, was a sugar village and is now an Indian township. Further on is Tongaat, and some 32 kilometres from Durban the Tongaat Sugar Estates mill—the biggest of its kind in the country—the head office of the Tongaat Group, and the Tongaat township.

It is an incongruity that a little past Tongaat, about a kilometre from the road, is **Compensation,** the site of the first sugar mill in South Africa, built by a pioneer who could find nobody to give him financial backing and was declared insolvent. He was Edmund Moorwood, who had visited the West Indies before he came to South Africa, and was stirred to interest by the reeds that grew along Natal's warm well-watered coast. Where they flourished, he prophesied, so would sugar cane; and in 1847 he made South Africa's first planting of it on his farm. The cane had come from Reunion, and just as Moorwood had believed, Natal suited it well: by 1851 he had made his own mill to crush it, and although nobody guessed it, Natal's sugar industry had been born.

The mill was a handyman's affair with rollers made from a spar from a wrecked ship, and was turned by handles operated by several Zulu assistants: the juice ran down rough wooden gutters into a pot, a little lime was added to it and it was boiled until the sugar crystallized. It might not have been sugar by today's standards, but it was a sensation when Moorwood showed it to Durban in the offices of the *Natal Times*.

Moorwood was not only a pioneer but a generous one. By 1852, when he was offering Compensation for sale because he could not make ends meet, he had already distributed seed cane to all who wanted it. The first steam mill was operating a few years later, and then came a factory on Springfield Flats a little north of Durban, and the sugar industry was on its way.

Moorwood died unsung in Brazil: a replica of his mill stands on Compensation, a memorial to him, and a national monument.

The journey up the old North Coast road a little beyond Stanger and from there along the coast to Durban, is worth doing for its interest and contrasts. Along the sea are the resorts, swimming, fishing, and the opulence of places like Umhlanga Rocks.

Right down the coast as far as Port Edward—indeed, round South Africa's whole 4 000 kilometres of shore—there is good and sometimes superb fishing, here in Natal with fish like sharks and barracuda, Natal silver bream which some call stumpnose, silver with golden scales, that is a marvellous angling species; shad, musselcrackers, mackerel, spotted grunter and white steenbras of estuaries, and others.

The fish of which everybody knows is the shark, because of its potential danger to man, and at Umhlanga Rocks is the headquarters of the Natal Anti-Shark Measures Board—NASMB—which at certain times is open to visitors. Its work is mainly the protection of bathers against shark attack, an ever-present danger that was highlighted in the early 1950s when there was a series of attacks that horrified South Africa. Shark attacks most often occur in warm water and this is why they have been particularly prevalent in Natal waters which reach a temperature of well over 21 degrees Celsius in summer.

To safeguard bathers nearly 40 Natal beaches have now been protected with specially knitted gill nets of strong, black polyethylene trawl twine, an Australian inspiration that has proved extraordinarily effective. In the first 60 years of the century over 80 shark attacks were made along the South African coast, mostly in Natal, in which 38 people died. Durban in 1952 was the first place to use the shark nets, and others soon followed, and in the following 24 years there was not a single fatality in protected places, although there were two attacks at Amanzimtoti on the South Coast in 1974 under the conditions that most favour shark attack—it was evening, the water was turbid, and the nets had actually been fouled.

The nets—well over 200 of them—are serviced regularly by NASMB staff, whose task it also is to declare an area safe or unsafe for bathing.

Not all sharks are man-eaters—of the 270 species in the world's seas, only some 27 are dangerous to men. Nevertheless, when they attack, they cause more terror and alarm than almost any other creature. Professor J. L. B. Smith, South Africa's great fish expert, classed those with really powerful teeth among the most ferocious and dangerous of animals—known to have killed elephants, and able to cut a man in half 'as easily as a donkey could a carrot'.

Most people know sharks by sight, if not in the sea than in oceanariums, the bodies made for speed, the horrible fins, the under-slung jaws and terrible teeth, the restless movement—for a shark has to swim to breathe. There is no bone in their bodies, only gristle, nor have they scales like other fish. Their sense of smell is phenomenal and, says Professor Smith, they can *taste* with their rough skins. So it is that when a shark sometimes brushes against his victim, he is tasting him with his skin before making his attack: some people, Smith believed, are naturally attractive to sharks and therefore always in danger of attack in the sea.

The bathers along Natal's coast might remember Smith's quip that more people die from falling downstairs than from shark attack. At the same time, when asked if he bathed in the sea, he replied briefly that it was seldom, and then only in a rock pool!

Our favourite memory of Umhlanga Rocks is that of a tea garden where we ate pancakes in the shade of a huge wild fig tree.

This tree, and the others in the garden, were remnants of the wild coastal forest that had once swept down the coast, that is now preserved here and there on dunes, in gardens and parks, on farms and on golf courses, along roads and in reserves, and that are part of the character of the coast. Not that people consider them much—they are props in the immense holiday act—but if the trees were gone, the coast would have a blank, undressed, alien look for which not even sea and beaches could atone.

The coastal forest is at its best in Zululand; it is there at Umhlanga, at La Lucia where the homes owe much of their beauty to the setting of wild trees, at Durban—built originally in and by a forest—and southwards in remnants along the famous holiday South Coast.

The resorts are packed close to one another right down the length of the coast. There is **Amanzimtoti** nearest Durban, with river banks still wooded in parts; Doonside, Warner Beach, Winkelspruit, Kingsburgh, Illovo Beach, Umkomaas—the river of the cow whales—Scottburgh and dozens more right down to Port Edward, the last Natal resort, with the Transkei the other side of the Umtamvuna River. We remember **Scottburgh** for the dune aloes growing on the sea shore, just beginning to open their yellow and orange flowers to the May seas.

Most of the way down the road from Durban we had noticed the tall wild croton trees near the road laden with salmon-pink fruits, between Scottburgh and Park Rynie there were ilala palms, picturesque with their large leaves, and every now and then there were the wild bananas, *Strelitzia nicolai*, with their big, handsome tattered banana leaves—the noise they make in the wind, like flags flapping, is a true coastal Natal sound.

Umdoni Park, further south, the Prime Minister's official holiday home on the South Coast, is named after the umdoni trees that are so common there. The golf course is a marvellous place, like a glade set in wild forest, with mahogany trees, spectacular dark giants, along the verges.

Ifafa Beach is one of the resorts that really does owe most of its attraction to its trees, and even casual holiday-makers remember the little idyll, with rondavels under flatcrowns and picnickers under an Egossa red pear, and a wild-tree and bush-lined lagoon.

This is a side of the South Coast that exists along its length, wild things among sugar-cane, subtropical fruits, holiday-making and hotels. Holiday-making, of course, wins hands down: it is for the sea, the beaches, the hotels and their life that people mostly come. They fill all the resorts—there are fairly big ones on the lower South Coast like Uvongo, Margate—the biggest of all—Ramsgate and Southbroom, and there is plenty of gaiety and socializing, with golf courses and country clubs as well as beaches.

This coast is also the fisherman's joy, especially at the time of the sardine-run. Next to the July handicap, this is Natal's most important event, when—from about mid-June to the end of July—immense shoals of sardines or pilchards arrive from the south and travel up the coast, accompanied by every game fish imaginable and by sea birds that travel with them, diving and eating as they go. When conditions are right, the sardines come into the surf close to shore, where excited and enraptured crowds scoop them out with everything from nets to wastepaper baskets. The crowds follow the shoals much as the birds and game fish do, and anglers have fine sport then with game fish of many kinds.

North of Durban, the shoals disappear and the excitement peters out, but in full flush the 'run' is a major news story featured by all Natal newspapers.

Where do the sardines go? Who knows? Professor Smith suggests they return to the Cape by way of the Agulhas current, but if this is so, the story remains to be told.

After the sardines in early spring come the shad—or elf. Vigorous fish, and smallish as a rule, with great appetites, they give thrills to everyone who wields a fishing rod—it is perfectly possible to land more than 200 in a day. Some experts maintain they give 'more pleasure to holiday makers than all the rest of the small fish put together'. Shoals have been depleted, and there are now restrictions (with heavy penalties for infringement) for overfishing of shad in Natal waters.

It is an interesting coast and combination—sophistication, sardines and shad—all blending to give a special South Coast atmosphere. There are people who have it in their blood, seeking the same thing, in exactly the same place, over and over, and finding a year without it meagre and ill-spent.

CHAPTER TWELVE

Transskei and the Eastern Coast

♣

There is now a bridge across the Umtamvuma River linking Natal with the Transkei. Once we used to cross it by pont, which was an exciting way to approach this brand-new countryside. Even now it has a simple uncluttered look compared to southern Natal, and although it also has a holiday coast, it is a very different one.

The Transkei became an independent state in 1976 so that this technically is not South African coast any longer but a 'homeland', less exploited than Natal's and thus more beautiful—and more difficult by far to explore. There is no coastal road along it and all the little holiday and fishing spots are reached by side roads that branch eastwards to the sea from the main road N2, the country's backbone and well inland.

Plateau and rolling hills decorated with clusters of round huts, and cattle kraals ringed with aloes, are what travellers remember most of the main road, N2, that runs through the capital, Umtata, to the south. South of Kokstad a road that is a good deal more picturesque branches off eastwards to **Port St John's,** the holiday village between forest and sea, that is one of the most beautiful along the entire cost. That stretch of beach and sea with the village at its heart held many memories for us as we travelled along N2—wild bananas with great leaves framing vistas of bright blue Indian Ocean, shiny green parrots feasting on little yellowwood fruits, and wide beaches empty of everything save black women picking shellfish on the rocks, and an otter's paw prints on the sand.

A little north of Port St John's is the most famous shipwreck site of the long dangerous coast, that of the *Grosvenor* which met her end here on August 4th, 1782. She was no Cunard liner, but a mere 700 tons, and she was homeward bound to Britain from Madras carrying cargo, crew and passengers. She struck at dawn and 136 people aboard scrambled ashore. The story of their long death-walk southwards— only 17 were known to survive—has been recounted many times.

What made the *Grosvenor* famous among countless wrecks was the legend of her treasure, six million sterling it was claimed, in gold,

177

silver and diamonds, that men have sought since for 100 years. Coins and trinkets have been picked up from time to time, and five cannon recovered, but this is all. Of course people still turn down the country road to treasure-hunt—who could be so cold-blooded as to leave unsought the diamonds, the crusados, the Star Pagodas, the pieces of eight? But the sea at the base of the wild cliffs guards the treasure well.

Among the greatest attractions for visitors southward bound are the clothes worn by the African women and sometimes by the men, the styles and colours changing from area to area. A whole industry has been built up on these for all visitors long to buy them, and the ornaments and beadwork too. Now they can, at the **Wonk'umntu Centre** five kilomtres south of Umtata on the main road to the south.

In the north, still known as 'Pondoland', it was pale blue clothes that riveted us (the colour derived from Reckitt's Blue), and southwards apricot and orange, colours of the earth. Those long full skirts of the women of the south, orange-red braided in black, swinging as they walk, and great black turbans embroidered with white stars, are one of the sights of Africa. We had the luck to see a group of women sitting on the ground outside a store gossipping and smoking. One old veteran had a pipe fully 50 centimetres long. It was made of the root of a thorn tree with long pale-yellow, scented flower tassels that grows along the rivers: and she had bought it from a pipe-maker who lived south across the Kei—a king of pipe-makers—who had taken days to make it using a knife and a piece of red hot wire to bore the stem.

Those who have not seen an African store have missed a world. We spent a long while in this one admiring the umbrellas that the women bought and decorated with beads, a saddle girth, beads of all colours, rolls of coarse sheeting to make skirts and cloaks and bras, black melton cloth for turbans, white blankets for the men and red for the boys, bowls of ochre used for dye, and the *mutis* that had a shelf to themselves. There was *inKanyamba*, meaning tornado, which glows at night and is painted on arms and face to chase away evil spirits; an ointment containing phosphorus which smokes when the lid is taken off and chases away evil spirits (both made in Johannesburg). There was also hippo fat, and lion fat which brings strength—smeared on the body or burnt it overcomes great difficulties; and a root concoction that was a love potion. We came away with five centimetres of tree bark which, said the store-keeper, we were to use in a decoction and drink when we had a cough. It would cure it without fail.

'If you want to know what you are looking at', someone said to us as we were examining the beads on the counter, 'read Joan Broster's *Red Blanket Valley.*'

Mrs Broster comes of a family that for generations owned and ran a trading store in the Transkei, and beadwork was—and is—her hobby and her passion. African beadwork is something that has received a good deal of publicity recently but when *Red Blanket Valley* appeared about a decade ago it was the first popular book—certainly the first of which we knew—to explain that the designs and colours in the gorgeous beadwork had their own symbolism.

It was from the women and girls buying beads that she learned that young people had certain colours—mainly turquoise blue and white, the older navy and white with some rose pink; pregnant women and young parents others, that there were special beads for social and ceremonial occasions, and that different combinations of beads recorded different messages and love-letters.

When we read of the miner's wide necklace, *isimamhlaba*, made for him by his sweetheart, of blue and white beads, decorated with three rows of pearly buttons and cerise pink bows, of the courtship rites with the young boys flaunting long bead tails with cerise pompoms and small brass bells, of the design *isadunge* which was a 'pattern of the past representing pools of water in a dry river bed', we knew we would never be parted from the book. We never have been, and we recommend it to every traveller, every discoverer, wishing to unlock this rich new world.

After *Red Blanket Valley* came Aubrey Elliott's *The Magic World of the Xhosa* with its emphasis on magic and superstition in Xhosa life.

At **Kentani** off to our left we were close to the scene of a tragedy, the belief in the power of ancestral spirits to control events, that unwittingly broke the power of the great Xhosa people in the 19th century.

That century—even before the days of the Zulu wars—saw a succession of frontier wars in the south-east, Black versus White, the Xhosas—the southernmost African people—versus the colonists who were slowly spreading northwards. The struggle took a strange turn in 1856. In that year a Xhosa girl, Nongqawuse—perhaps a medium, perhaps a trickster or a dupe—sitting on the banks of a pool in the Gxara stream, was visited, she claimed, by Xhosa ancestral spirits. They had come, they told her, to help to destroy the white conquerers: a mighty whirlwind would arise that would blow these into the sea, the old Xhosa warriors and heroes would arise from the dead, and the land would again be the Xhosas. They were to slaughter their cattle, and burn their crops; new fat herds would arise in their place and new crops spring forth from the earth, but first the sacrifice had to be made.

So the people destroyed the food—the cattle and the corn—but on the day of the prophesied miracle, a February day in 1857, a golden sun rose—not red as word had gone out it would be—and set as usual in the west; and no hurricane came to sweep away the Whites. And in the desperate days that followed the people starved—25 000 are said to have died while of the 105 000 people who had lived in British Kaffraria, no more than 37 000 now remained. The Cape Government helped, but even so, many lay down to die: some turned cannibal. Many thousands streamed into white-owned land to find food and work, taking with them as they spread across the Eastern Cape and west into the Karoo their melodious speech, their circumcision and marriage and other rites, and magical beliefs.

How did it all happen? Was Nongqawuse honest? Was it a great spontaneous burgeoning of national spirit? Or was it engineered? Eric Walker, the historian, believes it was the carefully executed plan of wily Moshesh of Basutoland next door, who was behind it all. He spread and fed the prophetic stories, he arranged the cattle-killing, because he knew war was coming between him and the Free Staters, and this was how he would keep the Cape from helping them: he would give the Cape something of its own to keep it busy. If so, it was probably the most monstrous plot South Africa has ever known—it ended a fighting nation.

We talked of the Xhosa girl as we began the descent into the huge valley of the **Kei**—the Great River—a tremendous landscape of hills dropping away to the hot river bed with its spiky euphorbia and other succulent vegetation and thorn trees.

That ribbon below us was an important river. For a time in the 19th century, it was the boundary of the Cape: today it is the boundary between the Transkei and the Ciskei and divides the Xhosa people—who live south as well as north of it—into two parts.

Now we were running into the country where the early frontier wars had been most savagely waged. This country between the Kei and the Keiskamma to the south had in those far-off days been the Province of Queen Adelaide (of brief life), Harry Smith country, for as Colonel Smith he had been in command of the area, had marched and ridden and fought here, and 22 years later, as Governor, Sir Harry, had proclaimed this as the Province of British Kaffraria, a province that was separate from the Cape until 1866. The old crossing on the Kei had been called Smith's Tower.

We were to remember him again and again in the Eastern Cape, but now for a while we forgot him as we drove to East London through the green thorn tree country, the pineapple and banana fields, past the side roads to Morgan's Bay, to Haga-Haga and Gonubie Mouth and other little places on the sea. It was clear that we were still in Xhosa country and that this was a special occasion; for the people wore blankets and beads, traditional dress, fast disappearing in everyday life. This country south to the Keiskamma River is still their strong-hold, and that day they filled it for us with the same life and colour as they did across the Kei.

As we drew near East London, we began to think more and more of the sea, and it was to be with us for many hundred of kilometres southward. **East London** is the only river port of any size in South Africa, and it was both the river and the sea that made it. The river is the Buffalo, and the little port came into being in the times of the frontier wars as the harbour for the garrison town of King William's Town not far inland. The first boat here had been the famous *Knysna*, which had been built by George Rex at Knysna further to the west.

A Union Jack was nailed to a tree on Signal Hill near the entrance to the harbour, which itself was christened Port Rex. It was a name that should have survived, a royal legendary name as the story of the town of Knysna tells, but when 12 years later Harry Smith proclaimed the harbour British, it was named the Port of East London, and East London it has stayed.

It is a city today with a harbour that is both big and important, serving the Transkei, Ciskei, part of the Eastern Cape and the Orange Free State Goldfields, an export port, a big wool centre, a holiday city with dozens of resorts strung along the coastline, south as well as north, a gentle town of clear streams, kaffirbooms and old houses, bounded by soft green country and blue sea.

For us, East London's excitements are mostly sea-born. That ocean fronting the city is not always calm and its savage moments have made East London's story in as great measure as the gentle. Orient Beach takes its name from a ship wrecked here in 1907, and Quanza Terrace from another. In September a few years ago a huge ship, the 258 000-ton carrier *Svealand*, was damaged off the coast in a gale when a gigantic wave crushed its steel hatch. It is that wave, that type of monster wave, that has occurred over and over in the seas beyond the port—along all this eastern coast from as far south as Port Elizabeth to as far north at least as Zululand—that has made the most dramatic history of all.

What happens in these seas is that, when a certain combination of conditions arises—a south-westerly gale beating against the south-flowing Agulhas current along the coast, combined with the long swells which sweep up unobstructed from Antarctica—a freak wave is sometimes formed. Sea-goers who have lived through one have described it as a precipice of water, an immense vertical face, with a great watery gulf before it, into which the ships have fallen as if into a hole. 'It was a hole in the sea', a survivor later said, 'a bloody great hole, and we went in'.

How many ships, big and small, have disappeared in such a cavern, nobody knows. Since World War II over a score of big ships, including liners and supertankers, have been either sunk or damaged. During the war, the 10 000-ton British heavy cruiser, *H.M.S. Birmingham*, was submerged 18 metres over her gun turrets. The liner *Waratah*, whose disappearance off the Bashee River mouth in 1909 made one of the greatest sea mysteries, is now believed to have been another victim. The first loss of which we know was *H.M.S. Penelope*, one of a squadron that rounded the Cape in 1591. Somewhere off this coast a huge wave engulfed her; the crews of the other ships watched her masthead lights disappear. The *Svealand* and the 25 000-ton *Edinburgh Castle*—which survived the wave in the seas north of the city—are among the best known in recent times.

From England, from the Hydrographic Department of the British Navy, in 1973 came an Admiralty notice warning shipping of these waves, particularly between latitudes off East London and Richard's Bay and between the edge of the continental shelf and 20 sea miles further seaward.

In lighter vein, the ship *Lady Kennaway* was wrecked at East London in 1857. Her cargo was girls, 153 'respectable young Irish women', who had been put ashore just before the ship was damaged—it was the most luscious cargo the bachelor-frontiersmen had ever dreamed. Ship and cargo are commemorated on East London's beach front where the big three-star hotel is named the Kennaway.

An East London wreck brought South Africa a treasure of another kind, its own recipe for chutney—Ball's Chutney. In 1872 when the steamer *Quanza* went aground, the captain's wife, Mrs Adkins, hurried back aboard the sinking ship to retrieve a recipe for chutney which her American mother had bequeathed to her. Captain Adkins and his wife settled ashore and their daughter became Mrs Ball. Lawrence Green says Mrs Ball, using the recipe salvaged from the *Quanza*, began bottling her famous chutney during World War I. It has been going strong ever since.

East London's sea gift that is known throughout the world wherever there are scientists and nature-lovers came from the depths. It is a fish, which—when it was found in 1938—became in a news flash the most famous of all fish of all time, excepting Jonah's. The story has been told many times, and will be again, for it sounds as good in the present as it did 40 years ago when it set the cables humming.

Three days before Christmas in 1938 a fishing boat pulled into East London harbour with its catch. Amongst it was a fish which had been caught near the mouth of the Chalumna River close to the city, a fish unknown to the crew and so odd in appearance that the captain decided to save it for the curator of the East London Museum, Miss M. C. Courtenay-Latimer, a young woman of considerable enterprise. She went to the docks, looked at the fish—now dead—and because she knew it was unusual and she had the determination to back her hunch, she made the museum famous (and herself as well).

What she saw was a big blue-scaled fish nearly 1,5 metres long, with a great mouth and fins like legs. She manhandled it into a taxi and took it to the museum where she had it photographed, and sketched it, and then, it is said, herself pushed it on a little cart to the taxidermist.

At Knysna, 560 kilometres to the west, South Africa's great fish expert, Dr Smith, later Professor of Ichthyology at Rhodes University, was holidaying. It was to him that Miss Courtenay-Latimer wrote describing the fish and sending her sketch. Dr Smith looked at it and guessed what it was. It was a Coelacanth, and he identified it for sure from a book on *fossil* fish, because there was then no illustration of a living one: as far as science knew, the last Coelacanth had died 70 million years before. All hell, his wife, Margaret, remembered later, broke out in the house.

As we write, Margaret, on a television programme, has just recalled how her husband saw the fish later in East London, gazed at it enraptured, touched it, stroked it. 'You know, my lass,' he said to Miss Courtenay-Latimer, 'you've got something here that will take the name of your museum right round the world.'

Smith's pronouncement that the East London fish was a Coelacanth, a living fossil, and the close relative of the fish that was supposed to have been the ancestor of all land vertebrates, was a sensation. It belonged to the most marvellous group in the world, that had lived the longest of any back-boned creatures and had remained, through the millions of years, almost unchanged in form. It was then as startling as today would be a dinosaur bounding down East London's Oxford Street, and in Dr Smith's own words, the discovery was rightly accepted as one of the most remarkable events in natural history of any time.

In due course the Coelacanth travelled to Grahamstown to be described by Dr Smith and he named it *Latimeria chalmunae* after Miss Courtenay-Latimer, and the place where it was found. A police guard travelled with it.

Where could it and its kind have remained hidden and unknown for 70 million years? Dr Smith was sure from its appearance it was among reefs, that this one had been a stray, that there were more Coelacanths, that they probably belonged to East African waters, and that they were known to fishermen there. His search to find the second is a story even more dramatic than the first.

World War II delayed it, but in 1945 he began to distribute leaflets along the East Coast and in Madagascar describing the fish and offering a reward for a specimen, and he and his wife started their own numerous expeditions along the coast and to the nearby islands. It was a single-minded, dedicated hunt that lasted 14 years.

In December 1952, the Smiths were aboard ship at Durban on the way back from an expedition when they received a cable from a Captain Eric Hunt who ran a small trading schooner between Africa and the Comores, a group of islands in the Mozambique Channel between Madagascar and the African mainland. He had a Coelacanth, he cabled; Smith must come and get it. Later they were to realize that Hunt's fish had been found on 22nd December, the same day that Miss Courtenay-Latimer had found hers, 14 years before.

Hunt's cable was followed by a second. There was no refrigeration—it was torrid mid-summer—and the authorities were claiming the fish. The Comores were over 3 000 kilometres away and Smith was frantic. What he needed was a plane, but it was Christmas time and the world on holiday. Nevertheless a plane he got. 'Go to the Prime Minister,' his wife urged him, and he did. Dr D. F. Malan, on holiday at the sea, got out of bed after the agonized plea had reached him to telephone Smith. An Air Force Dakota, Prime Minister-ordered, picked Smith up in Durban, and they were off to the Comores. There at the end, safe on Hunt's boat, was the great fish, all 1,5 incredible metres of it, a true Coelacanth, and as he looked at it Smith burst into tears.

It had been caught by a native fisherman off the island of Anjouan, where Coelacanths were well known to the locals. The islanders used the flesh, well salted, for food, and the stiff scales to roughen punctured bicycle tyre tubes before putting on the patches!

Smith, the Coelacanth, and the Dakota crew flew back to Durban through rain and storm, to be met at the airport by excited crowds. This was an adventure all South Africa had followed and Smith was received with acclaim—those lucky enough to remember the day, will never forget the thrill. Smith made a broadcast on the spot which reached across the world; he slept that night with the fish beside him, and flew off next day to Cape Town to show it to Dr Malan before taking it back to Grahamstown. We remember a photograph of the fish in its wooden coffin being shown to the Prime Minister, one tentative ministerial finger exploring a scale, Dr Smith with his hair on end, Mrs Smith—that loyal partner in all the ventures—looking on, an historic study of intentness and of victory.

Smith named the fish *Malania* after Malan and *anjouanae* after the island near which it was found; so that centuries later scientists would remember this adventure, and the prime minister who climbed out of bed to help find a dead fish. South Africa is a country of bitter politics. What we also recall from that day is how people of all creeds clapped the old politician: he had done something the whole country adored.

Walk up Oxford Street to the top, and there is the **East London Museum,** with Miss—now Dr—Courtenay-Latimer's Coelacanth in pride of place at the entrance. There are also, among other things, a first-rate ethnological section (this is still Xhosa country), a good bird display and a Dodo's egg, claimed to be the last in the world. Most people turn back for another look at the Coelacanth; there is no doubt that it steals the thunder.

Another stimulating place is the **Library**, in Gladstone Street, under dynamic Miss M. H. van Deventer, which is integrated into the life of the town in a unique and exciting way.

The national road N2 continues from East London inland through King William's Town and Grahamstown to Port Elizabeth and the Tsitsikama, but it is possible to reach the port along smaller coastal roads over the hills and through the coastal bush leading to holiday villages along the Indian Ocean edge.

From **Port Alfred,** among the loveliest of sea-side villages, a road goes on to Kenton-on-Sea and Alexandria, and a little west of the Bushman's River Mouth on this route near Boknes, a rough road leads seawards to Kwaai Hoek or False Island and to the spot which most maps mark today as the **Dias Memorial.**

To every historian, to every person interested in South Africa's story, this is perhaps the most fascinating spot in the country. It is not only the place where the first mark of our history was made, but it is the site of the most exciting and successful treasure hunt of modern times.

It is possible—first along a path through the bush, then across a waste of sand dunes—to reach a dark hillock or headland, the most western of three and the crest of Kwaai Hoek, which overlooks cliff and ocean. From a ship's deck out at sea, the hillock looks like an island, but is not, for it is joined to the mainland, hence the name False Island.

185

It was on the top of this dark knoll amid the white blazing sands that the Portuguese sailor and explorer, Bartolomeu Dias, set up a stone pillar and cross, a *padrão*, on a March day in 1488, on his return voyage round the Cape, a momentous voyage on which he opened up a sea route from Europe to the Indian Ocean.

It was the heyday of Portuguese sea power, when the Portuguese caravels were pushing through the far seas, exploring the coast of Africa, mapping a new world and seeking new markets and new wealth, and the fabulous land of Prester John. The explorers on this romantic—and highly commercial—errand carried with them in the holds of their ships stone pillars or *padrãos*, made of Portuguese limestone, to be erected at suitable spots to serve as landmarks. In the words of Professor Eric Axelson, the modern South African authority on the early Portuguese explorers, on each of them the Portuguese king's coat of arms and an appropriate inscription asserted his country's rights to the seas around and the adjacent lands: the cross surmounting each pillar proclaimed that the exploration was being carried out in the name of the Christian religion. It was one of these pillars that Bartolomeu Dias erected on the knoll at Kwaai Hoek.

Dias, with his little squadron of three ships, had set off from Portugal in 1487 (the date determined by Axelson) and sailed down the west coast of Africa; and off the south-west coast of South Africa, perhaps near Lambert's Bay, had either been blown westwards by a storm or had stood out to sea: in either event he rounded the Cape without realizing it, sailed east and north and struck the coast again at the Gouritz River, west of Mossel Bay. Along this coast he sailed, past Plettenberg Bay, Cape Recife and into Algoa Bay, celebrating mass on the island of St Croix, past Bird Island to perhaps the Keiskamma River, where a dissatisfied crew forced Dias to turn back. He raised the *padrão* not—it was known—at the point where he turned about, but at another more suitable spot a little further west.

Within a century the pillar and cross—the first landmark known to have been made by any white explorer in South Africa and the first historic beacon—had disappeared from view from the sea. Even its site had vanished with the wind and the rain.

In 1935 when a young Eric Axelson began his historical research, he was urged to concentrate on the Portuguese period by Professor Leo Fouche, Head of the Department of History at the University of the Witwatersrand, to try to solve the Dias mystery, and find the cross. Axelson went to Portugal, read and swotted, studied and searched, came back, and *found* the cross in an adventure that is already a South African classic.

Dr—now Professor—Axelson and head of the Department of History at the Cape Town University, tells the story in his first-class *Congo to Cape*. He told it to us one day in those same precise, level, authoritative tones known to his students, through which every now and then the sparks break out.

Axelson was returning home to Natal after his Portuguese researches in a mail ship following, as he said, Dias' route along the coast to Algoa Bay. He knew the cross must be close by—the early chronicles made this clear, although the details differed and often contradicted one another. Nevertheless, one chronicle described the cross as being five leagues from Bird Island (near Port Elizabeth) on an islet that was *not* cut off from the sea. Was there such a place? The officer on the bridge was interested in the puzzle and showed him the chart of this coastal strip, and there it was, 'False Island or Kwaai Hoek'.

He had, he knew, to see the place at once. There was, however, one day only to look, while the ship was in Port Elizabeth. Knowing the transport problems of those days, that impenetrable coastal bush, and the winds that blast by day and night, we grinned as he told us. But he did it, spending his last money on a taxi to Kwaai Hoek beyond the village of Alexandria 120 kilometres away, found his way through the bush and the puffadders, and looked down for the first time on the dark knoll on which then stood only a modern survey beacon. There was no indication whatsoever of any cross; yet he felt this was—had to be—the place.

Soon he and his brother were back, camping in the bush, working in the vicinity of the modern beacon, the most likely site for the ancient landmark as well. As they worked in the deep sand, their probe struck something solid, and here they began to dig. What they struck was 'rock', whitish-pink, hard and smooth, that did not match any of the rock around. It was the first bit of foreign stone they found that could have been part of the cross, but more were to follow, one a piece clearly worked by hand. Then in a pool at the foot of the cliff below the knoll they found another piece, a sea-gift this, encrusted with the ages—he told us how they had staggered with it, nearly 90 kilograms in weight, around the cliff to a place of safety, and how donkeys had dragged it over the dunes, two paces up, one and a half back: *Congo to Cape* told us they had had a coffin made for it in which it had fitted snugly.

Later Axelson returned to unearth still more pieces—he and his helpers recovered 5 000 in all, including fragments with lettering: the sea gave up still others. When the column was assembled, a square topped with a cross, it was found—incredibly enough—to be almost complete, although the block bearing the arms of Portugal that they had expected below the cross, was lacking. After much publicity and speculation, it was, both locally and in Portugal, deemed authentic, truly the Dias Cross. The original is today in Johannesburg in the care of the University of the Witwatersrand: what stands now at Kwaai Hoek—Angry Corner—buffeted by winds, is a replica only.

Axelson did not find only stone. There were, as well, some bits of rusted iron, slivers of lead, fragments of charcoal and one of glass from an old hand-blown bottle that must have held sacramental wine used in the consecration of the cross. They were enough to reconstruct the scene.

The charcoal showed they had made a fire, almost certainly to melt the lead to fix the cross in position. It must, then, have been a fine day. There had stood the sailor group, redolent of glory and of daring, below them in the sea the caravels, high in the bow and the stern, before them the cross: there had been the priest in scarlet vestments, his Latin phrases lingering for the first time on the southern airs; the chalice raised, the wine bottle emptied, cast aside and left, a fragment lying there for 450 years for Axelson to find. If we knew this shore, there had also been almost blinding brightness, a fine wind plucking at vestments, the aromatic-salt smell of bush and sea. Bartolomeu Dias was mourning at having to turn back 'as though he had lost a son', and it must have been a vivid, perhaps a bitter memory, for the brief years he was still to have. He could not have guessed the full glory.

There was a fascinating supplement to this story. Professor Vernon Forbes, well known authority on the early travellers in South Africa, was recently examining the travel diaries of Colonel R. J. Gordon, military commander at the Cape in the late 18th century, when he came on a reference to the *padrão*. In 1786 Gordon had travelled from the Cape to beyond Algoa Bay and there, east of the Boknes River, he had found 'a shattered-to-pieces old monument' on a prominent hill. He gathered together fragments (Forbes thought those that had been inscribed), loaded them on to his wagon, and took them back to Cape Town.

As we read of this in Professor Axelson's book, we thrilled. To have the path of Gordon, adventurer-explorer, cross that of Dias was richness indeed. This was the most eastern point in which we met Gordon, but we were to meet him again and again as we travelled westwards, and he was to emerge for us as one of the greatest of the early South Africans for—even if the name had not yet been coined— of South Africa he was.

A soldier of Scots-Dutch blood, equipped with education, brilliance, and heavenly curiosity, he settled permanently in the Cape in 1777, and wandered through the far, little or unknown regions, mapping, sketching and recording what he saw. The recent and accidental discovery of his diaries, with the clue to the *padrão*, was a bombshell. What happened to the inscribed pieces of the cross is still unknown. Of course Gordon guessed their significance: he would have prized and guarded them, maybe planned, when he visited Europe, to take them to Portugal himself. He died at the Cape in 1795 and his possessions were dispersed to Europe and Australia. But if they remained in Cape Town—and surely they did—they may yet, like his diaries, make a marvellous reappearance to complete the epic of the cross.

From here as we travelled **Algoa Bay** lay upon our left. The Bay of the Rock, Dias had called it (the Rock was Cape Recife), although later it became the Bay of the Lagoons—Baia da Lagoa—a name which in time was corrupted to Algoa Bay. We saw on its far side the harbour of Port Elizabeth itself, with the Swartkops River a little to the east, and at its mouth, the little settlement of Amsterdamhoek— Amsterdam Corner. A Dutch man-o'-war, the *Amsterdam*, that was wrecked here in the last century, gave it its name; and it has remained part of the river and sea ever since. (From its Captain Hofmeyr sprang South Africa's famous Hofmeyr family.)

Thirty years ago when we first knew it, it was a fishermen's paradise with small, simple cottages strung out along the water front. When it started to become elegant, we do not know, but as we drove down the one narrow street, houses to one side, the river to the other, we could hardly credit what 30 years had done—the fine houses that had arrived, with their own landing stages, beautifully and expensively attuned to water, the boats, all colour, paint and sparkle.

We were looking for a cottage we had known then, no longer a single-storeyed river cottage now but **The Poop,** the double-storeyed house with the nautical air that everybody stops to admire, as famous, as studied and perfected a 'sea home' as anything could be. It was the home of Port Elizabeth's well-known architect, Mr Herbert McWilliams, and businessman Mr Albert Milde, as a *cordon bleu* chef and maker of fine parties also famous.

Herbert McWilliams had designed and built the house himself 40 years before; through the years he had altered it, and both men had filled it with treasures they had collected on their travels. Outside there were retaining walls of smooth stones from the river, terraces and little gardens, and a small memorable scene—the lead figure of a girl, backed by the dense dune bush and overhung by the fat, furry, grey leaves of a Madagascan kalanchoe. It faced the silver water of the estuary, and as we looked at it we knew that, however classic in form and spirit, it had been made for just this southern scene.

It was not a house and garden, however beautiful, that had brought us here. Herbert McWilliams is not only architect but artist—he was an official war artist in World War II—and is also famous yacht-designer and racer. He represented South Africa at the Olympic Games in 1948, and has designed well-known types of racing yachts. Inevitably the theme of sea and ships runs through the home, and it was a nautical treasure we had come to see, the figurehead of *H.M.S. Medusa*, Nelson's flagship, which stands at the entrance to the house. There are other figureheads, one from the *Queen Adelaide*, found in a back yard in Knysna, one of the Duke of Wellington, which had come from a small ship and been discovered in Berlin, but it is the *Medusa* figurehead, white figure entwined with golden snakes, that is the prize.

Of all the things we had seen along this historic coast, this was the one with the most immediate sense of history. It had been found by Mr McWilliams in a junk shop in Norfolk, authenticated by the Maritime Museum at Greenwich, and repainted in the original colours of white and gold. People sometimes think it an astonishing thing to find at the mouth of a little river in Southern Africa more than 9 000 kilometres from English shores. In a way it is not: British sea relics lie across the oceans. As we left, we reached up and touched Medusa's serpents— respectfully—for luck and for history too.

Fifteen kilometres further on, we entered **Port Elizabeth** itself. We had known it well once upon a time as a city of steep hills, narrow streets and traffic hazards; now we sailed *over* the streets, narrow as ever, and the house-tops on fly-overs which were part of the city's new freeway system, Settlers' Way.

The wind was blowing as of old. We were certain that it had blown for Dias, for the Dutch sailors who came later and planted their beacon at the mouth of the little stream, the Baakens or Beacon River: for the British who built the fort to guard its mouth, for the Settlers of 1820 who founded the town, for every occasion in its story. Along with the sea, the steep hills up which generations had panted, and the Horse Memorial high above the harbour, it *was*, for us, Port Elizabeth.

A few things, like the Campanile near the sea, were the same, but most had changed. In front of the City Hall was something new, a stone pillar topped with a cross, which was a replica of the Dias Cross at Kwaai Hoek that Axelson had found. It had been hewn from the same quarry in Portugal as the original cross, and presented to the city by the Portuguese Government in 1954.

We climbed up on to the **Donkin Reserve,** the big, open, grassy spot on the slopes of the hill which from the sea looks like a green handkerchief between 'town' and the residential area above it. When we turned and faced the sea, clutching our hair and dark glasses as the wind hit us, there far over to our right—out of sight but still intact, we knew—was **Fort Frederick** overlooking the Baakens River mouth, which had been built by the British forces in 1799 to guard landing place and water supply. It is the oldest British building anywhere in the Eastern Cape, and like so many names here, it has a royal ring—it was named after Frederick, Duke of York.

As we stood here on the grass, we looked down on a modern harbour, which was third largest in South Africa, with all modern amenities. As children, we had known the wood and iron jetties that had pushed out into the sea, from which we had caught tugs that carried passengers to the ships lying far out. We had been lucky. Those Settlers who reached the shore in 1820 had ventured from their ships in surf boats, and from these had been carried through the waves by the soldiers. How the other soldiers had managed we did not know, but it was legend that the Highlanders had proudly carried the 'Scotch folk' ashore without wetting the sole of a shoe!

Sir Rufane Donkin had been the Acting-Governor at the time. This grassy place had been set aside in memory of his young wife Elizabeth, the eldest daughter of Dr George Markham, Dean of York, and the stone pyramid next to which we stood had been built in her memory. Elizabeth had been 27 when in 1818 she died in India of fever, and Sir Rufane was still mourning her deeply two years later at Algoa Bay. He had not let grief swamp his duty to the Settlers—his kindness was remembered through generations—but here he had done something, in erecting this memorial, to assuage his grief. We turned and read the inscription.

'To the memory of one of the most perfect of human beings, who has given her name to the town below.'

A lighthouse stands next to the memorial now; otherwise, as Donkin stipulated, no buildings have intruded on to the open space.

Below us reared up the quite startlingly ugly red brick **Campanile,** which had been built in 1923 to commemorate the coming of the Settlers, and to mark the spot where they landed. With relief we turned our eyes back to the Reserve itself. We walked past a group of little boys flying kites that were careering to the heavens, and on the northern side came to Donkin Street, the terrace of small, charming old houses that are now a national monument. Beyond it was **Upper Hill Street** which we remembered as a length of derelict old houses: it was this no longer, but a street of fascinating little Settler homes in the process of being carefully restored. One, with sash windows and pink shutters, was 'The Sir Rufane Donkin Rooms', one of the city's most popular restaurants. Their food, including Prince Alfred broth and Lord Charles coffee, was—we knew—famous.

We turned back to No 7 Castle Hill Street, on the south side of the Reserve. This, the oldest home still standing in the city, had been built in 1827 by the first Colonial Chaplain, the Rev F. McCleland, and was now an historical museum of great charm, and a fine example of a Settler town house.

We paid a pilgrimage before we left this part of the city to see again the **Horse Memorial** which stands now, no longer at the entrance to St George's Park as we remembered it of old, but in Cape Road near its junction with Russell Road. It was the work of Joseph Whitehead and was erected, by public subscription, in memory of the thousands of horses that died in the Anglo-Boer War. It is a famous statue—it is said to be one of only two of its kind in the world—and has always been a city sight. We thought now as we looked at it, that there was something about the figure of the kneeling British soldier and the horse, bending its head to drink, that had the perennial ability to touch hearts: doubtless other generations as well would also equate this with Port Elizabeth.

This is an old city as South African cities go, yet unlike Cape Town, it seems very much of the present. Not that it forgets its old glories. In 1852 there was Peard, the most flamboyant salesman South Africa had ever known—later in Italy in the 1860s to be 'Garibaldi's Englishman' —but now representative of American Colonel Colt, selling the new revolving pistols, the Colts, to military and frontiersmen to win the Eighth Kaffir War. He held a great pistol competition in the Baakens River valley, to which everyone came—and beat the lot. Thereafter the Frontier Armed and Mounted Police, to a man, were armed with Colts! The first diamond auction in the country was held here in 1869: the first shipment abroad of gold was from the harbour in 1874: the first cricket test in South Africa was held here in 1889, when Sir Aubrey Smith (later of film fame) captained the British team, the first Rugby test in 1891.

Looking at Port Elizabeth, it was easy to understand the gold and diamonds, for this was one of the big industrial and commercial cities, and the biggest wool centre as well—those industrial areas had mushroomed since we knew the city last. We did not, however, spend any time with them, but headed for the sea.

Not for a moment can anyone forget this is a sea town—even in bed

The great herds of game as Thomas Baines saw them in the 1850s

A typical small-town donkey-cart

Overleaf   Four hazards of the road

it is about one with the fog horns blaring their drama. It has a true sea history, with its share of tragedy, like that of 31st August 1902, when—in a great south-west gale—19 ships at anchorage were wrecked, one of the greatest disasters in South African maritime history. There have been many other wrecks here and in the waters close about, and wreck and salvage have been a perennial conversation piece for as long as we remember. In January 1977 two young Port Elizabeth divers, David Allen and Gerry van Niekerk, sparked a new salvage adventure when they sighted a cannon in the waters off the city. It was one of many more that they and their helpers located, massive bronze hulks up to four metres long, rescued and brought by trawler to the city. They had belonged to the Portuguese galleon, *Sacramento*, that was wrecked on the rocks near Port Elizabeth in 1647.

It is on a different sea that Port Elizabeth bases its holiday fame today, seas breaking on to wide gently-sloping beaches, which draw holiday-makers by the many thousand, including kings and queens. Humewood, with its beaches, lies a little south of the city proper, and at one of them, King's Beach, the British Royal Family swam in 1947.

The most famous sight along Humewood beachfront is the **Oceanarium** with its performing dolphins. The 'new' Snake Park, Museum and Tropical House are part of the complex but dwarfed by the Oceanarium's pleasures: these include many things beside the dolphins. However, at 11 a.m., and at 3.30 p.m. when the dolphins perform, it is here that everyone gathers.

The seas around the South African coast are dolphin waters. Most people know them, often in large schools, gambolling far out to sea, or their black fins tearing through the water, but it is only of later years that they have learnt to call them dolphins instead of porpoises. Porpoises, the Oceanarium has taught everyone, are creatures with flat square teeth of northern seas, while these are true dolphins, warm water-loving, with cone-like pointed teeth.

Dolphins in general have received a great deal of publicity of recent years because of their intelligence, memory, friendliness and incredible echo perception, in every way showing clearly they are not fish but mammals of the sea. From ancient times there have been stories of dolphins that have helped drowning men and befriended others. In 1972 there was South Africa's own story of the Pretoria girl, Yvonne Vladislavich, survivor of a ski-boat disaster between Inhaca Island and Lourenço Marques, who was helped by dolphins while swimming for her life. They swam alongside her, shoving their noses, she said later, under her body when she sank under the water, and they saved her from drowning.

Such things even at the start made the Oceanarium dolphins of particular interest: and during the years that they have been performing there, they have made themselves, with immense showmanship and good humour, stars of the first order.

They have taught people so much in the last almost two decades that it is difficult to remember how little was originally known about them. Mrs Muriel Rowe, formerly Assistant Curator, records in her *They Came from the Sea*, how in the beginning she thought she heard birds chirping, only to find it was dolphins speaking to one another: the staff knows a good deal more about dolphin communication now. They know first-hand, also, of their high intelligence and of the rapport that can develop between dolphin and man (or woman).

All those old dolphin legends seem very close as people watch them here. Some years nearly half a million men, women and children visit them. This is a vast number for South Africa, and it is clear the dolphins give their audiences a good deal more than a mere circus act. At the moment, a new American trainer has the dolphins in hand and there appears to be something of a hiatus in the performance: everyone waits anxiously to see the outcome.

Out along the Humewood road is the railway station and starting point of the world's most unique train, the **Apple Express.** Nowhere else is there anything quite like it, the narrow (2 ft) gauge toy working train that runs from the city inland through the apple orchards of the Long Kloof Valley to its terminus at Avontuur 285 kilometres away.

A little steam engine pulls the Lilliputian carriages: these sparkle with care, for the staff adore their little train, giving to the odd narrow carriages the sort of devotion that is usually reserved for vintage cars. Because the coaches are so narrow, the conductor swings his way along *outside* on a narrow wooden platform to collect tickets.

During the season, the Express makes a Saturday excursion returning the same day, and during the remainder of the week carries out the more prosaic task of hauling fruit and vegetables to Port Elizabeth. Those Saturday trips are made by steam engine fans from every corner of the world. Of course nobody thought of fans when the narrow-gauge line was build in 1902: then it was a matter of expediency, for the Cape Colony could not afford the standard 3 ft 6 in. gauge.

Part of the pleasure of the train ride is the country through which the Express runs, scrub and forest, orchards and mountains. This is part of the pleasure of Port Elizabeth generally, for it has a hinterland which is easily accessible and is of beauty and interest—Uitenhage, the citrus orchards of the Sundays River Valley, the Addo Elephant National Park, the forests and mountain views of the Suurberg, and the Karoo beyond; and to the north-east Grahamstown and the Settler country.

Seawards is Algoa Bay. When Dias sailed through here 470 years ago, he landed on a rocky islet in the bay, thick with sea lions and birds—Axelson says Dias and his party pushed them aside and that they made more noise than the crowd at a bullfight. The men raised a wooden cross here, under which they celebrated mass, and named the islet Ilheu da Cruz, today's St Croix.

What the party heard were Jackass Penguins, and these tame, engaging birds are still the most remarkable things on the island. They have a special place in South African ornithology because they were the first bird species to be recorded in some detail—Vasco da Gama saw them near Mossel Bay west of Port Elizabeth in 1497, 'birds as large as ducks but unable to fly, and braying like asses'. They breed only round the South African coast, and are considered today an endangered species: 150 years ago there were millions. Epicures helped in the decline, for the pale green jelly of the boiled eggs was rated a delicacy.

The **Bird Island** group—guano islands where the gannets breed—lies farther to the east. Until recently, there was a manually operated lighthouse here and a tug from Port Elizabeth paid a monthly visit to them. Although this is no longer so, the group was in the news recently, not because of birds, but because of seals which breed extensively on the islands.

A violent gale washed away a number of seal pups, casting them up along the shores as far east as Port Alfred, still living but facing death from starvation—some new-born, others up to eight weeks old, all of them still of suckling age. Their plight was seen from an Air Force helicopter, and the Port Elizabeth Museum alerted. The director, Dr John Wallace, contacted South African Air Force headquarters in Pretoria, and the hunt was on. Two official helicopters went up and down the 200 kilometre coastline airlifting the stranded babes back to their home islands. On land, people turned out along the beaches, hunting the castaways and rushing them to the Oceanarium at Port Elizabeth to be specially fed before being dropped back by the helicopters into the sea off the islands. From here the bereft parent seals watched the helicopters hovering and dropping their dark bundles, one by one. The crews said later that the animals guessed almost at once what it was all about, dashing out to guide the pups home, and at the end of the lift, it was clear that—to the adult seals—helicopters meant simply pups come home.

We left Port Elizabeth and set off one autumn day westwards along N2, passing the turn-outs to Schoenmakerskop and Sea View, with their rocks and pools. A turn-off to the sea led to Van Staden's River Mouth, where the sand dunes are famous, but we passed this to take the road to the left farther on marked Van Staden's Pass—there was no notice to show this was the way to the **Van Staden's Wild Flower Reserve**—but it was, and finally we came to this fine place of hills, trees, flowers and birds. It was here, in a grassy place between the forest trees, that we for a moment saw a blue duiker or bloubok, the smallest antelope of all, the size of a hare, with a dark pointed face and big ears.

We turned back to the main road, about a kilometre further on passing over the spectacular new Van Staden's bridge across the gorge, leaving the branch road to the Gamtoos River Mouth behind us and taking instead the turn-off to Jeffrey's Bay in the great half moon scoop of St Francis Bay. In May it was out of season so that the little village was empty of holiday-makers, but the two things for which it was famous were before us, the beach and rolling breakers that make this one of the best surfing beaches in the world, and the multitude of shells. A few years before, the world surfing championships had been held here: as for the shells, we knew them as a sort of legend. We had come, in particular, to see the **Charlotte Kritzinger Shell Museum,** housed in the library, and to locate 'the shell woman', who made the shell ornaments to be bought as far away as Johannesburg.

The museum was a disappointment to us, who had been expecting a fine display of local specimens. The shell woman, however, made up for it. She lived in a cottage at 42 Diazweg—Diaz Road—looking appropriately enough onto the beach. We knocked and the door was opened by a Coloured girl. For some moments we stood still, so great was our surprise. It had appeared quite an ordinary-looking little house: but this room within was a museum of the fine and precious, stuffed with yellowwood and stinkwood furniture, silver and plate, Voortrekker and 1820 Settler relics. In the middle of it was Mrs Emma Wait, the shell woman, as the eldest daughter of Manie Maritz, one-time Boer leader, a bit of history herself. Her large, handsome, lively face burst into smiles. Shells? She would show us. Yes, she had been working with them for nearly 30 years. Coloured women collected them for her on the beaches, and she had a staff of other women to help her with the ornaments.

She had that day finished an order for 400 dachshunds for sale in the Carlton Centre in Johannesburg, all as big as matchboxes, charming little bits of nonsense with screw shells for bodies, trumpets for ears, and auger shells for the long personality tails. She took two and pressed them into our hands: those were for our interest.

We left unwillingly. Back on N2, we set our faces towards the Tsitsikama. On our left were more branch roads to the sea, to the swan reserve at the Seekoei River estuary and to the Cape St Francis lighthouse, the bay with its huge breakers, and to Sea Vista, the sleek monied holiday village with its thatched houses and great views.

On our right, beyond Humansdorp, was a little road past Kareedouw linking our southern with a northern road more or less parallel with it—that road was the Long Kloof, the famous apple valley. We turned up it briefly for the fun of it, through tall proteas with pale flower heads, on to this famous old Cape highway that we were to meet again on our travels further west. Our satisfaction was complete when we saw the Apple Express itself. Like every other motorist, we gave it a big wave, and it replied with a toy toot as we passed by.

CHAPTER THIRTEEN

The Tsitsikama

❧

Before us stretched the **Garden Route,** perhaps South Africa's best-known tourist road, although where exactly it begins and where it ends is a matter of individual choice. Jose Burman, whose *Guide to the Garden Route* slips happily into pocket and bag, sees it as the whole stretch between Port Elizabeth and Cape Town. For us, and most others, it is the country from a little east of Storm's River to Mossel Bay in the west, bounded on the north by the mountains, on the south by the sea. It is a land on its own, which in spite of its highway, its tourists, its crowded beauty spots, is a wild place of forest and shore, perhaps the last place in the world where a fisherman can find a leopard's paw print on his familiar sands.

The mountains to the immediate north are, from east to west, the Tsitsikama, the Outeniqua and the Langeberg, and from the moist southern slopes of these the forests—the deep green, impenetrable wild forests—sweep down to the sea. So also do the rivers pour down in the deep chasms they have cut through ages, gorges that once cut off the land between and behind them from the outside world so deep were they, so precipice-like their walls, so dense the forest in them.

It was the forest and the gorges that robbed this mild, well-watered coastal land of a full early history, for although the bold and curious did venture here, many more avoided it, seeking homes and travelling roads in easier country. Yet it was on this coast that White men first set foot in South Africa. On a February day in 1488 Bartolomeu Dias, on his way to plant his cross at Kwaai Hoek, cast anchor off Mossel Bay and sent a party of men ashore. Perhaps—as Herodotus has it—the Phoenicians knew this coast more than 1 000 years before Dias did, but it was Dias who left the first record.

Nine years later there was a 'first' of another kind. Vasco da Gama, the Portuguese sailor who found the sea route to India that Dias had yearned to do, stopped here and 'bought' a bull from the Hottentots—he paid three bracelets for it. It was the first bit of business transacted by a European on South African soil.

This was an historical titbit that had always amused us because the one thing that visitors seldom think of on this southern coast is 'business': they come to it for other things. We came one March day first of all for the forests, the scrub and the streams, hoisting ourselves and our goods up the steep track to the Formosa Mountain Hut in the Lottering Forest in the foothills of the Tsitsikama Mountains.

We were there by invitation of Gwen Skinner—known all over Port Elizabeth and its hinterland for her knowledge of mountains, trees and flowers—and her husband, Len, both mountaineers; and with them we explored the forests and the *fynbos* around, the *fynbos* that is the richest scrub vegetation in the world, and on those bright scented days when we took the footpaths through it, the most fascinating too. Every evening we swam in a brown pool of the Lottering River below the hut, all set about with red watsonia blooms, and then sat about a camp fire looking at the mountain peak, the Grenadier's Cap, and listening to the nightjars. But with the first morning light we would be off.

The southern indigenous forests may be neither as tropical or as rich in different tree species as those to the north, but—stretching somewhat brokenly from Humansdorp to Mossel Bay, a distance of nearly 250 kilometres—they are both the best known and best loved. Here are the famous trees around which the early colonists built their lives, growing straight and tall, packed so closely together that it is often only along a forest path or stream that one can see the shape of the crowns or glimpse the foliage, making a world of trunks, bark and lichens, of fallen leaves, with the scarlet of the wild grape here and there, and the blue of a *Streptocarpus* flower.

Everyone wants above all to know the stinkwood which furnishes the most beautiful and expensive wood in South Africa, and the yellow-woods, often the tallest trees. In both the Tsitsikama and Knysna forests to the west, the trees in certain areas are marked, and it is possible, with the keys provided, to identify them easily.

In a few hours we exhausted the official forest sights in the **Tsitsikama Forest National Park.** We had driven westwards over the **Paul Sauer Bridge** that spans the Storm's River, pausing (in this world of natural wonders) to admire a man-made beauty. Ricardo Morandi of Rome had built it, constructing two great halves which, on hinges, were lowered from the sides of the chasm to meet in precision in the centre. It is a single-span, just over 190 metres long, the highest in Southern Africa, unique and unbeatable of its kind.

The forest within the Park, known as De Plaat, lies on the northern, the landward side, of the national road close to the bridge. We walked the trails within it, Tree Fern, Bushpig and Big Tree—the Big Tree is an Outeniqua or Common yellow-wood, *Podocarpus falcatus*, splendid here as elsewhere in the forests.

Tsitsikama means 'clear water' or 'abundant water', and we soon understood why, for everywhere, it seemed to us, were streams and pools in which every pebble, every leaf, showed clearly. The soft brown colour of the water was not 'dirt' we were assured over and over, but iron oxide and vegetable matter: if dirt it had been, we would not have minded—it looked like the mountains whence it came and the forest floor that fed it, and it felt like silk.

It was not only in the forest here we found it, but south of the national road in the **Tsitsikama Coastal National Park,** where the rivers cut their way through gorges to the sea, and the paths crossed streams and skirted pools that we could never pass by. We always paused at least to touch the water, and this was one of the greatest pleasures of the long days.

This coastal park, quite rightly, receives a good deal of publicity. It is a young park still, not two decades old, and was the first coastal national park in Africa. It stretches along some 70 kilometres of shoreline in a narrow band between the two Groot Rivers, the Humansdorp Grootrivier in the east to the one of the same name near Plettenberg Bay in the west, and consists, not only of shoreline and of the ocean 800 metres out to sea, but on the landward side of a narrow coastal plain and the cliffs that border it. So steep and tall are they, up to 250 metres high, that they effectively cut off the shore from the busy life inland and the Tsitsikama Mountains to the north: fishermen know the few narrow paths leading down the cliffs, but motor-cars reach the sea only along the road to the Storm's River mouth, and it is here that the only rest camp is situated.

Much of the Park, so close to the busiest tourist route in the country, is therefore as remote as a 3 000-metre peak: those who want to see it in its entirety see it on foot and the going is often difficult. Round the camp are a number of short trails, easily managed and of interest, but it is the long trail from east to west, the **Otter Trail** that is famous, the great challenge and the thrill.

The trail follows the shore as far as possible but is not straight or level or always open to the sky. Where no path can go along the shore, it creeps upward to the coastal plateau, dips again and climbs again; sometimes it is a tunnel through the trees. There are streams to cross and rivers to wade or swim; and there are four rough shelters at strategic points, which mean at least a roof overhead, no small thing in Tsitsikama rain.

It takes two to four days to walk, is only for the active, and should be planned ahead. Only a certain number of people are allowed on the trail at any one time.

We came to the Trail twice, once in March and once in May, and both times we lingered first at the camp, walking the short trails around, studying the open-air museum, letting the forest and the sea seep slowly into our bones. At the mouth of the Storm's River we rode in a boat up the river, with perpendicular rock faces enclosing us on every hand, the dark crevices lit by the flowers of a white *Haemanthus*. We were too late to see the George lilies, the red beauties, that are a sight in summer time, and too early to see the winter aloes, so that this was a dark journey over brown water to caves where bats lived.

On the path back we skirted a cave, the home by the sea that the Strandlopers—those early Stone Age men of the Cape coast—had used once upon a time. This must then have been as hospitable a shore as now, for all along it have been found the signs of ancient man, not ape-man but later people who left in the caves of this southern coast middens which tell us today something of the story of their lives. In places they left their bones as well, the remains of skeletons ceremoniously buried, beads of ostrich eggshell, red ochre, and sometimes painted grave stones.

On the rocks there were anglers, for this coast as far westwards as Mossel Bay is an angler's paradise. In our rucksacks, we had a book on the fishes of the Park, which we had bought at the restaurant in the camp, a book written by Professor Smith—of Coelacanth fame—and his wife, Margaret, full of marvels. More than 400 species of fish had been found in the sea fronting the Park, they wrote. As we read it, we longed to accost every angler to ask for which of these romantic Smith creatures he was trying.

Was it a red steenbras, weighing 45 kg, in deep water off the rocks? We knew the reputation of this great glowing creature as a formidable fighter: from the Smiths we learned that it was reputed to charge even a boat. Or was it perhaps a *dageraad*, a dawnfish, with the bright dawn colours flowing over its body; or a huge musselcracker with a nose that gave it, in the Smiths' words, the look of 'an old man who likes his glass'; or rockfishes like the dassie from the Atlantic that, small as it is, is a doughty fighter; or a *galjoen*, found only in South African waters, that is a fighter too; or an orange-scarlet roman to dazzle the eye?

The ocean before us was bluer than the Mediterranean. It was also, we knew, a special sea with special attributes, cooler than that off the east coast, warmer than that off the western shores, which were cold with their Benguela ocean river flowing offshore along it. It was an in-between sea, we found as we read our book over and over, with a rare fish life: although there were fishes from the far east and west, almost half the species here belonged only to South African waters and were, so to say, true South Africans.

In these Tsitsikama seas were almost everything one hoped for, and sometimes fish one did not; fish with gaudy colours and those with strange shapes; salmon, scarlet and blue fish; striped fish, rosy fish with fins like butterflies; fish with jaws like spears or humps on their foreheads or like balloons or big triangles of flesh and venom. There were even fish with beaks, like the *kraaibek*, the adult teeth of which were fused together. Professor Smith wrote that he used to receive letters from anglers saying that they had caught a thing that was a cross between a fish and a bird: a *kraaibek* it always was.

We knew of the sharks out to sea, grey sharks and man-eaters up to nine metres long, that could easily swallow a man whole according to the Smiths: and there were all the fish that dealt in poison in order to survive. There were those that stung, like the stingray of the sea bottom armed with spines covered with poisonous slime, and electric rays, swollen, brown and spotted, that could give a powerful shock. There was the turkey fish, striped and opalescent with fins like turkeys' tails—a prick from one of those ethereal spines, wrote the Smiths, caused agony and a dangerous fall in blood pressure. And sea-barbels with hidden spines having downward-pointing teeth and venomous slime (a stab could send a man demented), the barbel eel, and the *blaasop*—the blow-up—known by almost everybody, that swells itself up into a spiky balloon. Its flesh contained a poison which, said the Smiths again, had effects like the toadstool, causing a dreadful death, and it had enough to kill a dozen men. We ourselves knew too well the jellyfish, with which we had rubbed shoulders often when swimming in the sea—its tentacles had stinging cells—and bluebottles, the little transparent mauvy-blue balloons that trailed stinging cells—*their* poison was akin to cobra venom.

The fish that were pure delight, small and neat and sweet, were the *klip* fishes of the rock pools. Those pools are one of the great delights of the Park, and it is not only children who love them but adults, with the same aloof dedicated expressions as fishermen, 'sea expressions', we called them. We watched them hunting the flowers of the sea, the sea-anemones, only for the pleasure of gazing at them—red, scarlet, yellow, purple, green—with tentacles like narrow petals; and starfishes coloured like red sealing-wax, crabs and sponges, sea cucumbers that were not vegetable at all but animal, and sea slugs too glamorous to bear the name of slug.

There were all the common things like periwinkles and winkles, and lower down on the beach barnacles, mussels and oysters; limpets clinging to the rocks from high to low water marks; and near the lowest water mark things like venus ears—when we found the shells on the beach we saw the inside was lined with mother-of-pearl. If we had known enough, every single thing would have been wonderful. Dr G. A. Robinson, Nature Conservator of the Park, described the barnacle as 'an animal lying on its back, its head firmly cemented in place, and the feathery ends kicking the food into its mouth', upon which this ordinary little creature suddenly flowered for us. Dr Robinson, incidentally, together with R. M. Tietz, wrote the official book *Tsitsikama Shore*, which is as full of fascinations as the Smiths' book is.

Even the spiders were special, for they were able to live beneath the sea in the intertidal zones. Those we saw when the tide was low, were able to stay alive for the oddest, most practical of reasons—they carried *air* below their *hair*. This was thick, we found, with a water-repellant coat and enclosed a layer of air. Into this the oxygen from the water was absorbed—and this was how the Tsitsikama spiders breathed below high tides.

We could have spent days at the camp, soaking up such details, studying the open air museum, reading the other handbooks on the Park—there was one on the seaweeds by Professor S. C. Seagrief and another on the plants by Dr Courtenay-Latimer (again of Coelacanth fame) and C. G. Smith—with luck talking to Dr Robinson himself: but the Otter Trail lay ahead, and soon we started on it.

From the first moment when, near the camp, we saw the otter sign, an otter eating a fish, the day was good. We took the path past it through the low curry bush, with the sea on our left—there was an underwater trail here—and dassies sitting on orange-lichened rocks, past midden remains, along a beach path, and a forest path, to a waterfall and a pool. We swam here, then took the path onwards to the first rest hut, Ngubo, on a hillside overlooking the sea: it was all set about with lion's tail, curry bush and arum lilies, and in the swamp below there were fireflies when dark came.

Ngubo was eight kilometres from camp. Further, on the next 60 kilometres, were Scott's shelter on the Geelhoutboom River—where the fishing was especially good—the Oakhurst shelter west of the Lottering River, Andre's hut on the Klip River, and finally the Groot River estuary and the wide sands of Nature's Valley.

Taken all in all, it was—we thought at the end—the best thing that South Africa could offer the reasonably active. Hugh Taylor of the Botanical Research Institute, who walked the trail recently, thought it was the wildest of the wilderness trails completed up till then. We thought it was the most beautiful and exciting path we had ever seen, with the beauty of a bare, bright, empty world, ocean and rocks and shadowed paths where the trees met the sea, and the excitements of rivers to wade, pools to swim in, cliffs to climb, and all the wild things of the wayside, drenched with the smell of *fynbos*, of forest mould and salt, and sounding with waves: the physical effort itself was a challenge that was good to meet.

The Elandsbos mouth was especially good with its little beach without a footprint on it. We longed for an otter's spoor—otters that gave the trail its name—but although we were sure they swam in the creek above us and hunted here, there was no sign of them. On the seaward side was a little bay, on the landward the river with brown water and green mossy stones. We picnicked on the sand, and then with our trouser pants rolled above our knees, we waded through the river. We had timed it well. It was low tide: at high tide people swim this with their packs upon their heads and their cameras and binoculars in plastic bags.

As we climbed out on the farther side, we heard a shout behind us, and there was a young man grinning and splashing and hurrying to catch us up. He was very thin and brown with a limp beard and moustache, and he had a bit of yellow string tied round his forehead. His luggage was wrapped in a bit of leather (from Afghanistan) and he carried a leather water bottle (from Spain). His name was Gregory, and he was walking 1 000 kilometres along the coast, his food in his bundle—it was mealiemeal, raisins and dried beans. We offered to send a photograph of him to his family, if the gremlins left the camera alone, and he answered seriously, 'There are no devils on the Otter Trail'.

Len Skinner had said an hour before, as we had looked down over the forest and sea, 'It's a well-favoured place', suggesting not only beauty but grace. He and Gregory were saying the same thing in different words.

On the high land east of the Bloukrans River we spent our best hour of all. We had pushed along the path through grass and the purple-pink bells of ericas, when we came to a pool only a few paces from the trail yet hidden from it by a pile of rock—we would have passed it by if Gwen Skinner had not known it. It lay along the top of the cliff, a long deep brown pool fed at one end by a trickling stream, at the other dropping down the cliff-side to the rocks far below. We swam in it for a long time. First we thought only of the water, but as we floated our eyes began to take in other things, ericas, agapanthus and everlastings in bloom, a deep rose crassula, and blue lobelias in the crannies, grass with long golden plumes swinging over the water and a passerina weeping from a rock. Seaward there was a wall of rock just higher than the water dropping steeply to the sea, and the empty sea itself stretching away to Antarctica.

Except for Gregory and the anglers on the rocks, we saw no human being on the trail. The otters too eluded us entirely, and so did the bushbuck, the bush pigs and blue duiker. There were dassies, baboons, monkeys and birds (200 bird species have been recorded here). The gannets were swooping but if the little Arctic tern was there, we did not see it. A dead one was picked up on the trail near the Bloukrans River recently, which had been ringed in Denmark six months before. Nor did we hear the wild cry of the fish eagle, which would have fitted ocean and cliffs so well, and which we expected to hear—the first one to be described came from the Keurbooms River not far away.

We were too early for the Southern Right Whales, which often visit the Tsitsikama waters in the winter and early spring. Nor did we have a chance to 'hunt' the seaweeds, some of which, like the fish, belonging only to this southern coast. But as we left the Park we met Professor Seagrief. Next time, we said, we would spend more time with his treasures. He opened our copy of *The Seaweeds of the Tsitsikama Coastal National Park* and wrote below the note that seaweeds could be collected only with special permission, 'Collect at Low Spring tide when the moon is full', which—with the salt still in our bones—we thought the most glamorous invitation we had ever had.

That name, the Garden Route, was, we thought, as we travelled westwards along it, not really appropriate, for although its flowers were many and gorgeous—the drifts and clumps of watsonias in particular—this was not a landscape carefully groomed; the gum and pine trees were regimented in huge plantations for use not looks, and the indigenous forest was too wild. But if 'garden' stood for beauty and for plants, then a garden in a sense it was. We had two passes to cross before we reached Plettenberg Bay, deep gashes through the plateau, and both were famous for their tree-made beauty.

First was the **Bloukrans Pass** with its precipices and its huge yellow-wood trees festooned with ghostly Old Man's Beard, and the big Cape chestnuts that in summer bloom colour the ravine pink and mauve. In the **Groot River Pass** there above all the tree strelitzias with their big, broad, untidy banana leaves, the *piesangs* from which the Piesangs River took its name. All through South Africa, and the Cape in particular, British royal families have been impressed on the most unlikely things by the most unlikely names, and

here were the wild bananas bearing the name of Charlotte of Mecklen-
burg-Strelitz, wife of George III.

It would have been a good deal more appropriate to have named them
Bainia after the man who made this Tsitsikama and Outeniqua world
first known, the road-maker, Thomas Bain, who in the 1880s took the
first roads eastwards through the towering forests and across the
chasms: the road we were on was more or less his route. We were to
know Bain, and his father Andrew, a good deal more intimately when
we travelled the inland roads, but we thought of them here with due
appreciation. Bain's work, we remembered, had been made somewhat
easier by one of the greatest disasters the Cape had ever known, the
Great Fire of 1869 which had opened up the country and in which had
perished ancient forest from Swellendam to Humansdorp. We could
still see the effects of the fire as we drove. The big patches of grass and
fynbos, empty of trees, that we passed had before 1867 probably been
forest.

When we crossed the Keurbooms River, we left the Tsitsikama
behind us to enter **Outeniqualand.** The river takes its name from a
wild tree, the keurboom or 'pick of the trees', a not altogether fanciful
name for in its pinky-mauve pea scented bloom it is one of the fine
sights of Cape mountain and forest. Its generic name, *Virgilia*, honours
the poet Virgil, who certainly never dreamed of these forest slopes, so
there they were—whoever could have dreamed it—Charlotte and
Virgil cheek by jowl!

Outeniqua is a Hottentot name meaning 'man carrying honey', and
considering the flowers and the 'thousand swarms of bees' the early
travellers saw here, it was a good name. If it signifies plenty, it is still
apt. Like the Tsitsikama, this land overflows with beauties—forest,
shore, estuaries, lakes—to which men have added many sophisti-
cations as well.

On our left was the estuary of the Keurboom River, the wide lagoon
and the salt marshes, which bring birds and ornithologists in numbers,
and the popular **Keurbooms Strand,** which was once known as the
Place of Little Shells, Schulpie Plaats. From near the Dunes Caravan
Park a path leads to the Matjes River Cave, one of the most famous of
these coastal caves to have been the home of early man, and now a
national monument. We turned to our right up the river to the 'public
resort', a term so interwoven in our minds with crowds and litter that
we could hardly believe this one was true, with its space and neatness,
and its wild trees reflected in the quiet waters of the river. It was run
by the province, and very well too.

At **Plettenberg Bay** we halted. To Transvaalers this is Plet, a

Mecca to which they stream in summer holidays, when in a week the population of the little town leaps from 1 000 to 16 000, and the 4-million rand, three-star Beacon Island Hotel overflows. This, one of South Africa's best-known hotels, is new, modern, expensive, slick and stunning in its way. Yet what makes it most memorable is that it is part of the old immutable things of this coast, the sea and the rocks. The dining-room, restaurant, lounge and bar are suspended over the sea; and even those who never choose to *feel* the salt spray, can sit here enjoying the sound of waves on the rocks nearby and spray on the closed windows.

The island on which the hotel stands, joined to the mainland by a tarmac road, was in fact as well as in name the site of a navigational beacon built here first in 1772: by its ships' masters set their chronometers. The present one, outside the hotel's north walls, is almost a century old. A big old iron pot in the hotel grounds is a sea relic too: in it whaling crews cooked whale blubber over a wood fire perhaps 200 years ago.

The first white people to know the bay in historic times were again the Portuguese, who called it first the Bay of the Lagoons and later Bahia Formosa, the beautiful bay. What they left for us was the name Formosa, not now the bay but the peak that is the highest point in the Tsitsikama range, and can be seen from the village. The Dutch who came later left a more concrete reminder. In 1779 Governor Joachim van Plettenberg erected a stone of possession or beacon on the slope of the hill, a replica of which still stands, at the same time changing the name of the bay to Plettenberg in his own honour.

As was true of so much of the southern coast, the forest as well as the sea made history. Cape Town, by the 1780s denuded of trees, cast eyes on Outeniqualand, and to Plettenberg Bay there soon came woodcutters. The remains of the old timber store still stand near the Central Beach and are a national monument. The harbour that was planned was never a success: nevertheless over the years men hunted whales with the bay as headquarters, and over a century later a Norwegian company started a whaling station on Beacon Island. After a brief life, it closed down about 1920, its old quarters in time giving way to a boarding-house, then the first Beacon Island Hotel, and finally the new one in 1973. Today a whale (of fibre-glass) stands next to the entrance.

It is the sea and the 18 kilometres of golden sand that make the modern town. We were aware of its swimming, sunbathing, sailing, fishing, water skiing, its golf and cuisine and dancing, but that out-of-season day, when we drove through the almost deserted streets,

we were making for something new to us, the peninsula of Robberg
five kilometres long, that juts out into the sea south-west of the bay,
which it guards and protects.

Robberg—the mountain of seals—was well named, for the early
sailors and travellers noted that it was alive with the animals: its point
thrusting out into the Indian Ocean is still Cape Seal. We left the car in
a parking place high above the sea near 'the gap', from where we took
a path along the rocky tongue.

The whole peninsula is a nature reserve, for although fishing is
allowed the land itself is protected so that this today must be very
much as the Portuguese saw it, nearly 500 years ago, with its red
cliffs, its dunes and thick scrub. We climbed along a narrow path on
the cliff side overlooking the bay. Now we could see why sailors had
called it 'Formosa': there was the wide deep sweep of the bay, golden
beaches, and in the background dark forest and the blue-grey Outeni-
quas merging into the Tsitsikama Mountains. Later, we knew, the
whales from the Antarctic would come into the bay as of old to breed:
their 'blow' was a winter sight the townspeople knew well even if the
summer visitors did not.

We were too late for the red brunsvigias blooming in great patches,
so bright that people had mistaken them from afar for fires in the bush,
but the *blombos, Metalasia muricata, the* bush of the dunes, was
covered with its tight little creamy brushes and we smelt their honey
scent as we walked.

High above Seal Point, among a tumble of rocks on the cliff edge,
we made our tea. The Skinners were not mountaineers for nothing.
They made a fire between two rocks and hung the billy of water by a
shoelace from a stick—even with the wind whipping we had mugs of
tea in 15 minutes, and we drank it looking across the sea. Below us on
the rocks at the sea's edge, were anglers, trying perhaps for the *leervis*
and yellowtail for which the point was famous. Professor Smith had
thought this almost matchless as a fishing spot, for the rocks protruded
into deep water where were game fish of all kinds.

On the seaward side of Robberg there was a small peninsula known
as the Balk or **Bellows Rock** with a blow-hole some distance from the
water from where, in rough weather, comes a loud roaring sound. On
the way back, we looked towards it and saw that for a distance the
calm sea beyond was boiling with life and flashing with dolphins
leaping through the air. They were hunting a school of fish—
yellowtails, said a fisherman peering through binoculars; he could see
the blue and golden gleams.

It was near the blow-hole that Professor Smith and his wife once had an adventure that was a warning to every holiday-maker and fisherman on these rocks.

All along this coast, where the water is deep, the phenomenon is known of a big wave arising suddenly and soundlessly and sweeping away the unwary upon the rocks. Not one of the many people, Smith had warned time and again, who had been swept from the rocks had ever been saved, for the 'undertow' always sucked them down and out.

On a beautiful September day he and his wife were collecting in the rock pools on the Balk. Professor Smith had moved towards the cliff, when something, he wrote, made him look around, to see his wife, net innocently in hand, and behind her one of these terrible silent waves, 'a wall of clear deep water, at least twenty feet high'. He pointed in frenzy. She looked, threw her arms around a pinnacle of rock beside her and clung fast: the water rolled over her and fell back, and he saw her head emerge. As he gazed another monster rose and once more engulfed her; once again he saw her form appear still clinging to the rock. He rushed into the sea through the swirling water, took her hand, and they escaped together.

Year by year these big waves take their toll. The anglers on the Robberg rocks knew this coast well, we were sure, and certainly the wave as well. We wondered if Smith's *High Tide* was in their rucksacks, both for light and sombre reading: it would have been in ours.

As we drove towards Knysna, we thought of the forest as much as the sea, for this little town—even more than Plettenberg Bay—is compounded of both. The forest roads came thick and fast. There was the turn-off to the Harkerville Forest and 16 kilometres short of Knysna, we stopped at the bit of wild forest called The Garden of Eden, took a leafy walk and looked at the numbered trees. Then there was the road to Brackenhill Falls, and only three kilometres from Knysna, the road leading northwards to Prince Alfred's Pass.

There are many roads, paths and glades in the main **Knysna Forest** and in the forest areas about, most with their picnic places. We took the road to the Deep Walls Forest Station (Diepwalle Bosstasie) to the right of the main road. Only a few months before a new short trail had been opened here known as **The Elephant Walk,** and it was this we had come to see. The station itself was ringed with huge trees, looking out over forest to mountains and sea. We got our permits here, and were off along the trail as soon as we could, for we knew we would stop again and again in the forest. So we did the 9 km walk, taking nearer five hours than the official three. But who, we asked, stopping at the tree ferns, at the streams, at the lichened trunks and the moss-covered stones, and all the other wayside attractions, would march or bound through such a place?

It was a circular trail, the long route 18,2 kilometres and an alternative one 14,3 kilometres. When we did the long hop we would start at 6 a.m., we promised ourselves, and take 12 hours not six to do it, drawing out every quiet mysterious moment. For this was a forest of dimness and of secrets—all our good indigenous forests are.

We looked everywhere for a Narina trogan, that shy pigeon-sized forest dweller that everybody wants to see and rarely does: even when its quiet hooting notes sound through the forest, it is mostly invisible. Gwen Skinner had seen one in these forests, and we guessed it was creeping about the branches around us, showing off its resplendent greens and reds to the forest trees alone.

It was a good place to talk not only of the forest officers, beginning with Captain Christopher Harison, who had guarded these forests from early days, but of ornithologists, and because we were talking of the trogan, we thought of Francois le Vaillant who had christened it. He was one of our favourites, a ridiculous, flamboyant, boastful late 18th century French adventurer who journeyed through the Cape leaving a romantic highly-coloured story of his doings, but who at the same time was a true naturalist—even as we laughed, we saluted him, for with him began the history of ornithology in South Africa.

It was a jump from him to present-day C. J. Skead, the Eastern Cape ornithologist, but it was he who once told us how the tropical trogan made one half of South Africa's biggest contrast—here it was, 'where the Knysna forests sweep down to the sea', only a few yards from a truly sub-Antarctic species, the Jackass Penguin. It pleased us, sitting on the forest litter, to think we were almost at the point where ice and tropics met!

We looked for elephants as well. From time immemorial there had been elephants here, and a few, perhaps 11, still remain. The brochure that we had got at the Forest Station described, with a touch of poetry, how the elephants had trekked through here year after year to their summer pastures, and back again in autumn to their winter home, and how the remaining ones still did so. There were elephant droppings on the tracks, not steaming, we were happy to see, for these animals had a savage reputation.

There is, of course, a crop of stories about them, sometimes fearful ones. Nevertheless, the story we have always relished most was the small tranquil one of Georgina, the little daughter of Thomas Bain, the roadmaker, jolting through this forest in a wagon in the rain and watching the elephant footprints filling with water. What had her father felt about the animals? Had he felt any kinship at all? After all, man and elephants together were the greatest company of roadmakers South Africa had ever known, the elephants making roads through the forests and over the mountains with superb engineering flair, their enormous jelly-bags of pads treading with butterfly precision along the trails. Somewhere in these southern mountains a 20th century scientist had spotted an old elephant route, along the only possible path in the whole area, where the animals had grasped the roots of a big tree with their trunks and levered themselves over the rocks.

So all in all, The Elephant Walk was a good name. We could not, as we sat there talking, think of anything better to suggest the forest's history or its ancient untamed look. As for the track, it proved for us, after the Otter Trail, the most rewarding thing we saw on the whole Garden Route.

CHAPTER FOURTEEN

The Garden Route Westwards

✤

After a day in the forest, we went down to the sea. **Knysna** lies on the northern shores of a lagoon or estuary, from which there is a narrow outlet to the sea, through the two massive cliffs known as the Knysna Heads. It is an old town on a hill which Winifred Tapson, who wrote the town's story in her *Timber and Tides*, likened to a sleeping cat. It has always seemed to us that there is water everywhere, silver and pale blue in late autumn with red aloes blooming along the shores.

That day when we came into it from the east we were in search of at least a fragment of the George Rex story. George Rex, who founded the town, was an Englishman who, legend has it, was the eldest legitimate son of George III and of the young Quaker woman, Hannah Lightfoot, whom he was said to have married before Queen Charlotte, and who was 'banished' to the Cape in 1797 where he was given a Crown grant until his death on condition that he remained there unknown and undemanding.

We are told now by Pat Storrar, who did a great deal of research for her book, *George Rex, Death of a Legend*, that the story is completely without truth. Nevertheless, through the years it has burgeoned. It is one that almost every South African knows and so good that, willy nilly, it will continue to be told.

George Rex *was* Knysna. He had come to the Cape as Marshal of the High Court of Admiralty, and in 1804 settled on his farm, Melkhoutkraal, at Knysna, which became the centre of great possessions encircling the lagoon, and from here he gave a liberal hospitality to many—soldiers, governors, scientists, travellers—so that his name featured in many early journals. He sired many children, although by the end of the 19th century, the Rex name had disappeared from the district. Through the female line, however, Rex blood is widely distributed through South Africa: and even today there must be many who believe their background was a palace.

Rex's grave is much visited today. A few kilometres east of the town, near the site of the original **Melkhoutkraal,** we found a notice pointing to the left and followed a country road to the small stone-

212

walled cemetery shaded by two huge pines. There were several graves, that of George Rex, those of his son George, and his wife, Jessie, and perhaps that of a daughter—it was unmarked when we saw it. The headstone of George Rex's grave carried this inscription:

> IN MEMORY OF GEORGE REX ESQUIRE
> PROPRIETOR AND FOUNDER OF KNYSNA
> DIED 3RD APRIL 1839

There are other reminders of Rex. On the western side of the lagoon is the farm Belvidere, which originally belonged to Rex, but was later bought from him by the Scottish soldier, Captain Thomas Duthie, who married Rex's daughter, Caroline. Caroline was 17 when Duthie had visited Melkhoutkraal on leave, and they had fallen in love, and it was here they lived after they were married and founded the well-known Duthie family; and here Duthie had built the tiny exquisite Holy Trinity Church, a Norman church of sandstone and wood from the forest, which is now a national monument.

Westford lies at the foot of the Phantom Pass between Knysna and George, and this was where Rex launched his ship, *Knysna*—both brig and slipway were constructed of stinkwood. The site of the slipway is now a national monument and the table and chairs in the Knysna Divisional Council are made from the slipway beams. As for the *Knysna*, it was this ship that sailed to East London harbour in 1836 with the first cargo the port had known. She was stout and true and sailed up and down the South African coast, and then the high seas, for years: the last we knew of her was hauling coal round the coast of Wales.

There were other famous Knysna names like Newdigate and Barrington, but none was better known than Thesen, a name we associate all over the country today with fine timber and with boats. In the depression following the Danish-German war, the Thesen family decided to emigrate to New Zealand and sailed from Norway in 1869 in a schooner, *Albatros*, which had been part of their Norwegian fishing fleet: the ship was filled with Thesens, 13 of them, with a Thesen as skipper. Their first port of call was Cape Town. From here they sailed round Cape Agulhas, were caught in a storm, and returned to Table Bay for repairs—Agulhas waters have changed the course of many lives, and they made the story of the Thesens in South Africa too. In Cape Town the Thesens were offered the job of taking provisions round the coast, so the first Thesen saw Knysna and its lagoon, and that was the end of New Zealand. The rest arrived from

Cape Town in relays: and in no time the Thesens were as much part of Knysna as the Rexs.

One of those first Thesen children to arrive was Blanca; 'lily-fair', Winifred Tapson called her, who married Cape Town's young advocate, Frank Reitz, later Chief Justice and then President of the Orange Free State. Their son was the author, Deneys, whose monument stands today at Mariepskop and is part of the Transvaal Lowveld.

Albatros had a brief life, for five years after she sailed between the Knysna Heads she was lost near Cape Agulhas. Her name was triumphantly resurrected in 1971 almost 100 years later when *Albatros II*, built by the Thesens to mark the centenary of the family's arrival, won the Cape to Rio yacht race—true to tradition, a golden coin, a R1 piece, had been sealed below the mast. Knysna went mad, everyone shaking everyone else's hand, the men who had built the yacht dancing in the shed, the Coloureds dancing in the streets and shouting, 'Sy's daar'—She's there.

The Parkes, who bought the first timber mill in the heart of the little town, have a name as well known in Knysna as Thesen. The first of them arrived from England some 11 years after the Thesens, and the family has been there ever since. Their throbbing mill and the smell of sawn wood were our first memories of Knysna: we walked past their sheds again to listen to the steady familiar pulse. Then we ate oysters afterwards in a little restaurant, as every oyster-lover in Knysna does.

Afterwards we drove round the lagoon, past Leisure Island to **The Heads,** a grand sight still in spite of its urban air. The first white man to live here was a sailor, James Callender, who during the first British occupation of the Cape—a little before Rex's time—had been appointed Inspector of Government Woodlands. It was he who surveyed lagoon and coast, and saw Knysna as a harbour, and this Rex as well was to press in the years to come. In due course it did become a harbour and from early in the 19th century many boats called here, members of the Rex family acting as honorary pilots for three decades, thereafter, with a few intervals, four generations of the Benn family doing the job. For sailors, once through The Heads, it must have been an enchanted stop in the calm waters of the lagoon: but as an official harbour it lasted for only 136 years. *S.A.S. Pietermaritzburg* was the last ship to enter the port in 1953: a Benn brought it in 85 years after his great-grandfather had been officially appointed pilot.

The lagoon may no longer be a harbour but it is a playground without parallel, with some of the best boating anywhere along the coast; and sought after as well by water-skiers and fishermen. This was the place where Professor Smith, then a shrimp of a boy, caught his first fish that started him off on his long, exciting, watery way, and it was here that he first heard of the Coelacanth from Miss Courtenay-Latimer.

What did the name Knysna mean, we asked? A glance through the Knysna literature showed that everybody had their own idea, some believing that it was Hottentot meaning 'place of wood' or 'fern' or 'straight down' in reference to the cliffs, or—according to Winifred Tapson—that it was based on a Bantu word for water, and because we are Tapson fans, 'a big sheet of water' it will always be for us.

There are two main roads from Knysna to George, the northern across the plateau known as the Passes Road, and the southern along the coast, which is the Lakes Road, both of quite different character.

In the old days Knysna was isolated from the west by terrible ravines and boiling torrents that cut through the plateau—on the Knysna side the old wagon road used Trek-aan-Touw, 'pull on the rope', the crossing across the Touw River, and the even more notorious crossing of the Kaaimans River near George, the Kaaimans Gat or 'alligator hole' track: the lamentations of the early travellers who used it reach down to us through the centuries. It was Thomas Bain again who smoothed the way, leading the Passes Road past the worst terrors and building the Phantom Pass near Knysna and the Homtini Pass nearer George.

We use this road whenever we can, turning our faces to the forest and its little settlements, climbing the Phantom Pass (named not after ghosts but after the phantom moths) to Rheenendal. From there, a gravel road branches north-east to **Millwood,** and it is worth doing those 11 kilometres to stand at the site of the Cape's first gold rush in 1886.

Both alluvial gold in the streams and quartz gold in the hills was found here, and a flourishing and feverish little town arose, only to fade away as the gold fizzled out and prospectors moved north to the Witwatersrand. The forest took over: today the ruins of the houses are hidden by the wild growth, and it is almost as if that small unexpected chapter of history in the forest had never been.

Homtini means 'passage' and a splendid old one it is with its great curves cutting through the forest. Beyond it are Barrington, Lance-wood and Woodville, from which a branch road leads north to Bergplaas and the forestry settlement at Kleinplaats, and from here it is possible to follow on foot a track into the mountains, which the Coloured people still use. It is the Duivelskop or Devil's Head route, which 200 years ago was the main one across the mountains into the Long Kloof.

All the way as we had travelled along the Garden Route, the **Long Kloof** had lain to our right, more or less parallel to us, but on the northern side of the mountains. This valley had had tremendous importance in the olden days a century and more before the Bains, because it provided an easy road between east and west without the difficulties of the coastal plain. Travellers usually left the coast and braved the dreaded passes through the mountains to reach it: however bad they were, they were less impossible than the coastal forest and chasms. We were to meet some of these passes later when we took our inland journeys but the start of Duivelskop lay almost at our feet.

Saasveld, the Forestry College, lies further along the road to George on the righthand side—when we saw it last the Outeniqua mountains behind it were covered with snow. All this road is history, and so is the Saasveld name, given in honour of the Dutch castle from which came the Van Rheede van Oudtshoorns, one of whom owned land here. In Le Vaillant's day this was Pampoenkraal—Pumpkin Kraal—a famous camping spot, and this homely name graced many old stories of adventure.

Although this was the first proper road linking Knysna and George, it is not today's national road. This is the **Lakes Road** which another road-building giant, this time a modern one, P. A. de Villiers, made from George along the coast. In its wake a whole new tourist world arose as the crowds poured along this route between sea on one hand and lakes on the other. We have always seen the lakes on mother-of-pearl days, when they were soft and gentle, with water birds and rushes, and the wild bush dove grey until the sun broke out momentarily and turned it green.

There were Langvlei and Rondevlei, both bird sanctuaries, Swartvlei and Groenvlei—Green Vlei—where the fresh water is tinged green and where the descendants of wild swans are bred today. There was Sedgefield, the little resort, on the bank of the Swartvlei Lagoon, and there at last was the **Wilderness** itself, one of the most famous holiday resorts of all with its long sweep of beaches, its breakers and blue lagoon, and its houses—often opulent ones—among the dense, green, shiny-leaved wild trees. In spite of its sophistication, the name suited it well. The thick wild bush crowding down to the beaches give it a wild country air: if left to itself, we guessed, it would engulf houses and hotels as easily and silently as the forest had taken Millwood. Nearly a hundred years ago, when it was christened, a wilderness it must have been.

The proper thing to do is to go from Knysna to George by the train which travels along the coast, and is said to be a journey of great views and much fun. This train passed through the Wilderness as we loitered, and continued on over the viaduct at the mouth of the Kaaimans River, while we took the north-western road to George, along the eastern banks of the Kaaimans River, as dream-like that day as the lakes themselves.

We crossed the Kaaimans River on a fine, curved modern bridge: below it was a causeway where the wagon road had once crossed the fearful Kaaimans Gat, and above on the top of the hill, were traces of the old road. Very soon we were passing on our left the turn-off to Victoria Bay, and on our right that to the Passes Road. Three kilometres further on we were in George. The road we had travelled from the Wilderness was even more dramatic done the other way, and before we left the town for good we took it again to the Wilderness to see views of sea, sand and forest emerge before us.

George is a pleasant little town, and also an important one, one of the principal stops on the Garden Route. It is a good centre to explore all the little coastal resorts along the coast, the forest roads, and the mountains to the north. Today these mountains are crossed from George by the old Montagu Pass which connects it with the Long Kloof, and the modern Outeniqua Pass to the west which runs to Oudtshoorn, and these can be happily explored for weeks on end.

George was founded in 1811 and named, as any historian could guess, after George III. Even in its infancy, it had an ampleness—the width of the streets and their long avenues of fine trees ensured this, and because of these and its gardens it has long had a reputation for lushness. With many of its old trees gone, it has lost something of its character, but fortunately at least one of its famous oaks survives. It is the one that stands in the library garden in the main street, York Street, and is a national monument.

George had two things that gave us great pleasure that day. The first was **St Mark's Cathedral.** In 1911 when the town had its one hundredth birthday and became the centre of a new diocese, and George (this time King George V) had presented it with a Royal Bible, it was the smallest cathedral in the world. We walked in. The light was streaming in through stained glass windows that had been donated 'By their son, Montagu White, in memory of Sarah Jane and Henry Fancourt White, the Founder of Blanco and Builder of the Montagu Pass'. We had known the pass well, so that in a flash the inscription brought back to us the steep old walled road with its smithy alongside it and the proteas blooming.

The other pleasure was the **Museum,** made and collected by Mr C. O. Sayers, a former editor of the George newspaper. It was a gorgeous hugger-mugger affair housed in one big room, soon—we were assured—to be transferred to better quarters. Wherever it now is, we hope it still preserves its character, for that day we hunted treasure in it for a morning, and found it. Among the butter spats of yellow-wood, oven scoops, old washstands, yellowwood shelves, painted wagon-chests and old gramophones, were Queen Victoria's black kid mourning slippers lined with silk that she had worn at the funeral of Emperor Frederick of Germany in 1889, and five generations of swords, which had been owned by Parkes of Wilderness. One bore the label: 'The Sword of the Frasers of Lovat, believed to have belonged to Charles Fraser, great-grandson of Simon Fraser, Lord Lovat, who was A.D.C. to Charles Stuart, the Young Pretender, at the Battle of Culloden, 1745.'

In our travels, these bits of history linking past and present, South Africa with the world, had always been of special fascination to us, none more so than this—in a city named for a Hanoverian king, under a range of mountains bearing a Hottentot name—a sword that might have fought for a Stuart prince 230 years before.

Mossel Bay, South Africa's fifth port, was the next stop. We came to it over rolling country and scrub—the grand scenery had gone although the sea views were rewarding. The town itself, of fair size, lies on a promontory which shelters the sea on the western side and forms the bay. It was here that on 3rd February 1488, Bartolomeu Dias's two caravels sheltered and Dias and a party went ashore. Dias had indeed rounded the Cape, but so far out to sea that he did not realize he had done so: he had sailed east and then north, and had seen the long-awaited land, a river bank on which were cattle and herdsmen in numbers. It was the Gouritz River a little west of Mossel Bay and, according to Axelson, Dias called it Rio dos Vaqueiros, or Bay of Cowherds.

Next day they sailed past the bluff, on which the town of Mossel Bay lies, and into the bay, both of which Dias named after São Bras, whose festival it was. The name of the promontory was in time corrupted to St Blaize, and the Watering Place of St Bras was in 1601 renamed Mossel Bay by the commander of the Dutch fleet, Paulus van Caerden, who had visited the bay and found a huge quantity of mussels in the big cave on the headland. Soon it became a regular watering place for Portuguese ships, and it was during this time that a number of other first records were made.

Dias's men drank fresh water here and took a supply aboard ship: it was the first time white men used the water of South Africa, which they were to seek ever after through all its history as the most precious of all things, more precious far than gold. It was the first time they ever saw the indigenous people, the Hottentots, or the cattle of the country, big animals with humps and wide-spreading horns that were the ancestors of the Afrikander cattle that pulled the wagons of the Great Trek; and it was the place where they caught fish for the first time off the Cape, and where South Africa had its first 'post-office' and its first Christian place of worship.

The Portuguese landed at an inlet (Munro's Bay today) where was a small spring of fresh water, the only one in the vicinity, and close to it a milkwood tree. Everywhere all over the world sailors have left signs and messages for succeeding mariners. Here was one of the most famous of all, a despatch left, not under, or marked upon, a rock as often happened along the South African shore, but in an old boot hanging from a branch of the milkwood. It is generally thought to have been written by a captain of Pedro Alvares Cabral's fleet which in 1500 had been sent from Portugal to uphold the discoveries in the Indian Ocean.

With the fleet was Bartolomeu Dias himself, bent on a new adventure, the founding of a fortress and point of trade at Sofala on the east coast of Africa, then seen by the Portuguese as the port through which they could gain the fabulous gold of Africa. In a fearful storm in the South Atlantic, Dias's ship, together with three others, was lost: and it was the news of this and of Dias's death that was contained in the despatch. It was found in 1501 by the commander of the next Portuguese fleet to sail to the East, João da Nova, who had left Portugal before the return of Cabral's fleet.

The milkwood tree, whose thick evergreen crown protected boot and letter, is now a national monument and one of the most romantic of all. It must be a very old tree, well over 500 years of age for in 1500 it was judged big enough to give protection from the weather. It is a huge mound of foliage now, living luxuriantly with all protection, unlike its brothers up and down the coast, often bent and battered by salt and gale.

Not only it, but the little spring of water—still flowing—is a national monument. Near them is a post-box in the shape of a sailor's boot, and letters posted here carry a special franking—few visitors can resist it. Of the first place of Christian worship in South Africa erected by Da Nova in 1501, only the record remains.

Mossel Bay is today a famous angling spot. The first fish that began this sport was caught here by Vasco da Gama's crew. It was a bad start to South Africa's fishing history, for the catch poisoned the sailors. Professor Smith believed they ate blaasops, the ludicrous-looking fish with the poisonous flesh that we had so wished to see along the Tsitsikama coast. So many foreign sailors, he wrote, had caught and eaten them with disastrous results, that once a special leaflet picturing the fish had been issued to all ships in Table Bay. Thus Mossel Bay had seen the first case of blaasop poisoning, another record.

It was also the only town which we know to have thrown away a Harry Smith association. In spite of its historic site, the town of Mossel Bay only came into being in 1848. Sir Harry Smith was governor, and the town was christened Aliwal South in honour of his Indian victory. The name did not stick and Mossel Bay won hands down. It is, of course, a better name.

The only memorable things along the road towards Albertinia and Swellendam were the twin rail and road bridges over the Gouritz River and the tall aloes with their broad spiny leaves, the Red or Bitter aloe or the Tapaalwee, *Aloe ferox*. For over 200 years these aloes had been the livelihood of many people living here for two reasons, almost as old as the aloes were their honey and their sap. Over a century ago a traveller, Dr William Guybon Atherstone, whom we talk of many times again, wrote that the farmers of these flats shore their aloes annually 'as we shear our sheep'. Today the Coloured people still cut the leaves and for the same reason, to collect the juice. It was aloe-cutting time and we knew that all over the district people would still be cutting the leaves, piling them over a big tin or trough, collecting the dripping sap, and boiling it until it was a dry, dark, bitter substance—the drug, bitter aloe, that has been exported from South Africa for two centuries. A glance at Jose Burman's guide warmed our hearts. He not only described its preparation but added a fact about this almost Biblical procedure that we did not know—that modern machines could not crush the leaves properly, so that this slow, clumsy ritual might be expected to continue for a long time.

Atherstone had also talked of the honey the aloes had yielded, together with that from the ericas, for which the country was famous, 'vast quantities, which, in the late drought, when all else failed, saved the inhabitants from famine'. The honey was made by wild bees, which one farmer had lured into candle and soap boxes, and which had made honey worth £200, a small fortune then—the English bees, which had been imported into Knysna, finding the climate so genial, with no winter and flowers all the year round, refused to work and made no honey.

The monotonous low grey scrub stretched on to Riversdale. This was *renosterbos*, the bush that covers huge stretches, especially of the Western Cape, a weed of some distinction for country people use it to cure influenza and indigestion, and to heat their Dutch ovens—when they still have them. Wherever it grows, it lays its stamp upon the country, one of which we soon tired.

Riversdale is famous for its flowers. It is a pretty little town, for us notable for the original Zeekoegat homestead of 1795 where Van Plettenberg, and better still Harry Smith, spent a night, and also because from it the Garcia Pass to the north and Puntjie on the coast can easily be reached. The Garcia is a fine pass with a famous old toll house.

If we had two weeks to do with as we pleased, the odds are that we would go again to Swellendam beyond Riversdale, that little town that in the mid-1700s was the Cape's most eastern, most remote village and point of civilization. It lay athwart the old wagon road from Cape Town to the east, soon becoming a famous stop where everyone outspanned, ate, drank and gossiped, and wagons were mended and oxen and horses refreshed. We would stop again in the town to look where the *Kaapse wapad*—the Cape wagon road—had run, at the simple fine old houses (the Drostdy above all) and we would use the town as many of the old people had, as a resting place before we struck out into the country round.

It is a particularly good centre to see the sights of the **Overberg,** 'over-the-mountain' as this country east of the Hottentots Holland mountains is called, and from here we would strike north to the mountains and south to the sea, seeing again the fascinating things we did in our too brief days.

Originally, we stopped in **Swellendam** itself. The little town was given its name in the 1740s, not because of its pleasant, rather melodious sound but because the governor of the day was Hendrik Swellengrebel, and the maiden name of his wife was Ten Damme. The name thus neatly honoured them both.

A good deal of South Africa's history has been made by farmers trekking away from authority, and it was out of an attempt to control the farmers who had moved eastwards from the nearest officialdom at Stellenbosch, that the drostdy here, the seat of local government, arose. It was built in 1747, one of the most eastern of the fine Cape Dutch houses which are so numerous further west, and it was geared, not only to authority, but to hospitality, for it stood close to the wagon road. In its early history, in particular, it welcomed travellers of all kinds, governors, lesser officials, explorers, scientists, including, in 1777, Colonel Gordon, then a captain; four years later Le Vaillant, and in the early 1800s, William Burchell.

It is a great house but not a grand one, a simple, wide, low building without the ornate gables of the west, with big rooms with high ceilings, casement windows with small thin panes of handmade glass, twin cypresses at the entrance, a pergola, and a very old vine, a Sweet Hanepoot, said to have been planted in 1794. It is a fine, quiet old place with yellow-wood and stinkwood, and the floors of bygone times, earthern floors smeared with dung, one of peach pips, and a painted limestone floor, now carefully restored.

This is one of the Cape Dutch houses that is open to the public for it is a museum now. We parked our car where the outspan once was, in front of the building, and went in to browse for a while, admiring the home-spun treasures, and the beautiful little wine cellar, with its plaster work of vine and oak leaves, and then we turned to the things outside. There was the Craft Museum, unique of its kind, with the smithy and wagonmaker's workshop (Swellendam wagons were famous once), the cooperage, coppersmiths, cobbler and harness-maker, a horse mill, and a mill that worked—a water mill for grinding wheat. There was, as well, the old wagon built in 1795, which is thought to be South Africa's oldest vehicle: it was called a *kakebeen* by the old people because the high sides sloped up at the back and reminded them of an ox's jawbone.

From here we went north to the **Tradouw Pass.** At the start we first drove east, until a short distance from Swellendam we took the road to Suurbraak on our left, and came into the little Coloured village. It had originally, we learned, been founded by the London Missionary Society and was now a Dutch Reformed Church Mission, a place to remember, with white or pink cottages with green woodwork and yellow mealie cobs in strings in front: all had big chimneys, and there were sheep tethered in the street and chickens, geese and dogs mixed up with the children as they played.

Beyond it was the Tradouw Pass with steep kranses, a winding walled road, and an old toll house. Thomas Bain planned it and in 1873 it was opened by the wife of the governor, Sir Henry Barkly. His daughter rode up it in riding breeches, the first the locals had ever seen. The sensation was terrific.

Tradouw was a Hottentot name meaning 'women's poort', and Cogman's Kloof near Montagu, through which we travelled later, was a corruption of another Hottentot word, the name of an early Hottentot tribe, the Koekemans. We took the road from Swellendam north-east through pleasant farming country, through the village of Ashton towards the Langeberg, and by way of these we cut through **Cogman's Kloof.** Here was a fantastic scene of orange-brown moun-tain, layer on layer, and a tunnel through the rock—Kalkoenkrans or

Turkey Krans—with a small fort perched upon the top, built during the Anglo-Boer War, which had been successfully held by Gordon High-landers. **Montagu** in the Little Karoo, famous for its hot springs, lay only a few kilometres distant, with Robertson to the west and Barry-dale to the south, and to the north and west the road through Burgers Pass and the lovely lonely Koo Valley to the national road, a country road we knew from other times.

This wild mountain scenery within a couple of hours' travel of the main road was a pleasure that we thought travellers, who now skimmed along the national road with not a glance northwards, would enjoy. Later we learned that at least one tour, 'Rediscovery Holidays', includes both Cogman's Kloof and Montagu.

From here we went seawards. A little south of Swellendam was the **Bontebok National Park** where are protected and bred some of the rarest buck in South Africa, the bonteboks, once numerous in this part—and this part alone—and at the beginning of the century on their way, apparently, to extinction. Today some 800 exist in the Park and on private farms in the neighbourhood. It helped, we thought, to even things up a little for Swellendam is sometimes said to have been the place where the last blue buck in the world was killed in 1791—not the little blue duiker of the coastal forests, but a larger animal related to the sable and the roan, which had ears like an ass and a blue velvet coat. Not even a single mounted specimen remains in South Africa, although there are some five in museums in Europe. It was one of the three South African species of mammals to have become extinct in modern times, and we were not proud of the record, so that the bonteboks, increasing so generously, gave us a special lift.

Two main roads south invited us, one to Port Beaufort, and the other to Bredasdorp and Cape Agulhas. **Port Beaufort** brings back stories of the Barry family—Barry and Nephews—Swellendam's 19th century merchant princes, whose kingdom the Overberg was, who 'made' the port, who traded with the farmers, held the goods in ware-houses here, and shipped them to Cape Town in their own steamer, and who issued their own bank notes—the £5 rightly enough with the design of the ox-wagon that had helped to bring them wealth—and whose fall in the middle 1860s ended Swellendam's golden days.

Only the name, Port Beaufort, given before their time, does not reflect the Barrys. It was bestowed by Lord Charles Somerset, the governor, the head of whose family was the Duke of Beaufort.

Malagas lies further up the river. It was from Jose Burman we learned that Joseph Barry had shipped wool and aloes from it in the 1840s, two things which are still the essence of big slices of South

Africa. It reminded us how some of the earliest wool farmers—the Van Bredas, Van Reenens, Reitzs and Albertyns—had lived in this country and bred merino sheep in the days when these sheep and their thin tails were despised by Cape farmers generally.

We travelled from Swellendam to **Bredasdorp** over undulating land patterned with ploughed fields where later wheat would grow, a bare world with dark patches of renosterbos and low scrub, with windmills, sheep dogs, and tall spidery trees in rows with bare stems and flat tops bending before the wind. It was so alien a country to us, so different from the country through which we had come, that we could hardly accept it as Africa. Three days later after we had gone to and fro across it, it was no longer foreign, but, it seemed, part of our bones. Bredasdorp lay in its heart. This is the southern-most town of Africa, 140 years old, named after Michiel van Breda, who had been one of the early merino sheep pioneers. We stopped here in what appeared at first to be an ordinary, pleasant little town, to look at the period museum that was to be opened shortly, and quite by chance found ourselves standing in the old Independent Church next door, an extraordinary thing to come upon without any foreknowledge. It is now a marine museum.

Almost due south of Bredasdorp is Cape Agulhas, the southern-most point of Africa, with a coastline on either side that is among the most deadly in the world. Shipwreck was the museum's theme. There were the usual dioramas, lighthouse and ship models, charts, anchors, winches, gems, trinkets, porcelain and other treasure trove, but the drama was the hall itself and the figureheads from the ships lost along the coast. The church windows had been filled in, and in place of glass in the niches stood the figures: one was a 17th century Portuguese warrior drawing his sword. The room was dark and one by one the figureheads were illuminated, jutting out into the backness in their pools of light in all their finery and colour: and we thought we had never seen a display so simple and so stunning.

How much ships' timber went into the building of Bredasdorp nobody will ever know for sure: there is a ship's door here and beams there, and so it goes. There cannot be a single farmhouse that does not hold some sea relic, like cabin doors, portholes, lanterns or whole chunks of upperworks. Each one tells a story.

We went first to **Arniston**—or Waenhuiskrans—on the coast north-east of Cape Agulhas, which had been named after the British transport *Arniston*, which foundered there shortly before Waterloo. She was bound for Britain from Ceylon, carrying mainly invalided soldiers, and the ship was put ashore by her captain when he was

224

Matjiesfontein—the Lord Milner Hotel

An ostrich flock outside Oudtshoorn

Somewhere under these red Kalahari dunes lies the Lost City

Moffat's church at Kuruman

trapped on a lee shore. Only six of the 378 on board were saved. On the shore at the little village was a memorial to four Murray children who were drowned in the trooper and in the hotel were two human skulls salvaged from the sand. The tragedy came through to us clearly over the 160 years.

There was a huge sea cave nearby, the **Waenhuiskrans,** which gave the village its second name, which we approached through sea foam over rocks and through pools: it was big enough to house a wagon and ox span, as the name had suggested. Then we walked to the fishermen's cemetery on the dunes nearby amid the scrub, where we found sand and wind, wooden crosses with faded lettering, and shells upon the graves. It had that melancholy charm that graveyards, and particularly simple ones, always have: but we were glad to find Kassies Bay beyond it on the eastern side of Arniston, full of life and Coloured fisher families.

Tumbledown as it was, it was picturesque with the thatched cottages, the geese at the back door and the fish drying at the front. As we write, the whole village is being refurbished through the 'Save Arniston' committee: money to restore it has flowed in from many quarters. So many of these simple, charming little houses in the Bredasdorp district have disappeared of late, that these at Kassies Bay have provisionally been proclaimed national monuments.

A particularly good example of one, white-walled, thatched, with jutting chimney and oven, stood beside the road at the Bredasdorp entrance to the village. As we admired it, the Coloured son of the house emerged, and asked if we would like to see the inside. It was as unpretentious as the outside; but our host's manners came from a palace. We were not, however, as concerned with cottages as with shipwrecks, and with these in mind we turned west and south past the seaside homes of Struis Bay (Straw Bay, because of the thatched roofs), to **Cape Agulhas.**

As the southern tip of Africa we had been expecting the cape to be grand and dramatic. What we found instead was a gale-torn low land with ragged rocks, tufted with wiry, wind-cropped grass, peering rather than thrusting into the sea. There was nothing in the land itself to suggest it was a punchbag for powerful currents and mighty winds, for tropical and Antarctic marine climates: nor did the sea tell that it was one of the great ocean meeting places, of the Indian Ocean and the South Atlantic.

Bartolomeu Dias, as he sailed westwards round the coast on his homeward voyage, put into Struis Bay and remained there for three weeks refitting his caravels. This was just over to our left as we stood

225

looking out to sea. Then he sailed westwards round Cape Agulhas—which he called after St Brendan, the Irish saint who, legend has it, discovered America in the sixth century. He missed its significance altogether and who can blame him, for from the sea the cape must have looked even more insignificant than from the land: he thought when he passed the Cape of Good Hope later, that here was the tip of Africa, and this the Portuguese maps showed for a long time to come.

Later sailors named this Cape Agulhas, meaning—according to Axelson—the Cape of the Compass Needles, because at that point at that time there was no magnetic variation and the compass needles pointed true north.

Insignificant the cape might appear, innocent it and its waters have never been. Before us lay their latest victim, the *Oriental Pioneer*, a bulk ore carrier of 59 000 tons, which had laid her R5-million worth of bones alongside those of at least 108 other big vessels which had failed to pass by Cape Agulhas safely. In 1974 the ship, with a full cargo, had developed a severe list and been beached in about three fathoms. All salvage attempts failed and, in order to prevent pollution of the coast by her bunker oil, a novel device was tried out—a jet fan to suck the oil from below decks and burn it. The glow from it, like the yellow eye of a dead fish, stared unblinkingly at us from out of the mist. When it went out, the *Oriental Pioneer* would be truly dead.

Three years before, the super-tanker *Wafra* had gone aground close to this spot. The *Wafra*, spilling thousands of tons of oil, was finally pulled clear and sunk out to sea by rocket-firing aircraft to prevent pollution of the coast. She could have carried Dias' ships on deck with room to spare.

We took the road to Elim. Far over on our right was **Zoetendals-vlei,** once owned by the Michiel van Breda who had kept here a pioneer Merino sheep stud, and had come over the mountains from Cape Town every year to fetch his wool. It was Audrey Blignault, writing of this southern world, the Strandveld, who as a child had been shown the mounted horn of one of the first rams, with the dates 1817-1830 inscribed upon it.

Elim is the Moravian mission in the plain, which is possibly the most picturesque village in all the Cape, with its thatched cottages fronted with their little fig trees, and the working water mill. We went through it and out into the veld with its marshes and pools, its milkwood trees, its birds and in spring its flowers, the most beautiful in the world, Audrey Blignault, child of the Strandveld, had called them.

West was Gansbaai—Goose Bay—with a gravel road from it to

Danger Point a short distance away, and beyond it to the north, on the same Walker Bay, the plush holiday resort of Hermanus. That stretch of shore told in a nutshell the story of the whole coast from Zululand to Cape Point its age-old, perennial sea terrors, and the beauties and pleasures of the long sea shore.

From **Danger Point** one can see over the sweep of Walker Bay: almost one can distinguish the solid, costly Hermanus homes, the scenic road and the beaches for play and leisure. Here at Danger Point was the lighthouse and two kilometres offshore the hidden rock on which the *Birkenhead* was wrecked on a calm night of February 1852.

The *Birkenhead* was a troopship carrying soldiers to the Eighth Frontier War. She struck a rock in the early hours of the morning and sank within 25 minutes. Two boats were launched in which the women and children and some men were placed, while a few others found safety in the gig which landed safely nearer Hermanus. Four hundred and fifty-four men died, the young soldiers setting an example of courage and staunchness that makes this not only a disaster but an epic. Only three men broke rank and jumped overboard to swim for their lives. The remainder—a heterogeneous collection drawn from ten different regiments (none had ever been under fire), followed the example of their commanding officer, Lieutenant-Colonel Seton, and formed up on deck where they stood until the ship sank under them and finally broke in half.

The story echoed round the world and finds its echoes still. The King of Prussia had the story of the *Birkenhead's* men read aloud to his regiments. Queen Victoria placed a monument to them in the colonnade of the Chelsea Hospital. There is a plaque to them, erected by the Navy League, set into the base of the lighthouse at Danger Point.

Beyond Walker Bay and fashionable Hermanus, we took the road to N2 again and soon were on the **Houhoek Pass,** climbing from the hills, the undulations and the grain lands of the Overberg towards the Hottentots Holland Mountains and Sir Lowry's Pass across them. However beautiful the old roads through the Houhoek mountains might have been, this modern pass is not particularly impressive, but it was the entry into what we considered Cape Town's world—the country beyond Sir Lowry's Pass. The name Houhoek pleased us: it is said to have been derived from the common 'hou'—stop—shouted to oxen on a trek, and 'hoek', meaning a bosky place.

To our right as we drove through the pass the double-storeyed building a little way off the road gave us more satisfaction still. It was the Houhoek Inn, the oldest coaching inn at the Cape, a fine building with an enormous gum tree—over 100 years old—standing outside it. We knew its reputation for good food, hospitality, and Dalmatian dogs—for as long as anyone can remember a spotted dog has always been there. A Dalmatian greeted us, and that was a propitious start. It was the middle of the morning and we settled for tea. Later, when we sampled the meagre and expensive teas of Cape Town and its environs, we realized the worth of Houhoek's.

Let no one say this was a poor way to end a chapter of a journey or start a new one. We had Harry Smith's word for it that it was a good cup of tea that gave him the strength to ride his 600 famous miles and for us Houhoek's friendly cup set us well on the road for Cape Town and all its joys.

CHAPTER FIFTEEN

Orange Free State—Eastern Cape

❧

Whatever our first plans, Cape Town in the end usually becomes our Mecca. That it is a world away, with whole countries in between, is splendid—exploring them makes a good adventure even better. There are the roads to Cape Town lying in the east, those of the west, and a central one we use when hard-pushed for time.

The first part of the journey is usually through the Orange Free State, a country that as a rule we do not loiter through. The flat rich uplands the Vootrekkers knew moving with game and smelling of flowers present a different face today, with mealie lands and ploughed fields alongside the road, stretching away it seems for ever.

Yet there is a way through it in the east skirting the mountains that is a scenic road, rich in history and prehistory, which—running southwards into the north-east Cape—is becoming known as the Highlands Route. Beginning at Harrismith, it passes through Kestell and the Golden Gate Highlands National Park, and from there runs southward close to the Lesotho border through Rouxville to Aliwal North and Barkly East, after which it loops through the mountains of the north-east Cape to Dordrecht and East London.

The route from Johannesburg to Harrismith is one of the main ones to Natal, continuing over the Drakensberg via Van Reenen's Pass to Ladysmith the other side of the mountains. Harrismith stands on an old wagon route from Natal to the Orange Free State and Kimberley diamonds. Time here, however, should be counted not in decades but in millions of years, for this is one of the rich fossil areas of the country. The first fossil dinosaur outside Europe came from here; and the area was the stamping ground of some of our early fossil hunters, like Joseph Orpen, the land-surveyor, who found the dinosaur; and Arthur Putterill, who was Harrismith's blacksmith, and a good one, yet is remembered today mainly for the fossils he found in the dongas round the town and sent to South African museums.

Most of the country from here southward to the north-east Cape has yielded fossils, often of other dinosaurs and the creatures associated with them. The rocks in which they are found are those that geologists term the Red Beds and Cave Sandstone of the Stormberg Series of the Karroo System, a tremendous mouthful yet worth remembering, for nowhere in the whole country are ordinary people, as apart from scientists, more aware of rock and soil than here (Karoo, confusingly, has two 'r's in the scientific usage, one in more usual parlance.) Outcrops of the rocks make the red and cream striated cliffs that dominate the countryside; weathering shaped the sandstone forming the cavities—the caves and rock-shelters—which gave the Cave Sandstone their name. These shelters hold Bushman paintings for which the area is famous.

From Harrismith we drove one day to Bethlehem, then south to the Golden Gate Highlands National Park, about 400 kilometres both from Pretoria and from Durban to the east.

Near Clarens, on the way, is a cave on the farm **Schaapplaats** with well-known Bushman paintings. **Clarens** has the other part of the twin treasure, as well, fossils. In 1976 Dr Kitching (of the Bernard Price Institute for Palaeontology) was fossicking in a stream bed in the area, when he found five fossil dinosaur eggs. They were gentle swellings in the red rock, twice the size of a hen's egg. In excavating them, three were split open to show the embryos within—the whole rib cage was no bigger than a finger nail, and there were minute teeth in the little jaws.

They were the first to be found in Triassic beds and set fossil-hunters everywhere vibrating. Now, as we followed the road to the **Golden Gate Highlands National Park,** through the golden autumn landscape with the Lombardy poplars like bright fingers, we longed to stop at every gully, every stream, to find an embryo dinosaur ourselves. Then we were in the Park, among the foothills of the Maluti Mountains, ringed with the massive cliffs that are not cream in many lights but of that brilliant dramatic blazing gold that gives the Park its name.

This is not a national park resembling any of the other ten. It is high—2 770 metres at its highest point—snow-covered in winter, a place to walk and climb in, to enjoy the scenery, the wild flowers and the animals on the high slopes—black wildebeest, eland, grey rhebok and mountain reedbuck among others—and, as well, the considerable comforts of the Swiss chalet-type Brandwag camp at the foot of its golden cliff.

There were two things in the Park that we wished to see in particular, the black wildebeest—the gnu the early Cape and Orange Free State colonists knew—and the lammergeyers.

James Clarke once called this wildebeest a sort of devil horse, 'cloven-footed with wicked horns and a flowing white ghostly tail', and it is a fiercer, more noble creature than its hang-dog cousin, the blue. It was also, until recently, in danger of becoming extinct: now, through the great efforts made, largely by the Free State Province, its numbers have increased so substantially that it is off the danger list.

It was a success story we saw first-hand on the open slopes. Of the lammergeyers, there was that day no sign.

For ornithologists, these birds are the big attraction of the Park, a species once common from Europe to China and southwards to most of the mountains of South Africa, and now exterminated over large areas. They still live here, however, and in the high mountains close by in Lesotho, Natal and Griqualand East.

They are territorial birds, 'owning' a piece of country and the nesting sites and hunting rights within it. One pair nests in two spots high up on a sandstone krans within the Park, using both nests at various times. Standing in front of the Glen Reenen rest camp below Brandwag, we could, even with the naked eye, see the two dark spots against the cliffs that were the nesting places.

We knew the bird from museums and books, this great eagle-vulture with a wing span of nearly three metres, its beard of black feathers, its eagle's beak, its vulture's claws, and the controversy that had raged about it—eagle or vulture?—and how its egg had proved its vulture kinship. We knew its place in legend—it was a lammergeyer that had killed the Greek poet, Aeschylus, by dropping a tortoise on his bald head; and it was the bird that the early colonists supposed to be the raven let out of the Ark. Now we hoped to see it in the flesh.

This was the only place we knew of where we could *expect* to see the birds without climbing a mountain to do so. We were unlucky and missed them, yet hours before they had shown themselves, soaring and gliding above the cliffs, and delighted visitors with their peerless flight.

There were fossils and rock paintings all the way further down the road south. Close to Wepener on the farm Ventershoek on the eastern road to Mafeteng is the painting of a famous raiding scene, now a national monument (part of it was once removed to Paris!) At Rouxville there are not only paintings but fish, and fish of an extraordinary kind. In the 1890s the town gardener at Aliwal North—immediately south of Rouxville—was an Englishman named Albert Higgens, who was also a fossil collector, and it was he who found a deposit of fossil fishes on the farm, Bekkers Kraal, in the Rouxville district. Among these was a shark, and a Coelacanth that was of the same family as the Coelacanth salvaged by Dr Courtenay-Latimer in

1938 that made history. A shark and a Coelacanth in the land-locked Free State; we were as enchanted as those early fossil-hunters must have been nearly 90 years ago.

Aliwal North is no longer Orange Free State but north-eastern Cape, known today mainly as a health resort, for its thermal hot springs are famous. It is, as well, part of the Harry Smith saga, for it was named after Aliwal, his famous Indian victory.

There are rock paintings in this district, too, and like all those along this eastern route, they are worth an expedition: some are faded, some glowing with colour, all are filled with history and with story. As for where they are—we always ask a policeman—for those country police often know their territory inside-out; and if they fail, there is always the town clerk. The farmers themselves are usually friendly and permit people to visit the paintings on their property. The Knowledge Seekers, based in Johannesburg, run Rock Art tours to these shelters of the eastern districts which are said to be good.

The Highland Route swings east here towards Lady Grey and Barkly East in the Witteberg.

Joseph Orpen, who found the Harrismith dinosaur, laid out many of the farms near **Barkly East,** famous now for their merino sheep and the wool known as Barkly Blue. We remember the area for a night of piercing cold—this is a skiing district—its trout, and Bushman paint-ings. Rhodes lay beyond the village (Cecil Rhodes presented pine trees to the village), and then we were on the road over the Drakensberg by Naude's Nek Pass, the highest road in the Republic that is open to the public. We drove it in winter time, the best time to learn its character, into a high harsh country. There were wild roses towards the top with bright hips, a legacy from the seeds in horses' forage in some distant frontier war: they made dense thickets on the mountain side, but besides them there was nothing except heights, ragged high cloud and a gale that cut like icicles. To the north-west was Ben Macdhui, over 3 000 metres high—the highest peak in the Cape Province—and under our wheels a twisting dirt road that snaked below us in long curves marked with white stones, so narrow we wondered if we could pass another car with safety.

This country, it is claimed, is the Switzerland of South Africa, but the only touch of the northern hemisphere was the roses: for the rest it was as South African as the *cheche* bushes in the gullies, and the Xhosa girls in the foothills who came stepping down a kloof with bundles of wood on their heads. They gathered round our little gas stove with cries. 'Can it cook?' 'Can it really make water hot?' and laughing and exclaiming, they went on down the valley.

From here we turned southward, coming into a land of grassy undulations speckled here and there with thorn trees—'a succession of parks', one early governor called it—of hills, gentle and sombre, and mountain forests, thick bush and scrub and aloe-covered hills, of river valleys that were a different world, hot, arid, filled with an assortment of low trees and plants, all spikes and spines and angles or with fat fleshy leaves, marvellous places both for botanists and birds.

It is a distinctive sort of countryside in many ways, this Eastern Cape, wedged in between the Karoo on the west and the Indian Ocean on the east, with its own sights and smells, produce, accents, history and monuments, and its own sort of names—King William's Town, Queenstown, Adelaide, Port Alfred, all tell their own bit of empire building. For a peaceful looking country, it has known an inordinate amount of blood-letting, for it was here that the white settlers moving east and north first met the Xhosa tribe moving south and clashed, so that many of the historic landmarks have a military flavour.

This was the home of many of the Voortrekkers and it was from here they moved north on their Great Trek; and it was here, too, that the first big British settlement was made in 1820, which was to gentle the Eastern Cape and change the life of South Africa.

Queenstown was a frontier and military town and shows it in its lay-out, although few today are aware of this: six thoroughfares radiate from its heart, a six-sided open place, the Hexagon, which gave it, 125 years ago when it was laid out, an unobstructed line of fire from every angle. From here are two main roads south, the one via Stutterheim and King William's Town to East London, and the other via Fort Beaufort to Grahamstown and Port Elizabeth. We drove to Stutterheim.

Queenstown and **Stutterheim**—their names tell something of their very different stories. One was named after an English queen (Victoria), the other after a German baron, Baron Richard von Stutterheim, who commanded the party of German immigrants who, in 1857, settled in the area between the Amatola Mountains and the sea. Like the British Settlers of 1820, they were meant to be a buffer on the frontier. Unlike them, however, they were semi-military, a legion of German mercenaries who had been recruited by Britain to serve in the Crimean War, and who were later settled here. Soon they were joined by other German immigrants, and towns and villages with names like Berlin, Braunschweig, Frankfort and Potsdam sprang up. Today, 120 years later, family names are still often German, as is sometimes the speech in the homes—even the liver sausages are a fine Teutonic breed.

233

The memorial to the British German Legion is at King William's Town; but before we reached it, we turned off south of Stutterheim to the hamlet of **Keiskammahoek** to see a little hotel born of this German countryside and furnished now with its relics.

This is Ciskei, African territory today, but the hotel we had come to see, The Grosvenor, was still there as we had known it of old, doing a thriving trade. The village—once the Camp in the Mountains—was a military base in the frontier wars, and the overflow of soldiers from the fort were lodged in a building where later The Grosvenor arose.

The one-storey building was much as we remembered it, built about a courtyard bright with flowers, a Cape cart outside, and inside an incredible assortment of fine old things ranging through every corner, in the public rooms and bedrooms and on the stoeps, all formerly the treasures of the German immigrant families who had later moved away.

We remembered, too, Mr Teddy Radloff, the proprietor, whose grandfather had come from Pommerania with the immigrants and who had himself been born and grown up in Keiskammahoek, his identification with the village and the hotel, and his pride in both.

He gave us the welcome we had looked forward to ever since we had left Pretoria, and took us in. We slept that night in a fourposter bed in a room where the furniture was yellow-wood from the Amatola forests; but it was a room the settlers never dreamed of, complete with private bathroom where the water was piping hot, and a bell to summon tea.

The next day we walked into the village: as we remember it there were three streets only shaded by big trees, with open furrows and little cottages slick with paint.

Outside the hotel we noted a wagon wheel, red ornamented with black and white. It was a Ballantyne wheel, from the Ballantyne wagon shop across the village, and we walked across to see it. The shop was no longer working. Years before we had seen it busy, the big high old rooms roaring and squealing and shaking with noise and action, the water wheel that supplied the power turning in the stream outside. We stood outside, looking at the old double storey, at the gables, the big, small-paned windows, the bell, the clock painted on the wall (seven minutes to one, it said), and the battered old wagons in the yard.

At the door still stood old Mr Ballantyne. He had once told us about the Ballantyne wheels, like the one in front of the hotel, and the colours and pattern that were his trade mark; and of how this shop had turned out nearly 5 000 wagons in its working life, all with the same patterned wheels. His father had started wagon-building here in the late 19th century and he had carried on.

Under great pressure, he remembered, he had turned out three wagons a week. Not from scratch, of course; he had built up stocks to use when needed. 'I once had 100 000 assegai spokes on hand', he said wistfully of the great years. No, the motor lorry had not killed his business directly. People still wanted his wagons—he did not tell us but others did, that his wagons were perhaps the best of all. One had delighted crowds at the Rand Easter Show not long before. It was not lack of custom, it was because he could no longer buy iron axles. Nobody wanted wooden ones these days, and he had searched for iron ones across the country, as far north as Rhodesia, without any luck. So one day a few years before, he had quietly shut his shop.

Now—he was nearer 90 than 80—brisk and cheerful as ever, he took us in and showed us his empty shop, empty, that is, except for the old machinery, the ancient cogwheels and saws, some yellow-wood and blocks of wood, and a wagon wheel strung up to the beams above our heads.

It was not melancholy because Mr Ballantyne would not have it so, but it was the end of a brave chapter, or almost the end—there was still a working wagon-shop in Stutterheim, he said. It was also the end of one of the most remarkable vehicles in the world, designed to ride plains without roads and mountains without passes, which could be taken apart and floated across a river, and was not only home but fortress. It was part of pioneering history, and for many, of childhood memories as well.

In the little cemetery nearby we found the perfect end to a nostalgic day. Passing by the graves of the soldiers and the young children—there were many of both—we came to a headstone that halted us. It read:

ERECTED TO THE MEMORY OF BARON JOHN DE FIN
BORN IN PRAGUE
LATE CHAMBERLAIN
TO THE EMPEROR OF AUSTRIA
DIED AT KEISKAMA HOEK
FORTIFIED WITH THE RITES OF THE
CATHOLIC CHURCH
15 APRIL 1887
AGED 86 YEARS

R.I.P.

The legend locally, we learned, was that the baron had fought a duel in Austria, killed his man, and fled to South Africa. Why here? Had he come with the German immigrants? And how did he fare among these green hills? Nobody could tell us.

King William's Town is another town with a military history and a background of frontier wars—in keeping with its name, it was an imperial garrison town as late as 1914. It was next on our route and important to us for various reasons. There was its early colourful history, and its present pleasures, chief among them its museums, the Kaffrarian, which is late 19th century and famous, and the new South African Missionary Museum, the first of its kind in the country. Missionaries, as well as bringing the Christian religion, played an enormous part in the opening up of South Africa, both in the almost unknown north-west and in the Eastern Cape; and it was a missionary, the Reverend John Brownlee of the London Missionary Society, who was the first white man to live in the King William's Town area. He brought his family to settle here in 1826 and opened the Buffalo Mission Station—which is still in existence and still functioning.

After Brownlee the missionary came Harry Smith—gay, vain, imperious, generous romantic, dashing soldier and ardent lover—who warmed South African history through two decades, and even from this distance we smile at the contrast Harry offered.

The year 1835 was one of war for these frontier districts, colonists and military desperately fighting the Xhosa warriors who were pouring southwards. It was into this scene of blood and panic that Harry Smith erupted with all the force and *éclat* of a good soldier, Wellington-trained, with Glory and Empire in his blood, and a drama that was Harry Smith's alone.

At **Grahamstown** further on our journey we were to remember how he saved the town that January of 1835. Soon after, he was here at King William's Town, ruler of the new territory between the Keis-kama and the Kei River, the Province of Queen Adelaide, which had been created as a semi-military buffer against the Xhosas to the north.

He did not rule for long. On instructions from Britain the territory was handed back to the Xhosas and Harry Smith, wild with pain and passion, was shouting of philanthropists who led people to the devil for God's sake! Chaos would follow, he warned, and it did. Years after the Great Trek, Harry was sure that it was *his* recall that had caused it—had his system been persisted in 'not a Boer would have emigrated!' Good old Harry—how easy he made history sound.

We thought of him as we drove through King William's Town's streets. Here he had had his tent, and then the little house of the 1830s, which he had shared with Juana, his adored wife—'my dear, faithful, adventurous and campaigning wife', he called her, who had set out from Cape Town to join him, travelling by wagon with two servants, her maids and dogs, and nurtured and befriended by the Dutch farmers as she passed.

Theirs at the time—perhaps for all time—had been the great love story of the Eastern Cape, and the Cape colonists, Dutch and British, revelled in the romance: it was one of those tender scintillating affairs that touched everyone. Harry had first seen Juana when he was a young man fighting with the Duke of Wellington in Spain during the Peninsula War. After the sack of Badajos the countryside was in all the terrible disorder of war, when a girl of 14 was brought into camp by an older sister who begged the British officers to protect the child. Harry Smith, then 24, looked at her, fell in love, and married her forthwith.

He taught her how to ride a horse, and she was with him everywhere, including many of the fields of battle, enduring all privations and dangers with gaiety. 'She laughed herself warm,' he remembered, when a mud hut in the Pyrenees fell in upon them in a night of biting rain, turning them black as chimney-sweeps. All the soldiers adored her spirit and laughter, begging her to ride with *their* company; and the commanding officers knew her charm. In action once, Harry found her holding her umbrella over a general who was suffering from rheumatism!

These stories travelled before them to the Cape, and everybody was prepared to enjoy the lovers. Juana was 23 years older here in the bush of the Eastern Cape, yet only 37, still blooming, still campaigning, still beloved. So they camped in King William's Town and left it, mourning, together. Eleven years later they were back in South Africa as Sir Harry Smith, the Governor, and his lady, and the Cape frontier was delirious with joy.

All that Harry had feared and come about in his absence. The Boers had emigrated and there was bitter war between Black and White. That same month he landed, he was in King William's Town again where 2 000 Xhosas awaited him sitting 'in a great hollow circle'. He rode in among them and halted to read a proclamation. We imagined that green grassy world, Harry on a splendid horse, his nose—so like the Duke of Wellington's—more prominent than ever, his eyes flashing, roaring out his message to that great boiling assembly of men. The country between the Keiskama and the Kei was now to be British Kaffraria, he told them, no part of the Colony but under the sovereignty of the Queen. He called for a sergeant's baton—the staff of war—and a stick with a brass knob, the staff of peace, and demanded of the chiefs that they touch the one they chose. They touched the stick with the brass knob and Harry's cup was full: and he had this town laid out in squares and streets, seeing it as the 'perfectly magnificent' capital of a peaceful independent land.

It had already been named, and there was nothing he could do about this, but a military village he established in the territory not far distant was firmly called Juanasburg.

History seldom ends as neatly as this, and Sir Harry's way was to be beset with sharpest thorns. But for us that day when we came into the town, he *was* King William's Town, and his story and Juana's coloured everything we saw.

King William's Town was not only a military centre, but since Brownlee's day had been a missionary centre as well. The American missionary, Daniel Lindley, and his wife stayed here on their way to Natal. He was the minister, famous and beloved, to the Voortrekkers, and there were many others who visited this mission or worked in the vicinity. So the town is a particularly good centre for a museum which collects everything connected with South Africa's mission history. It is to be housed in the Wesleyan Church in Berkeley Street, itself an old mission church, both beautiful and historic.

The **Kaffrarian Museum,** under whose wing it is, is packed with delights, with military material, particularly that associated with the Cape Mounted Rifles: there are also a German Settler display, good ethnographical exhibits, and a reconstruction of an old African trading store. Above all, there is the mammal display, which is one of the best in the country covering most of the large and small mammals.

The museum houses, too, the Shortridge Mammal Study Collection of about 20 000 specimens. Captain Guy Shortridge was a director of the museum and a noted author and wild life expert: the collection he built up is one of the most comprehensive but it is purely scientific and is not on display.

There are two other things we always associate with King William's Town, giant earthworms and birds, above all Cape parrots. These can usually be found in the lovely Pirie Forest of the Amatola Mountains nearby: there is a good viewing spot about nine kilometres out of town on the Stutterheim road, where their shrieks and bright colours reveal them even to the ignorant.

The Rooikrans and Maden Dams under the Pirie Mountains have a big bird population, while the Maden Dam and the footpaths into the forests nearby make some of South Africa's finest beauty spots.

Seeing the earthworms is a matter of luck. From time to time stories have come from the country round King William's Town of worms 9 metres long, and so thick that a small piece can just be squeezed into a bottling jar. Scientists, of course, distrust the figures—they say earthworms stretch like a nylon sock—although they accept a length of two metres happily. We ourselves once saw one nearly a metre long, although the giants eluded us: but what everyone can see is the plain at Kommetjie Vlaktes close to the town on the Fort Beaufort road, which is studded for kilometres with deep basins up to four metres wide—made, say the experts, by the giant worms that ingest the soil at the bottom of the holes in wet weather, casting it up to make the saucers' sides.

The more western road from Queenstown to the south has its own attractions. **Fort Beaufort** on the Kat River had its beginnings in the military post of 1822 which saw a good deal of action—the round stone fortification known as the Martello Tower, now a national monument, dates from the early frontier wars.

The countryside around also knew war and peace, missionary endeavour and frontier valour. To the east is **Alice** (named, it is thought, after Harry Smith's beloved sister) on the main east-west trunk road, which grew out of the mission station, Lovedale, founded in 1824, a famous name that is still borne today not only by a mission and school but by a hospital, a press and farm. Close to the early mission, a fort was built called Fort Hare, and this in turn gave its name to the African University College of Fort Hare which was established here.

A little way beyond Alice on the main road is **Middledrift.** All this Eastern Cape is aloe country, but this section of the road is perhaps the most famous of all, for here *Aloe ferox*, the Red Aloe (which provides the aloe sap for the Gouritz River people of the south) grows in such abundance that in late winter it turns the countryside red. Red Hill is here, taking its name from the aloes close beside both the railway line and the tarred road. C. J. Skead—his name is associated with mammals, birds and plants throughout the Eastern Cape—still tries to have it proclaimed a national monument, but nobody heeds his plea.

It is impossible to journey in this area, westwards to Graaff-Reinet, northwards to the southern Free State, to the river valleys of the Transkei, and along the coast to west of Swellendam, without meeting these most magnificent of aloes again and again. They stand on the plains and hill slopes with an almost human air—the troops in the frontier wars often mistook them for men—and in flowering times, from early winter near the sea to spring in high inland places, when they send up their dense cylinders of red bloom, they are matched by nothing else. The veld and bush of this east, rich as they are in variety of plants, are often drab; knowledgeable travellers always try to travel through them in the aloe season.

To the north are the mountains with their resorts like the Hog's Back near Alice, and the Katberg Inn on the Katberg mountains near Fort Beaufort, and further west are the little towns of Adelaide and Bedford. This is Settler Country: and it was to a valley of the Winterberg north of Bedford that in 1820 a Scottish party of immigrants came; their Baviaans River valley was the most remote part of the territory assigned to the Settlers and one of the most beautiful as well. The small party was led by Thomas Pringle, most famous of the Settlers, who was to become South Africa's first poet to write in English, and first champion of the freedom of the press.

They called their highland glen, **Glen Lynden,** and with the help of their Dutch neighbours, built a stone church here—it was a Dutch Reformed Church built in the traditional Scottish T-form. Pringle himself settled on the farm Eildon further up the valley, and here he built his beehive cabin under the 'umbra tree' he immortalized in his poetry: it was here he wrote some of his best known work.

The Baviaans is still a beautiful valley, today with prosperous farms. The Glen Lynden Church is a national monument, and Eildon a fine place with an old gabled farmhouse, built in 1846 and enlarged later, still lived in by members of the Pringle family—Mr Alan Pringle and his wife, Mavis. The site of Thomas Pringle's cabin is a national monument as well, and the neat little umbra tree, shown on the title-page of Pringle's *African Sketches*, is still alive. It is a shepherd's tree, *Boscia oleoides*, and one of South Africa's famous trees.

Pringle, most people remember, was forced off the land by bad times and became sub-librarian of the South African Public Library in Cape Town; later, together with his friend, John Fairbairn, he started South Africa's first literary journal. In an article on the difficulties and privations of the Settlers he antagonized the governor, Lord Charles Somerset: his fight for the right to write as he chose—for the freedom of the press—is legend now. Deprived by Lord Charles of the means of earning a living in South Africa, he went back to England where he died in 1834 at the age of 46, and was buried in Bunhill Fields cemetery.

In 1970 his remains were exhumed and brought back to the Glen Lynden valley. They were reburied, in the presence of hundreds of the scattered Pringle family, in the 1820 Scottish Settlers' Memorial Church on Eildon: it was a ceremony that, via radio and press, South Africa shared.

This time when we drove to the Eastern Cape, it was the road from Fort Beaufort south to Grahamstown that was our paramount interest, the military road through the wide valley of the Fish River that was called the Queen's Road in honour of Victoria, who was crowned Queen the year the road was begun. It is, in a way, the most important road in Cape history, not so much because it linked Grahamstown with Fort Beaufort and the mountains that sheltered the Xhosa hordes, but because it was the first road built by South Africa's greatest road-maker, Andrew Geddes Bain, who was to change the history and the economy of the Cape.

Because it was a huge success, it was Bain who later made the roads of the Western Cape, the great roads and passes through the mountains that encircled Cape Town and its immediate hinterland, and which locked them away from all South Africa beyond. Cape Town had always had the freedom of the sea; it was Andrew Geddes Bain, and later his son Thomas, who gave it the freedom of the land as well.

His work was like a marvellous snowball gathering precious snow. Because he had to make roads, he looked at the soils and rocks about him. At the age of 40, the year he started Queen's Road as an untrained road-maker with the Royal Engineers, he borrowed a copy of Lyell's *Principles of Geology* and was captivated: he too would study geology. So he did as he worked on the roads, 15 years later making the first geological map of South Africa and earning himself the title of 'Father of South African geology'.

Queen's Road passes over a small river close to Grahamstown which is called the Brak today, but which in Bain's time was the Ecca; and this was the name he gave—the Ecca Series—to the rock formations at the base of the **Ecca Pass** leading to it: it is a famous name because it is in the rocks of this series that South Africa's coal deposits are found.

Because he made roads and studied rocks, Bain became something else, the first great fossil hunter of South Africa—as late as the 1930s, half the Karoo fossils at the British Museum had come from him. The mammal-like reptile fossils that set the 19th century scientists agog were first found by him—certainly it was he who first introduced them to the world.

Much of his collecting was done in this Fort Beaufort area. It was while he was road-building through Blinkwater just north of Fort Beaufort that he one day spotted a small bone sticking out of a rock that turned out to be part of the skeleton of an immense creature, an ancient giant lizard, with a large mouth, wide open, with 60 teeth, which became known all over the scientific world as the Blinkwater

Monster, *Pareiasaurus*. It was in this area, as well, that he found, among other creatures, his first *Dicynodon*, one of those famous mammal-like reptiles that he called bidentals because they had only two tusks in the upper jaw and no teeth.

When he had made a collection of these and other species he offered it to Grahamstown as the nucleus of a museum. His great-grand-daughter, Margaret Lister, records that this 'parcel of old stones' was rejected, and that Bain, nettled, made up his mind to send them to the Geological Society of London. Before he did so, however, in 1844 he exhibited them in Grahamstown, and this had its own sequel. Dr William Guybon Atherstone, a medical practitioner in the town—the same man who had remarked on the Gouritz aloes—looked at them and was entranced. They led to his study of soils, stones, and fossils through the succeeding years, and to work and friendship with Bain: and thus it was that 23 years later, when a 'stone' was sent to him to identify as he sat in his Grahamstown garden, he knew it was a diamond. It was the first of South Africa's diamonds, and in a way it was Bain who had set it rolling round the world.

But he was thinking of something a good deal more precious to him than diamonds when he packed up his bones in three casks and five packing cases: these, together with his first 'geological letter', were the first intimation the world had that a new race of animals had been found at the Cape.

London fortunately, was more receptive than Grahamstown. The scientists looked at the bones and found them marvellous, and they encouraged Bain to continue with the work.

Sixteen kilometres before Grahamstown on the right-hand side of the road at the top of the Ecca Pass is a monument to Bain. It is worth stopping to look at, and to spend a moment thinking about the 19-year-od Scot who came to South Africa the year after the Battle of Waterloo, who was—in the first part of his life here—saddle-and-harness-maker, explorer, trader, soldier, farmer, before he ever became a road-maker, a scientist or a great man. We like to remember as well that people enjoyed his bright blue eyes, and that two minutes after he had joined a gathering, 'all was laughter and gaiety': the little details give him an extra dimension.

We headed south along Queen's Road, passing **Fort Brown** just across the Fish River, once a border fortification. Few people remember it for its past history; instead there is a brand new Fort Brown legend.

In early 1974 heavy rains caused the rivers of the eastern districts to flood. Many of the modern bridges were swept away, but not the old iron bridge here. People had gathered on the banks watching the torrent bearing past dead horses, still with their saddles, concrete mixers, tractors, beds and motor-cars and houses, when they saw an ostrich floating down the river.

With its wings spread out on the water, it sailed by, bending its long neck now and then to peck, with every appearance of pleasure, at the pumpkins rushing by beside it. The crowd held its breath as it neared the bridge, for the water was almost level with it. Almost, they could see it think, 'Oh goodness, my neck!' for at the crucial moment it bent its head, laying its neck along the surface of the water, and was borne unscatched below the bridge, where it appeared again with its neck upright, bending its head as if bowing from left to right. It had been a dismal crowd: now it gave a great roar of delight.

Further south still on the road to Port Elizabeth lies **Grahamstown** in the district of Albany, a town that is like a pocket of another world, 19th century, English-flavoured, with its own legends and traditions. It has the first-rate **Albany Museum** with its research scientists, Rhodes University, and is packed with famous schools and churches, all things of the urgent present, so that it is strange it should appear so much a city of the past. Perhaps it is the touches of old wars, the signal towers on the hills around, the fort, the old houses, the feeling generally that time moves slowly here.

It was for a while the hub of the early frontier wars, and it was to this countryside that there came the bulk of the British Settlers of 1820, with their top hats and silk slippers, their ignorance, innocence and courage, the people who were planned to act as a shield to the old established parts of the country against the Xhosa hordes, and to civilize the frontier.

Fifteen years later they faced huge Xhosa forces avalanching across the Fish River, killing, and devastating the countryside: the Settlers took refuge in the churches and fled with families and possessions to Grahamstown and other villages.

It was Harry Smith's moment. Here he was again, full of courage and swagger, on New Year's Day, 1835, beginning his historic 600-mile ride from Cape Town to Grahamstown to take command of the forces and save Grahamstown, an epic ride that people remember when they have forgotten the rest of history—14 miles an hour, 100 miles a day, in six days, over mountains and rough tracks, in sickening heat, on 'Dutch horses living in the fields without a grain of corn', with his orders and warrants sewn into the lining of his jacket by Juana.

We remembered that ride when we travelled through the southern mountains that he had crossed. Remounts had been arranged for him and some he begged and one he stole. It was near Uitenhage, lying now further to our south-west, that—when his own horse was exhausted—he had seen a farmer with a good saddled horse that he would not part with to the stranger. So he had knocked him down, 'though half as big again as myself', jumped on the horse and galloped off. (The Boer knew Harry's reputation and hastened after him to apologize—the stranger's tactics had convinced him it could only be the Colonel!)

His fame went before him: he reached Grahamstown, proclaimed martial law, reorganized the defence, drove out the Xhosas, saved the missionaries, restored confidence. Afterwards, 'Men moved like men', he wrote. It was a good Harry Smith note.

Then there were forays into the thick bush of the Fish River. It was at Fort Willshire east of Grahamstown, that Harry one morning just before daylight desired his bugler to blow the 'rouse', or at least something that he knew. So the man blew the quadrille, at which Harry began to dance by himself in the dawn. Who could resist such a leader? Not Harry's men nor any country colonist. And it was here that he met Juana travelling from Cape Town, her wagon appearing on a height one side of the fort as he appeared on the other, and—dreaming of her, thirsting for her—he was united with her 'in gratitude to Almighty God'.

Of the things remaining in Grahamstown from the early days, the most romantic—the ivory market—has vanished. Here, in the centre of the city, near where the Publicity Association building stands today, elephant tusks were piled up for purchasers to view, and of this nothing remains save a Thomas Baines painting. There are many buildings left, however, reflecting troubled times. The Settlers built what they knew in England, sturdy cottages and solid, geometric Georgian houses, one- or two-storeyed, flat-faced, with thick walls, and here with pitched roofs. (The little stoep in front they borrowed from the Dutch.) War showed them soon the danger of thatch (in Harry's war over 450 farmhouses were burnt in a year by the Xhosas) so they built roofs of slate, shingle and tile, and the fortified farmhouses with their loopholed walls, their watch towers, guard-houses and stone kraals.

Some of the fortified farm houses, like Barville Park, are still there, while the Settler cottages, as those in Artificers' Square in Grahamstown, beautifully restored, are one of the city sights. Looking at them, we remembered that Piet Retief, the Voortrekker leader, who had shown much kindness to the Settlers, built some of Grahamstown's old houses.

There are over 40 churches in the town. The oldest is the **Cathedral of St Michael and St George,** which incorporated part of the original St George's Church of 1824, which was arsenal and refuge in war. It is a beautiful building in the Early English Gothic style—Sir Gilbert Scott, the well-known British architect, designed the tower and spire—and is the oldest cathedral church in the country. We remember with most pleasure two diverse things, the chancel windows designed by Hugh Easton, who did the Battle of Britain window in Westminster Abbey, and the pulpit that bears the carved face of an old friend.

It is that of an early bishop—Nathaniel James Merriman—and he is depicted as one of the disciples of the Resurrection scene—the others have the faces of three former bishops as well, Armstrong (who founded St Andrew's College), Cotterill and Webb. Robert Bridgeman from Litchfield, England, did the carvings.

Merriman, father of a Prime Minister of the Cape Colony, was the famous Walking Parson of the mid-1800s, who—because he could not afford a horse—made his visitations from Grahamstown across half the country on foot. He died nearly 100 years ago, but his *Cape Journals*, lively and devout, made a popular broadcast series a little while ago.

St Patrick's Church nearby, built by Roman Catholic soldiers, was also used as a place of refuge and defence in later wars—there were loopholes in the vestry.

Commemoration Church (Shaw Hall) in High Street not far away, built by the Wesleyan Methodists, was a memorial to the whole Settler group, erected in thanks for 25 years in their new home. It was the first formal memorial to the Settlers. The last was the R4,5 million **1820 Settler Monument** on Gunfire Hill above Grahamstown, designed to be the heart of English culture and as a symbol of peace, non-racialism and co-operation. It is big—twice as big as the Voortrekker Monument outside Pretoria—honey-coloured, handsome and functional, with conference rooms, offices, and a splendid theatre with a revolving stage. The first production, rightly enough, was a play, *Take Root or Die*, by Professor Guy Butler, head of the Department of English at Rhodes, a descendant of the 1820 Settlers, and prime mover in the festival that launched the opening. 'We had to take root and grow or die,' the Reverend Henry Dugmore, of the original Settlers, had said 150 years before, and this in time became a Settler watchword.

We were all very conscious, at the time of the opening of the Monument and the festival, what the British Settler heritage was—not only of the 1820 Settlers but of those who came at other times as well—a British-type parliament, freedom of the press, organized education and agriculture, roads, bridges, harbours, railways, industry, science, fossils, Georgian houses, bathrooms, books, and what our friend Newman Robinson, writing on the Settler Monument, called, 'a fresh injection of that old-fashioned but still useful commodity; good manners'.

Now, driving through Settler Country—very much pineapple land today—we were reminded of something else. This had given us our South African brand of English speech. The South African English, flat and clipped, is distinct: in this country we believe it a completely local accent, peculiar to ourselves. Not at all, says 'Wits' professor of phonetics and linguistics, Professor L. W. Lanham. Our *thenk* instead of *thank*, our *berrel* instead of *barrel*, our *kittle* for *kettle*, our *pen* for *pan,* our *naan* for *nine,* and scores of other such words, are English. They belong to regional English dialects and the Settlers brought them to the Eastern Cape, whence the accent spread—so that what we speak across South Africa today is, in fact, fine rural English and very much a Settler legacy.

CHAPTER SIXTEEN

Orange Free State—Port Elizabeth

We drove out of Pretoria one early autumn morning on the long haul, via Bloemfontein, to the Cape, the central route that is the busiest of all. We had arranged the time carefully so that when we reached Johannesburg the sun would be rising; and when we passed over the De Villiers Graaff motorway, there was that first warm light turning the city and the immense cooling towers pure gold. Johannesburg is not beautiful by broad daylight, but at this time it was magic, and as always we found it stirring.

Past Uncle Charlie's we rode, the roadhouse that is a Johannesburg landmark on the south, and on to the Parys road, and now that the light was there, we could see the cosmos. They grow, these tall beautiful daisy flowers, over all the South African uplands in every province, bursting into bloom—white, red and pink—in autumn, often round Easter-time so that people think of them as Easter flowers. Weeds to the farmers, they are a joy to travellers, who at this time pass for many kilometres through flowery plains and sometimes through flowery tunnels. They are so much part of our landscape, they seem indigenous, but are not. They came from Mexico, perhaps in fodder for horses in some war, the fodder that brought other strangers to South Africa, including the wild roses we had seen on the mountains to the east.

We breakfasted at Parys in 'Mimosa Gardens', under a *blinkblaar* on the Vaal River's edge—we choose this spot every time for the first picnic of a southward-bound trip, loving the water and the little boats, the tree with its shiny leaves, and the turtle doves calling.

It is the best place to stop on the road for many hundred kilometres. That main road, N1, is not well endowed with pleasure spots: the official picnic places beneath solitary trees are boons, but seldom gracious ones, while the food to be bought along that long interminable road makes people blanch as they recollect it. So, like other wary travellers, we had our vacuum flasks and gas stove and picnic basket, and at Kroonstad we visited the bakery to stock up with their warm delicious things.

This is the quickest route for most Transvaalers to reach the Cape, and a main thoroughfare; otherwise few would use it. This is not the Orange Free State at its best, although sometimes, when big clouds throw shadows over the grass and mealie lands, it can be beautiful. And there is always the Allemanskraaldam and the **Willem Pretorius Game Reserve,** off the national road north of Winburg, to show one what the Free State can look like—grass, densely wooded kloofs with wild olive and other trees, sounding with running water, stretches of water alive with fish and birds, plains speckled with animals—the species that were indigenous here—guineafowl on the roads, and from many points, stupendous views across the plains.

At **Winburg** we were back with the Great Trek. This is the oldest white town north of the Orange River and an important point in Afrikaner history, for it was the meeting place of all the five main Trek parties which had set out from various places in the Cape, and the spot where they worked out a simple system of government for themselves. On Kruger Day, 1968, a monument to the Voortrekkers was opened here, with five tall symbolic towers, back to back.

A little way north of Bloemfontein, national road N1 is joined by a more westerly road which leads from Pretoria and Johannesburg to Bloemfontein, through Odendaalsrus and Welkom, today's Free State Goldfields, the fields that sprang to life with such drama in 1946. Here on a mealie farm in April of that year, gold was discovered which led to the opening up of the fabulous new rich fields, and the quickest, hugest development South Africa has ever known. Today the Free State mines yield a substantial part of South Africa's total gold output.

Johannesburg came, higgledy-piggledy, into being. Not so the towns of these new fields. Their development was planned every centimetre of the way. Odendaalsrus was the only one that existed at the time of the strike: in just over 30 years since then a string of towns has developed, with Welkom, the largest, as the centre of the fields.

We sometimes use this road, and it is usually to see the flamingoes. The mines have done more than produce gold: the saline water pumped from them has made dams, big shallow pans, in the grassy plains, and these—particularly at **Odendaalsrus** and **Welkom**—attract tens of thousands of birds, above all flamingoes. The road passes close to the mine dumps and the dams; and there are the flamingoes in broad white bands, delicately feeding, showing off their startling white and when they move their even more startling crimson-pink. The landscape is so ugly, and they so entrancing in form and colour and movement that it is a specially good as well as incongruous sight.

We always take our binoculars. Both the Greater and the Lesser flamingoes are here, and it pleases us to distinguish them—those in full adult plumage with the tip of the bill dark and the bit next to the head light, are the Greater, and those with the bills uniformly dark the Lesser. It was Skead who told us years ago how to distinguish the birds in the field, a tip we have made use of many times.

Brandfort, the village before Bloemfontein, was once on the main road south so we know it well, a tiny spot on the wide plateau, remarkable only because here a man built an aircraft in 1907, only four years after the Wright brothers had made the first powered flight in the world. He was 34-year-old Maximilian Weston who had been born in an ox-wagon in the Vryheid district of northern Natal in June 1873. He rebuilt his aircraft in Paris, providing it with a 50 h.p. Gnome engine, and with this gave a flying display in Kimberley in 1911. Later he built another engine out of the spare parts of planes that had been destroyed by fire, and this, our first indigenous aircraft engine and the oldest in the country, is a national monument.

We think of Maximilian Weston as we go through Brandfort. He was the town's most famous son, and his aircraft was the beginning of the story of aviation in South Africa—an extraordinary thing to have come out of a Free State dorp.

The aircraft engine is in the **National Museum in Bloemfontein,** the next stop, and is an irresistible attraction to every boy. The museum itself is the largest general museum in the country. The city has, as well, the country's only literary museum which is in the Old Government Buildings, a centre where everything to do with Afrikaans writers is to be kept—even their medicine bottles, it seems.

There is very little left in Bloemfontein now to remind us how it got its name—Flower Fountain (or was it named after a *Bloem*—a man, an ox or a cow?) This was what it was early in the last century, the site of a perennial spring in a grassy plain jewelled with flowers, which in time became an outspan, a farm, site of a British mud fort (Fort Drury), and heart of the Orange River Sovereignty—the country between the Orange and the Vaal Rivers—proclaimed a British territory by our old friend, Sir Harry Smith, in 1848. It was taken by the Voortrekker leader, Andries Pretorius, retaken by Sir Harry, and handed over to the Voortrekkers in 1854, when the country became a republic and Bloemfontein the capital.

Bloemfontein is today the heart of Afrikanerdom, so it is altogether incongruous that its two most obvious landmarks, the hill that dominates the city and the 'white horse' outlined upon its slopes, are both linked intimately with British sailors and soldiers.

The hill is **Naval Hill,** named after the naval brigade that camped on its top in the Anglo-Boer War, after Lord Roberts had occupied the city. On the slopes was the remount camp for the Wiltshire Regiment: it was the men of this who laid out the big white horse here, picking out the outline in whitewashed rocks.

Bloemfontein is the judicial capital of the country and because it is the centre of South Africa, a general meeting place of all kinds. Farmers think of it for its ram sales, and their wives for fashion. They plan their clothes for the sales months ahead. Why talk of high fashion at Durban's July Handicap? they ask. South Africa's fashion peak? Barr! Let the world come and look at the ram sales.

We drove through the city and then through Edenburg to Trompsburg. Away on our right was Jagersfontein (from where came the world's third largest diamond) and beyond it, **Fauresmith.** We did not turn off to Fauresmith this time, although train enthusiasts often do. They go to see the main street shared alike by motor-cars and trains—there probably isn't another village like it in the world. Walter Battiss, the noted South African artist, spent some of his youth there and remembers how their rather wide side-gate, when opened, passed over one of the railway lines, and how the station-master sent one of his staff to ask him politely to close the gate 'so that the train could pass'.

In generations, there have been only two casualties, one chicken run over and one car dented (the owner forgetfully parked it in the street too close to the line).

There were gasps of horror in 1973 when the authorities announced that the Fauresmith line was to be relaid. But even the Minister of Transport, Mr Ben Schoeman (who himself graduated to cabinet rank from the footplate) had fallen under the Fauresmith spell. The line remained in the main street—relaid, reballasted, smartened up, it is true—but still down the middle.

At Trompsburg we took road N1 running southward to the Orange River, a Free State road of which we are fond, running for much of the way straight as an arrow's flight between grassy plains and koppies to the hills about the river. Just short of it, we turned off westwards to the village of Oranjekrag and the **Hendrik Verwoerd Dam.**

This is an exciting place, and the first glimpse travellers from the north have of South Africa's stupendous scheme to bring water to dry territory of the south and west, the Orange River Project. The Orange is the biggest river in the country, with its tributaries draining two thirds of South Africa. Rising in the mountains of Lesotho to the east—and there it is not much more than 250 kilometres from the Indian Ocean—it flows 2 200 kilometres to the Atlantic, for more than half its way through dry or desert country, irrigating only the narrow band of ground in its valley. It used to be an unbridled river, its water—that should have given life to men and animals—pouring away to the sea, at times flooding its banks and bringing chaos, at others dwindling and drying up, bringing destruction of another sort.

That idle, 'unemployed', and sometimes dangerous water posed a problem for a hundred years. Men thought constructively about it for a long time, and the scheme that evolved—the Orange River Development Project—was the climax to the most detailed and dramatic planning South Africa had known, to make the river work, to take its waters where they were needed for irrigation and for power.

Dams and power stations were planned from near the mouth of the river in an arc across the interior, a R900-million project which would take, by stages, 30 years to complete. The appearance of the Midlands and Eastern Cape would change—there would be dams, tunnels, canals, power stations, and green growing things where there were few before, and industries to follow: it would halt the drift of people to the cities, said experts hopefully, and tourists would flock to the great new lakes and the·delights they offered.

We had with us a tourist map of the area already showing broad green bands labelled Orange River Project, running southwards from the Orange River, one through Cradock following the Great Fish River, the other through Graaff-Reinet and the Sundays River, with a green link through Somerset East joining the two: these were the areas—the hot dry Karoo lands—to which the Orange River water would come, and when it reached the ocean it would be, not the Atlantic, but the Indian.

Here at the Verwoerd Dam we were seeing the first step in the project, the largest and most important single work, for on the water caught and held by the dam the success of the whole scheme depends. It is the largest dam in the country, covering 373 square kilometres: its wall is 90 metres high, and it holds 3 000-million cubic metres of water. Already it is a tourist draw. From it, water goes to the P. K. le Roux Dam in the north-east, second largest dam in South Africa, and into the longest tunnel in the world, the Orange-Fish Tunnel, which starts the water moving southward to the Indian Ocean.

We had seen the dam in the making, the foundations being laid, the wall going up across this gorge of the river. One early morning years before we had looked out of the motel window which overlooked the valley, and seen it filled with cloud, with the dark peaks of the hills rising through it. 'This is what it will look like when it's full,' we had exclaimed; and now we saw we had been right. The water had taken the place of the mist: it was silvery-white and later blue, filled with islands, and it gave us the sort of electric shock that water in a dry place always brings.

It was so sea-like that we could not comprehend its size; but as we walked over the wall looking at the water rushing through the outlets to the river below, and the huge tower of spray with its rainbow, and listened to the roar, we did realize something of its magnitude.

We crossed to the southern bank—to the Cape—to the outlook on the rocky ridge overlooking the river. Eight kilometres away was the village of Norvalspont, a much-used river crossing in the old days, and not far upstream, a little short of Bethulie, the place where Colonel Gordon, that soldier-explorer who had carried away part of Bartolomeu Dias's cross at Kwaai Hoek, had first seen the Orange River. Up till then the colonists had called the river Die Groote Rivier and the Hottentots the Gariep: it was Gordon who christened it the Orange, not once but twice, here informally in late 1777, and later ceremoniously at the mouth of the river near the Alexander Bay of today. It was Gordon who as well made the first charts and drawings of the river.

The hippo that Gordon saw have gone. Had the Great Snake as well, we wondered, the monster up to 9 metres long that people had claimed to have seen up and down its length? All sorts of people had seen it, we remembered, including reputable witnesses, yet no giant cast skin or dead monster had ever been recovered. Dr Hans Sauer, who wrote *Ex Africa*, saw a huge serpent when he was a boy, bathing in the river at Aliwal North—his friends and his father saw it too. A trader at Upington ferrying stock across the river saw one emerge close to him: its 'neck' was three metres long, and his Hottentots screamed. And there was the story to back it up of the American companion of the prospector, Fred Cornell, who saw a gigantic serpent in the river near the Augrabies Falls—it seized a calf from the shore and disappeared. Sir James Alexander well over a hundred years ago wrote of a big snake at the mouth of the Orange River, 'whose trace on the sand is a foot broad'. Hottentots have told tales about it ever since.

Could there be any truth in the stories? Certainly F. R. Paver, well-known editor of *The Star*, suggested there could be, that there might be a giant breed of python, a specialized variety, some shy retiring giant, living mainly in water and among rocks. We bandied this about. What fun, what horrific wonder, if the Verwoerd became one day a Loch Ness Dam with an Orange River monster to give it mystery as well as fame.

Colesberg lies a little west of the Verwoerd Dam, and it was there we spent the night. We were happy to reach it, this little northern Cape town with its old houses and fine old Dutch Reformed Church, that had once been a gateway to the north: the hill dominating it, Coleskop, had been the best-known landmark in the whole countryside once upon a time. The main road bypasses it now, but we always turn in to see it; it has a look and smell of the Cape Province—*die Kolonie*, the Coloured men say who fill the petrol tank—and it is the first we meet on our way.

We think of the district today mainly for its horse-breeding; but once upon a time it was diamonds and lions. Through here much of the diamond traffic passed to the early Kimberley fields, while the first diamond discovered came here to be viewed and considered by the Civil Commissioner, Lorenzo Boyes, who used it to scratch a pane of glass—the pane is still there in the Town Clerk's office.

That day we were more interested in lions than diamonds, for it was on the flats near the town that the last Cape lion in all that huge Karoo area was shot by Captain Peter Copeland-Crawford in 1836. It was not the very last of the Cape lions for a few lived on in other parts until the 1850s, or possibly even later, but it was the last in this territory that had been so much his.

In a way we had grown up with him. The first lion stories we had heard had been of him: he was Van Riebeeck's lion and that of the first colonists and Voortrekkers; and now zoologists were telling us that he had been a creature on his own, not a Transvaal or Kalahari lion of today but a distinct sub-species, larger and heavier than the northern race, with a longer body—up to 3,3 metres, it was claimed—with a snub nose, and a luxuriant black mane and a thick dark fringe of hair below his belly.

That he had been a 'different' lion was fascinating; that he, who had disappeared from the Cape not much more than a century ago, had left behind him only stories, was fantastic—he had gone from this land where he had lived in such numbers leaving behind hardly a skull, a bone, a skin. We remembered, as we drove through the Colesberg flats, how zoologists had longed for concrete details and found so little, and how that last lion shot here was now not in South Africa at all, but in the British Museum of Natural History, the only mounted specimen in good condition in the world. We had gone to see it once, but it was being refurbished, and, said a museum official, precious and not for casual visitors. Now it is on show. We would go and look for it again in London, we promised one another, this glorious sad old relic: it might no longer smell of karoo bush, but it was still part of the Cape story.

Perhaps we will not need to go to London: perhaps we will see the

Cape lion here in the flesh. A long time ago Dr Austin Roberts had told us, when we visited him at the Transvaal Museum, that he was sure that the lions in the Dublin zoo, which had been bred there for a long time, and which had the typical black mane and belly fringe, were descendants of Cape lions. Dublin once served as a lion clearing house, and from here lions, almost certainly from the Cape, travelled to many zoos. What that means, says James Clarke today, is that its genes may still be alive and 'living in Europe', and that if this is so, it might be possible to recreate it. After all, he says, the Germans have been trying for 30 years with a fair degree of success to recreate the big black auroch, ancestor of modern cattle, which has been gone for 350 years. Why not the Cape lion which disappeared relatively lately?

We talked about this bizarre possibility all the way to Cradock. From Colesberg two roads lead to the coast, the main south-west road, N1, through Hanover and Richmond, and the southern one, which—a little way south of Middelburg—branches again, one arm going to Graaff-Reinet and Willowmore, the other to Cradock and Port Elizabeth. It was the Cradock road we chose.

Cradock, on the Great Fish River, is one of the busy towns of the Karoo, on a main road and railway line. Like most other Karoo towns, it is dominated by its Dutch Reformed Church. This, however, is a church with a difference, for it was modelled on St-Martin's-in-the-Fields in London. When we had first looked as this famous church off Trafalgar Square, we had been perplexed, it had so familiar an air. We were right. We had seen it often here, bounded by dusty Karoo streets.

Cradock was important to us personally for two things, firstly because it was closely associated with Olive Schreiner, South Africa's first great novelist, and secondly because of the national park close to it, the Mountain Zebra National Park, which is one of our favourites.

A good many South Africans grew up with Olive's *The Story of an African Farm*, that wild, dark, stormy, ludicrous, magical book that took the world by storm in 1881. Olive had conceived and written it on a farm here in the Cradock district, Ganna Hoek, much of it before she was 21. She had been born on a mission station (now in Lesotho) in 1855, had a strange hard nomadic childhood—largely in the Karoo—and at the age of 19 was serving as governess to a family in the Cradock district: she lived and wrote, with labour and passion, in a little outhouse, crouched under an open umbrella to protect her from the rain pouring through the leaking roof. The book she wrote was a few years later to be one of the most famous to have come out of Africa.

When she had finished writing it, she had to find someone who would help her get it published: she packed it up in a coarse cotton cloth and then in brown paper, and sent it off to England to a friend of Karoo days, Mrs Mary Brown, of the well-known Solomon family of Cape Town, who was then living in Burnley, Lancashire. Mary remembered later that when she opened it there poured out on the Lancashire winter air the strange pungent smell of the smoke of wood fires from a Karoo farm. She folded away the cloth and kept it all her life.

The manuscript was written with many blots, many erasions, and here and there a grease mark 'as though the tallow candle had dropped a tear'. Mary Brown, shaken with homesickness, sat up half the night reading it. She and her husband eventually sent it to a friend in Edinburgh who submitted it in his turn to an Edinburgh publisher. He suggested certain alterations, and the manuscript was returned to Olive in South Africa. She revised it, feeling 'a little heartsore', and in 1881, at the age of 26, took it herself to London.

Even now she had trouble finding a publisher, although in the end Chapman and Hall published the book. It was a sensation. As one literary critic wrote, 'The faults of the book stared at me, but the magic of it was in my blood.' In one leap, Olive was the rage, the New Woman, the young genius from the South African desert, lionized by all London. It was to be her only great novel. She was to have happiness with her husband, unhappiness and heartbreak later, but this was her triumph, and this, we thought as we drove through the Cradock countryside, was where it all began.

A good many South Africans were, as it happened, thinking of Olive Schreiner at the same time as we were. PACT, the Performing Arts Council of the Transvaal, was presenting the first dramatized version of *The Story of an African Farm*. How, we had wondered, could that story, that passionate, undisciplined cry from the heart, ever be contained upon a stage. But André Brink, writer and poet, had done the adaptation from the book, and Annelisa Weiland was playing both the part of Olive and of her heroine, Lyndall, of the book. As soon as the curtain went up on *Kopje Alone* (*Ganna Hoek*), on the farmhouse and yard and the ladder to the loft, the audiences were transported: the old dark magic flooded into the theatre, and there was André Brink leading them in and out of the familiar story, and Annelisa, with passion and poetry, as they had thought of Olive and of Lyndall.

Olive died in 1920. Her husband, Cronwright, had her buried on top of a sugarloaf mountain a little way outside Cradock town. Her private collection of books is now part of the Cradock Library. The descriptions of the countryside she left are as valid as when she wrote them over 90 years ago: today if people want to know the essence of this northern Karoo, they only have to open Olive's book and read the first magic page.

The **Mountain Zebra National Park,** our destination that day, lies 27 kilometres from Cradock among the mountains; it can be reached from the Middelburg-Graaff-Reinet road where there is a turn-off some 11 kilometres from the town.

This is a small park as national parks go, some 6 630 hectares in size, a place of arid Karoo hills and mountains, steep valleys and immense views, which was created in the 1930s to preserve the mountain zebra, a distinct zebra species, from extinction. These charming, neat animals, with their compact little bodies, their brilliant stripes right down to their precise hoofs, their dewlaps and big donkey ears, once lived in numbers in the mountains of the Cape. Zoologists know them as *Equus zebra* whereas the common zebra of the north is Burchell's zebra, *Equus burchellii*. They went the way of so many wild animals after the coming of the hunters, until by the 1930s a few herds only were left—when the farm Babylonstoren, now part of the park, was taken over by the National Parks Board in 1937, the herd of zebra for which it was famous consisted of only six. They were some of the rarest animals in the world. There were 140 of them that autumn day in 1975 when we saw them on a Karoo mountain slope here, and we looked at them with awe—it is not often men can bring back to life a vanishing species and mend the mistakes of another age.

Except for the eland that leapt out at us from a thicket of thorn trees, and the kudu in the bush, all the animals in the park were easily seen, which proved a big advantage. There were springbok, blesbok, rooi ribbok, duiker and steenbok, and gemsbok brought back after an absence of a long, long time, and birds by the score. C. J. Skead, who knew the park well, thought the bird song seemed to be louder, and more, and more persistent, and could not find the reason. We went up the mountain road, past the koppies with the dassies basking in the sun, and the *kiepersol* trees with their big blue-green leaves and candles of bloom, into a sharp, high, wide world where even the smells were sweeter: and we knew at once why the birds sang more persistently and louder.

There were Bushman paintings as well as animals here. We followed a path along a mountain stream to reach them. There was an ochre-coloured eland on a rock face in a shelter above the water, a *kiepersol* and silver, pungent-smelling bushes about the entrance, two

256

Lilienfeld's shop (now Rosen's) at Hopetown. Geoffrey Jenkins points to the scratch marks still visible on the window made to test Van Niekerk's great diamond. The marks are, indeed, rather more visible than the author.

The Big Hole at Kimberley

Pomona today, derelict and abandoned. Once men saw this desert strewn with diamonds glittering in the moonlight

The loneliest graveyard in the world—Pomona

black eagles above soaring and dwindling, and as we stood a sudden thunder of hoofs and a herd of mountain zebras dashed across the valley floor and vanished into the bushes on the far side. We knew our luck. Nowhere else in the world, not even in other parts of Southern Africa, could we have experienced just this combination of marvellous things—the mountain, the wild olives and the rushing stream, the eland painted on the rocky wall, and finally those fleet wild little animals, rescued from oblivion, charging, all colour and dash, through their own remote mountain home.

We visited the museum on Doornhoek farm, within the park, a farmhouse filled with old farm things, the dairy with a reed ceiling and all the butter-making apparatus, smooth and honey-coloured now, and the wagon house with the bellows and forge, and the wagon built in Cradock in 1902 with the water barrel slung below. Then we went on to the farmhouse at Weltevrede to spend the night. We had heard about the two farmhouses in the park which offer accommodation and what fun they were. This time there was nobody else but us. There was the big old house with a heap of wood before the door but not a glimmer of light nor any voice. We opened the door and went in. Everything was neat as a pin, a pile of blankets in the bedroom, the little refrigerator working, the stove in order, candles on hand. We made a roaring fire and ate our supper before it, with a bottle of good wine and the flames flickering, and wondered if there could have been a better day or a better way of ending it.

The road south to Cookhouse runs through the valley of the Great Fish River, through which also the water of the Orange River Project now flows. We took this route next day, at Cookhouse abandoning the main road to Port Elizabeth—a road with few pleasures—to take the old road from Somerset East over the Suurberg to the sea, where we found beauty and interest round every corner.

Somerset East made a famous start. This small old town, which grew out of an official experimental farm, was founded in 1815 by Lord Charles Somerset. It lies in a shallow valley at the foot of the lovely Boschberg, with one main street running right across the valley from a 'great house' at the foot of the mountain to the farther slope two kilometres away, and the town spread out symmetrically on either side. Since we knew it of old, it had lost its fine avenues of oak and plane trees.

There was one thing, however, as good as we remembered of old, and that was the 'great house' at the head of the main street, that long axis laid out 150 years ago. It is the old parsonage, the double-storeyed, Georgian farm manor house, facing south in the tradition of

Settler homes, that is not only one of the best-known houses in the Eastern Cape but one of the most beautiful as well. Somerset East is only on the fringe of Settler Country proper, yet this is an English home such as the Settlers might have built in Albany.

It was built in 1818—which makes it probably the oldest great house of the Eastern Cape—as part of the government farm. It is popularly thought to have been the Drostdy, the seat of the landdrost, but this it never was. Instead, in 1828 it was owned by the Wesleyan Church and a chapel made within it; by 1834 it belonged to the Dutch Reformed Church and was its parsonage or pastorie, and it remained this for over 100 years. Here came George Morgan, and following him John Pears (friend of Carlyle), strange names today for Dutch Reformed Church ministers, but then in keeping with the times, to be succeeded by the Hofmeyrs, father and son. Hofmeyr is one of the famous South African names, and the Hofmeyr ministers here made it widely loved as well.

The house is now a museum so that it is open to the public, and it still has an atmosphere of life and history. In the Hofmeyr day rooms were built on 'like swallows built a nest'. We knew the house when it was erupting with handsome lively Hofmeyr children—the ingenuity of one of these, Jan Hendrik, is still legend in the town. Walking through the house, over the yellow-wood floors, we climbed up to the children's room, and here we heard how, when renovating the house, the workmen pulled out the ceiling and found a thick layer of acorns and oak leaves (from the oak-lined streets of Somerset East) to deaden sound. We thought of Jan Hendrik and laughed.

We wandered slowly round the town. Over the mountains beyond Bruintjeshoogte to the west, the towns and villages were built by Afrikaners in their own tradition: but here in Somerset and its surrounds, the British Settler note lingers still in the houses and the roofs of slate, probably carried to South Africa as ballast in sailing ships.

The westward road from Somerset East over Bruintjeshoogte to Pearston and Graaff-Reinet is now becoming known as Under-the-Mountains, a good name for this Karoo route hugging the blue mountains for many scores of kilometres. It is a route we know well for many things, including the big dam on the farm **Cranemere,** 16 kilometres beyond Pearston on the left hand side of the road. This, after good rains, is a fine stretch of water which is famous for its blue cranes, and it was here that the artist, Dick Findlay, sketched the crane that adorns the five cent coin. This time, however, we left Bruintjeshoogte on our right and headed south.

This southern road to Port Elizabeth runs a good part of the way through Karoo plains, flat and dry, to the Suurberg—the mountains which here separate the Karoo from the coastal plain. Over 150 years before us Thomas Pringle, the Settler-poet, had ridden to the **Suurberg,** or Sour Mountain, from Somerset East, probably following much the same route, noting the dry desolate veld without a single spring, the vultures, the bustards and ostriches, and snakes and lizards, and little else. He had found a farmer living against the mountain in a 'wigwam' and had supped there on mutton and potatoes dressed with wild honey, and then climbed the steep slopes by a cattle path.

We passed Ann's Villa, near where Pringle had dined, and from here snaked up the mountain on a good gravel road, seeing the same things Pringle had, the slopes with the wiry sour grass, glens and deep ravines, and finally the Hottentot bread trees that he had written of. We stopped at once. He had thought them palms: we knew they were cycads, of the same fascinating race as the Modjadje's palms of the north-eastern Transvaal, but of the species called *Encephalartos longifolius*, which almost changed the course of history. The kernels of all the cycad species that have been tested contain a potent liver poison. In the Anglo-Boer War General Smuts and a Boer commando camped in this Suurberg, ate the seeds and were poisoned. They all recovered —but how easily they might have died, and what then would have been the course of South Africa's history for the next 50 years!

At the Zuurberg Inn on top of the range we had, not mutton dressed with honey, but tea; and from here we followed what we fancied might have been Pringle's path, looking out over his 'billowy chaos of naked mountains, rocks, precipices and yawning abysses', his deep-sunk dells and dark impenetrable forest, and at the mountain's foot the forest-jungle stretching to the coast, with the Sundays River, like a dragon's path, winding through. The immense view could have changed very little, we thought, as we looped down the mountain, past the streams and yellowwood trees and candelabra-like euphorbias, although the elephant alleys that Pringle had talked of had long ago disappeared, those paths arched over like a summer alcove that the elephants had once made to climb the mountain.

At the mountain's foot we were in the low, dense, spiky, succulent jungle of the Addo Bush, still with its elephants, the last anywhere inland in the Cape, no longer roaming as in Pringle's day but confined now in the **Addo Elephant National Park.**

They are the same species as those in other parts of Southern Africa today, but smaller, short-tusked and bad-tempered; and when, in the old days, we drove through this bush, along a sandy track in temperatures exceeding 40 degrees Celsius in the shade, we knew why the elephants were vicious—it was the hottest, most suffocating place we had ever known.

It was because the jungle was inhospitable that the elephants here were saved. Elephants, like buck, make bad gardeners, and when the fertile Sundays River Valley began to be intensively farmed more than 60 years ago, elephant damage to property and life became a burning problem. In 1920 the almost legendary big-game hunter, Major P. J. Pretorius, was commissioned by the Province to wipe out the elephants. He did almost this. He went into the bush—the death trap of a jungle—with dogs, and a ladder with which he spotted the elephants and from which he sometimes shot. His only assistants were a bunch of Hottentot ex-jailbirds for no-one else would take the job. He killed over 120 elephant, sometimes when they were sleeping, sometimes at danger to his life, and when public opinion was roused and it was decided to protect the last, only 16 were left that he had not been able to find in the dense bush.

Everybody in the Eastern Cape in those days talked elephants. A little girl, Sita Osmond from the Sundays River Valley, went with her father in an old Tin Lizzie to visit Pretorius. Now a grandmother, she talks still of the big open arena of the compound with the huge rib cages of the slaughtered elephants upside down, the little yellow men, the ex-jailbirds, standing in the pool of blood within the swaying ribs, hacking off the flesh; and a woman in a khaki helmet standing on an elephant measuring its ears. There was Pretorius in his braces, spare and small and sallow, like a piece of biltong, eating elephant meat and hard-boiled eggs with his gun beside him, and telling stories, and herself crouched behind a bush, longing to listen, afraid to look.

The park is only 72 kilometres from Port Elizabeth, and is a tremendous attraction. It is a kind little place, enclosed now by an elephant-proof fence; no longer do the animals hold up the trains or threaten railwaymen and farmers. Instead, visitors can watch them—there are over 60 today—eating oranges and pumpkins.

It was the Addo elephants that reminded us how the early colonists refused to eat elephant meat, not because it was poor eating but because the great animals were thought to have the emotions of men. South Africa's most famous elephant, Hapoor, the old bull with the nicked ear that was for many years the leader of the Addo herd, had a human's reasoning power, and—could one say—compassion? The Nature Conservator told the story of how he had darted a sick elephant cow, Ouma, in order to immobilize and treat her. She fell, when hit by the dart, got up, and was then helped by Hapoor and another elephant towards a dam. She fell again, and this time Hapoor ended her life by stabbing her with his tusk between ear and eye and behind the ear, stabs which the Conservator found later were clearly in the direction of the brain. Hapoor then returned to the herd and led them back to Ouma's body around which they all stood, Hapoor trumpeting the while.

Hapoor was the elephant that showed the others that the first fence around the park that was electrified (and a failure) need not necessarily contain them. He taught them that only the wires were dangerous, and that if they pushed the poles only, they could destroy the fence without shocking themselves.

A little while ago the Conservator here saw something else that set people talking, a new baby elephant that could not reach its mother's teats. He watched two other elephants lift it up in their trunks, wait while the baby had a good long drink, and then set it back gently upon its feet.

Who indeed, we asked, turning our faces towards Port Elizabeth and the sea, could eat an elephant after that!

CHAPTER SEVENTEEN

Karoo

❦

We had, on that previous journey, taken the Cradock-Port Elizabeth road, but far more often it is the more westerly roads to the coast that we choose. Although the Graaff-Reinet road to Uniondale, Knysna and George is our favourite, the Colesberg road through Beaufort West—the quickest route from Pretoria to Cape Town—and its branch road to Oudtshoorn, have many things in common with it.

They are all, for much of their length, Karoo roads, and they all break through the barrier of mountains separating the **Karoo** from the coast over passes so spectacular that travellers often plan their routes around them.

The Graaff-Reinet road, with New Bethesda to the west and Pearston to the south-east, runs through softer Karoo than the western route—if, indeed, Karoo can ever be described as soft. The very name is a Hottentot word meaning dry, and so it is. Even at its most lush, it is semi-desert. More than half South Africa is semi- or true desert, and of this only the Karoo is known to most South Africans. Many would rather not experience it at all, but are forced to, because it stretches across two-thirds of the Cape Province as a huge, arid, dusty plain, covered—depending on the season—with roasting sand or icicles, which travellers cross when going north or south.

Flat as the sea, as parts are, there are mountains, and hills like table-tops, koppies with dark blue-black rocks of ironstone that ring like metal when struck, and a dwarf vegetation of the hardy and the brave, plants adapted to struggle and exist, each in its own way a small miracle.

People travelling through the Karoo by train or motor-car often believe it is devoid of living things, devoid even of anything man-made except sheep-grids, gates or windmills. In actual fact, it did once support an abundance of wild things, but because it is farming country now, and fenced, these have dwindled, although there are still a surprising number which are seldom seen because they are shy or nocturnal. Instead have come the sheep and goats, the wealth of the Karoo, which have made this one of the great wool and mohair centres of the world.

Even the sheep, say travellers bitterly, are seldom seen; and it is true that on the main Karoo roads almost nothing seems to stir. The sheep on the vast farms are always over the *randjie*; there may be a group of springbok, or a ground squirrel dashing across the road, a secretary bird, a couple of blue cranes hunting insects, and a little hawk or chanting goshawk on a telegraph pole. But usually there is little to suggest the teeming life that lies about, the kudu in the bush, the baboons and eagles on the mountain, the dassies in the rocks, all the creatures in their holes below the ground that venture out with darkness, the snakes, the scorpions and spiders and the other abundant life beneath the stones.

Travellers know little of the Karoo's insect world—it is, above all else, *their* world. They see perhaps a swarm of locusts or moths, or hurrying ants when they stop for a picnic tea, and often this is all. But even to guess at this insect life, at what stirs around the roads and railway lines, is richness (sometimes of an unusual kind, but richness still).

There are the cicadas, the Christmas bees, shrilling away—their vibrating cry through the hot summer days is as much the Karoo's song as the coo-coo-roo of the turtle doves. There are house flies, horse flies that bite people and blowflies that eat holes in sheep, and a horde of others; and bees and wasps in enormous numbers—Karoo honey has it own wild tang.

There are butterflies, not rare or splendid species but, in particular, the little Lucerne Butterflies, fluttering or flying fast and low in huge numbers over the lucerne lands like orange clouds—they can sometimes be seen from the highway.

And there are moths. There is the small yellow one which in its larval stage feeds on old damp horns lying upon the ground. The little runs it makes upon the horns are root-like, and for generations foxed farmers here who maintained that the sheep horns on their ground took root and grew! There are, above all, the brown moths speckled with cream that every farmer knows very well. They are there, billions and billions of them, of a summer's night fluttering in a fog about insect-proof wire doors of houses to reach the lights beyond, and in the Karoo villages enshrouding lights everywhere. Their dark caterpillars —Karoo caterpillars—do not make roots but webs: they look like spiders' webs enveloping the little Karoo bushes, and they eat the bushes clean.

There are the Brown Locusts, endemic to the Karoo, lively little creatures as tough as the Karoo bushes themselves, that can still, in their times of abundance, hold up a motor-car · upon a highway.

Fourteen years ago swarms in the Karoo stopped the Cape Town-Johannesburg train. There are their relatives of all kinds, armoured ground crickets or *koringkrieks* that are not crickets at all but monstrous spiky creatures with eyes on stalks; true crickets with legs like kangaroos, and Hottentot gods, green mantes lifting their front legs as if in prayer.

There are beetles, those with the long-drawn-out, high-pitched cry that local people know as *Langasem*—Long Breath—and ones so small they seem like particles of moving earth, and dung beetles, snout beetles, and large tiger beetles that bite; mosquitoes larger and better, we are certain, than in any other land; ants by the legion and termites, and ant-lions that make the round dimples in the cinnamon sand—the list could continue without end.

There are as well all the things people think of as insects but are not, like millipedes—sangololas—long, dark, shiny, supple pencils with prussic acid in their blood, winding along on bellies and legs after every shower of rain; centipedes and spiders—sand spiders with plump red bodies; funnel spiders waiting in their holes between Karoo bushes for their prey to twang their front-door steps of web; trapdoor spiders with picks on their jaws for digging, and baboon spiders that live in holes, terrible creatures with great fangs and furry paws; hunting spiders, red and striped, so fast they look like a flicker in the veld, and Cape scorpions with thin tails and big pincers that bear in their stings a nerve poison like a cobra's—their holes can be spotted by the insect remains (the middens!) at the entrance.

They all are made for searing days and hot breathless nights; and they can sometimes surprise even entomologists with their hardihood. Cronwright Schreiner, Olive Schreiner's husband, who collected trapdoor spider nests in the Karoo for the South African Museum in Cape Town, once melted solid paraffin and poured this, boiling hot, into the sand around a nest: after a little while the spider walked out from under the lid unharmed, leaving a little arch in the paraffin where it had travelled.

On every side of us as we drove to Graaff-Reinet were the sheep. Even if we did not see them, we knew they were there—we knew their camps and paddocks spread out over the veld, the kraals where they were dosed, the sheds and lucerne lands of the rams, and the sheds where they were shorn and their wool sorted, the wool bales, and the smell of merino wool, a lanoline smell but warmer and greasier still.

Tradition has it we were in the best sheep country in South Africa: this Sneeuberg land near Graaff-Reinet was 'the best nursery for sheep in the whole colony', wrote John Barrow nearly 200 years ago. Only then he was not talking of merinos, the large, sturdy sheep of today with their fine big fleeces and Roman noses: he was not talking of woolled sheep at all, but of the Cape sheep the settlers found here, runts by today's standards, spindly creatures with long legs, sharp noses, long lapping ears, and short frizzled hair in place of wool, with no fat anywhere except on rump and tail.

It is easy to look down on them from today's merino heights, but what a race they were and how both the Hottentots and the early farmers prized them. Like locusts, they could live off the veld where other animals perished (they could live off their tails like camels off their humps, men said); certainly they had come far enough and hard enough to toughen their breed, probably from Syria many centuries ago, for their fat tails resembled the tails of Syrian sheep.

It was their tails for which men—and housewives—loved them in particular. They were enormous lumps of fat, which greased the Hottentots' skin and the farmers' wagon wheels, made their candles and soap, and were their oil and butter and their finest delicacy. Proud farmers claimed the tails could weigh up to 20 lb and had a standing joke with strangers at their tables: 'You have no appetite,' they used to say, 'you are not able to manage a sheep's tail.'

Plenty of people thought the tails tasted good, like marrow-bones or richest butter. They even reached England, for when Thomas Southey visited the Earl of Sheffield at Sheffield Place in the last century, he was served the tail of a Cape sheep dressed by a French cook. About the middle of the century, well over 1 000 lb of sheeps' tails were exported from Port Elizabeth in one season.

It is not likely that many Cape sheep survive in these Karoo midlands: instead, there is another fat-tailed non-woolled species, the Black-head Persian, which has a smaller tail but one that is a delicacy too. It is a sheep that came to South Africa by chance.

About the year 1870 a crippled sailing ship limped into Port Beaufort near Swellendam on the southern coast, with four black-head sheep aboard, a ram and three ewes, which had been carried to provide fresh meat on the voyage. Although they had been shipped from the Persian Gulf, they were indigenous to Arabia, and they were so surprising and curious to Cape eyes that when two farmers, who were visiting the ship, saw them, they at once decided to have them. The captain was satisfied with substitute slaughter stock, and the Persians were taken to Cape Town, and then inland, to become the founders of South Africa's Persian flocks.

One of the ewes from the sailing vessel gave birth to a lamb with a red head: her descendants had red heads too, and although we had never seen them, we knew there had been a famous pure-bred red-head stud descended from that lamb at Somerset East, away to the east.

Today merino wool from close on 30 million sheep—a major part of it from the Karoo—is South Africa's most important agricultural export: but for a long time it was fat tails versus wool, and the tails won hands down.

The first attempts to introduce woolled sheep in the 17th and 18th centuries were met with derision: a few did come then and later and the farmers split their sides—what, the back worth more than the tail of a sheep! and they slaughtered their spindly flocks and rendered down the huge tails into the oil-like fat that was their gold.

It was Colonel Gordon, whom we had thought of last on the banks of the Orange River, who in 1789 imported the first merinos that were to leave a mark on South Africa. They were six genuine Spanish sheep, four ewes and two rams, which had been part of a Spanish royal gift to Holland, and they settled down near the present town of Malmesbury in the Western Cape, multiplying and enriching the local breeds. A few of their progeny went to farmers like the Van Reenen brothers, Jan and Sebastiaan, who crossed them with native ewes, and gave neighbouring farmers the use of their rams: and soon famous sheep names, like J. F. Rietz and M. van Breda, were appearing in the south-west.

Colonel Gordon's little flock was not only the first to influence South Africa's sheep to any extent; it was also the basis of Australia's flocks. In 1795 when the British occupied the Cape, Gordon—then military commander—committed suicide, a tragic end to an illustrious life. On May 5th, 1796, at a sale in Cape Town, his widow sold 26 of his merino flock, for the sum of four guineas apiece, to two ships' captains, Waterhouse and Kent, whose ships were lying at anchor in Table Bay. They shipped the sheep to Sydney in the warships *Reliance* and *Supply* (oddly prophetic names), and of the 13 that arrived alive, five went to Samuel Marsden, farmer-missionary, and eight to Captain John MacArthur. The sheep were the ancestors of Australia's merino flocks, and Marsden and MacArthur the founders of Australia's wool industry.

In 1801 MacArthur took some of his merino wool to England, to be told it was the equal of the Spanish. At the time he was turning South Africa's merino wool into Australian gold, Cape farmers were still plugging tails. They did not for very long, for under British rule, new thoughts began to move.

Lord Charles Somerset, the governor with whom Pringle had crossed swords, imported merino sheep for the government experimental station near Darling, and some of the rams from the farm came here to Graaff-Reinet. Away to the east the 1820 Settlers were doing their bit to popularize the sheep, and it was at Bathurst in Settler Country that the first wool mill was built.

Today Australia and South Africa provide most of the world's fine merino wool, and this is a joint Gordon legacy. Australia produces a good deal more than South Africa does; but wool is a moneyspinner in both countries.

Goats came by a different route. The first settlers found goats of a kind at the Cape: and these were improved by new blood from Europe. By the 19th century the Boer goats had become a South African breed on their own, tough as the fat tailed sheep themselves. They are still to be seen, although in these Karoo Midlands another breed of goats largely took their place, the kings of the goat world, the Angoras, with their curled silky-white lustrous hair and pointed clever faces, that today make South Africa the world's principal mohair producer.

The devious ways they reached the Karoo make splendid stories. Angoras were the famous speciality of Turkey, in particular of the country round Angora. Their hair was important even from early days, and because of this the Turkish Government did not originally allow the export of any that was unspun. The time came, however, when the rest of the world began to want the little goats that produced this marvellous hair, and among them was South Africa. In 1838, at the same time that merino fame was spreading, a flock of 13 Angora goats—12 rams and one ewe—was imported. They had come by a roundabout way, via India, to the Cape. How the Turks must have laughed at colonial innocence—the rams, it was found on arrival, had all been castrated before they left Turkish soil. What nobody reckoned on, however, was that the ewe was pregnant, and on board ship gave birth to a pure-bred Angora ram kid.

That kid goat was reared as an emperor in South Africa, and it gave a royal return in its long life. The best all-white Boer ewes were put to it, resulting in a flock that was, if not pure, nevertheless in many instances good, 'yielding in some cases hair of splendid quality'. Some of these belonged to the Graaff-Reinet district, and when the first pure-bred Angoras came later, eight were sold—on an autumn day in 1857—on Graaff-Reinet's Church Square amid much interest and speculation.

From the road and railway, the Karoo farmhouses among their clumps of trees can often be seen, sometimes fine ones with gables and wide stoeps, filled with beautiful things. They were mostly built on wool and mohair.

There are sheep and goat in the kitchens too. This is a country of good cooks, and we have memories of exotic roasts and other dishes, a fat Boer goat leg stuffed with bread, herbs and whole eggs and pot-roasted, and spiced Angora *frikadelle* laced with rosemary like the baby lamb of Rome. With luck there is Persian lamb, a small delicate leg with aromatic flesh that melts in the mouth, and pastry and rusks made of Persian fat tail.

The farmhouses here are sometimes well over a century old. We knew one with a high ceilinged pantry with a big table with one thin leg (shaped by generations of cats' claws), with a brown jar on it full of *kaaings*, the little bits of crisp rich fat left after a fat tail has been rendered down, a delicacy in days when calories were not counted. There was also bread made of home-grown wheat or sometimes of minced fresh mealies, and naartjie *konfyt*, yellow peach pickle, bottled peaches and apricots, and quince 'leather' in rolls, prickly pear syrup, loquat honey, and apples of marzipan made of fresh almonds and coloured pink and green. Besides, there was springbuck biltong drying on a stoep, pickled hams; sausages made of venison and mutton, dried wholewheat crumbs, coriander, lemon rind, garlic, black peppercorns and thyme, and turkey cooked slowly in a big black pot in the back yard.

Travelling, as we were, southward, we were coming to 'Cape cookery' country, and all these farm dishes were redolent of it. The older homes both on the farms and in the villages still often have at least one of the old cookery books on the Cape art, besides their own home books of handwritten recipes, handed down through generations.

We saw *Hilda's Where Is It* on a shelf in one farmhouse, the cookery book that was one of South Africa's earliest, written by pretty, lively Hildagonda Duckitt, who was born in the Western Cape nearly 140 years ago and left a book on local food and cookery that people still use. There was Alice Hewitt's little square yellowish *Cape Cookery* as well, now an Africana prize, and Mrs Dijkman's English translation of *Kook, Koek en Resepten Boek* of 1904. We paged through it. She had set the tone for the time—'Born not for ourselves, but for our friends, our country, and for the glory of God', and what a window on the age it was, with its medicines for scab in goats and worms in lambs, its cure for drunkards, and drink for a tired horse, its directions how to mend umbrella handles and to treat wounds (an application of bluegum vinegar), to keep flies from pictures, and what to do for children with weak legs (rosemary brandy rubbed on the skin did the trick). Then there was a fat black book with three generations of farm recipes, mixed up—in good tradition—with remedies: there was a recipe for *kop-en-pootjies* (head and trotters), and one for walnut tart (made with walnuts grown on the mountain nearby) to be eaten with fresh cream and rum, alongside a remedy for eczema—'put hands in sheep dip'—and for diabetes, made with a prickly pear leaf and a *silver* spoon.

Karoo riches of other kinds flooded us as we travelled. On our right was the turn-off to **New Bethesda,** that enchanting little village. With that signpost, we knew we were back in fossil country. From here down the road beyond Graaff-Reinet and westwards to Victoria West, Beaufort West and Laingsburg, we were in the richest fossil country in the world, yielding bones of ancient dragons, and the creatures— perhaps the most important that ever lived—that were on their evolutionary way from reptiles to mammals.

They have drawn palaeontologists from all over the world: yet they were not discovered in the early days by scientists at all, but by simple, 'ordinary' people with the eyes and the spirit to see a story in the rocks about them. The great Andrew Geddes Bain, who was such a person, had been a road-builder, and here in New Bethesda had been another. He was a big gentle man, C. J. M. Kitching, who one day as he was crossing a river bed with a wagon near New Bethesda saw bone in the rock in the bed. It was the skull and skeleton of one of the mammal-like reptiles that were fascinating the world's scientists: and it was the first of many he was to find. Bain's discoveries went to the British Museum, many of Kitching's to another of the great museums of the world, the American Museum of Natural History.

Many people are inclined to think of C. J. M. Kitching as the father of Dr James Kitching, whom scientists call the greatest vertebrate palaeontologist in the world. He was, however, a great fossil-finder in his own right. Perhaps he would have been the greatest of all, but he died in his early forties of war wounds and malaria contracted in North Africa. After his death, when his family opened his kitbag, they found the fossils, the shark vertebrae and invertebrates he had collected in the Western Desert: even his socks were stuffed with them.

His father and the Karoo rocks were James Kitching's background. And there was somebody else as well, whose story we were to glimpse nearby. It was Dr Robert Broom, whose work we had met in the Transvaal Museum and in the caves of the ape-men. His love had been mammal-like reptiles before it was early man, and he had blown in and out of the Kitching home in New Bethesda breathing fossil exuberance and fire, sitting on their kitchen table cooling his coffee in his saucer and talking, talking, as the piles of rocks and fossils grew about him and Kitching, and feeding fossil literature to the Kitching family in a continuous stream.

Broom, a medical doctor and amateur palaeontologist, had—in a circuitous way—come to the village of Pearston not far from Graaff-Reinet in 1900, a place he had chosen carefully because it was on the edge of this fossil-rich country. It was C. J. M. Kitching and his brother who lured him to New Bethesda close by with talk of bones in rock; and soon he knew this whole Karoo area well.

We could not see New Bethesda from the main road, but we could spot from it a farmhouse encircled with trees some 30 kilometres before we reached Graaff-Reinet. This was the farm **Wellwood**, where a sheep farmer—he called himself 'a simple man'—without any scientific knowledge, made a museum that is without parallel anywhere in the world. He was Dr Sidney Rubidge, and he built up here a collection of fossil mammal-like reptiles from the local Karoo rocks that draw palaeontologists from everywhere.

Broom, of course, had a hand in it as well. He described the first fossil that the Rubidge family ever found on Wellwood—he called it *Dinogorgon rubidgei*—and most of the hundreds of others that followed. 'I became obsessed,' said Dr Rubidge after that fossil. Broom was already this. Thus was a marvellous partnership born, Rubidge collecting and employing others to collect for him, and Broom arriving at Wellwood throughout the years to study and name the specimens, both vibrating with the thrill of it all. The fossil specimens went into what became known as the Rubidge Museum, which is housed in a special building on the farm.

Dr Broom died in 1951, Dr Rubidge in 1971. The museum is as it was, beautifully cared for today by Richard, Dr Rubidge's son, and his wife Pam, still open (by appointment) to the public, still a farm museum, still a scientific wonder.

Graaff-Reinet is a prize at the end of the road. This fourth oldest town in South Africa, named after governor Van der Graaff and his wife Reinet, is not only a bit of turbulent frontier history, but a little place of great charm with some of the old frontier simplicity, that is emphasized now by good restoration work.

It lies in a big horse-shoe bend of the Sundays River, next to Spandau Kop, the conical hill that is a landmark, and is still as surprising a green place in its arid setting as it was a hundred and fifty years ago when travellers across the Karoo plain heard at night the croaking of the frogs in the river and knew that water, gardens and hospitality were near.

Not many South African towns date back to the 18th century, but Graaff-Reinet does, for it was founded in the 1780s. People often talk of it as 19th century (which it mostly is), but its streets, its open water furrows and homes belong to an older colony. For the Karoo-born, travelling southwards from the Transvaal, this is a coming home to something that the Transvaal for all its exuberance lacks, a sense of establishment and 'roots'. However hurried we are, we always linger here, not so much to look at the great houses—and there are some among the finest in the country—but to drive slowly round the back streets, soaking up the pleasure of these old, modest, enchanting Karoo cottages that look as if the soil had sprouted them, so right are they, so perfect in every detail both for a frontier village and a modern semi-desert town.

There are so many of them—built originally by ordinary men who were no skilled artisans, with the materials immediately to hand, with a likeness, a style so definite—that people sometimes talk of it today as Karoo architecture. The houses are there in other Karoo villages as well—Colesberg, Hanover, Richmond, New Bethesda, Aberdeen, Prince Albert, among others—but it is in Graaff-Reinet we think of them in particular, symmetrical, square, small houses, flat-roofed (there were no reeds or thatching grass in those early days for thatched pitched roofs), thick-walled, white-washed, with green shutters and projecting chimneys, and fanlights above the front doors. They are backed with gardens full of vines and fig trees, quinces and pomegranates, with a high stoep in front, and a tree—perhaps a cypress or an oak.

The town was laid out with broad streets lined with trees, terminated by fine buildings. The avenues of orange and lemon trees the early visitors admired have gone, but the streets are still treelined and the town views are as fine as ever—better in some cases, for the old buildings that so splendidly terminate vistas have, after years of dilapidation, been restored to their old beauty.

The Dutch Reformed Church—the **Groot Kerk**—is still the centre of it all. The Gothic church of the old Cape, the hub of so many villages, is here in the form of England's Salisbury Cathedral—only it is built of local stone! The Cape Town architect, J. Bisset, designed it, and it was opened in 1887 during the ministry of the Reverend Charles Murray.

The townspeople love to tell visitors that the ecclesiastical Cape silver still used in the church is the finest collection in the country.

We walked down Parsonage Street to the building at the end, which we have always thought was one of the loveliest homes we knew. A home it once was, and a home it appears now although it is today a museum filled with the period antiques (for which Graaff-Reinet is famous) arranged as they were when the house was lived in a century and more ago. It is the Old Parsonage—the *Ou Pastorie*—now **Reinet House**, essentially a Cape Dutch home of the 18th century, built about 1812 by the Dutch Reformed Church, H-shaped, gabled and thick-walled, with a flight of graceful outside steps, and a hitching post beside it.

It is linked with a family whose descendants today populate half South Africa. Andrew Murray, the Scot from Aberdeenshire, who came to Graaff-Reinet in 1822 as minister, lived here until his death in 1866. At the start he shared it with young Robertson, a teacher and fellow Scot—ancestor of the conservationist, the incomparable 'T. C.' Robertson of today. They had arrived in South Africa together as part of Lord Charles Somerset's scheme to import young Scots ministers and teachers to serve the Dutch community. Soon Murray was married to 16-year-old Maria Stegmann of Cape Town—she travelled from Cape Town to Graaff-Reinet after the wedding by horse-wagon, dressed in 'pure white muslin with embroidered bodice, very short in the waist and low in the neck'. There was little other frippery in their lives. They were a devout, courageous, hard-working couple: here they had 16 children, raising 11; here they were hosts to many—to all missionaries, including Livingstone—and from here Andrew Murray went out to minister to his wide-spread flock.

In 1972, the 150th anniversary of Andrew Murray's arrival in South Africa, his descendants gathered in Graaff-Reinet to celebrate. There were Stegmanns, Hofmeyrs, De Villiers, Neethlings, Marquards, Luscombes, Meirings—names all South Africa knows—and many more. Fifty years before they had also streamed into Graaff-Reinet for the same purpose, some travelling by ox-wagon. They were all seed of this old house.

After the death of Charles, Andrew's son and successor, the house fell on hard times and was rescued from increasing shabbiness by Graaff-Reinetters themselves, and restored under the supervision of the architect, Norman Eaton, so that by 1956 it had returned to its former glory.

Inside there are the walls a metre thick, high rooms, fine old furniture, and a splendid kitchen in which had surely been cooked the same sort of robust good food as we had eaten on the farms round about. We stood there remembering Andrew Murray. Fate had brought him to a pleasant place, yet when he had set out from his Aberdeenshire home that day in 1822, the future must have looked uncertain, frightening perhaps. Andree Luscombe—a scion of this same home—later described that parting day, how Andrew's brother had walked with him to the highway where he was to catch the London coach, and how they had sung together 'Oh God of Bethal, by Whose Hand the people still are fed', as they waited, and how this had become a family hymn in South Africa, sung many times in this house.

At the back, down the famous curving flights of steps, there is a cobbled yard, a paved garden, and the grape vine that is one of Graaff-Reinet's sights. It is a Black Acorn, or Black Hamburgh to visitors from Europe, the trunk measuring more than two metres at breast height, and is the largest vine in South Africa (the townspeople believe in the world): certainly it is bigger than its relative, the famous vine at Hampton Court. It was planted by Charles Murray in 1876 and still bears abundantly.

Reinet House is a national monument, and so is the house across the street from it, the **Residency.** We admired its lines, its gables, and in particular the fanlight above the entrance. It is a great interest walking Graaff-Reinet's streets to admire, among other things, the fanlights and count the number of their designs—it is clear, as one walks, why the whole town is called a living museum.

All **Parsonage Street** is being restored by the Simon van der Stel Foundation to look as it once did. At its other end, opposite Reinet House, is Graaff-Reinet's newest restoration project, the **Drostdy,** which for so long has been the rather dilapidated double-storeyed Drostdy Hotel, but which is now once again the single storeyed elegant old building (originally designed by Louis Thibault), an hotel still but one that is probably destined to be great.

Behind it is the little street which became famous a few years ago as Stretch Court or **Drostdy Hof.** Originally a street of cottages for slaves and Coloured workers, it was restored by the Historical Homes of South Africa—which does restoration work on a commercial basis—becoming an enchanting alley of little flat-roofed cottages, complete with slave bells and lamp posts, and gay with fresh paint and red geraniums. These have become part of the hotel.

Nearby, on the opposite side of the road, is the **Hester Rupert Art Museum,** the Dutch Reformed Mission Church of 1821, the sixth oldest church in South Africa, now a museum of contemporary South African art. It was saved from demolition in 1965 in the nick of time by Graaff-Reinet-born Dr Anton Rupert, business tycoon and philanthropist, and named after his mother.

Before we left the district, we drove the 14 kilometres past the Van Rhyneveld Dam to see the **Valley of Desolation,** this much publicized Karoo view of a desert valley carved in the rocks, with red precipices and rock columns, and below an immense landscape marked with the threads of dry stream beds. If anyone were to ask us to show them the essence of the Karoo in one swoop, we would bring them here.

Aberdeen is some 50 kilometres down the road. This little village was named in honour of Andrew Murray's birthplace. Conservationists remember it sadly because the last wild quagga in the world was shot on the flats here in 1858. When it disappeared—this beautiful defenceless cousin of the zebra—it left Aberdeen's Karoo more desolate than ever. Desolate it is, but like the rest of the Karoo, rich in desert plants. In the hills about the village grows a famous one, *Pleiospilos bolusii*, which is one of the mimicry plants that send plant-hunters crazy with delight. This one 'mimics' stones, for its pebble-sized fat leaves are not only the brownish-grey touched with green of the stones about, but rough to the touch, 'weathered' like the stones. Dr Rudolf Marloth, the famous botanist, thought it the most remarkable of the so-called mimicry plants. Marloth had the keen eyes and the blazing enthusiasm of a great botanist: he had gone succulent-hunting here on his hands and knees, creeping passionately and victoriously through the Karoo bushes, so that for us this country where he had collected could never be uniformly dull.

We hurried through Willowmore further south on the road—we had memories of trying to buy fresh bread here and being told 'it had not arrived from Port Elizabeth'—which sent us (with our memories of Karoo largesse) chattering with fury on the southern road.

Outside the town is a road to the east which takes adventurous travellers through the **Baviaanskloof**—the Kloof of the Baboons—to Hankey and the coastal road. It is the wildest, strangest, most spectacular road in Southern Africa, part of the way a river bed (impassable in heavy rain), rearing up to mountain tops, with views of a thousand peaks beyond, red cliffs, caves, yellow-woods and proteas and endless ever-flowing streams and—on the day we drove it—a farmer who, seeing a stationary motor-car on the roadway near his home, brought us a basket of oranges as a bit of Baboon Kloof hospitality.

Through Uniondale we came to the **Long Kloof,** running east-west between the mountains and parallel to the southern coast. It is a prosperous gentle valley filled with old white farmouses with long outside ladders to the lofts above, and fruit trees by the million that in spring are a cloud of blossom. It is then one of the most paintable scenes possible in a soft gentle way: but the village in it, **Avontuur,** hints at another side as well.

Avontuur means Adventure, and the valley saw more of this in the early days than any national road today. Here we were back in travellers' history. South of us were the mountains, range upon range, and beyond them the coastal strip along which we had travelled on the Garden Route. There we had seen the forests and chasms that had turned the early travellers to the north to find an easier east-west road, which was this Long Kloof. Now we ourselves were on this historic route along which they had ridden and jolted in comparative ease, the one-time ivory road to the east, and the hunters', soldiers' and explorers' road.

Soon we began our 20th century crossing of the mountains that had daunted the old-timers, on a road professionally constructed. It was the pass closest to Uniondale, Prince Alfred's, running from Avontuur to Knysna, its head in the mountains, its feet in the forest, our favourite passage through the mountains and one of the greatest beauty. This 'modern' road—now well over 100 years old and the longest of the passes through the southern mountains—was a Bain's work, not an Andrew but a Thomas Bain, and is still very much as it was in 1867 when it was finished.

We travelled down it on a leaden day with the immense bowl below us filled with rain and mist, and the peaks and rocks appearing for a moment and disappearing as we drove. As we descended it began to snow: and part of the way down, when we passed a clump of pink gladioli drooping from their rocky wall, we paused among the flakes to see if they were real.

Soon after Avontuur we found De Vlug on our left, the place where Thomas had lived with his wife and children while he was building the pass. The family came to us across the years, with all its freshness and vigour, and we thought of Johanna, Thomas's wife, and her contralto singing voice that had not only enchanted Cape Town's young men when she was 17, but which delighted and comforted the Bain family in the years that followed. All the early roads that Thomas built, including this one, knew the sound of Johanna—travelling, at work and at play—singing to her family: and sometimes of Johanna and Thomas, bumping along in the wagon in the moonlight and singing, while Thomas played the violin or the concertina.

It was a good note to end on, and we entered the cool dense coastal forest through which Thomas had made the roads, thinking of them and of Georgina watching the deep elephant footprints filling with the rain, and so came into Knysna.

CHAPTER EIGHTEEN

Little Karoo—Matjiesfontein

✤

A good deal thirstier than the eastern Karoo roads is the Colesberg-Beaufort West route N1. We travelled it last on a late autumn day, driving through the huge empty landscape, burnt umber, domed by an empty sky, talking of the true desert road it once was, when men, crawling across it with their wagons, cried with joy when they reached a water-hole that was not dry. South of Richmond, we passed on the side of the road an old wood and iron pump, a 'flesh and blood' reminder of that trail—beside it was a mesquite tree of Wild West fame: we stopped, pumped the water, cupped our hands, and drank.

Soon we passed the **Three Sisters,** the dolerite-capped hills that are a landmark in the countryside, where the alternative Transvaal-Cape route via Victoria West and Kimberley joins the main road N1—we had turned up it once especially to see the country museum at Victoria West, a delicious jumble of unexpected things, including what must be the best fossil fish in the world.

This time we did not turn north: we were hurrying to Beaufort West, with its pear trees in the streets and open water furrows, to see Napoleon's wine glasses. There were two of them in the museum that is part of the library, heavy and unusual-looking, that Napoleon is reputed to have used on St Helena. Although we knew the treasures to be found in some of these little towns and villages, we found this the most extraordinary of all.

Beaufort West leapt into the news recently, not because of Napoleon, but because of the announcement that a Karoo national park is to be established here. It was a substantial bit of good news that delighted nature conservationists everywhere, and would, they hoped, be the forerunner of other parks in the drier areas. (Conservationists keep pegging away at the fact that although South Africa has some of the world's most famous national parks, there is less land set apart from them—2,4 per cent of the whole—than in many other African countries.) The park, in scientific jargon, will be 'a conserved endemic South African ecosystem'. For ordinary people it will mean that a piece of this barren, strange, haunting Karoo will be preserved.

As we drove south-west down the Cape Town national road, we saw rising up before us to our left a line of far mountains. They were the Swartberg, the Black Mountains—blue as blue that day—the first range of mountains between us and the sea, with the Outeniqua Mountains lying beyond. At Prince Albert Road we turned eastwards towards them and the village of Prince Albert.

We were in the heart of **The Koup**—or the Goup or Gouph or Kouf or Kaup or Cope, depending on spelling whim—that desert reaching from the Swartberg to the Nuweveldberge north-west of the national road we had left. (This road, N1, still carries the name Koup, a station slightly off the road between Laingsburg and Prince Albert Road.) The name was Bushman, meaning 'fat'. Fat what? we asked ourselves, succulents or sheep tails? But no, an early writer had written, it was—to Bushmen—fat in the sense of richness, for this was a country with ostriches, honey, baboons and scorpions, and what more could a man ask?

The country had been surveyed in the 1840s, after an old trekboer, who wished to settle down, had applied to the governor of the day, Sir George Napier, for a farm here. In Cape Town this had caused a sensation. 'They'll be applying for a grant in hell next,' Sir George said; and an official who had done an inspection of the country, bellowed with laughter—'Give him the Gouph, Sir George, *Give him the Gouph.*'

The early farmers did very well, when there was no drought (as do the present ones). Their stock was big and sleek, and they obese, and it was all, claimed Dr Atherstone who later roamed the country fossil-hunting, because of the fossils, the bones of those ancient reptiles that had yielded up their phosphates and so enriched the land! It might have been apocryphal, we knew, but his theory amused us. After all, this was part of the great mammal-like reptile country. The first specimen known—a tooth of some old monster—which had belonged to the land-surveyor, Chrisbrook, had been picked up by a boy here: and it had been one of the most famous collecting grounds ever since.

Atherstone did not come only to collect fossils. Men have treasure-hunted on the Karoo ever since they knew it—10 years ago when we travelled through it there were oil derricks etched against the sky, where men were oil-hunting. Atherstone came on the track of gold, and with him was Thomas Bain, then Inspector of Roads. They came to investigate an extraordinary find, a fair-sized gold nugget that a 13-year-old boy had found among some lamb droppings in the veld on what is now the road to Seekoegat, east of Prince Albert.

They interviewed young Lodewyk Luttig, an intelligent honest lad, brown as the Karoo itself, and he showed them the exact spot where he had seen, as he thought, the dropping of a new born lamb. It was in a sheep track about two kilometres from the homestead on the very watershed of the Koup from where the waters flowed east and west. Kicking the dropping aside, he felt it *couldn't* be. So he picked it up and took it home where it lay in the family wagon kist for weeks until a neighbour who saw it pronounced it to be gold or copper. Gold it was, a nugget weighing 2½ ounces, which Atherstone thought was probably alluvial. It sent a nerve tingle of excitement through the Cape: everyone in the area, and around 'nugget farm' in particular, began to hunt for gold; and the government sent Atherstone to find out what it was all about.

The men made a survey of the whole area next day. Atherstone found no formations to suggest gold, and no stream that could have brought the nugget, so—as it had not grown there—it must have been a human agency at work, but *who*, *why*, *when* and *whence*? Bain, differing from Atherstone, thought there was possibly gold in these rocks, and that the nugget could indeed have come from here. They argued about it endlessly and their theories proliferated—perhaps a baboon could have brought it to this remote spot. Neither of them ever worked it out for certain, and the nugget became 'the mystery of The Gouph'.

That must have been the gayest, oddest official enquiry in South Africa's history, with Atherstone and Bain bent on fossils even more than gold. 'What a scene of excitement. No time to breathe. Hammer and chisel, and echoing shouts of indignant baboons. How we joked and laughed and argued and chaffed,' wrote Atherstone.

It was January, mid-summer. 'This is a country,' he wrote 'in which no blotting paper is required, for the ink dries faster than you can write,' a pretty fair description, we thought, as we drove towards **Prince Albert,** seeing the whirlwinds chasing each other across the plains.

Prince Albert was a duck of a village, he had written, and it still is, with its old houses and open water furrows, and a watermill some 125 years old which still grinds wheat which—locals say—makes bread with a special Prince Albert flavour.

From here the **Swartberg** seemed very close, the mountain range that is incomparable in Southern Africa for mighty rocky towers and gorges and brilliant flaring colour. It is this formidable barrier that separates Prince Albert from Oudtshoorn to the south, the Great from the Little Karoo of which Oudtshoorn is the centre.

Until some 120 years ago it was a barrier that was impassable, to the grief of the people of the Little Karoo, trapped in their strip of country between this and the Outeniqua Mountains on their coastal side. So eventually a way was found at the eastern end through a kloof or valley that was called Meiringspoort, and then another was constructed towards the west and was christened Seven Weeks Poort, why, nobody today knows for certain. Those cuttings go to show how desperate people were to cross the mountain, for both followed river beds and were impassable in heavy rain. In the end it fell to Thomas Bain to build a road, the Swartberg Pass, not through but over the mountains between the two kloofs, safe from flooding rivers—but not from rain, wind, snow and ice, which travellers on it today frequently meet. (Thomas Bain inspected the route first on Christmas Day and was caught in a snowstorm.) From the point of view of excitement and drama, this is probably *the* pass in South Africa, not that it is the highest—it is only 1 585 metres above sea level—but because it is steep, and there is almost no let-up as one snakes up and up, no time to draw breath to take in the views across half the world, only to give thanks for a motor-car with a stout heart.

We stopped at the summit. The wind whipped away our voices, and we leaned against it, looking down at the famous hairpin bends and the stone walling which was the hallmark of Thomas Bain's work. Then we went down the southern side, with the Little Karoo before us, and its own spectacles and thrills.

As for the two poorts, **Meiring's** and **Seven Weeks**, through the mountains, we had travelled through them at various times and found them both magnificent, with their orange-ochre and red sandstone rocks standing on end, towers and ramparts and strange contortions, the sandstone turning burning colours with the evening lights. Even today these roads are impassable when the rivers flood. It was through Seven Weeks' Poort that Atherstone had travelled to The Koup, and he crossed and recrossed the river 30 times. We did not count our crossings, but they were probably the very same.

At **Oudtshoorn** we were with ostriches and feathers. This is the last remaining citadel of ostrich farming, its world centre, from where the white plumes travel across the ocean to wherever the great fashion houses want them, and the lesser—the blacks and browns—are made into the feather dusters used across South Africa.

There are still some 300 ostrich farmers here. Once there were thousands both in the Little and the Great Karoo, in the boom days before World War I, when 1 lb of ostrich feathers sold for R200. It was a period of quick easy money, and it changed the appearance of the district and its way of life. It was then that the extraordinary homes arose that were dubbed ostrich palaces, vast, often single-storey affairs of sandstone shaped by imported masons, with wide stoeps with pillars and trellis work, turrets and spiral staircases, and big high rooms with fine steel ceilings. They stood, opulent and masterful, among the aloes and the lucerne lands.

In the 1914-18 War nobody wanted ostrich feathers, nor did they in the years that followed; the feather bubble burst overnight. People could not believe it. One day ostrich feathers would come back into fashion, they were certain, and all over the ostrich districts for many years after the war farmers kept some breeding birds and their incubator in order waiting for the new boom to come. It never did; but a modest demand did grow up. In recent times plumes have sold for about R40 a lb; the ostrich skins make first class leather, the leg meat is used for biltong, and the firm bright yellow fat for soap.

Oudtshoorn itself has two ostrich sights, 'The Story of the Ostrich through the Ages' display (including the fabulous feathers) at the **C. P. Nel Museum,** and the ostrich feather sales—the most unusual regular auctions anywhere at all.

Outside the town people can still experience the birds. On one of the dusty roads leading through the ostrichs' lucerne fields, our way was barred by a little Coloured man, clearly of Hottentot blood, waving a red flag and followed by a flock of ostriches. They padded past us, these largest of living birds two metres tall, and we did not know at which extremity to gaze more ardently, those great two-toed feet with the horrifying dinosaur claw, stirring up the dust, or the long long necks, topped with the ridiculous little heads, and the marvellous, film star eyelashes. It was gratifying to think that at that particular moment ours was probably the only motor-car in the world to be held up by an ostrich.

On the ostrich show farms close to the town like **Highgate, Safari** and **Riempie,** tourists can see and even touch the birds—those chicks that look like speckled fluff have feathers like little spiky quills! Everything is arranged for the tourists with dash, from the information —how wild ostriches were captured near Oudtshoorn in the 1850s, and how they were farmed and the industry developed—to plucking pens and ostrich nests and eggs, ostrich races with Coloured jockeys, and a picnic meal (also the rarest in the world) of ostrich steaks, eaten sitting on a lucerne bale.

We did not sleep at Oudtshoorn but turned west to **Calitzdorp.** It was evening when we came into the tiny village and in the dusk we looked at the square white box of the hotel with an outdoor stairway to one side, fronted by a furrow so broad that it was a river—as we

crossed the little bridge to the hotel we saw that all the buildings up
the street had their own little bridges, too, across the water. Would it
look so good in morning light? We hastened out with the first sun to
see if it was true. It was. There were also two geranium trees—and
they *were* trees—a pink and a red, hanging over the water; and houses
with latticework, sash windows and potted plants—praise be, not a
new one among them. The people, yawning on their front stoeps and
on the pavement, called out to ask what we were doing in Calitzdorp
and if we liked it, and the Coloured men and women on their way to
work greeted us as they passed. It was a Cape village, and even if we
had not known where we were, the early walk down the main street
would have told us.

Calitzdorp is one side of the Little Karoo, the **Cango Caves**
another. They lie, these great limestone caverns, still largely un-
explored, 27 kilometres north of Oudtshoorn, and are reached along
a tarred road. They were discovered almost 200 years ago, by a
slave, it is said, who was searching for cattle; and it was the farmer,
Van Zyl, the slave's owner, who first descended into the depths and
reported their wonders.

We had seen them twice, once in early childhood, when the caverns
stretched away full of blackness, and the stalactites and stalagmites,
seen by the light of tapers, were of unearthly mystery. When we went
again there was electric light, tourist patter, and caverns called by such
names as Crystal Palace and Lot's Wife. To those who have no
comparison, these are still a natural wonder and beauty: but that day
Calitzdorp and its simplicities had set the tone for us, and we
wandered out on a new route, along a valley called Coetzeespoort,
parallel with the Swartberg to the north.

It was one of the loveliest things we had seen, with green lucerne
lands set between orange-red precipices, vineyards and Lombardy
poplars, and the sound of running water, and in the distance—set
about with green and gold—white farmhouses and stone-walled kraals.
Calitzdorp is said to produce the best dried fruit in the country, and we
thought we would find it here too, only there was nobody at all on the
road to ask.

We would have liked to have spent a week in the Little Karoo,
driving up the kloofs and passes, looking at the aloes, goats and
donkey carts, talking to the friendly people, and rereading, as we did
so, what Pauline Smith in her *Little Karoo* had felt about it all long
ago. Instead we rode southward through the Outeniqua Pass to George.

We should not have travelled it after the Swartberg, for although the
motor-car enjoyed the high-speed pass—a magnificent example of

what a modern motorway through mountains should be—we missed the drama of the older roads. It was not until—descending towards the coast—we reached the 'Historic Passes' viewpoint on our left, that we felt the adventure of these roads begin to stir. As we stood there, we could see the first pass by which men had crossed the mountains in this area, indicated by white beacons on the far mountain side. This was **Cradock Kloof,** known locally as Voortrekker Pass, the dreaded ascent which replaced the even more dangerous Duivels Kop pass to the east.

This view was of tremendous interest to us, for these old passes into the Long Kloof to the north had figured so much in the books of early travels that we knew them well in theory; now here they were before us. We picked up the route of the Montagu Pass as well, the narrow twisting road that in its turn superseded Cradock Kloof, and which is still used. Also quite clearly visible was the railway line of 1913, and a few paces behind us the modern Outeniqua Pass of 1951, the work of engineer P. A. de Villiers of the National Roads.

We slipped into George, spent a night comfortably at Hawthorndene Hotel, and next morning early were on the **Montagu Pass** itself, one of our favourite routes with its loops and climbs, the proteas glimpsed beyond the stone walls, and the ruined smithy at its side. It was specially important in the story of our roads because it was the first fruit of the road-planning of the Surveyor-General, handsome, romantic-looking Major Charles Mitchell, and the Colonial Secretary, John Montagu, who provided the know-how and the money for so many of the new 19th century roads. If it had been Bain who had built the pass, the trio would have been complete. But it was Henry Fancourt White instead—his camp at the foot of the pass was Blanco (White), the name surviving today.

Which is the most famous of these southern passes? It is hard to say. North-west of Mossel Bay is the old Attaqua Kloof, mercifully no more, that was as dangerous as Cradock Kloof, and near it the modern Robinson's Pass between Mossel Bay and Oudtshoorn, Garcia Pass and Plattekloof to the west, and then the Tradouw Pass and Cogman's Kloof—sensational, almost every one—and far away to the north-west, the Hex River Pass through the Hex River Mountains, on the main route N1 that we had left at Prince Albert Road to travel through The Koup. This is probably the best known route of all, a gentle pass (at least, comparatively so) leading into a civilized fertile valley of vineyards backed gloriously by blue mountains.

Lovely and established as it appears to Transvaal eyes, we would never travel that last bit of Karoo road, Prince Albert Road to the head of the pass, just for its own sake. We go because of **Matjiesfontein,** just short of the entrance to the pass.

There are few South Africans today who do not know the name of this absurd and altogether delicious fantasy in the middle of the Great Karoo. There it lies, a small huddle of houses almost hidden by trees, beyond Laingsburg on the left-hand side of the road, not quite 300 kilometres from Cape Town. Everyone who can do so, turns off to look at the village, to eat there (supremely well), and sleep. Two men dreamed it, and it was our luck to find one at home.

What this is, is a Victorian village—not a cardboard one but an old village brought to life as it once was, plus considerable gloss and sparkle. A Scotsman, James Douglas Logan, built·it in the last century: David Rawdon, the present owner of Lanzerac (the well-known hotel on the outskirts of Stellenbosch), resurrected it.

When Logan saw it in the 1880s, the village was a tiny settlement of corrugated iron shacks on the north-south railway line, a speck in a wide desert world. Jimmy Logan had magician's eyes: he looked at Matjiesfontein and saw what it could become and made it. He himself was one of those extraordinary people South Africa threw up in its young days, a 19-year-old from a waterlogged sailing ship that put into Simon's Bay in 1877, who walked to Cape Town (his clothes were all he had); porter, station master, district superintendent of the Touws River—Prince Albert Section of the railways, head of the Cape Railways Refreshment Department, and—among other things—politician, cricketer, and gambler. He also had TB. He must have known well how to turn misfortune into gold: in a search for the dry air that would cure his lungs he found Matjiesfontein.

First he served refreshments to passengers of passing trains in an iron shed; soon he owned the land and was building a village. Queen Victoria was on the throne and it was a village of the time, its one main street lit by street lamps, the hotel—he christened it the Milner Hotel—with crenellated towers he had designed himself and a wrought-iron balcony (a cross between a castle, a fort and a Victorian mansion), heavy shining old furniture, a fountain, a croquet court, a cricket field. He got the finest builders he could, from Britain when necessary; only the best would do.

The village became the rage. Here came dukes and earls and lords and generals, not to mention the Sultan of Zanzibar. In the Anglo-Boer War British wounded were nursed here, for Logan had offered the hotel as a hospital: the tower made the most frivolous look-out of the war. Olive Schreiner lived in a cottage in the village. Passengers to Cape Town knew her thick-set figure and brooding look as she stumped up and down, up and down, within sight of the train. Long afterwards they used to talk of her as if they had seen a lion upon the platform.

Logan was now 'Laird of Matjiesfontein'. How odd a porter he must have been as a boy when as a man he filled the role of Laird so triumphantly. He was now someone in his own right; and when Edward VII was crowned King of England, there—by invitation—at the coronation were Jimmy Logan in tailcoat and breeches, and Emma his wife in a lilac gown. On view still are the stockings and shoes she had worn, pink silk stockings and lilac silk shoes.

Logan died in 1920, and so, in a sense, did Matjiesfontein. It was David Rawdon who brought it to life once again. He had looked at it with the eye and the knowledge that had made Lanzerac, and in 1968 he bought—in one swoop—the whole village. The new one was going to be as like the old as possible, with some additional glamour, but basically it was to be a bit of true Victoriana. To do this he stripped and uncovered and restored—old photographs, as always, helped—and searched for the right old furniture, here and in England.

He made in the end something that was a heavenly lark—a lark in the sense of something so odd and delightful and warming that the name Matjiesfontein brings the same reaction as the fizz of a champagne bottle overflowing.

We slept in a bedroom in the hotel—the Lord Milner now—all green and cream and great red garlands, wrought iron, marble, and lamp shades trimmed with beads, a red chaise-longue, a Victorian pincushion to match the curtains, and on the walls flowery prints—Suttons' Amateur Guide in Horticulture, 1891, their Bulb Catalogue for 1889. In the night it blew, and we lay in our sumptuous beds listening to a living house responding to the wind, glorying in every creak.

When we walked through the hotel to the courtyards, cottages and gardens beyond, all amusement left us. What David Rawdon had created here was not the Victoriana of the main street—delightful gimmicks—but something belonging to no one age. The walled, bricked courtyards and fountains were not the extravaganza of the main street; we had seen something like them, we remembered, with the same sturdy simplicity and the same weeping pepper trees, in Spanish mission gardens in America. Around us was desert. These things seemed the answer to it, its extension, perhaps, and this enclosed shade and privacy and the sight and sound of water—a vine, an evergreen against a white wall—offered in a desert everything man could ask for peace and pleasure.

We found the best 'simple' food in all the country here—its fame is founded not on its gimmicks but on excellence. 'We hear your food is exquisite,' we said to David Rawdon, and he replied, 'It's absolutely simple.' We were both right.

We lunched at the Laird's Arms next to the Lord Milner, a Victorian pub, warm and noisy, smelling of hot soup, fresh bread and beer, laughing at a bowler hat, everyone talking in between the gusty harmonium's honky-tonk, honky-tonk.

The dinner was first-class—paté, for which the place is famous, in tiny pots; Karoo loin of lamb, a dozen puddings on a table to themselves: candied orange and grapefruit peel with coffee. But the breakfast was the best we had ever tasted, and as important, *ever seen*. It was 'Help yourself' at a groaning board; a young black chef in a tall white hat; hot porridges, and cereals in fat blue jars; omelettes, boiled eggs in a china hen; sausages of many breeds; a huge pink ham; new wholemeal bread and hot Matjies muffins; eighteen preserves and honeys to eat with them; a watermelon piled high with watermelon balls; a china 'fountain' of purple grapes and golden plums.

We have a dream now, and that is to go to Matjiesfontein for Christmas: to travel in the Blue Train and have it stop at the station (which it does not do); to be greeted by David Rawdon and his staff, all wearing crowns—because in their way they are royal—to drink a 1975 Montpellier Gewürztraminer with David, laughing and squatting on his heels beside our dining-room table, and then to bed in the red room and to think of Matjies Christmas breakfast and sleep and wake, and find it.

CHAPTER NINETEEN

Desert Route

✤

Our favourite road is to the far west, the desert road. Everyone has his own idea of what is truly Africa: for us this is the most 'African' road of all. It runs straight and level between the horizons in a great empty bowl of a world filled with light, where the rocks are smooth and dark and the sand dunes red, the flower colours burn, and the very lions are heraldic beasts, bigger and prouder than ordinary flesh and blood. Here the frosts and the heat can stupefy, and as men walk at midday the beetles hurry over the sand on long thin legs to stay within their shadows. It is a country where water is life and shade far more precious than gold, where the last Bushmen in South Africa live, and there is a wild animal sanctuary complete with unicorns.

In Pretoria we are a long way from the Kalahari Gemsbok National Park; but when we pack the car, check our water and equipment, our hats, the oranges and cabbages for the ranger, our field-glasses and cameras, we are filled with expectation. The distance does not matter —almost every kilometre of the road holds interest of some kind.

Always we start with the dawn. Last time, it was a spring morning, but even so we were still shivering at **Lichtenburg,** as we looked at what remained of the great diamond rush of 50 years before; the most dramatic reminders lay north of the town on the Zeerust road. We did not linger, for it was not diamonds we were after but birds, and we hurried along the Vryburg road to **Barberspan,** the famous bird sanctuary now controlled by the Nature Conservation Division of the Transvaal Provincial Administration.

The Western Transvaal highveld is not an inspiring countryside nor is this pan beautiful; but it is a bird-lover's dream, a vast stretch of shallow water that has never been known to dry up, spread out not so much in a wild countryside as one devoid of anything, flat as a table, desolate and dusty, with the wind—on the day we saw it—biting our bones, blowing past the tin building on the pan's edge, and the lamentable exotic plants.

In a way, the dreariness made the birds more unforgettable—the flamingoes and pelicans, geese and pochards, yellowbill duck and coot and herons, the turnstone and avocet, whimbrel and ruff, greenshank and godwit. Many were here already, others would come soon, like the Little Stint, the smallest migrant; it had not yet arrived from Russia 10 000 kilometres away. How many millions of creatures had used the pan, we wondered, since springbok hooves had hollowed it long ago—it has been known as an outstanding bird spot for nearly 150 years. Ornithologists today claim that well over 300 species of birds have been recorded here, many of them travellers, like the Little Stint. A ruff ringed at Barberspan was found in Siberia north of Vladivostok only two months later, so that it is to study migration, among other things, that many ornithologists come.

Vryburg on the edge of the Kalahari Desert was our next stop. It is the centre of South Africa's largest cattle district—but we remembered it not for cattle. Coming out of the desert one winter's day we had stopped at the bakery to buy a cake—we had eaten dust for days. It was warm, scented and plump with cherries, soon to become a family legend, and the baker's little shop a sort of Mecca about which we told other hungry travellers.

Vryburg does not look romantic—it is solid and hot, with abattoirs and supermarkets—but it did have a picturesque beginning. Nearly 100 years ago it was laid out as the capital of an independent state, the Republic of Stellaland, founded by a group of white mercenaries who had fought in one of the local African wars and had been rewarded with farms. Their republic lasted a year: the South African Republic laid claim to it, and so did Britain, and in 1895 it became part of the Cape Colony.

The name Vryburg—free town—remains but Stellaland is history only. As we passed over the wide grassy plains, we mourned the name. The vast, dark, velvet sky with its glowing stars is part of Southern Africa, and of the desert lands above all: travellers, hunters and farmers knew them as well as they did the hills and pans and wild animals of daylight. But in the names they gave there are no Plains of Orion or Rivers of the Milky Way—there are instead plenty of Salt Pans, Lion's Pans, Kareekloofs and Teebus and other such: it took a mercenary, lying on his back round a camp fire looking upwards at the stars, to make them into a name for men. He and others in the party were talking of the name for their new state. 'Let's call it Star-land,' he said. So they did, but in another form, 'Stellaland'. It was a name which deserved to live but did not; but we thought of it as we left Vryburg behind, and its magic was still there.

We talked, too, of the quite extraordinary romance of associations. Vryburg town hall is a long way from Windsor Castle; yet the green

Stellaland flag with its stars which is now in the town hall once hung in Windsor Castle. It took a king—George V—to return it.

Everyone who travels into the west should think of its past story. This great, arid, empty world made history before the Transvaal and Free State did. The roads to the east were made by the Voortrekkers. Although it is true that before them went missionaries, traders and hunters, yet the Voortrekker story in its magnitude eclipsed theirs. The roads here in the west were beaten by missionaries (and their wives) and travellers when the Transvaal was so-to-say unknown. They came alone or in small groups with their ox-wagons, their Bibles, guns, scientific books, printing presses, and a lion courage, and they brought to this hinterland both the first Christianity and the first 'science'. It is impossible to travel west without crossing their tracks; they give distinction even to today's journeys.

The greatest of the traveller-explorer-scientists was William Burchell, bent on knowledge; the greatest of the missionaries was Robert Moffat (the same Moffat who described the Inhabited Tree in the Western Transvaal), sent out to South Africa by the London Missionary Society to spread the gospel. Although their routes met, they did not, for Burchell preceded Moffat by some years.

They had many things in common, courage, determination, the ability to endure hardship, keen eyes. Burchell was English, Moffat a Scot, but when they arrived they were both innocents in the ways of the desert and veterans when they left; they both succeeded superbly in their jobs, leaving written records that are part of the history of the west.

As we turned south-west from Vryburg we talked of both of them. We were a good deal north of the Orange River in the chunk of the Cape Province between the Orange and Molopo Rivers, heading for **Kuruman,** the little desert town with its famous spring of water, the 'Eye.'

In 1812 Burchell had arrived at the African town of Litakun, some way north of the Kuruman of today, and had been entranced by it, the multitude of houses, and the size—the town measured not less than a mile and a half in diameter: he looked at it all, noting every facet of its life with delight. As we drew near, we remembered some of Burchell's adventures, how his drawings had so pleased the people that they had crowded into his wagon and packed round it, with great laughter, the ochre with which they were smeared turning the wagon and himself red; how he had held a banquet in his wagon for the chief and his relatives consisting of boiled beef, melted sheep fat, boiled rice and tea, and how the tea had been a hit; and how he had given peach-stones to the chief to provide food without work, all these little

Sociable weavers' nest beside the desert road

The famous Kat Balcony in Cape Town, the combined work of the early masters, Thibault and Anreith

The splendid pulpit in the Lutherar Church, Cape Town, carved by Ar

touches that bring his journal so brilliantly to life.

Moffat visited Litakun eight years later, not Burchell's town but one which had been moved nearer the river. It was a terrible summer journey he had made to get there, with lions roaring, he and his companion searching for their paw-prints in the night by striking flint with steel to light the sand, their lips and tongues so swollen that they could not speak, their eyes inflamed, the mirages of the day with their lakes and pools sending them half demented, cowering in the shade of the few low bushes, burying their heads in antbear heaps to get brief relief from the sun.

A year later he brought his wife and family to Litakun, and in 1824 the mission station was moved to a spot five kilometres north of Kuruman.

Burchell left no solid mark upon the desert: Moffat left a church. It was the first mission church building in the North-West Cape: it is today a national monument—'the most famous chapel in Africa'—and is still in use.

We came to it along the dry river, turning into the mission grounds. T-shaped, stone-walled and thatched, it is still not only sturdy but beautiful. We went in. It was large—it can seat a thousand—and quiet, the pulpit in the centre, the floor, as of old, of dung. The roof beams, we remembered, had been brought by wagon from the Western Transvaal and were of white stinkwood; the silver Communion cups and plates, still used, dated from Moffat's day. The nave had once held the printing press on which the New Testament in Tswana—the first African Bible—had been printed: Moffat had done the translation.

It must have been Mary Moffat's church as much as Robert's— Mary who had come here as a pretty, plump, determined girl—and standing in it they seemed very real to us. Outside was the homestead they had built, where both had laboured prodigiously for most of their lives. When we first saw it, it was derelict with the calico floating in ribbons from the ceiling and the windows broken and boarded up, but later it had been restored. Two other buildings, a cottage and wagon house, were still derelict when we saw it that day, the cost of repairs being great.

The garden that Robert had planted had mostly disappeared. To make it he had led a water furrow from the spring, the famous Eye. Had Moffat planted the parent of the big old syringa trees in the grounds? Nobody could tell us. But the remains of one tree was there, carefully preserved. It was the stump of the fruit tree under which David Livingstone, the great missionary-explorer, had proposed to Robert's daughter Mary. He had been mauled by a lion nearby, Mary had nursed him (so the story goes) and they had fallen in love. Robert had married them in the church in 1845, and they had had their wedding breakfast in the living-room of the Moffat home.

We left the tree and turned to the family cemetery. Here were the graves of Robert and Mary's children, including that of their infant son who was the first to be buried here. (Those children's graves in distant places occur so often where pioneers passed, they tell their own story.) But this cemetery spoke of continuity as well as death. All over South Africa where people pause and look, they see the signs of other—of ancient—men, the stones they shaped for tools and weapons and left upon the surface of the ground. Sometimes they lie in hundreds, and nowhere is this truer than in the bare dry west around a pool or river.

Our young son, stopping at the gateway, picked up a stone and held it out. It was a flake, a rough tool, fashioned by some Stone Age man, who had found this spot a good one, perhaps ten thousand years before Moffat had built his church.

We left Kuruman before the dawn heading for the west, driving through a long white tunnel bordered in the headlights with pale ghosts: we knew, but could scarcely believe, they were trees powdered with earthly dust. Daylight showed us our strange road, on and on in the dry bed of the Kuruman River, red dunes on either side, farm-houses upon them (all pale pea green the year we saw them) and camelthorn and *witgat* trees.

We cooked our breakfast under a *witgat* on the little gas stove that travels with us: it was bitterly cold and the wind blew and we ate red sand with our bacon. Later we passed the little hotel at **Vanzylsrus,** an odd little green box on the red road, which is reputed to be good; but the **Gemsbok Park** lay at the end of the road and we did not stop.

At Witdraai we turned north for the entrance gate. On our right was the Molopo River, almost parallel to the Kuruman, two great dry river beds almost side by side. Ahead was the Park. We knew the map of it by heart, this great stretch of land 400 kilometres from north to south, running in a broad wedge between Botswana and South West Africa, and narrowing toward its northern end. Through this ran two rivers traditionally dry, the Auob to the west and the Nossob to the east, making the boundary with Botswana. Adjoining it, across the river in Botswana, was another game sanctuary just as large, managed jointly by the South African National Parks Board and Botswana. It was a huge area, formidable, yet an ecological whole, 'unique and un-rivalled', said our little guide book to the national parks, 'with drift sand and dunes'.

We had studied all this, how the Park lay between the Auob and the

Nossob, how the two main roads ran along their hard bare beds and the sand between the rivers was piled up, and how the Dune Road ran across them, connecting the river beds. We knew how the country was geared to heat and dearth of water, that although there were the animals of the softer east, this was most truly the kingdom of the things that did not need to drink—the lion, the gemsbok, the spring-bok, the eland and steenbok, the little desert rat, the ostrich, the big Kori bustard. We had seen the desert plants, the *tsamma* melons and the wild cucumbers. We knew the heat and cold, and how the rain could come, the rivers flow and the desert bloom; how the Kuruman had come down in flood in 1974 cutting off the Park from the south, how even the springbok drank and drank when the rain came and the bat-eared foxes grew fat on the mice escaping from their holes along the river banks. We knew the grass and bush, and the camelthorns in the river beds, and the lions in their shade near a waterhole.

But when we turned in through the entrance gate at the southern camp, at Twee Rivieren, it was as if we had known nothing. Every-thing was brighter and cleaner and more exciting in the flesh, and the anticipation was hardly to be borne.

The first thing we saw was a herd of camels! Camels had once been used on patrols here and these animals remained. Perhaps they should not have looked at home in a park of indigenous animals, but in fact they were superb.

Just outside **Twee Rivieren**—Two Rivers—the Nossob and the Auob meet. We went up and down them many times, and both river beds gave liberally. In the wide hard bed of the Auob there were gemsbok, both on the flats and outlined against the red dunes above, with buff-grey coats, black-and-white faces and long straight horns. Brian Barrow, whose book *Song of a Dry River* is a loving and magnificent tribute to the Park, writes that the colour of the red sand brings a peach blossom tint to their coats, and so it can.

These were the colonists' unicorns, we reminded one another. Tradi-tionally the unicorn had the head, body and tail of a horse, the hind legs of an antelope, and a single long sharp horn. Today it is thought to have been, in fact, the oryx of the north and north-east Africa—he is a great fighter, in battle often losing one horn altogether. Our gemsbok is an oryx, too, *Oryx gazella*, and when we eyed its strong pony-like body, its tail and its horns, side-on appearing as a single horn, and saw several one-horned animals in the flesh as well, we *knew* that what we were seeing were unicorns.

We never tired of watching them, their heads nodding as they walked, or galloping with their horns lying backwards on their shoulders, one of the handsomest sights in all the Park.

There were springbok too, sometimes in big herds, trotting delicately among the old camelthorn trees, the prettiest little antelope in the world, and, when they raced and sprang and bucked, spreading their white fans—the long snowy hairs upon their backs—among the most dramatic too. They love to be able to see around them, and the river beds suit them well.

Springbok migrations once made the strangest animal story in Africa. Millions of them would band together and trek as a vast moving sea regardless of danger, stopped by nothing, devastating the country, sometimes marching into the very sea, at other times disappearing mysteriously and often for ever. Books have been written about them, and zoologists still argue the reasons. What may have been the last migration may have taken place in the Gemsbok Park. Brian Barrow tells how Joseph le Riche, Chief Conservator, in 1945 saw a 'small' migration of some 15 000 buck within the Park itself across the Nossob River bed. The springbok came in waves in a solid mass, moved out of the Park, and disappeared.

In the Nossob valley towards the north were eland—we could scarcely believe how these great cumbersome animals could achieve such grace and beauty scaled to a desert world as tremendous as the sky. There were red hartebeest as well, with sloping backs: they looked so clumsy and yet were fleet; and blue wildebeest as ludicrous as their brothers in the east.

We saw cheetah once upon this road, and many lions. This is by far the best place to see them. Not that it is as easy to spot them here as in the Kruger Park, but while a lion in the lush grass and the shade of a fecund marula tree is good, a desert lion is better—a wild animal in a fierce wild world.

Watching one one day walking slowly to a drinking-place in the open Auob bed, tawny as the ground beneath him, with the astonishing red dunes behind, we thought he had an heraldic splendour: and when we considered it, we were sure we were right—those proud lions of early crests must have been desert lions as well, most likely from northern Africa.

They are really of the desert, all those 250 pale tawny cats of the Kalahari Park. In the east, lions need to drink in order to survive. Not these. When necessary, they are almost independent of water, true desert kings.

This is the last place in the Cape Province where a wild lion's roar can still be heard, that tremendous sound that Stevenson-Hamilton compared to an immense bass organ. And this is the last place in the

Cape, too, where an ostrich's booming call can be mistaken for it.

Often in the old days in the Cape the two were confused, and the Bushmen told the story why. The ostrich, they said, called so well that the lion was jealous. It called with its lungs, the lion lamented, with its chest and with its chest's front, and its voice was so resounding and strong and sweet that the women cherished it and it alone. As for the lion—'he sounds as if he had put his tail in his mouth,' the women mocked. So the lion killed the ostrich and ate its lungs so that he could call with its voice. Often he does.

That is the lion in fable. At Twee Rivieren a lioness made grand comedy a little while ago. She entered the rest camp and took up residence in the toilet block—for 36 hours nobody was able to enter. What the visitors thought is not recorded: but by the time a sedative dart had flushed the lioness from her lair she was news and a gale of laughter had travelled round the country.

The two animals that we enjoyed most in the Park were relatively humble creatures, the bat-eared fox and the honey-badger. The little foxes with their gentle pointed faces and great ears, silver-grey fur rippling with light, and thin, delicate little legs, are the prettiest animals in Southern Africa—the only true foxes also. We watched them on the Auob road searching for insects, bulbs and mice.

We saw honey-badgers (ratels) everywhere, and whereas the foxes in small groups had looked at us attentively and moved away, the solitary honey-badgers cared not tuppence for us: they jogged along with their rolling sailor gait in the grass beside us, and we were close enough to see the low-slung forms, even the black hairs among the broad grey-white back bands, their pigeon toes, their long curved claws, their beady eyes. They are absolute monarchs of their own domain—no teeth or fangs or sting can penetrate their skin. As we watched, we knew *they* knew this: they made it perfectly clear.

They pleased us for another reason. They are part of one of South Africa's oldest stories, the partnership of a bird and beast. The little brown bird, the honey-guide, the story goes, leads the honey-badger to a bees' nest: the honey-badger breaks open the nest and the two of them then share the pickings. In 1950 Herbert Friedmann, who wrote a book on honey-guides, came to Africa to find out if the story were true—and found it was.

This was exciting in itself, but more was to follow. Here in the Gemsbok Park people noted another bird relationship the honey-badger had. The Pale Chanting Goshawk is the eagle-like, pale-coloured, long-legged bird that everyone notes in the dry west sitting on the tops of telegraph poles or on trees. This is the honey-badger's companion here. The badger is a great hunter, digging mightily in the ground with his great claws for rodents and other things and disturbing many small creatures as it digs: these are goshawk food. Some people have watched bird and beast together and say the goshawk follows the honey-badger: others go further, saying they have seen the bird guiding the honey-badger to holes and burrows in the first place, then waiting expectantly in a tree nearby for its share. It is the old story brought up to date, and fascinating.

There is a varied bird life in the Park, which after good rains is remarkable—visitors then have remarked on the birds of prey such as bataleurs, steppe eagles and tawny eagles, hawks and kestrels. Birds that always pleased us were the little Namaqua Sandgrouse. Waiting at waterholes in the Nossob, we would see the flocks come, settle on the trees around, and then fly down to the water to drink, plump little birds, miraculously built to cope with their world. Perhaps fifty kilometres distant were their feeding grounds (and their nests as well), where old and young fed on the dry seeds round about—a diet that made daily drinking necessary. The adults could fly to water but the chicks could not—so the fathers brought the water to them. Into the water along the Nossob they went, soaking their feathers as they bobbed and dipped—then out and back to their nests on the bare ground, the water securely trapped in their belly feathers, surely fashioned in the most marvellous pattern in the world to hold water for that desert flight.

We saw one end of this little saga. Dr Gordon Maclean of the University of Natal described the other, the arrival of a male bird at the nest, and the chicks running out as he landed to drink the water from his plumage, 'looking for all the world like a litter of puppies'.

'Kelkiewyn, kelkiewyn,' the birds call on the wing. We have heard them not only here but in other parts: they tell of small miracles and great dry open spaces, and we listen to them always with a stir of pleasure.

There are three rest camps in the Park, at Twee Rivieren, at Nossob, and at Mata Mata on the Auob River on the South West African border. All are good but small, scarcity of water restricting their size. Near Twee Rivieren there is a special interest, a few Bushmen encamped in the desert, tame Bushmen now but worth visiting because they are almost the last in South Africa.

We remember **Mata Mata** in particular because here we spent the coldest night we have ever known in Africa. Desert cold strikes deep, and the anti-freeze we had in our car, we found in the morning, had frozen. It was nevertheless here that the ranger told us a story of

Kalahari heat. Two visitors from Europe, travelling to Mata Mata from Windhoek over the dune roads in summer-time, had ignored the standard 'desert' advice—keep to the road, take food and water—and had pulled off the road to picnic under a camelthorn. The sand was loose and deep and here they had stuck. Five days later a passing farmer found them and took them into Mata Mata, half-crazed, half-blind, their tongues so swollen they could not talk. They were lucky. There have been people who left the road—and left their bones in the Kalahari dunes.

There are those who go to the Kalahari not to see wild animals but in pursuit of a legend—to find the Lost City—and when they drive up the Nossob they look not west but east.

The Lost City—mirage or reality?

Nearly a century ago an American showman named Gilarmi Farini, travelling through the central Kalahari, claimed to have found the ruins of a city half-buried in the orange-red sand. Their whereabouts has fired the imagination of three subsequent generations and sparked at least 26 expeditions of many nationalities to locate them. None has. The ruined city has also triggered a flood of speculation, ranging from coldly erudite to wildly romantic. Either could be right.

What is known is that Farini on a hunting trip travelled up the Nossob to Ky Ky (now in the Gemsbok Park) where he and his party branched eastward into the desert, covering a large area as they hunted and explored. Modern expeditions braving this country in four-wheel drive vehicles have reported a tale of broken springs, fouled radiators, burst engines and crippled gearboxes. Farini, travelling by ox-wagon, appears a superman.

It was somewhere in this tract of territory, on his return to the Nossob, near a muddy pan on the homeward leg, that Farini found the City—how researchers since have tried to pinpoint that pan!

His party camped at the foot of a mountain 'beside a long line of stone' which looked like the Chinese Wall after an earthquake and which, on examination, proved to be the ruins of quite an extensive structure, in some places buried beneath the sand, but in others fully exposed to view. They traced the remains of the wall over a kilometre, noting many details, digging down, finding a pavement of carefully laid stone, including some in the shape of a Maltese cross, in the centre of which, they surmised, an altar, column or monument had stood.

Strangely, Farini never made much of the discovery, mentioning it somewhat casually in the book he wrote. Afterwards, when he gave a lecture to the Royal Geographical Society in London, he gave its position, about 23½ S latitude and 21½ E longitude. Expeditions found that the city apparently did not lie at this position, while it became clear that Farini's directions and map on which he based his route were full of inaccuracies. Still—he had, as far as can be ascertained, neither sextant nor compass. And so the arguments continue.

Some people believed in the City and some people did not: but the excitement got into their bones and even some of those who did not believe went to see. Dr John Clement of Oranjemund was one. He is a sceptic, but in his splendid book, *The Kalahari and its Lost City*, he weighed up the evidence for and against impartially.

Somebody who does believe is Wing Commander Clive Beadon, a British expert in the art (or science) of map dowsing and teleradiesthesia—the detection of objects by parapsychological powers.

Dowsing can be likened to water divining by the diviner's rod, but has a wider application to other things, such as oil, diamonds, gold and other minerals; it has been used as well to locate missing persons and to diagnose illness. In map dowsing the dowser holds a pendulum over a map, in the other hand often holding a sample of the material or object he is seeking. From the 'pull' of the pendulum the target is then located. It is magic to some and rubbish to others, but a good many people claim that it works.

We wrote to Wing Commander Beadon, sending him Farini's map and account of the Lost City, a photocopy of the sketch his son had made of the ruins, one of John Clement's maps, and a modern largescale map of Botswana. Could he with the help of these locate the Lost City? Back came the answer as rich and mysterious as anything in Africa. With the help of the sketch, which he had used in the dowsing, he *had* located it, and he sent an exact 'fix' of the Lost City in terms of latitude and longitude, plus course and distances to be flown. The City was, he added, at the time he wrote also buried under 6–7 metres of sand.

Why not? we thought. Farini had said the City looked as if it had been struck by an earthquake. We knew that the geologists claimed that the sand dunes had been stable for centuries. Yet Botswana was an earthquake 'hot spot'; since 1950 there have been no fewer than 30 earthquakes, mostly exceeding Force 5 on the Richter Scale. Why could not an earthquake upheaval have buried the city Farini saw?

So at Ky Ky on the Nossob, where Farini had turned east on his outward journey, we watched the gemsbok drink and thought of him, and what fun and drama it would be to follow the dowsing clue, go east, and find the City. Africa is full of pipe dreams, and this was ours.

When we left the Gemsbok Park, driving south along the road to Upington, we were still on Farini's track. He had approached Twee Rivieren from the southwest, and on the way may have passed a rock formation which Dr Clement thought he had mistaken for city walls. This is **Eierdopkoppies**—Eggshell Hills—lying a little to the west of the main road. Here large slabs of rock are perched one on top of another, square-cut, apparently mortared together with a cement-like substance which is no more than a natural deposit of calcium carbonate. We made for the hills, but when we got there we were certain they were no clue. Who could ever have believed these rocks a ruin? Not Farini, who was a keen observer. No—either the Lost City was real or Farini was a fraud.

Soon we stopped thinking at all of the Lost City. The Kalahari has many gifts, and if there was no Lost City there was something else. We turned on to the nearby **Hakskeenpan,** the biggest pan in the central Kalahari—25 kilometres long—a huge bare, hard, level sheet without that day a drop of water in it. There was no road but we drove across it smoothly: and to meet us came two ostriches running in a lake, upside-down with their legs in the air; and minutes later a locomotive and train that passed and trembled and disappeared. We were seeing the mirages—the famous mirages—of the desert pans. We cooked our breakfast, trying to keep the tiny blue floret of flame alive in the wind, and as we did, two men appeared on bicycles, bush-hatted, heads down, pedalling steadily in unison. They passed us— silent men, dark men—three metres away, and we heard no sound. They never raised their heads (they must have seen us) or greeted us, in this, one of the world's lonely places: nor did we wave to them. We looked at one another. Were they flesh and blood? We did not know then and we have never decided since.

CHAPTER TWENTY

Diamonds

There is another road to Upington, for most of the way also a desert road, that we love as much as the Gemsbok route. Over the Western Transvaal highveld we go, through Klerksdorp, Wolmaransstad and Christiana to Kimberley, and west into the southern Kalahari, through Campbell and Griquatown to Groblershoop, and then hugging the Orange River to Upington. From here to Kakamas is a river road, and beyond a desert road, far barer than the Kalahari, that runs through Bushmanland and Pofadder to Namaqualand, down the escarpment to Port Nolloth and north on the bleakest road of all to the Orange River mouth.

This Bushmanland road is not one that many choose to take, yet it is a unique part of one of the most exciting roads of all, beginning at Kimberley and ending where the Orange River flows into the sea. **Kimberley** stands for diamonds—it *is* diamonds—and the historic Diamond Road was the one linking its diamond fields with the south. Yet in a way the Kimberley route to the west is the diamond road of today for at its other end, on the Atlantic 1 150 kilometres distant, are the greatest diamond fields the world has ever known, discovered much later than the Kimberley fields and richer by far. Prospectors have been up and down the Orange River between the two searching for treasure but little has been found; it is at the end of the road that the fortunes still lie.

The story of diamonds did not, in fact, start at Kimberley at all but a little south 120 kilometres away near the village of Hopetown on the Orange River. It was here, in the blinding hot summer of 1866, that the first diamond in South Africa was picked up, which set in motion the greatest series of diamond rushes the world has seen.

There is a mystery about all diamonds, and there is a mystery about South Africa's first. It is not clear who found it.

One story goes that it was picked up by a Hottentot boy; another, which is more generally accepted, that it was a farmer's son, 15-year-old Erasmus Jacobs, who found it on the farm De Kalk, on the southern side of the Orange River. The boy's own statement, made when he was an old man, can be read in the Mining Museum in Kimberley.

He had been searching the veld, he said, for a thin branch to clear a water-pipe that was blocked and had sat down to rest in the shade of a tree.

'I suddenly noticed, in the glare of the strong sun, a glittering pebble some yards away. I became curious, and went and picked up this *mooi klip*—it was lying between some limestone and ironstone. The spot was quite a distance from our homestead, but only a couple of hundred yards from the bank of the Orange River.

'I had no idea, of course, that the stone was of value. I was wearing a corduroy suit at the time, and simply put the stone in my pocket. I did not feel at all excited about finding such a beautiful stone.'

On this tranquil scene appeared a new actor, Schalk van Niekerk whose name (like that of the trader John O'Reilly, still offstage in his travelling wagon) is indissociably linked with the first diamond.

Erasmus was playing a game called Five Stones—four river stones and the diamond—with his sisters and brothers when Van Niekerk happened to pass. He collected pretty stones, saw the diamond, and was interested. Although an amateur, he apparently knew that a diamond could make a deep scratch—a score—in glass, and the story goes that he scratched a window-pane in the farmhouse with it. Nobody knows what he deduced, but Erasmus' mother gave him the stone, and he passed it on to a travelling trader, O'Reilly, to see if he could find out anything about it. O'Reilly took it to Colesberg, where it was to spark another drama.

Now the fate of the diamond-fields-to-be hung in the balance. It was the Acting Civil Commissioner at the town, Lorenzo Boyes, who tipped the scales—the right way. Boyes told O'Reilly that he considered his stone to be a diamond. But the town's chemist, Dr Kirsch, was so sure that it was only a topaz that he bet Boyes a new hat that he was right. Boyes took on the bet. They agreed on the Cape's top scientist being the judge in the contest. He was Dr William Guybon Atherstone, who was a great man in his day, and who lived in Grahamstown.

The men posted the diamond, in an ordinary envelope, to Atherstone and when the letter was delivered to him, the diamond fell out and rolled away. Atherstone and his daughter scrabbled for it in the dust and grass. The world knows they found it.

Atherstone tested the stone. Boyes won his bet. It was a 10-carat diamond, which was later bought by Sir Philip Wodehouse, the Cape Governor, for £500 and then exhibited at the contemporary Paris Exhibition.

This historic diamond, which was called the Eureka, now rests in a place of honour in the Library of the Houses of Parliament in Cape Town. During the tercentenary celebrations of the Cape in 1952 the stone, set as a tiepin, was presented to Parliament by Mr Harry Oppenheimer, the South African diamond magnate.

When Atherstone's verdict was confirmed by M. Héritte, French consul in Cape Town and probably the best judge of a rough diamond in the country at that time, the hunt was on. Nevertheless, the find was met with a barrage of scepticism and doubt, while even those who accepted the stone as a diamond doubted that there could be more.

Then, in March 1869, came the clincher. Schalk van Niekerk—the same Van Niekerk who had spotted the first diamond—spotted the second as well. This time it was a Griqua shepherd on the farm Zandfontein who owned it, and Van Niekerk paid him the unheard-of price of 500 sheep, 10 oxen and a horse (worth in all about £400) for it. He was risking everything he had, and the gamble paid off.

Presumably this time, out in the veld, there was no window-pane on which to test the diamond, so it was to Hopetown that he brought it, to the little corner shop with its sign, Lilienfeld Brothers, and here, on a front window-pane, he made two scratches. When he and the Lilienfelds saw them, they were sure his stone was a diamond. There was no eye-witness to record the scene that followed: but the Lilienfelds, with an eye to a bargain, bought the stone on the spot for £11 200. It was a good deal. It was a superb blue-white diamond weighing 83 carats, to be called the Star of South Africa. In Cape Town it was exhibited in the Commercial Exchange which was heavily guarded. It rested—big as a pigeon's egg—in a small box which was held by a police inspector who opened and shut it—one-and-sixpence a time—to show visitors. He made a small fortune for the Ladies' Benevolent Society!

On a grander scale the Earl of Dudley paid £30 000 for it; and early in the present century it was sold and bought again anonymously, only to disappear from public view for more than 60 years. Who would pay a fortune for a diamond only to keep it hidden? It was a mystery which tantalized the diamond world. Then in 1974 out of the blue it appeared again at a jewellery auction in Geneva, as a pear-shaped stone in a pendant cut, then, to 47,70 carats: buyers from all over the world attended to bid for it, and it was sold for R333 000—the seller's name remained a secret!

In 1869 when the value of The Star became known, it brought fortune-seekers by the tens of thousands to Hopetown and the banks of the Orange River, and the Vaal which joined it west of Kimberley: some prospected eastward into the Orange Free State, striking it rich at

Koffiefontein and Jagersfontein. It was the gravel of river beds—
sometimes dry ones only—that yielded the treasure, and it was here
that they first looked. Then came news of further strikes on farms
south of the Vaal where Kimberley soon arose. The diamonds here
were not in river gravel but in 'dry' diggings, in pipes of a soft rock to
be known as kimberlite, yellow on the surface, blue below—the 'blue
ground' that has yielded diamonds worth billions.

It was here that the diggers concentrated, and that the world-famous
mines developed—Bultfontein, Dutoitspan, De Beers and Kimberley.

When we came to Kimberley we did not stop but slipped out of the
city southwest on the main road to begin the diamond story at its
proper end. An hour and a half later we were cruising down **Hopetown's** sun-blanched main street looking for the store where Van
Niekerk had 'proved' his diamond. It was still there—the faded sign
says A. Rosen now—a little corner shop with an overhanging roof,
pulled down like a hat against the sun, an ordinary platteland trading
store smelling of Manchester goods, mealie-meal and paraffin, but
with the most dramatic display window in South Africa. It was a big
one, we saw, behind safety mesh, and at shoulder height were two
diagonal scratches, those made over 100 years ago by Van Niekerk's
diamond.

We stepped inside and were cordially welcomed, and shown the
visitors' book. Kings, princes, dukes, film stars, the famous and the
not-so-famous, all those who had thrilled to the diamond story, had
come to this store and signed the book. A veteran assistant, in
rolled-up shirt sleeves and braces, made some puckish remarks about
the great and said he had been with the Lilienfeld brothers before they
had finally sold out. Then the book—a simple affair—was tucked
away again beneath the window among the soft goods, and we left
amid warmth and invitations to call again. We paused as we went out,
and felt the incisions in the glass. It was as near as any mortal would
get to the Star of South Africa, and we could feel it there beneath our
finger-tips.

We turned the car around and made for Kimberley.

Like every other visitor, we headed first for the **Big Hole.** This, the
largest man-made hole in the world, was dug by diamond-hunters over
decades: after the Kruger Park, it (and the museum of which it is part)
are South Africa's biggest tourist draws.

It is near the centre of the city now, but in 1869 when Van Niekerk
tested his diamond, there was not a dimple in the earth where the Hole
now gapes to suggest its future—there was instead a small koppie with
a single camelthorn on it. Then in 1870 diamonds were discovered on

three farms nearby, on Dorstfontein (Dutoitspan), Bultfontein and on Vooruitzicht where the Big Hole was to be excavated. The farm was owned at the time by two brothers called De Beer, whose name was to become synonymous with diamonds forever after.

Among the early diggers on Vooruitzicht was a group from the Karoo village of Colesberg known as the 'Red Cap Party' because of the red woollen caps they wore. They made this nickname famous, because it was they who pegged the claims on Colesberg Kop, the little hill with the camelthorn atop, that was named after them. It had first been called Gilfillan's Kop, and was to become the New Rush, then the Kimberley Mine—the richest of Kimberley's mines—and finally the Big Hole today.

It is popularly held that the first diamonds on Colesberg Koppie were found by a drunken Coloured servant named Damon, who had been dismissed by the Red Cap Party and told not to return unless he could bring diamonds—and he brought them back, from the top of the koppie. It was in fact a woman, looking for a little Sunday diversion, who walked here with her family and dog and found the first, and this was some time before Damon's adventure. She was Mrs Sarah Ortlepp, who rested under the camelthorn and—while playing with the sand as she did so—found the first diamond there marooned between her fingers. It did not apparently cause even a ripple of excitement. The little girl with her was Florence, later to be Lady Phillips.

To Colesberg Koppie came half the world, including 18-year-old Cecil Rhodes. Here he began his meteoric rise to the top. He imported—and it was a simple but colossal brainwave—pumping machinery to suck the water out of the honeycomb of claims in wet weather.

There are plenty of records of those early days captured by photographer and artist, like the action picture of diamond sorting against a backdrop of thatched huts that shielded sorters from the sun. Alpheus Williams used it in his book, *Some Dreams Come True*. Frank Rhodes is sorting, Herbert Rhodes is screening, Cecil Rhodes is sorting, Dick Lauder is shovelling, while looking on is no less than Dr Atherstone himself, the man who set the diamond boom in motion with his Hopetown identification.

The artist, Mary Elizabeth Barber, left some of the best records of those lively early days in her watercolours—of the single camelthorn on top of Colesberg Koppie and under it hundreds of men digging waist-deep in what to modern eyes look like foxholes. She showed the tents, the wagons, the piles of wood, the scotch carts and oxen, the transport wagons, the sieves, the water-barrels. Thelma Gutsche, who wrote the biography of Florence Phillips, noted that Mrs Barber showed also a lady with a parasol and a little girl among the toiling diggers on the koppie, and these were surely Florence and her mother, Mrs Ortlepp.

The camp at New Rush, together with that at De Beers adjoining it were united and renamed Kimberley in 1873—the name was given in honour of the British Colonial Secretary at the time.

We stood on the viewing platform and looked down on the Big Hole, this huge chasm with a diameter of some 1 500 feet and a circumference of nearly a mile. (The traditional measurements are so hallowed by time that to metricize them seems almost blasphemy.) The steep sides were ochre and cream with green pepper trees studding the less perpendicular slopes towards the top: far below was a pool of deep green water looking like a bottomless pit.

A piece of the side broke away and toppled into the water, pocking the surface as with machine-gun bullets. After an appreciable time-lapse, the sound wandered up to us.

A thick-set young man standing next to us laughed. 'That's nothing,' he told us. 'In the early 1880s the lining of the Big Hole detached itself and thousands of tons of ground covered the workings to a depth of 90 feet in places.'

We eyed him curiously. 'The Big Hole has something special for me,' he went on quietly. 'I come here at least once a day to gaze—sometimes more often. It has an irresistible fascination. Look at those rock doves!'

A group, disturbed by the slide, was circling around.

'There was a big splash here the night before last,' the young man went on. 'Someone took a header from the top of the far side into the water.'

Another section of the wall slid, almost in slow motion, into the water and again the far-off noise of the splash came up to us, as if emphasizing his words. 'They haven't found his body—probably won't ever. Bodies don't often surface—they remain trapped in the rocks deep down.'

The Hole has seen many things—the first attempts at organization, the coming of amalgamation, mining companies and new techniques. It saw the rise of 18-year-old Barney Barnato, who had *walked* to Kimberley and ended up as a millionaire; and of Rhodes himself who dreamed of consolidation, who fought Barnato to gain control of Kimberley Mine and won, and who in the end controlled the diamond mines. De Beers Consolidated Mines emerged in its working life, with Rhodes as chairman, and great names associated—Barney Barnato,

C. D. Rudd, Alfred Beit, and others. In the Anglo-Boer War women and children were lowered into the Big Hole to escape Boer shells, and in 1902—the year Rhodes died—it saw, too, the arrival of a young man, Ernest Oppenheimer, from Germany, who was to be the greatest figure in the modern diamond world.

This is the richest hole in the world having produced 14,5-million carats of diamonds. What we were looking at was, we knew, the spectacular symbol of South Africa's diamond industry. This was the beginning of modern South Africa. From here came the riches to finance Johannesburg—gold rode on the back of diamonds, and this is something Kimberley never forgets. When the gold of the Witwatersrand was discovered, diamonds had already made South Africa famous.

We went on to see Kimberley as it is and was. It is a modern city now with all amenities, far removed from the tin-can town of the 1880s. Then it was wood and iron, dust, heat and flies, to which came the toughs and adventurers of the world, 'the libertines, forgers, bird-catchers, the outcasts of Europe . . . the Houndsditch Jew and the London rough'. There also came men of courage and genius, integrity and vision, and a vast number of ordinary people to share the money and see the fun.

Many South Africans today had grandfathers or great-grandfathers who took transport wagons to Kimberley and made their money, or had a flutter on the diamond fields themselves. One young hopeful named Patrick Campbell never made money. His wife in Britain took up acting to support herself and family—so Kimberley gave Mrs Patrick Campbell to the world!

The diamond road from the Cape to Kimberley was not only one of adventure but of incredible hardship too, littered with dying animals, the bones of those already dead, vultures, broken dreams, empty bottles and discarded food cans. Farini of Lost City fame travelled along it in 1885, through 'the most terrible, arid, parched-up, kiln-dried, scorched, baked, burnt and God-forsaken district the sun ever streamed down upon, not even excepting the Sahara'. Near Kimberley the road was a tunnel of empty tins piled high on either side, and in the town itself they made—with hoop-iron and gunny sacks—the houses of the poor.

As tents and tin disappeared, homes of wood and corrugated iron appeared, and then of brick, and sometimes fine spacious homes with high ceilings and imported wrought iron work that was to become a feature of the homes of the wealthy in Johannesburg too. Round the Big Hole were the wood-and-iron offices of the diamond-buyers and sharebrokers, and in the centre of the bustle was Market Square.

Some of the old buildings in the town still stand, like Rudd House and Violet Bank in Belgravia, with fine wrought iron, and elegant old Dunluce, which was the home of the John Orr family and is today owned by the **Alexander McGregor Museum**—when it was restored recently it was found that the walls were made of chicken wire stuffed with mud and horsehair!

Market Square is a national monument, and visitors wonder why. If it seems very ordinary today, it was once a frontier heart, a big, open central spot crammed with life, with tents, men, oxen, wagons and the things they brought—everything from potatoes and complete houses to firewood and ivory. Everyone came here to buy and bargain, talk and plot. In 1886 this was the place which had the first electric street lights in the Southern Hemisphere (a few other spots in the town had them also). Then in the same year amid scenes of great exuberance, Frederick Alexander showed—and panned—a gold-bearing ore from the Witwatersrand. It was his exhibition that first sent Robinson, and later Rhodes and others, to the Rand; so that Johannesburg, historians claim, was born on Kimberley's Market Square.

It was the territory of George St Leger Gordon Lennox, better known as Scotty Smith, highwayman perhaps, certainly South Africa's most illustrious horse and cattle thief and bandit: there are still people who knew him, described as a mixture of Dick Turpin and Robin Hood. One of the places he frequented was the Market Square, where he is reputed to have dealt in illicit diamonds; certainly the best-known Scotty Smith story was set in the Square at a horse sale.

Everyone should have been on the alert for Scotty, but nobody apparently was. Up for sale was a particularly fine riding horse, which the auctioneer invited would-be buyers to test. Scotty Smith sprang on to its back, his broad-rimmed hat pulled down over his face, along the road, and was gone. 'It's Scotty Smith,' yelled someone in the crowd, at which the auctioneer roared back, 'Gone!' So the horse had, and never came back.

In the Anglo-Boer War, when Kimberley was besieged by the Boer forces for four months, food was distributed from the Square. A relic of the siege, a 28-pounder gun called Long Cecil, stands in front of the Monument to the Honoured Dead which commemorates those who died defending Kimberley. The monument was designed by Sir Herbert Baker; but the gun was a purely local and rush affair, designed by the De Beers chief engineer, an American from Michigan named George Frederick Labram, from books in the local library. It was built in the diamond workshops in Kimberley in 27 days and proved to be a splendid job. (Labram was later killed in his hotel bedroom by a stray Boer shell as he was dressing for dinner.)

In one way or another all this local history, every monument, every splash of Kimberley colour, is linked with the Big Hole, which is not only the centre of Kimberley but the central exhibit in South Africa's biggest open-air museum, the **Kimberley—or Big Mine—Museum.**

This is far and away the best thing of its kind in the country, a part of it being a period museum executed with meticulous care and considerable dash, providing plenty of hard facts, and fun and sentiment as well: people react to it with a shout of laughter or a tear in the eye, and this is probably how Kimberley was.

For decades, local Africana—including whole buildings which had been removed *in toto*—had been collected round the Big Hole. Then in 1969 the general manager of De Beers, Mr Ken Loftus, issued an ultimatum. Either the museum had to be organized properly 'or we pull the whole thing down and toss it into the Big Hole'. They did it properly. Where the Kimberley Mine had been, Old Kimberley arose —the gay, bawdy, rough pioneer town of diamonds and brothels, poker, faro, of corrugated iron churches brought by wagon and lovingly reassembled, of spittoons and kid gloves and painted fans.

We spent a day at the Museum and it should have been a week. We did not see a brothel but we did see a bar, a ballroom, the sort of houses that rich men and poor men lived in, the shops that served them, the places where they fought and said their prayers—often the original buildings and not reconstructions at all.

Barney Barnato's Boxing Academy, where some of Kimberley's great fights were held, is not a reconstruction but the same old building moved to the museum in 1955. Barney was an extraordinary man, millionaire and mining magnate, the little London East End Jew who made a fortune in the toughest company South Africa has known, and who fought great battles with both wits and fists. Nothing for us was stranger than his photograph, a cocky little sparrow with butterfly collar, bow tie, check suit, moustache with the ends neatly waxed, and pince-nez. It was, we knew, the face of a supremely successful adventurer—but who would ever have dreamed it!

'The Diggers' Rest' is one of the 128 old bars, 'a relic of the days when Kimberley had more saloons than was good for it'. It is, we thought, the greatest bit of fun of all and what most people look for first, and where they linger longest, savouring the old counter and swing doors, the mirrors and gramophone with the great horn, the footrails and spittoons, hearing—and it does not need much imagination—the laughter, glasses clinking, corks popping. There were also, we remember, 58 brands of cigarettes displayed, and a shock treatment for hangover.

We went to see the ballroom with the regimental ball invitations displayed—they were on fringed silk, with gold and scarlet tassels—and the streets of shops, which everyone delights in. Old Kimberley, we saw, had known advertising techniques. 'Have your hair cut in the same chair as the late Mr Rhodes,' was the notice in the shop of a cigar importer and hairdresser.

There are, above all, diamonds. Whatever one wants to know about diamonds, the Museum tells—what they are (carbon, crystallized in the earth's depths at great heat); how they are the hardest things in nature with an age of from 150-million to 50-million years; how at Kimberley the 'blue ground' in which they occur lies in volcanic pipes; how they are mined, how recovered, how sorted, what they look like, filling in the background both of science and of glamour. We learned how Harry, Sir Ernest Oppenheimer's son, became chairman of De Beers when his father died in 1957 (between them they have served as chairman for over 50 years); and how Kimberley mines, together with Koffiefontein and Finsch, still produce more than 3,5-million carats of diamonds a year.

As for the great diamonds themselves, there was Kimberley's Tiffany—287 carats rough, 128 when cut—a golden stone found in 1879 and bought by Tiffany and Co of New York, who still own and display it; and the champagne-coloured, flawless Kimberley, recut in 1921, which was once part of the Russian Crown Jewels. The Oppenheimer came from Dutoitspan Mine in 1964, an almost perfect diamond weighing nearly 254 carats in the rough—it was bought and presented to the Smithsonian Institution in Washington by the New York dealer, Mr Harry Winston, in honour of Sir Ernest Oppenheimer.

On the human side, there was a photograph of Erasmus Jacobs, who had picked up the first diamond, and of his wife, and a reconstruction of the De Beer's farmhouse with its reed ceiling, deep wall oven, bunches of onions and old iron bed. Above all, there were Barney Barnato's pince-nez, and the diamond scale he had used. He had bought and sold diamonds when he first came to Kimberley, and his scale survived him. It was so small and fine and delicate it looked like a toy. Standing in front of it—we went back half a dozen times to look—we knew its power; it was stronger and harder even than a diamond, the stuff of which history had been made.

CHAPTER TWENTY-ONE

To Namaqualand

❧

A hundred years ago Kimberley's was a country of camelthorn trees, the sturdy desert trees that give shade and shelter to everything that walks and flies. They were also the first fuel for the diamond diggings, so that within a few years the countryside had been stripped of them: even the tree that spread its branches over the claims of the Red Cap Party had disappeared—there must have been diamonds between its roots and they had surely sealed its fate. As we drove from Kimberley to Campbell we saw the trees still, with a young, orphaned look—we were to keep company with the camelthorns, young, middle-aged and great old sages, almost all the way to the Atlantic.

A party of bat-eared foxes ran across the road in the early light and we stopped to admire them: then it was on again, over the Kaap Plateau and into **Campbell Kloof** and the little village which bears the name of John Campbell of the London Missionary Society, who came to South Africa in the second decade of the 19th century to visit the Society's missions, and had passed here.

The mission had been one of the earliest centres of Christianity north of the Orange River and a resting-place for many early travellers such as Burchell, George Thompson, Dr Andrew Smith, and Livingstone himself. The little church with its dung floor was opened in 1831, and under the casuarina—the tall beefwood tree—nearby Livingstone held services in the early 1840s. It is still called the Church Tree. In the mission house that had stood close to it Livingstone first met Mary Moffat, whom he was to marry later in the Kuruman church.

Forty-eight kilometres further on we came to **Griquatown,** the Klaarwater of the early travellers and once a well-known mission station. It was the centre once of the Griquas, a miscellaneous collection of Hottentot and other blood, calling themselves—proudly—The Bastards: their leaders, Adam Kok and Andries Waterboer, figured largely in the history of the area.

A main road runs west from Griquatown to Groblershoop on the Orange River, but we turned north of this, through the Langeberg mountains to **Witsand**—White Sands or the Roaring Sands—one of the strangest phenomena of the Kalahari. It was a road worth travelling, past camelthorn trees with sociable weavers' nests, like haystacks in their crowns, through rocky mountains covered with fragile scented trees, the little boegoe that washed the slopes silver and mauve. When we saw them we knew we were in Burchell's own country—he collected them on these very slopes and christened them as well.

Then we were on a road blazing with colour, red, red Kalahari sand burning the eyes, and a sea of stunted silver trees reaching away to the horizon. The dunes rose out of the plain, ten kilometres long and one to two-and-a-half kilometres broad, light pink or white, a long pale tongue in a red land. That pale strip intrigues everyone for three reasons—its colour, the water close below the surface (below the red sand it is hundreds of metres deep), and the fact that it roars—or talks, as the local people say.

The colour and the surface water, experts explain, are allied. The redness of the surrounding plain, the typical Kalahari red, is given by a thin coating of iron oxide which covers the grains of sand. At Witsand, once upon a time, red sand collected and piled up above a supply of strong surface water: the water acted upon the sand, washing out the iron oxides and turning it white. This was now not only a white but a smooth sand with a large contact surface which, when disturbed, produces intense friction between the grains of sand, vibrations and sound. So it is, when the sand is disturbed, the dunes roar—they roar, incidentally, only in dry weather for moisture silences them.

Geologists have been enthralled ever since they first knew the dunes. Seventy years ago one came here on horseback to get samples: he moved four fingers up and down in the sand and produced a roar, with higher and lower notes which he thought were exactly like men snoring. Others took away bags of sand to Pretoria, which roared when the bags were tilted, became silent in the moister climate, and roared again when heated in an oven. It was a game everyone could play, and many did, loving it perhaps more when there was no scientific explanation.

We longed to hear the sands roaring but never did. The dunes themselves, though, were worth the climb—for every two steps up we slipped back one—for when we reached the top they spread out before us, not white here but pale pink with silver trees upon them: their wood must almost have matched the sand on the surrounding plain for they were *Acacia haematoxylon*, the Acacia with the blood-red wood. They drooped their soft feathers of leaves over the sand: we picked one and marvelled, for the leaflets were almost too small to see—as small as atoms, Burchell thought.

Early visitors to Witsand used to come on horseback or by donkey-cart and sleep in the sand; there are fair roads now and a rondavel resort. In spite of this, it remains a remote, exciting spot. We left it unwillingly and headed for the Orange River.

This North-West is an empty place. The long road ran on over a plain with never a sign or a noticeboard, and when we turned off to a little farmhouse in the distance to ask the way, it was empty, too. Newly colour-washed, neat as a pin, it stood there abandoned. When we shouted there was no reply—no dog's bark or hen to scratch. The hair prickled on our heads. We crossed the river to Groblershoop and were back with people.

From here we followed the river road to Kakamas, pausing for a while at **Upington.** It is a hot little town, and an important one, a major refuelling stop for long-distance jets flying to Europe. It is also the main gateway to the Kalahari and the town through which most people travel to the Gemsbok Park.

Scotty Smith lived the last years of his life here, a bearded old gentleman with a genial smile, although—some claim—with a devil in his heart. He was buried in the cemetery, and on the plaque on his grave are the words, 'Gone but not forgotten'. Above is his name, 'George St Leger Gordon Lennox'—people love to point out that Gordon Lennox is the family name of the Dukes of Richmond and Gordon.

It was close to Upington that Farini searched for diamonds. Diamonds, not a lost city, had brought him to South Africa. At a show in America he had, incredibly enough, met a Coloured man from the Kalahari, Gert, who claimed to have found diamonds on the banks of the Orange River near Upington. So, imagination alight, and accompanied by Gert (who, such were the days, was presented to Queen Victoria en route) to Kimberley and the Kalahari he came. They found the *witgat* tree under which Gert's 180-carat diamond was supposed to have come, but 'no diamond was to be seen', then or after.

Although the Orange proved no diamond river here in the central North-West, it brought another sort of riches—top soil. When we drove down the river on the northern bank from Upington to Kakamas, we saw what rich silt could grow—lucerne, cotton, grapes, wheat: in a desert these are splendid and exciting things.

We slept at **Keimoes**—mouse nest—a little half-real village with palms and a giant waterwheel in the main street, and in the night we were awoken by a strange noise. There below us, in full voice, filled with wine, was a man serenading his camel under the full moon.

From Keimoes a road runs southward to Kenhardt, with a branch to

Verneukpan where in the 1930s Sir Malcolm Campbell tried in his 'Bluebird' to break the world's land speed record. It is as much a world of pans, of heat and mirages, as that of Hakskeenpan near the Gemsbok Park in the north.

We did not turn south, however: instead at Kakamas on the river we branched northwest to the **Augrabies Falls.** These are not falls as the Niagara and Victoria are falls: there is no wide river and sweep of water here, no verdure or softness, but instead a torrent in a narrow rocky winding gorge plunging down cataracts and in one or more streams over a rockface to a whirlpool 90 metres below—190 metres in all from the cataract's top. The spray rises in a cloud above, and the roar of the waters sounds over a great distance—'the place of the big noise,' the Namas called it, for this is what the name Augrabies means.

This is one of the five great waterfalls of the world. Because there is nothing to give it scale, however, it does not appear very high and, except in time of flood, it is not the river water which is the wonder but the spectacular gorge through which it flows, worn by the river out of solid granite. Geologists say it is the finest example in the world of the weathering of granite by water.

The rocks spread on either side as we stood above the falls, grey, shining and polished—deadly we thought them, and this was true for before the safety fences were erected, people had slipped and plunged to death.

The area is a national park now with good accommodation and a restaurant, as well as a fine aloe garden and—what we enjoyed in particular—a grand avenue of kokerbooms. From here to western Namaqualand the kokerboom is the tree of the country. A giant desert lily, some call this famous tree aloe, and sure enough when we look at the yellow flowers, lilies they are. Early travellers thought it looked like the Dragon Tree of the Canaries (which it does) but 'quiver tree' the first explorers called it, because the Hottentots used its bark for quivers. We were to see its spiky form everywhere as we went west, in little cemeteries and desert gardens, alongside the road and on the hills and plains near the Orange River.

We returned to Kakamas, then turned west along a dirt road to **Pofadder.** We were in Bushmanland now. Where does it begin, this territory (from which the last Bushman has gone) so seldom marked on any modern map but which we hear mention of every day in the weather forecast? Everybody has his own idea; for us it begins at Kakamas and stretches westward to the Kamiesberg which runs north-south across Namaqualand; to the north the Orange River is the

311

boundary and its southern—it is somewhere north of Calvinia, we say, and leave it at that.

All of it is desert, not one of Kalahari dunes but of stony sandy plains, of biting cold or of broiling heat, of dust, of mica gleaming on the surface of the ground, Bushman grass in round tufts, and *driedoring*—the gaunt three-fingered bushes of the desert that Burchell named for botanists—of farmhouses like little boxes, of lonely roads and lights—midday lights that blind, and those as well of evening and early morning, purple and mauve and mother-of-pearl, soft and dreamlike, to touch the heart.

Pofadder village was not named after a snake, as we had always hoped, but after a local chief. Its reason for existence was its springs, the soundest possible one in the North-West Cape. Pella lies to the north, with its date palms and Roman Catholic mission, and west is Aggeneys, centre of a new mining venture and a countryside now known to be rich in minerals—copper, silver, zinc, lead, manganese, iron ore, asbestos.

When we first knew the road here there were no fences. Along it went the trekboers, the wandering farmers, in search of grazing and water, with their wagons and carts and possessions jammed into them, their donkeys, their flocks of fat-tailed sheep and goats, and crates of fowls. They outspanned where they wished, the women baking their bread in the oven of the nearest farmhouse, watering their animals and moving on, an other-world scene, unique and timeless, it seemed to us then. But time changed it very soon. We saw no trekboers and every road was fenced. When we return, there will be a mining town where we knew the Black Mountain rising out of the uninhabited lonely plain. Some people will rejoice, but it will not be us.

We stopped on the plain to make tea—there was not a single bush to cast a tiny shadow—and thought we were the only living things. Then, waddling purposefully towards us came two *koringkrieks*, gigantic crickets 10 centimetres long, like repulsive dark tanks on crooked legs: they live because they eat everything they meet (even hair from human heads, say people who have tried it out) and finally, with gusto, one another!

We remember, too, that when a drop of water from our flask touched the sand, it hissed.

We do not know how many people have hunted for minerals—for diamonds above all—in this North-West; it must be thousands for the legends are there (fields of diamonds, pot-holes crammed with the precious gems) although nobody has found them. On our right as we drove lay the hunting-ground, up and down the river, of the most famous prospector of all, Fred Cornell, bald-headed, tough as a bit of leather, poet, writer, dreamer, who left his name, Cornell's Kop, in the Richtersveld near the Orange River, and a book, *The Glamour of Prospecting*, that is South Africa's best true story of adventure.

He himself, the book makes clear, sought not only diamonds, but all that lay 'beyond that last blue mountain barred with snow'. He had his own idea of what a prospector should be, a man with the love of wild things in his bones, who knew soil and minerals, who could ride, shoot, walk and swim, who should be 'an adventurer in the older and honourable sense of the word'. As we drew nearer to Springbok and Namaqualand's Atlantic coast, he began to assume heroic proportions in our minds. There one of the last great diamond rushes had taken place—too late for him—yet he had given the prospectors as a breed a stature, and glamour too.

We were to see Cornell's Kop later, now we were almost at **Springbok** passing through the grey Namaqualand hills to this historic little town. It was a new world where the dust was pale and the rain fell in winter, still a thirst-land but a different sort. Although we were still on a diamond road, this was copper country and the hill at Springbok a copper mountain.

Springbok has a different background to other places in South Africa also. While Voortrekkers and hunters made Transvaal and Free State history, and missionaries that of the North-West we had left behind, soldier-explorers, the first explorers of all, made history here. This was Cape Town's first hinterland. Not ten years after the settlement had been born at the foot of Table Mountain, soldiers of the Dutch East India Company were travelling north towards Namaqualand.

It was the dream of Monomotapa, the fabulous kingdom of gold, that lured the Dutch into the far-off Transvaal Lowveld across the Lebombo Mountains, and it was Monomotapa also they sought here. Instead of gold they found copper. In 1684 Sergeant Isaac Schrijver presented the samples he had taken from Springbok's copper mountain to Governor Van der Stel in Cape Town, and next year the Governor was off to see it all for himself, an epic journey in a lumbering Dutch coach with a great entourage. (For many, the greatest point of interest was the artist, Claudius, he took with him—the official photographer, so to say—who left curious and charming little records of the trip.)

Historically, the most important thing Van der Stel did was to sink three shafts, from which copper ore was taken—the shafts can still be seen at Springbok. Although nearly 200 years were to pass before the transport of the copper could be organized and mining could start in earnest, yet it was Van der Stel who set it all in motion: those crude shafts he sank were the beginning of South Africa's mining industry, and people today view them with respect.

In the mid-19th century men began to haul the copper by wagon and mule train from Springbok and O'Kiep nearby down the escarpment to Hondeklip Bay and Port Nolloth on the coast—the mule train was a bit of transport history people still talk of with amused delight. Those who wish, can follow the old route today with Willem Steenkamp in his *Land of the Thirst King*, sharing its outspans and nostalgic delights.

It took us two hours, stopping frequently on the **Anenous Pass**—up which the mules had pulled the trucks—to get to the sea from Springbok via Steinkopf. **Port Nolloth** is a rather characterless little port today, yet it is full of history. Palaeontologists remember it because the first fossil record in South Africa came from near here when the two famous explorers, Colonel Gordon and Lieutenant William Paterson, travelling northward along the coast towards the Orange River mouth, noted 'petrifactions of shells' in the rocks well above sea-level. They were both amateur scientists, Paterson a botanist and Gordon, as we know from his exploits in the east, a man of many parts and a keen observer. Nonetheless, they missed the treasure the fossils marked—they went slap past the diamonds which were later found to be associated with the fossil shells.

They went on up to the mouth of the Orange River, and on 17th August embarked in a little boat they had brought with them in a wagon. Gordon hoisted the Dutch colours, drank a toast to the State, the Prince of Orange and the Company, and solemnly named the river in honour of the prince. They did not think of diamonds.

Nearly a century and a half later, however, this coast was the scene of a diamond fever just as great as Kimberley's. People had hunted diamonds here with enthusiasm but without any great success until, in 1926, a young man named Jack Carstens, working on his father's claims just south of Port Nolloth, found a diamond. That was when the fever began. Soon there was another find up the coast at a spot to be called Cliffs Fields—as far as can be reckoned today it was the place where Paterson and Gordon had seen their fossil shells, if not the exact spot, then certainly close by.

Soon there were more strikes. Every prospector who could rushed to Namaqualand and claims were pegged everywhere, north, south, east, west. It was a frenzied scene of unco-ordinated finds, on which late in the year appeared the geologist, Dr Hans Merensky. It was he, patiently following every clue, examining the ground and noting the traces of fossil shells here and there, who first established the fact—

314

startling at the time—that deposits of fossil oyster shells and diamonds were linked. It was a hunch to begin with that he backed, pegging and buying up claims along the 'Oyster Line' just south of the Orange River mouth. They were to make him a millionaire.

Up till then, diamonds had only been found in kimberlite pipes or alluvial gravel. But here the 'oyster beds' which held them were ancient beaches now raised above the level of the sea. This much is known, although even today the origin of the diamonds found on these ancient beaches is not. Merensky thought they were truly marine, born of some volcanic pipe under the sea; other experts maintained that they had come from the land, had been washed into the sea by floods and rivers, and had been flung back on to the beaches by the action of the sea.

Whatever their origin, there they were in multitudes. Very soon, to save the diamond market, the government took a hand, banning prospecting and establishing the state diggings at Alexander Bay—where Colonel Gordon had launched his boat and named the Orange River 150 years before.

Alexander Bay is south of the river. North, even greater things were to follow. Since 1908 diamonds had been found sporadically up the terrifying desert coast of South West Africa—the Sperrgebiet or Forbidden Territory, the Germans called it—at places like Bogenfels, Pomona, Kolmanskop and Elizabeth Bay, and these were operated by small German mining companies. In 1920 Sir Ernest Oppenheimer was able to merge these into the Consolidated Diamond Mines of South West Africa (C.D.M.), one of the great names in the diamond world today. Six years later, when Merensky had made the mouth of the Orange River news, C.D.M. began to prospect on the northern bank; and here, too, the marine terraces were found to contain a fortune. Today they are the richest fields in the world.

Dominating everything is the highly efficient, watchful, security-tight mining machine which is Consolidated Diamond Mines, with headquarters at Oranjemund.

At Port Nolloth we turned north along an incredible flat desolate desert road towards the Orange River and **Oranjemund.** The diamond mines are not open to the public, although it is possible, by arrangement, to see them. Through the generosity of C.D.M. we did see the workings, and from the air Merensky's famous Oyster Line in the south, as well as the spot where the first prospecting trench was begun.

We flew by helicopter 100 kilometres upriver, clattering low above the brown waters, into 'Cornell Country'. The story is still told that Fred Cornell found the diamonds of the Oyster Line before Merensky and had gone to London to form a syndicate to finance their exploitation, when he was run down and killed by a London taxi (and not accident either, men breathe.) That he did not know the oyster shell secret, that he died quite otherwise from a chance blow, these are facts that people seldom accept because they lack true diamond drama.

We flew into the Richtersveld to see his monument, over the jumble of mountains—Cornell's own adored mountains—where the Orange loops to the north, the loneliest and least-known corner of South Africa, and low down over Cornell's Kop where the plaque to his memory stands. It says very simply, 'In memory of Fred Cornell, 4.2.1925'.

From there we flew north. Diamonds in the Forbidden Territory belong to an even stranger world than in the south, a pitiless Namib Desert of marching dunes and ghost towns, once diamond centres and now—with the greater riches at the river's mouth—abandoned. At **Kolmanskop** near Lüderitz we stood on the railway track where Zacharias Lewala had found the territory's first diamond in 1908. He showed it, we remembered, to August Stauch, who test-scratched the face of his watch with it! It was real, and South West Africa's diamond rush started here.

We followed the old, neglected road to **Pomona.** Pomona, a ghost town dominated by a graveyard on a scarp overlooking the Atlantic, embodies all the magic of the legendary discoveries of the past.

We drove to a high point and looked down on it—a post-cart, axle-deep in sand, stood outside the former German police station, into whose smashed windows breakers of sand washed. Not far away a narrow-gauge train, with old-fashioned open carriages, stood in a non-existent vanished station, as it had done through the upheavals of two world wars and the predatory gnawing of innumerable gales.

This same Namib was empty one January night in 1909 when three men looked down on it from our vantage-point. One of the men was August Stauch, who had tested the first diamond a year before; the others were Dr Scheibe, a German geologist, and Jacob, an Herero.

At nightfall, as they were preparing camp, Jacob, a little way off, started scratching idly in the sand. Suddenly Stauch and Scheibe heard him yelling. They sprinted up to him and found him clutching a handful of diamonds in both fists—and his mouth was crammed full of them too!

The moon came up, the men looked across the valley: the floor of it was aglisten with diamonds sparkling in the moonlight.

Dr Scheibe was so stunned that all he could say, over and over, was, 'This is a fairy-tale'.

Elizabeth Bay is another abandoned town. Offshore, like a whale surfacing, is **Possession Island,** biggest of the guano islands. It was more exciting for us than diamonds. Captain Kidd trod its guano-splashed rocks—3 kilometres long, half a kilometre wide—on his way to a raiding voyage in the Indian Ocean. The preserved and mummified bodies of New Bedford whalermen lie in coffins strapped to the rocks because there was no soil in which to bury them. The shoreline is strewn with wrecks, some old, some new; and there is a legless woman ghost as well and the ghosts of her gigantic boarhounds.

At **Bogenfels** we saw the great soaring arch of rock, pierced through its centre, which juts out from the yellow-striated cliffs into the sea, one leg standing in the boiling surf. Bartolomeu Dias on his epoch-making voyage was the first white man ever to sight Bogenfels; he noted it in his log on Old Year's Eve in 1487. No voyager since has missed it: it is the biggest feature of the coast where palomino-coloured dunes ripple right down to the sea's edge and wind-scoured, hillocky dunes march away endlessly inland.

It was a strange nostalgic world, as ghost places are, and we turned back from it to living Oranjemund. After we had refuelled from an emergency dump in the desert, dusk came, then night. We moved slightly inland, away from the coast, flying low between the sandhills. They turned from dun to gold to grey; the sand ahead and on either side and the dead light above gave the impression of a tunnel, with no beginning and no end, a sealed journey into sherry-coloured space. Night came; there were only the stars. Then ahead was a whole configuration of stars low down on the horizon, where the night-fields of the Namib were seeded with Oranjemund's lights, like another floor of diamonds.

We have said this is a world of diamonds, and it is; yet such are the security regulations that few visitors today come to see them. They come instead to see succulents and flowers, often unique to Namaqualand.

All South Africa's arid regions are famous for succulents, the fat-leaved, moisture-filled plants adapted, with detail and drama, to the desert; and **Namaqualand** is the richest part of all. Here are the strange shapes and forms in abundance, fat smooth dwarfs, spiky columns, stone plants indistinguishable from the brown stones around them, as small as a little finger-nail or taller than a man.

Two of the rarest succulents of all belong to the Richtersveld, attracting botanists and collectors from far corners of the world. One is the *Half-mens* or Half-man, *Pachypodium namaquanum*, that grows on stony hills near the Orange River, its tall bottle-shaped form extraordinarily human as it inclines its head, with its few small leaves and

317

flowers, gently to the north. Legend has it that these succulents are the spirits of a people from the north who were stranded here and died and who now—in new form—look always to the land they left behind them. It was Fred Cornell, dealing now not in diamonds but in living matter, who took the first plants to botanists in Cape Town, one of which later went to Kew.

There is also one of the rarest aloes, *Aloe pillansii*, a tall sparse tree, which the Coloured people of the Richtersveld know as 'The Long One'. It was named after N. H. Pillans, the botanist who collected it on Cornell's Kop near the plaque erected to Cornell's memory the year after he died.

We went to see them. Not the guests of C.D.M. this time, we camped on the banks of the Orange River just outside the diamond security fence. What a place it was, a sandy nest among the wild trees that made a belt along the river, full of monkeys that weaved about us, ghost-like in the evening light. We put our sleeping-bags side by side in the sand and, with our backs to the diamonds, slept like kings.

Next morning we followed the river eastward, the Orange on our left, mountains, canyons and old river beds upon our right, until we came to Cornell's hills. When we climbed into them, we found they were bare of anything but stones—flat stones that leapt up and bit our ankles as we passed—and 'the Long Ones' whose thin gaunt forms made a Namib etching against the pale sky. We did not see a human being, going or coming, or any single living thing on the hills on which they grew. It was a vast landscape, rimmed with mountains, the right place in which to remember Fred Cornell, who had loved the space and mystery of the Richtersveld above diamonds.

Most of Namaqualand's tourists come to see the spring flowers. This is a land of winter rain—scant rain for it is semi-desert—after which follows a spring blooming that, in good years, is of superlative quality. The best time to see the flowers is usually in August or early September but exact dates are dependent on the time of rain, and they vary. Nevertheless, early spring is Namaqualand's tourist season when every bed in every hotel is booked in advance and every camping-place is full.

We were lucky in our spring. It followed a season of unusually good rains which had fallen at the right time, and in late August when we turned back from the Richtersveld to **Springbok,** Namaqualand was alive with colour. There were many scores of different species, although it was largely the daisies that painted the hills and plains— the Namaqualand daisy is horticulturally one of the world's famous flowers now.

From Springbok they radiated every way. When we first approached the town it was late afternoon and the daisy flowers—which mostly bloom in sunshine and warmth—were shut. Even so, with every petal closed, the country on either side of the road was a subdued orange—we had not thought that closed flowers could colour a landscape, but, packed side by side in millions, they did.

In sunlight they were all that everyone had ever said they were. They were even better because nobody had told us that part of the shock of Namaqualand spring flowers was contrast. Here were no gentle fields of flowers but poor, inhospitable semi-desert laced with sombre granite hills. We saw swathes of flowers pouring over the land, solid tides of brilliant colour, that did not hide the nature of the country. Nobody could ever look at them and think they were the fruits of easy living: one look at the hills and sand from which they sprang and they were clearly desert-born. Those myriads of small, ephemeral, delicate, glittering forms when seen against the dark everlasting hills were as near to perfection as anything we had ever seen.

At **Concordia,** to the north of Springbok, were fields of yellow cotulas, Duck's Eye, surrounding little farmhouses—every step we took was perfumed with their fragrance. To the north we found a farm that welcomed us and then left us to ourselves to walk as we wished. For a day we zigzagged quietly over a plain and climbed the hills encircling it, stopping and starting, with sand in our shoes and certainly fever in our brains.

On the hills were bushes of silver peas, *Lebeckia sericea*, with yellow flowers set in silky leaves—we had passed them everywhere but now we touched them to feel their silk. They grew among the rocks together with the *kokerbooms*. Simon van der Stel's artist had figured one two-and-a-half centuries before, so it was with a sense of history that we climbed the hills between the trees, running our hands over the smooth, yellowish bark with its cracks and dimples; but when we walked among the flowers on the flats, history deserted us. All we thought of then was colour.

The sand was pale salmon-pink, gleaming with minute mica flakes, and on it burned the great double heads of the double Namaqualand daisies, *Arctotis fastuosa*, with orange 'petals' based with black and blackish shining centres. We could hardly bear to leave them. There were huge orange gazanias and smaller Namaqualand daisies, *Dimorphotheca sinuata*, and wild cinerarias in pink and yellow. The pinkish-purple showed in between the orange of the daisies, with salmon sand between. In a garden we would have turned our eyes away; here the mixture was stupendous.

There was the heavenly blue of the little daisy, *Charieis hetero-phylla,* and yellow daisies big and small, *Oxalis* species in different colours, pink diascias and succulents in flat clumps with grey leaves tipped wine-red bearing pink ostrich feather flowers. The whippy stems and blue flowers belonged to *Heliophila* —blue flax—and there were white as well, frail plants growing in sheets and as the wind moved the white bells, the green calyx and thin stems revealed themselves in a wave of sea-green.

There were a multitude of plants, although few bulbs; these we found farther to the south. Many we did not recognize but longed to know them all. On that day we tramped the farm, there was no popular book to tell us what we saw. Later, Sima Eliovson, the garden writer, produced *Namaqualand in Flower*, with colour photographs and descriptions, a beautiful and exciting book that should go with every visitor to Namaqualand.

Kamieskroon lies south of Springbok and as we drove towards it the candle-snuffer church tower of the little village rose up to meet us. We were approaching it from the north, and the flower heads on every side were turned toward us—toward the sun—so that we saw them at their best, and we stopped to study this gay, charming sight of the church that had apparently sprouted with the daisies.

We turned toward the mountains, the Kamiesberg; topping a rise, we came upon a white drift in a valley below and shouted, 'Snow!'

Namaqualanders would have smiled at us. The snow was flowers, myriads of white flower petals packed close together and shining in the sun. They were wild flax, *Heliophila* species, and we walked through them—they were hardly up to our knees—wondering that flowers so small could make so dense a sheet of colour.

Namaqualand ends south of Garies and beyond it is the south-western Cape. In spring the road south is still a flower route, although the flowers are often of a different kind. There are arums in the ditches and proteas in the mountains, ixias and sparaxis, gladiolus, freesia, moraea, babiana, erica, all those flowers that made the south-west tip of Africa famous long before diamonds and gold were dreamed of. We loitered down the road, past Vanrhynsdorp—a famous wild flower centre—and Clanwilliam: on our left was the Bidouw Valley jewelled with flowers, ahead Citrusdal and Piketberg; and so we came into Cape Town, a little drunk with pleasure, on an early September day.

The gateway to the Castle

Mrs Dollie on 'The Parade' in Cape Town

The kitchen in the Koopmans de Wet house, typical of early town kitchens

CHAPTER TWENTY-TWO

Cape Town

꧁

The classic way to approach Cape Town is from the sea, standing on a ship's deck, gazing at the blue water and the city beyond at the foot of the great flat mountain, Table Mountain. When colours and lights are right it is a sight of stunning beauty. People come now more often by air or by road: but still the city and the mountain are unique.

So is the whole Peninsula, the 51-kilometre, narrow, half-moon hatchet thrusting southwards into the ocean, Cape Town to the north, and in the extreme south Cape Point, its rocks and cliffs so full of might and drama that they, and not the flat tongue of Cape Agulhas, should be the tip—the end—of Africa. This Peninsula is for many people one of the most beautiful places in the world, beginning with Cape Town and Table Bay, continuing southwards with its mountains and rocks, its valleys and vines and old Cape homes, and its long coastline with its incomparable views of sea and cliffs with all the warmth, the spectacle and colour of Italy, but the wind and the smells of Africa.

At the same time there is no part of South Africa where men's foolishness is more apparent or the ugliness they have brought more obvious—gross buildings despoiling classic views, tatty suburbs, places of history and beauty gone before the bulldozer, mountains denuded, a flora—from early days known as the wonder of the world—endangered. It is a never-ending list. Yet in spite of all the crudities, the Peninsula remains a world beauty.

We stood one morning in Cape Town's famous Adderley Street. At our backs was Table Mountain and the Peninsula behind it, before us Table Bay and the sea. It was a wonderful moment. We knew exactly why we had come to this corner of the South-West Cape; to see first-hand this first town of all, to learn again our beginnings, to look at the old homes and beautiful and curious things that had helped to make the South African story, to eat the food, drink the wine, and see the flowers. It was a tremendous programme, and here we were at the beginning with the boulevard of the Heerengracht ahead of us, and the harbour docks, a streamlined modern world of ships with their tang of salt and adventure.

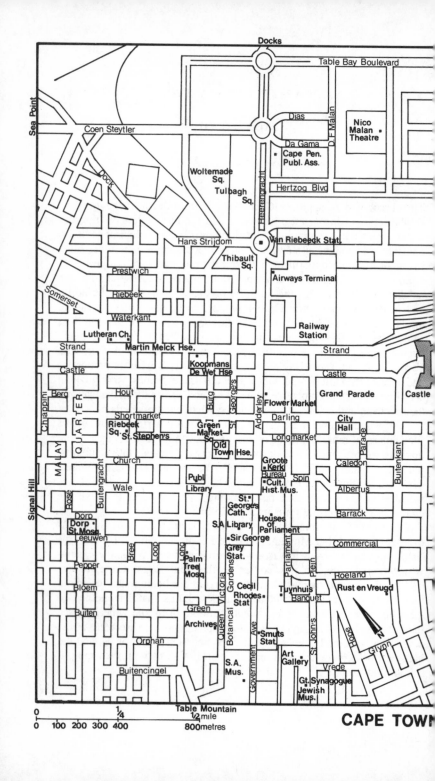

We began at the sea-end of the street because it was from the sea that the story had started. It was in Table Bay that the Dutch ship, the *Haarlem*, had been wrecked in 1647, almost 330 years before. It is true that Bartolomeu Dias had rounded the Cape and landed on the Peninsula 160 years before the Dutch ship had foundered, that in 1503 Antonio da Saldanha had anchored in the bay (and named Table Mountain), and that thereafter British and French ships had also stopped here in the safety of the harbour to get fresh water from the streams that ran into the sea and bargain with Hottentots for meat. But the sailors from the *Haarlem* did something more, something no others did—they made a vegetable patch.

That patch was the beginning of South Africa.

It grew and flourished at the right time in the history of the seas. The route to the East was open but for the sailors that voyage of 200 days and more from Europe to India was still heavy with death, not only from the sea itself, but from scurvy, the sailors' scourge.

By the 1600s men knew that the disease could be kept at bay by a diet which included fresh vegetables and fruit. And now, at a time when Dutch sailors had been urging the need for a settlement some-where on the African coast to provide food, came the *Haarlem* survivors with their story of fresh vegetables, self-grown at the mouth of the Fresh River where it entered Table Bay, and of fresh meat. In Holland it tipped the scales. Five years later three little ships, the *Dromedaris, Reiger* and the *Goede Hoop*, sailed away to establish a settlement at the Cape to provide fresh food for the ships of the Dutch East India Company.

The party anchored in Table Bay and went ashore on April 6th, 1652: and at their head was Jan van Riebeeck, the Commander, the first 'man of authority' South Africa ever knew.

Every school history we had ever known had told this, and the succeeding story, how five years later Free Burghers had been granted land to become our first farmers, and how 27 years after Van Riebeeck's landing there had come the first man who had looked at the Cape and seen it not as a vegetable garden, a granary or a pasturage, but as a home. He was Governor Simon van der Stel, who had backed his fancy, built his great house on the Peninsula, and died here, leaving at his death a thriving little colony. In his time came the French religious refugees and immigrants, the Huguenots, bringing South Africa, among other things, French names and dark eyes.

In 1795 the British arrived, occupying the Cape when Holland was overrun by the French, in the name of the refugee Prince of Orange—it was the time at the Cape of Major-General Dundas, and later Sir

George Yonge as Governor, and of Lady Anne Barnard wife of the British Colonial Secretary, hostess and letter-writer, from whom we know much of Cape Town of the day.

The year 1803 saw the Cape once more, by the Treaty of Amiens, Dutch: it was handed over to the Batavian Government of Holland—but not for long. Its strategic position on the route to India was too valuable and three years later it was again taken by the British. Now there followed a string of English governors—Cradock and Somerset, Donkin and Cole, D'Urban (under whom the slaves were emancipated) and Napier, Sir Harry Smith and Sir George Grey—and all the frontier wars they fought. In 1867 diamonds came like a gift from heaven to boost the Colony's finances: five years later Responsible Government was granted, and by 1890 Cecil John Rhodes was dominating the scene as prime minister and millionaire. There came the Jameson Raid, the Anglo-Boer War, and the South Africa Act of 1910 by which, with a fanfare of trumpets, the Union of South Africa came into being.

Now we stood there, in a city which bore the mark of every person and every happening—part of a republic now—looking across Adderley Street to the spot where it all began.

Across the road to the right were huge excavations. They were on ground being cleared and dug for a big new business complex soon to be built—the site was popularly known as the Golden Acre because of its business value. It was close to here that Van Riebeeck landed, for in his day the sea reached almost to the foot of Adderley Street—all the land in front of us, we recalled, had been reclaimed. Some 70 years before, the first old pier had been discovered in excavations at the Golden Acre. Now the remains of that ancient reservoir, built by Van Riebeeck's successor in 1663 to hold water from the Fresh River (which ran down Adderley Street) had been found, and a canal leading from it as well. It was here that sailors had filled their water-casks. This discovery of the first construction of all thrilled people, and the remains were, we found, to be preserved in the complex in a glass piazza for the world to see.

We left the docks, the fishing harbour and the seals, the Fish Market and the Penny Ferry for another day: we would eat a crayfish tail at the famous Harbour Café on a more leisured occasion, we promised ourselves. Now we turned to our right down Strand Street towards the Castle, a few blocks away from Adderley Street, which to us symbolizes the Cape's past.

The **Castle,** although later than Van Riebeeck's day, is the oldest building in South Africa, the only 17th century one left. The wood-

and-mud fort Van Riebeeck had constructed was on a spot close by. The early Dutch Reformed Church services were held here in a room hung with skins; we remembered how the stuffed zebra at the entrance had been removed before the service began lest it should prove too fascinating for the congregation.

We parked near the entrance to the Castle and paused outside its walls. Star-shaped, stone-walled, with bastions topped with cannon (that never fired a shot in anger) and a city gate straight from the old Netherlands, the Castle was once surrounded by a moat, and a drawbridge had linked it with the outside world. Even without the moat, it was a splendid sight, but at the same time the most un-African thing in Africa, a medieval fortress from Europe set down in the shade of Table Mountain. Simon van der Stel who had arrived at the Cape in 1679, had designed the main gateway, which now bore his name.

It was tremendously impressive, not only a fortress we saw as we entered, but a fortified palace, the whole area divided into two by a great wall (a typical medieval plan), with courtyards on either side. Here had been the Governor's home and the government offices, and from the flat-roofed buildings within the walls the settlement had once been administered.

From without we had looked through the open gate in brilliant sunlight towards a wonderful balcony on the far side of the courtyard. Now we examined it from close at hand. This was the lauded Kat Balcony in front of the Governor's residence—added about 1800— from which proclamations had once been read. Balcony, we thought, was a poor term for it, for it looked as if it had been designed to house a throne, and with its teak ceiling and parapet, panelled door and heraldic carvings, its iron balustrades and graceful steps, it was one of the loveliest things we saw in the city.

It was of special interest for another reason—it was a fine introduction to the work of two men who in the late 1700s and early 1800s had changed the face of Cape Town. They were Louis Michel Thibault— who came to the Cape in 1783 and was the first architect of note in South Africa—and his contemporary, the German sculptor and wood-carver Anton Anreith. It was Thibault who designed the balcony and Anreith who executed the outstanding carvings, and the two lions flanking the gateway.

On the balcony stood a sturdy little bronze cannon bearing the monogram of the Dutch East India company. It had been hauled up out of the sea in the net of a fishing trawler, *George Irvin*, 29 sea miles WSW of the Cape—where for two centuries it had lain on the ocean bed 300 fathoms deep. It set us off later on a cannon hunt in Cape

Town (we found cannons everywhere, cannon muzzles making a fence around the Castle garden, cannon as bollards in the harbour, as old hitching posts in the streets, at old batteries, as decorations in front of private houses).

Now we left the little gun to pass into the Governor's apartments with their beautiful things belonging to the William Fehr collection. People interested in Cape glass come to the Castle to study the collection of elegant pieces of this distinctive glass of the past, white and most often with the fern-leaf pattern, all collectors' items now. Cape silver addicts haunt the silver collection too, and there are copper and bronze beauties, fine furniture, and pictures. There were also, we found, a maritime and military museum of interest, and dungeons which we did not visit—Madame Tussaud's Chamber of Horrors had cured us for good of any taste for the macabre.

There were not only old things about us but plenty of new. The Castle today is the headquarters of the Cape Command of the South African Defence Force, so is filled with activity, often with dash and colour. The ballroom is the same as that in which Lady Anne Barnard, first lady for a period at the Cape, received her guests some 175 years ago. She would have approved the modern military balls, with their 19th century uniforms, a guard of honour for the brigadier, a carriage, white horses, and a military band. Amid today's glitter, perhaps some remember her feast: 'Our lamps well lighted with the tails of the sheep whose saddles we were eating.'

The Castle faces on to an open square near which the first vegetables were grown. From early times it was known as the **Grand Parade,** where garrison troops were once trained (and where Captain Cook's sailors from the *Resolution* and *Adventure* camped and his sheep grazed). It is today only half as big as in the early 18th century, but big enough for business and fun—here on Wednesdays and Saturdays is an open auction and flea market, noted for colour, humour and good bargains; Lawrence Green, the prolific writer on Cape Affairs, wrote that a three-roomed house of papier mâché was once sold here. We enjoyed it all, sizzling with life, the apricot-coloured city hall (Italian renaissance and Bath stone) beyond: palms below with orange dates, a pigeon sitting on a statue, the head of Edward VII we found; bargain hunters by the hundred; Mr and Mrs Dollie selling 'high-class' materials, Mrs Dollie with a dishcloth pinned to her hat and hanging down the back of her neck to protect her from the sun. There were dozens like them, many Cape Coloureds, as full of life and humour.

The Castle and the Grand Parade made for us a pocket of Cape

Town complete in itself. Now for the rest. We turned our backs on the Castle and walked westwards along Strand Street, crossing Adderley Street as we did so. This had once been on the waterfront—Zeestraat or Sea Street it had been called—a busy place full of merchants' homes where great people had lived, such as Captain Cook, William Burchell, and the Abbé de la Caille who in 1751 was the first scientist to stay a long time at the Cape. He had come to observe the southern sky and so built a small observatory behind his lodging-house at the corner of Adderley Street. Here he laid the foundation of South Africa's study of the stars, among many triumphs plotting the positions of 9 766 stars. A plaque commemorates his stay.

His clever, full, long-nosed face accompanied us along the street, but further on, beyond Bree Street, he gave place to little gentle William Burchell, the ecologist—a 20th century word of which he never dreamed—with the sharp eyes and the great spirit who in 1810 had lodged in the building on our right, No 96 Strand Street. It was from here that he had set out to explore the almost unknown hinterland, to write his careful, detailed journal, the story of courage and adventure, and to bring back his 60 000 specimens which today are spread across the world.

Only Burchell fans stop at No 96 to think of him. Everybody else does because of the interior decorating shop which flourishes superbly there today, or because the building is one of Cape Town's most famous. It is the Martin Melck House, one of the Lutheran Church complex, with the old **Lutheran Church** beyond it; on the other side is a smaller building which now houses the Netherlands Legation: together they make the only group of three 18th century buildings left in the city.

Lawrence Green, who loved the group, thought the church was possibly the most beautiful in the country. It was built by Martin Melck, the famous 18th century soldier-settler, and some of Anreith's work can be seen here, a carved door, a balustrade, the pulpit and lectern in the form of a swan. The swan—that beautiful strange bird—is the unlikely emblem of Lutheranism. Based on the words of the martyr Jan Hus, it has a savage origin. Hus, when he was about to be burned at the stake, made a prophecy around his own name ('hus' is a Bohemian word meaning goose). 'Today a goose may roast, but a swan will arise that will be invincible.' The swan was Luther.

The **Martin Melck House** next door was the old Lutheran parsonage and had still, we thought, the air of a home. This 18th century house, double-storeyed with courtyard and big high rooms, is supposed to have been the combined work of Thibault and Anreith.

The most fascinating feature of all to us was the *dakkamer*, the little room on the roof, with its four windows set in a gable, crowned with the Lutheran swan. It is the last *dakkamer* in Cape Town, although once such rooms were common. Their purpose is not always clear— some claim that they were vantage points from which to view the shipping, and certainly this is how we would have used this one, hanging out of the windows to enjoy the tremendous sweep of the bay.

We crossed the road and walked back until we came to the **Koopmans de Wet House** between Long and Burg Streets. This is one of Cape Town's sights, a house and museum preserved as a wealthy Cape Town home of the past two centuries, complete with furniture, pictures, silver and glass. We stood outside the elegant, double-storeyed, flat-roofed old place, admiring the triangular pediment and fluted pilasters, the tall windows, the door and fanlight with a lantern.

That flat roof told its own story, one of wind and fire. In the early days there had been thatched pitched roofs. But thatch caught fire easily and Cape Town's notorious winds carried flames from roof to roof: so out went the old roofs and in came flat ones of brick and clay with a low parapet or cornice in front, all comparatively fireproof. We knew the early pictures of Cape Town with these picturesque homes: but most had gone, the Koopmans de Wet House remaining to show us how a fine house of those days could look.

Part of the building may date from 1701, which is very old for South Africa. It was enlarged by various owners (some credit Thibault with the main work). In 1809 it was acquired by Mrs Margaretha de Wet, widow of the president of the Burgher Council, and in due course became the property of her two granddaughters. One of these was Marie, wife of Johan Koopmans, an officer in the British-German Legion, who was called Mrs Koopmans de Wet. She became one of the great of Cape Town, champion of the Boers and their language, contemporary of Rhodes—hostess, collector, and defender of the old and beautiful in the city.

It was she who saved a section of the Castle from demolition when it was planned to route train and tramlines through it. We treasure the story of the envoy Rhodes sent to her to assure her that only a little buttress of the Castle walls would be removed, to whom she answered that Rhodes's nose was only a little point on his face. 'Let him cut it off and look in the glass.'

We went into her house, walking slowly through the rooms, which indeed looked as if a careful housewife had kept them in trim. In particular we admired the furniture. For anyone wishing to see old

Cape furniture at its best, this is a fine collection to study, with its wall cupboards and chests, and other massive, gleaming pieces. We remember in particular a stinkwood and camphor cabinet with silver fittings made by the Cape silversmith Daniel Heinrich Schmidt, 'master craftsman in the making of furniture fittings': it had a rose inlaid above the keyhole.

There is a wonderful lot of old Cape silver, too, the rare, mostly 18th century silver which has now become precious Africana, and is eagerly sought by collectors. We noted a silver snuff-box with the letters W.L. and a silver *tessie* inscribed C.L.—magic marks, those of Carel Daniel Lotter and William Lotter, of the famous Lotter family of silversmiths. There were forks by the English John Townsend, and best of all a tumbler cup made by Heinrich Schmidt, and on it the name and initials of Colonel Robert Gordon who had left his work on so many things we had met in our travels.

What the elegant old house did not have was a bathroom! Mrs Koopmans de Wet had a hip bath carried in and out of her bedroom, and this was once quite customary; we remembered those hip baths from our own sojourns in country places. It was the English who in the early 19th century had brought bathrooms to ordinary city homes, and fireplaces as well—in the early days the Dutch people in cold weather had copper footwarmers of coals or warming-pans filled with hot chains, and coats in which they shivered—the English even brought the coal from England. The many chimneys on Cape Town's skyline were thus theirs as well.

Adderley Street was only two blocks away, and when we reached it we halted. If we wanted history, it was about us now. Here the Fresh River had once run down to the sea. The first road here had been Burgwal, later changed to Voorste Straat, and then to Heerengracht—the present boulevard, Heerengracht, had been christened to revive this historic name. The name Adderley dated only from the 1840s when a shipload of convict settlers was prevented from landing at Cape Town largely through the efforts of British parliamentarian Charles Adderley, who spoke up for the Cape Town cause in the House of Commons. The convict ship, *Neptune*, went on to Australia, and the Heerengracht was renamed Adderley Street in gratitude to that faraway politician.

It might have been named Harry Smith Street—for he was then the Governor—if he had fallen in with Cape Town's wishes, but whatever his private opinions, he was too loyal a servant to his Queen and government. Poor Harry! He was not used to being unpopular, and now Capetonians tried even to block the food going to Government House.

We looked up the street towards Table Mountain. The vegetable garden that developed into the famous botanic and ornamental garden had stretched from the top of the street in the direction of the mountain. Over the years it was gradually cut up, a bit going for government buildings, a cathedral, a museum, and so it went. Now there remained the old avenue with its trees, Government Avenue, and the Public or Botanic Gardens to remind people of the distinguished garden that once had stood there, and of the part it had played. We began to walk towards it.

We had not yet found John Muir's *Know Your Cape* or his short guide to Cape Town, or Betty Hughes' *Walking Through History*, so that it was an erratic pilgrimage, stopping frequently and turning off here and there. That day, however—and it was a long one—exploring old Cape Town, now fused with the New, was the purest urban pleasure we had ever known in South Africa.

On the left we passed the flower-sellers, just off Adderley Street in Trafalgar Place, and the Standard Bank building topped by its statue of Britannia, and a little farther on a big church, the **Groote Kerk,** a building that architects describe as 'half Greek, half Gothic', and which was the first Protestant church in Africa of which a part remains. It is the Afrikaner mother church and much loved.

It took us back a long time to Willem Adriaan, the son of Simon van der Stel, who succeeded his father as governor and who laid the foundation of 'the old Cape church' in 1700. There was space for vaults and graves; and here his father was laid 12 years later.

The building went apace and was finished in 1704. One of the first people to be married here was a Coetzee—what could have been more indigenous.

In its early life, the church had a wide generosity: not only the British worshipped here but Coloureds, and here French and English as well as Dutch governors and other notables were buried with honour. In the time of the Governor Ryk Tulbagh, a large lady, stirring in her pew, disturbed the flooring-boards and sank below: she was found 'sitting on the tomb of an early governor'.

Obviously the church needed attention and was repaired from time to time. It finally became so unsafe that it was demolished and a new church built on the site by Hendrik Schutte, the Dutch-trained builder-architect, who with Thibault and Anreith made the famous building trio. In this, the old steeple and some walls were incorporated. The beautiful pulpit carved by Anreith and Jacob Jan Graaf in 1789 was carefully preserved throughout the building operations, but the vaults, tombs, monuments and memorials were destroyed or lost, even the tomb of the great Simon van der Stel, so that part of the story of Cape Town vanished forever.

This has, incidentally, the only church floor in the country which acts as a barometer. We had heard this and hoped the story was true, and it was. There were stones of Batavian saltstone let into the floor that changed colour with the humidity, darkening in stormy weather, lightening with the fair.

The Groote Kerk stood on ground that once had been part of the Gardens, and so did the building next door, once the Old Supreme Court and now the **Cultural History Museum.** In the book by Hans Fransen and Dr Mary Cook, *The Old Houses of the Cape*, in which the old buildings of importance are listed and described, the maximum number of stars—four—are given to this, so that it is important on two counts, not only for what it holds, but for itself as well.

Originally this was built as the Company's Slave Lodge, and it is possibly the second oldest building in the country. Thibault and Schutte rebuilt it in 1814 as government offices and Supreme Court—the first—and Anreith did the plaster pediment over the Parliament Street doorway. The British lion sculpted here is a drooping sad old specimen which we viewed with amusement—it was intended as a good enduring crack at the British victors!

What we enjoyed most was the charming cobbled courtyard with its oak trees and well, and with the tombstones of Jan van Riebeeck and Maria, his wife. There are many mellow old courtyards in the Cape, none better than this, and none more full of atmosphere.

We fell into conversation here with a woman. 'What!' she exclaimed tartly. '*Transvaalers* admiring a Cape cultural museum!' We replied mildly that we were Cape-born, which made everything all right at once. It was the only time we met the Cape snobbery that is supposed by lesser breeds to rule the city.

There were wonderful things to see in the museum, Cape silver—the famous David Heller collection—coins, stamps, a famous collection of weapons, ceramics, costumes, and much besides. We spent most time on the section on the Malay people, their history and customs, learning here something of this most colourful of the city's folk before we walked into the streets to see them, their homes and mosques.

The Malays—a Muslim people—have been in the Cape almost as long as have been the Whites, much longer than the Blacks. They came humbly, of a Javanese group, as slaves and exiles. They have remained—with a good deal of pride—for 300 years, and if in three centuries their blood has become mixed, their religion, their great uniting bond, remains pure and strong. The founder of this Muslim faith here in the Cape was the holy man, Sheik Yusuf—Sjech Yussuf or Sheik Joseph—whose tomb is still a place of pilgrimage. There are other tombs also venerated, those of early Muslim saints and wise men, and a rough circle of these stretches round the Peninsula—the tomb of Sheik Yusuf at Faure, the others on Robben Island, on Signal Hill, Oude Kraal and Constantia. This is the Circle of Islam which protects the Faithful from 'fire, famine, plague, earthquake and tidal wave', as was prophesied over 200 years ago: some say that disasters have indeed stopped short of this holy ring.

In the Cultural Museum there was a model of a mosque and worshippers within, and a description of the ritual, all of which we studied.

There are over 30 mosques in the Cape Peninsula, which we had already seen from a distance, buildings of pink and silver, blue, green, pale apricot, green and white, built almost on the streets, glimpsed up an alley or over a roof, the crescent and star of Islam silhouetted against sky and mountain slopes. They were mostly beautiful with their domes, and minarets from which the muezzin calls the Faithful to prayer, with their exotic Eastern air and touch of mystery. Later, we were to enter one and see the interior first-hand for ourselves.

As we stood again at the museum entrance on Adderley Street we looked to our left to the **Houses of Parliament.** Once upon a time we had attended debates here, but now we remembered only General Smuts's neat little beard and Malmesbury burr from the debating-chamber. What was of present interest was the Parliamentary Library, which includes now the **Mendelssohn Library.** Sidney Mendelssohn was the Englishman who became a South African diamond magnate, one of the greatest of all collectors of Africana, and compiler of one of the earliest and finest bibliographies, *Mendelssohn's South African Bibliography*, which is still the basis of most of the work and research on Africana today. He willed his Africana collection to Parliament, and now across the road it was—in terms of his will—being expanded. One of its acquisitions, acclaimed as a particularly rare and precious bit of Africana, had just become news. It was the collection of 165 watercolours of Francois le Vaillant, the traveller and ornithologist, whom we had thought of last in the southern forests.

Straight ahead of us was **St George's Cathedral,** an imposing building, begun in 1901 and designed by Sir Herbert Baker. The old one on the same site had been modelled on St Pancras in London, the design being adapted by the Colonial Secretary, Colonel Bell. He did very well too: and when it was demolished Cape Town mourned it.

This was originally St George's Church for Cape Town had no Anglican bishop until Bishop Gray, who arrived in 1848. One of the stained glass windows in the Cathedral is in memory of his wife, Sophie, a pious woman who rode horses and designed churches. In 1827, when the land for the first St George's was granted, the Bishop of Calcutta visited Cape Town. He was the first Anglican bishop to set foot on Cape soil.

This top end of Adderley Street had known considerable gaiety of late. In April 1977 when Cape Town held its second Festival—which is likely to become a regular feature of the city—it was briefly closed to traffic, and here instead of motor-cars was the Tavern of the Seas, the restaurant under the umbrellas, where everyone—White, Black and Brown—ate their food together (R1,20 a meal, well done) with much laughter and good humour, while acrobats performing high overhead added to the fun.

We left all this behind us and turned into **Government Avenue,** South Africa's most famous street. This was once the main walk of the Company's Garden, starting below the Groote Kerk we had left at our backs. The straight, tree-lined path of today is the Dutchman's road of 300 years ago, although the oaks on either side which give the street their character are mostly younger.

We had always loved it for its link with the past, its cosmopolitan colour, and for the fat squirrels and doves of the present. That morning it was a dappled tunnel alive with moving things. Nothing on wheels rode here, but a throng of people passed up and down on foot, men, women and children of all ages and colour, the old rested their bones on the benches, and a young couple made love, oblivious of the world: there were peanut-sellers, housewives, businessmen, tourists with their cameras, and Capetonians amusing themselves by looking. There was Miss Farieda Ebrahim, her Malay beauty stunning under her headdress of white and gold, laughing with her family as they viewed the passing world. There were squirrels eating peanuts and rushing up and down the trees, and we noted that particular peanut vendors had their special squirrel friends.

Cecil Rhodes introduced the first of these grey squirrels from America after 1900, and they are generally regarded as a pest—but not in the Avenue, where they are part of its charm.

Going upwards, we turned to our right. The big pillared building was the **South African Library,** with a vast collection of books on Africa and today one of South Africa's great libraries. The building was completed in 1860 in the time when Sir George Grey was Governor, and it was he who had boosted the young library by giving it his own personal collection of books, which included priceless items like ancient manuscripts and a Shakespeare First Folio of 1623. It was his marble statue outside the building, the first statue to be erected in the country.

Up the broad walk from the statue—one of the old paths from the Company's days running parallel to Government Avenue—we passed the sundial and turned right to see the old pear tree in the lawn that Van Riebeeck had planted—how strange that his fort should have gone and his green tree remained. Then we turned back to the walk and passed Rhodes's statue on our way to the tea garden.

Tea here is always fun, watching the pigeons and other birds strutting between the tables and accepting offerings. Skead once said that the white-eyes here were bold enough to steal the sugar and jam on the tables, but this we missed. We waited to hear the Noon Gun fired at 12 o'clock from Signal Hill, and to see all the birds take off in a cloud together. Then we walked back, admiring the magificent old trees, to Government Avenue, and passed southward up the walk.

On our left, standing well away in formal gardens, was a long low building different in character from other Cape Dutch buildings we had seen, so solid and simple, for this was a light gay rococo creation topped with a plump infant Neptune and an equally fat, arch little Mercury, holding a drape between them with the initials V.O.C., the monogram of the Dutch East India Company. It was **Tuynhuis,** the House in the Garden, which through its almost 300 years of life had been a guest house for important visitors (Holland wanted no prying eyes in the Castle), Government House after the time of the British Occupation, the home of the Governor-Generals after Union, and now the winter home of the State President during the parliamentary session.

Thibault in his day remodelled it, and it was fully restored as a presidential home only in the 1970s, work—assisted by the 'restoration architect', Mr Gabriel Fagan—which has earned much praise. The figures of Neptune and Mercury that we had so much admired might have been Anreith's but were not, for his models had long since gone, so that these were done in his style by the Cape sculptor, Sydney Hunter.

It was not a big or grand building but had an engaging air as if it had known a lot of people and enjoyed much gaiety—which it had. Harry Smith used to hold his Waterloo balls here—the Duke of Wellington had been his hero as well as mentor and later he was standard-bearer at his funeral. There were many that followed, including one of the greatest balls in South African history, held over 100 years later, the coming-of-age ball of Elizabeth II of England. She had danced in the ballroom in the left wing on that night of 1947 when—as a young solemn princess in her glittering gown—she had made her dedication speech. Looking through the barred gate now, we were touched as we had been 30 years before.

At the top of the walk, we found the **South African National Gallery** on our left which, besides containing a good deal of work of artists from abroad, has the most comprehensive collection of local art in South Africa, including, among other things, the carved doors of the Atrium, and other panels, done by the master carver, Herbert Meyerowitz.

In front of the gallery was the controversial **Smuts Statue** done by Sydney Harpley that had caused an uproar in Cape Town when it was finished in 1964. Beyond was the **Great Synagogue,** with the Old Synagogue, now a museum, close to it. To the right along the walk, at right angles to Government Avenue, was the **South African Museum.** This is the country's oldest museum, established—by Lord Charles Somerset—in 1825.

It is famous for many things, from its first superintendent, the great Dr Andrew Smith, to its fine collections and research and educational work of today.

We went in pondering South Africa's debt to Scotland—Smith was a Scottish army doctor, the son of a Border shepherd, whose passion while stationed in South Africa was zoology and who—at Lord Charles' invitation—established this museum in Cape Town. The father of South African zoology, he is sometimes called.

In the 12 years which followed his founding of the museum, he remained an army officer, launching and maintaining the scientific work 'for love'. Wherever he went on military duties he collected—in Namaqualand, Zululand and in the Transvaal. This latter expedition was led by him through the Orange Free State and North-West Cape to the Transvaal in 1834, complete with artist Charles Davidson Bell, astronomer and taxidermist. It was by far the most important scientific expedition up to that date. Kuruman was his base for many months, and Moffat his host.

It was S. Meiring Naudé and A. C. Brown who reminded us all that the museum tradition in South Africa went back to Jan van Riebeeck's day when skins and stuffed specimens were displayed in the Fort—we thought of the stuffed zebra and the church services— and that there had been a small museum in the Gardens.

What a sequel to those infants this museum was. We thought of all the associated names that had since been part both of South African science and ordinary lives since, the names of noteworthy pioneers. There was Layard who published the first bird book in 1867; Ronald Trimen and his butterflies; W. L. Sclater, another bird man; and the brilliant, formidable Louis Péringuey with his vast enthusiasms and his beetles and prehistory. There were the modern scientists as well, like Dr Leonard Gill—what bird lover does not know his *First Guide to South African Birds*—Keppel Barnard and his sea creatures; A. W. Crompton; and now Dr Tom Barry, today's director.

Bushman research has always been a notable part of the museum: the Rock Art Recording Centre is here, while the most popular exhibit in the whole place is the Bushman, with paintings, implements and ornaments, and its famous group of casts done by the Scot, James Drury, who was museum taxidermist for 40 years. Drury began taking casts from living Bushmen in 1907 when there were still some of these vanishing people in the Prieska and Carnarvon districts, and over the years assembled a unique collection. His process—coveted at the time by other museums of the world—was a secret one, evolved by himself, and it resulted in figures that were completely natural and realistic. He had never had a lesson in the art when he began, but Péringuey wanted life casts and so he started. At first he used Old Tom, an odd-job man about the museum, as a model, going on to practise with many others until gradually he perfected his unique technique. 'You won't find my secrets in any text-book,' he told Lawrence Green once.

Today the figures have been recast in fibre-glass, and go on exhibition to Britain and Europe.

We emerged from the museum and went on up Government Avenue to admire the fine gateways, the work of the famous trio, Thibault, Anreith and Schutte, leading to the Little Theatre.

We could not resist walking on into Orange Street to look at the **Mount Nelson Hotel** near the top of the Avenue, that stately old Victorian pile that serves the best breakfast in Cape Town.

We made our way down Orange Street, through Greys Pass, to Queen Victoria Street—home of the Government Archives—on the far side of the Public Gardens, and down Wale Street that ran across it. We wanted to see the old **Reserve Bank building,** now owned by the Board of Executors, between Adderley and St George's Streets, not old at all but a 1928 version of Florence's Pitti Palace. Italy has often transplanted well into the Cape, and so it was here. The Scots architect, James Morris, had designed it, and South African Ivan Mitford-Barberton had done the sculpturing. Mitford-Barberton was the sculptor whose fine craftsmanship had embellished South Africa from the Transvaal to the Cape. He died only recently and Cape Town, in particular, has many of his works. In Wale Street he had done, as well, the decorations outside the African Homes Trust and that of the Provincial Administration Building.

We had one more sight to see before our day was done. We walked two blocks down Adderley Street and two blocks to our left along Longmarket Street to Greenmarket Square, the big open space that once had been a vegetable market. Dominating it was the **Old Town House,** which was formerly the Burgher Watch, headquarters of Burgher Guard, a building to which Fransen and Cook give four stars. This fine old building, with its carved fanlights and mouldings—probably Malay-crafted—above the windows, which give it much of its distinction, dates from 1755. In its history it has been the seat of the Burgher Senate, police station, and town hall. Now it houses the Michaelis Collection of art.

It was the end of the day, and we knew where we were going to dine—at one of those little restaurants with no liquor licence that have become a feature of South African night life. They can be exceedingly good and are frequently inexpensive, and one takes one's own bottle for good cheer.

Cape Town meets this local wine need well: bottle-stores (open until 6 p.m.) keep wines that are specially chilled for diner-customers. We went into the nearest, and out of the refrigerator picked a Nederburg Johann Graue Special Bin (which was well packed for us in insulating layers of paper) and a little later drank it, still chilled, at the restaurant of our choice. It was the **Kaapse Tafel** in Queen Victoria Street, and we drank it with a Malay chicken pie—it was one of the best simple meals we ever had in Cape Town and the restaurant the best value for money. It specialized in some of the Cape's traditional old dishes, and what better could one do in Cape Town than sample them.

At three o'clock on a Saturday afternoon we arrived at the entrance to Government Avenue to find Mrs Betty Hughes under the first oak tree in the avenue, and around her a small crowd of people, hatted and low-heeled. They were going on her Malay Quarter and 18th Century Cape Town tour of two hours, and we joined them.

Mrs Hughes, inspired by a walking tour she had made in London years before, had undertaken a similar one in Cape Town, making use of her knowledge of the city, not only of its 'sights' but of its oddments and charm. She took us first through the Avenue and Botanic Gardens which we already knew, out through Queen Victoria Street and along Keerom into fascinating Long Street, still with its old houses and shops, and so into Leeuwen Street. This, the approach to the **Malay Quarter** stretching towards Signal Hill, was new ground to

337

us. On our right at the corner of Dorp and Long Streets was our first
mosque. Across Long Street, we all looked backwards as Mrs Hughes
directed, to a flat-roofed building with two palms in front, the Palm
Tree Mosque. Across Loop Street to our left was the Loop Street
Mosque, pink with a pink-and-silver minaret, an artist's dream, and
still ahead were Buitengracht Street and the Malay Quarter proper.

At the **Dorp Street Mosque** almost on the Dorp Street corner we
halted, and then went in. Bare-footed—the shedding of our shoes was
the only observance asked of us—we looked into the interior, the tapes
stretching across the carpet, the prayer mats side by side between them
pointing towards Mecca, the niche facing in the same direction, the
pulpit, the big simple unadorned room, its entrance guarded by a palm
grown from a date stone brought from the Prophet's birthplace at
Medina, and the line with the day's washing hung beside it: we had
never seen prayer and living more inextricably mixed.

This was Cape Town's first mosque, built 250 years before, and the
story goes that the Malay saint who founded it, Tuan Guru, provided
Cape Town's first 'copy' of the Koran—because there was no Koran
in the town, he wrote down every word of the blessed book *from
memory*. Miraculous his powers were: he once punished a churlish
farmer by turning his potatoes into stones.

Now we were outside among the Malay homes, looking at the flat
roofs with their little cornices or parapets, high stoeps, old fanlights
above the doors, the suggestion of a courtyard behind. It was, we
knew, a part of the city that had been Malay for a long time: the
Malays had begun to take over the quarter in the 1830s when they
became freemen, and had remained a community ever since, close
knit by custom and religion.

Mrs Hughes led us along Chiappini Street into an area between this
and Rose Street where all the houses on the steep cobbled hill streets
had been declared national monuments, and on to Rose Street itself.
In a builder's storehouse filled with oddments we found the most
fascinating thing in all that fascinating quarter. It was an old stable in
which stood two landaus and three milk-white horses. They were the
city's last remaining landaus—used for ceremonial occasions—and the
horses that pulled them: and the Malay men who were grooming them
were the last Malay coachmen. Cape Town knew them well, driving
through the streets in their *toerings*—traditional conical straw hats—
and many people remembered how such a coachman drove General
Smuts through Cape Town in triumph after the end of World War II.

The horses were Anna, Ivan and Big Boy. Anna, in the yard
drinking out of a bathtub, was scintillating, her coat gleaming, her

hooves jet black and glittering. 'Polish?' we asked Mr Samuels, the senior coachman, but he answered hotly that her hooves were *natural* —too late he saw the shoe polish tin and brush in view.

A few months later, landaus and horses disappeared from Cape Town's streets; the upkeep had been too much, we heard. Cape Town, however, is not letting the matter rest: and 'tomorrow', we were assured, all of them—horses, men and landaus—would be back again.

We missed one thing in the Malay Quarter, the restaurant specializing in Malay foods that is promised for the future. All those who value good eating in South Africa will welcome it, and the fragrant spicy food the Malays introduced into Dutch kitchens 250 years ago, and which has now become a Cape tradition. Few restaurants present it today, and it took Hilda Gerber, a modern cook and South African writer on food, to re-introduce many South Africans to that inner world of the Malays, that discreet, courteous world of religious and family festivals, of black hair and dark skins glowing with jewels, of fragrant smells of spices and of Eastern foods that go with it. We hoped the new restaurant would be as delectable as her book.

Crossing Buitengracht Street again, we came to **Riebeeck Square** where farmers once outspanned with their ox-wagons, and paused to look at a grey rectangular building with a fine high flight of steps on to the square. This was South Africa's first theatre, built in 1801 when the unpopular Sir George Yonge was Governor, to entertain the British troops: 38 years later it became a church for freed slaves, and still later was taken over by the Dutch Reformed Church. It has a most surprising name, **St Stephen's:** it is the only Dutch Reformed Church in the country with an English name and is the only one called after a saint, while the Coloured people give it a more unorthodox title still—they call it *Die Ou Komediehuis*—the Old Theatre.

As we admired it, a Coloured wedding party emerged, and for a moment the bride, cream skin glowing under her veil, and her groom stood at the head of the steps, bringing the simple, elegant old building to brilliant life.

We said goodbye to Mrs Hughes. It had been a good afternoon packed with interest and entertainment, and not arduous. Her tour had ended our two days on foot in the city, when we had glimpsed most of the town's sights, all within a fairly small radius. She also does a harbour tour and sometimes impromptu little trips as well.

As for John Muir's *Guide to Cape Town and the Western Cape*, no visitor should ever be without it: it fits into pocket or bag and tells one everything from sights to parking garages, and where to eat and shop. It is not merely factual—a good deal of the Cape Town atmosphere creeps in as well. There is, of course, the Visitor's Information Bureau of the Publicity Association on the first floor of the Cape Town Centre in the Heerengracht, which we found very helpful.

Before we left central Cape Town between Table Bay and Table Mountain, we climbed **Table Mountain**—once on foot, once by cable car. We had looked up at it from below countless times, this famous beautiful mountain rising up sheer from the lowest gentle slopes, that had been a landmark and welcome throughout the centuries. There was Devil's Peak to the left as we gazed up, the flat-topped Table Mountain the centre, and on the right the parts of the mountain known as Signal Hill and Lion's Head.

Cape geography is often confusing to visitors, but the layout can be easily understood when it is seen from the mountain-top, with the help of telescopes and maps supplied. We looked at the great panorama of sea, mountains and suburbs round us, and everything fell into place. There was central Cape Town, the harbour and the sea below and immediately before us. From the western edge of the table top we could see the Atlantic coast and the splendid buttress known as the Twelve Apostles; and from the eastern, the Cape Flats, the low-lying sea of sand that once was an ocean, and that today connects the Peninsula with the mainland. South of it was False Bay, with the warm water that brings swimmers by the thousand to Muizenberg and Fish Hoek and other resorts along the coast; and far beyond was Cape Point with its lighthouse and rocks.

Apart from its beauty, the mountain was a great, famous hunting-ground. Countless visitors had climbed there since Antonio da Saldanha in 1503, first a trickle of them, then a stream, young and old, men and women, out of curiosity, wonder, and for the pure adventure: of these, a great many had been the early scientists and collectors of various kinds. Some had been botanists like Thunberg, or later Marloth, or Smuts, the great amateur, for the plants on the mountain had had that immediate, passionate appeal. But here, too, the study of animal life in South Africa had begun. Mammalogists came, and ornithologists admiring the Cape sugar bird with its long tail streaming in the wind, the orange-breasted sunbirds, the red-winged starlings of high places, the rock pigeons and thrushes, the eagles and hawks, the vultures that Le Vaillant declared were thrown down in Cape Town's streets by the south-easter.

Others came to find snakes and lizards—for the Peninsula is rich in both—and frogs like the rare ghost frog which lives in streams in Table Mountain kloofs. The first insect collectors had had field days on the slopes, and here, well over a century ago, had come the Frenchman,

340

Goudat, to find for the first time one of the world's strange creatures, the little Peripatus, that had brought other scientists, too, turning over logs, hunting in caves, to find more of these little curiosities. It had all been a great Peninsula—a great Table Mountain—adventure, for Peripatus, the wanderer, was a zoological curiosity of southern lands, part worm, part of the group to which insects and spiders belong, a strange ancient velvety harmless little worm-like wonder, whose place among living things was established here by a zoologist from the *Challenger*, which had put into Table Bay in 1873.

Not far from us as we stood at the top of the mountain was a big sandstone cave where Dr Keppel Barnard had once found a Peripatus which Dr R. F. Lawrence named *Peripatopsis alba*—it was completely white and eyeless. Dr Lawrence himself had spent a lot of time 'messing about' in this enormous, damp, slimy dark place, guiding overseas entomologists down it. Now for us it was a marvellous association—our old friend Lawrie, who is a Peripatus expert and can bring wonder to everything he deals in, and this rarest creature in the world. We did not ask him, but surely it is the rarest, for nowhere else in the world but in this cave on the top of Table Mountain has it been found.

It was a beautiful clear day with no south-easter blowing, that wind Capetonians take for granted and that to all visitors is a frantic gale. It brings moisture that condenses to make the famous Table Cloth, so that day there was no cloth either. We walked about the flat top near the cable station for a long time, enjoying the spectacular scenes and their associations.

John Muir says that there are 450 different routes on the mountain. It had once taken us three-and-a-half hours to dawdle up the mountain by the Platteklip Gorge route, an easy path without the mountaineering drama of many of the others; by cable car it had taken seven minutes. They were both fine ways. Whatever way one takes, it is a good thing to remember that the mountain is a national monument; that it is dear to Capetonians (many of whom are ardent conservationists), and that the plucking of a flower or tossing away of a lighted match can earn quick retribution.

CHAPTER TWENTY-THREE

The Peninsula

✦

Cape Town's suburbs lie mostly beyond Table Mountain to the east and south; and south, too, is the Constantia Valley with its vineyards and old homesteads, most important among them Groot Constantia.

This was South Africa's first great home and still remains the most important historic house in the country, a large solid building of beauty in its vineyard setting.

People go to see it for various reasons: for its history, for its wine, or for the house itself, as a particularly fine example of the style of Cape Dutch architecture, which in the last 30 years has become the thing to see and know about. Like red wine, it is a fashion revived, and like it, too, the background has become increasingly important to people—a whole modern literature has grown up around it.

This is easy to understand for the homesteads—with their background of mountains and their setting of vineyards and orchards—have come to epitomize the Cape for people throughout the world.

This is because they are not ordinary houses at all, but something indigenous, homesteads with hints of Europe but shaped by local needs into a unique form, the single-storeyed long low houses, often of farm and country, with white-washed walls and high-pitched thatched roofs and gables: houses with handsome entrance doors, often half- or stable doors, with the fanlights above that are so lovely and distinctive a part; and on either side, symmetrically arranged, the small-paned sash windows with shutters on their lower halves alone.

The shutters (to protect the interiors from the bright Cape sun) and the trellis-covered stoep, were Cape adaptations as well. Even the main gable, which most people think of as the essence of the style, brought originally from northern Europe, was altered to suit Cape taste, while its plaster mouldings, frequently so gay and free-flowing, had a grace and lightness that northern Europe lacked. Malay workmen brought their own imaginative touch, so that this as well was peculiar to the Cape.

Cape building materials gave the homes their own individuality too. The lime-wash was made from shells collected on the beaches. The floors were of dung, often polished with blood, and the ceilings of reeds. The old floors and ceilings have disappeared in the great houses—although they sometimes linger in the humble—but the flooring boards and the beams that took their place were as indigenous: they are most often of yellow-wood from the Cape forests, giving their own light bright sheen to the high interiors. The *brandsolder* is sometimes still there, the fireproof layer of clay or bricks laid over the ceiling to catch burning thatch and so save a home from destruction: sometimes it worked and sometimes it did not, as the stories of the houses tell.

Today people avidly study every detail of the old Cape houses, and take great pleasure in their beauty and simplicity, the oak trees so intimately associated with them—if not the ones the Van der Stels introduced and made popular, then their descendants—their shadows dappling white walls, the oak avenues, the old gardens, fountains, pigeon house and slave bell, and the old wine cellars, sometimes still in use.

It was not always so. Incredible as it may seem today, the Cape Dutch houses fell as far out of fashion as they are 'in' today, and by the end of the 19th century, theirs was a style largely forgotten or despised.

It was left to four English-speaking people, four 'foreigners', to restore their popularity—Cecil Rhodes, who did it with vision, money, and his architect, then plain Mr Baker; a woman, Alys Fane Trotter and her pen and sketchbook, and an American, Arthur Elliott, and his cumbrous old-fashioned camera. Edmund Garrett, famous editor of the *Cape Times*, helped; and between them they launched the old houses on a new wave of prosperity and respect.

We often today forget Rhodes, the lover of old Cape things, in Rhodes, the politician: yet his passion for Africa, the old and beautiful, is more in evidence in the south-west Cape today than any empire-building. He built Cape Dutch houses and bought others which Baker restored in authentic detail, in the face of criticism and ridicule, and by doing so he made people consider and appreciate them all over again.

While he was operating in the 1890s, Alys Trotter was also at work. She was an artist and wife of the electrical engineer invited to the Cape in the 1890s to advise on the use of electricity, and although she only spent two years here, she spent them well. Enchanted with the beauty, the history, and the old homes, she rode about the south-western districts from farm to farm on a bicycle describing and sketching the houses she saw. Her books, *Old Cape Colony* and *Old Colonial Houses of the Cape of Good Hope*, and her sketches are charming (and priceless).

Soon she was collaborating with Edmund Garrett. Anyone who cares to go to archives or library may see the Christmas number of the *Cape Times* of 1898, a rare bit of Africana, the whole issue on old houses written by Alys Trotter and illustrated with her drawings and *Cape Times* photographs: it was, said Garrett in the foreword, fulfilling an ambition of his. Many Cape Town people, who had never given a thought to the old houses about them, must have looked at them with new eyes in 1899.

After Mrs Trotter, from the time of the Anglo-Boer war onwards, came the American photographer, Arthur Elliott, who also had an eye for the beauties of the Cape. His photographs include hundreds of the Cape countryside, its houses, gables, bells and walls. His camera may have been antiquated but the results were first-class and their detail has been valued in modern times when old homes have been restored.

Alys Trotter was followed by other authors, notably Dorothea Fairbridge, and after World War II, which was followed by yet another explosion of interest of fine old things, a number of modern more technical writers, producing books of authority and sometimes of charm, all gobbled up by an eager public.

It was Alys Trotter we were concerned with, the day before we drove round the mountain to visit Groot Constantia. We walked up Buitenkant Street, the thoroughfare to the far left of Government Avenue, to number **78, Rust-en-Vreugd**—Rest and Gladness—and passed through the splendid carved door ('the finest door in the Cape'), into what, between ourselves, we called 'Alys Trotter's Place'. It might have been irreverent, for this was once Lord Charles Somerset's home, and now—in its magnificent interior—houses a William Fehr art collection, but it is also the home of Mrs Trotter's sketches, and—we were delighted to find—her photograph as well. There she was, in 1961 aged 99, at her home near Salisbury, England, still as upright as when she had ridden her bicycle sketching through the Western Cape.

The sketches were very up-to-date, very close to us, that day. She had had a companion on occasions, a Miss Muir, and we had at last tracked her down. She was Sir Thomas Muir's daughter, now Mrs Lillie Cameron Cornish-Bowden, and was still living in Somerset West. She and Alys Trotter had ridden some of the first safety bicycles in South Africa, over hard and lonely plains and passes where later motor-cars had laboured, as well as the more hospitable valleys, so that Alys could write and sketch—in the 1890s they had both been adventurers in the old heroic meaning of the word, riding as no other women and few men had ever done before them.

'What do you remember of it all?' we had asked Mrs Cornish-Bowden, and she had replied, 'Dust, heat, dirty faces and perspiration.' She did not say glory, but—they were undoubtedly a dashing pair—they must have tasted this too.

'I am now in my ninety-third year,' Mrs Cornish-Bowden told us in 1975. So that Rust-en-Vreugd was not only Alys Trotter's place but a little bit of Lillie Muir's too, and between them, they launched us on our expedition to see the old things beyond the mountain with a tremendous sense, not only of the past, but of the lively present.

From Buitenkant Street we drove to Roeland Street and over the De Waal Drive, passing **Groote Schuur Hospital** on our left: always well known, it has become world famous because of the heart transplant operations done here by Professor Chris Barnard and his team.

Then we were in Rhodes Drive with **Mostert's Mill** on our left, the Dutch windmill, built in 1796 and beautifully restored—together with the original threshing floor—that is now a national monument and open to the public. This was the suburb of Mowbray, and we were in the heart of an historic area. When Van Riebeeck, more than 300 years before, found that the wind blew the grain out of the heads of the wheat he had planted, he, too, had come round the mountain to plant his wheat lands here in a more sheltered spot near the little Liesbeeck River—the Stream of Reeds—which rises on the southern slopes of Table Mountain and flows northwards into Table Bay.

He called the place Koornhoop, Hope of Corn. The land nearby, where grew a round clump of trees, was used for another garden, and close by he built a great barn, Groote Schuur, in which grain was stored, and a Company House at Rustenberg where later governors lived. For himself he made a farm at Bosheuvel in an especially lovely spot a little further south. There were three little forts on the Liesbeeck to protect settlers from the Hottentots—they were called Turn the Cow, Hold the Bull, and Look Out—a few farms and gardens, and further in Van Riebeeck's day there was little.

Today Koornhoop can still be spotted near the Settlers Way bridge over the Liesbeeck, with the original dovecote surviving. The clump of trees is Rondebosch, a well-known suburb, and Groote Schuur the Prime Minister's home. Of Rustenberg only the summerhouse, restored by Sir Herbert Baker, remains in the grounds of Groote Schuur, while Bosheuvel is Bishopscourt, the seat of the Archbishop of Cape Town.

We were in Rhodes Drive now. Across the road from Mostert's Mill on the slopes of Table Mountain was the vast area of land that Rhodes had bought to preserve for all time, his Groote Schuur Estates, and further along it, still on the Estates, stood the University of Cape

345

Town, with its backing of mountain, one of the most beautifully sited universities in the world.

Rhodes was much in evidence. There was not only Rhodes Drive but Rhodes Avenue, and the **Rhodes Memorial** above the road on the slopes of Devil's Peak, with a far view over the Flats. We turned up to it along a road that passed buck grazing and drove up the slopes through the stone pines, to the spot where Rhodes used to sit and brood and plan, and where the memorial to him was later built. Sir Herbert Baker designed the Doric Temple—Rhodes had sent him abroad to study the buildings of Greece, Italy and Egypt—and this was one of the fruits his travel bore. The bronze head of Rhodes in a niche in the temple was the work of J. M. Swan, and the inscription above was Rudyard Kipling's: 'The immense and brooding spirit still shall quicken and control: living he was the land and dead his soul shall be her soul.'

Swan did, as well, the bronze lions—clearly Sphinx-inspired—guarding the granite steps: below stands the bronze statue of a man mounted on a splendid horse, which is the original 'Physical Energy' sculpted by G. R. Watts in England and given by him to South Africa—the London statue of today is but a replica. It is a fine monument, and on a clear day when colours sparkle and one can see across the world, magnificent.

We stood on the mountain side below it looking down and across Rhodes Drive to **Groote Schuur,** the Great Barn. This was the very site where Van Riebeeck built his barn to store the grain, and although the house below us was comparatively modern, below it were still Van Riebeeck's foundations—the earliest in existence in South Africa—and the arches: they were traced when the later house was built.

Today it is the official Cape Town home of the Prime Minister, Rhodes's gift to all the Prime Ministers of South Africa, unfortunately not open to the public. When he bought it in 1893 as part of his scheme for preserving a piece of the Cape, it had been a private house for a long time, and was owned by the De Smidt family. Restored by Sir Herbert Baker, it was burnt down three years later, and the present house was the second one built by him on the site—as like the previous building as possible.

This is not, therefore, an 'old' Cape Dutch house, for Britishers built it within memory: yet a Cape Dutch house it is, in the grand manner. By building it, Rhodes gave value again to the old style, and so it has a special significance in the story of Cape houses.

It is also the only Van Riebeeck-Rhodes project in our history!

Rhodes had another house close by built by Herbert Baker in the

Cape Dutch style, known as Woolsack. It was here that his friend Rudyard Kipling lived as his guest for some time, and wrote the poem 'If'.

Across the drive from Groote Schuur was another home, once known as **Onder Schuur,** and later as Westbrooke after one of the owners, Judge William Westbrooke Burton. In the days when it had been owned by the De Smidt family it had been leased by the British Government as a country home for the governors, and now it has become the official Cape country home of the State President.

It has almost as famous a history as Groote Schuur, and knew distinguished visitors, none more captivating than Aliwal, the Arab horse that belonged to Sir Harry Smith. Harry had ridden him in India through all his battles, and had named him after his victory, and—during his term of governorship at the Cape—had stabled him here. The Peninsula knew them both, man and horse, dashing along the roads and over the hills, Sir Harry shouting to the children.

We remembered another thing about the house. Such were South Africa's interwoven family relationships and society, that a girl who was a road-builder's daughter could live here as her right. She was Georgina Bain, and her grandparents were the De Smidts who owned the house, so that her early memories were not only of ox-wagons but of wonderful days and nights here and at Groote Schuur, of governors and good company, chandeliers and silver.

Back on the high road we drove through Claremont, further on passing the road to Kirstenbosch and Constantia Nek upon our right. We turned south through Bishop's Court to **Wynberg**—Wine Mountain—close by, where vines had been planted centuries before, and where a military base later grew up. Now there were names like Waterloo Green, Wellington Road and Wellington Avenue, and they went very well too with wine—the Duke of Wellington, then Brevet Colonel Arthur Wellesley—had had quarters at the Officers' Mess here more than 170 years ago and had much enjoyed the famous wine from Constantia, the estate which we were on our way to see.

Incidentally, the Wynberg Girls' High School in Aliwal Road (shades of Harry Smith again), had its 90th birthday a few years ago, when permission was given the school—in the duke's stronghold—by the present Duke of Wellington to use the Wellington crest. He sent the school, as well, some seeds of the cedar planted by Wellington on the grave of his famous charger, Copenhagen, which he rode through the Battle of Waterloo. Perhaps there were little Copenhagen cedar seedlings now in the grounds of the school. We knew that some time we had to find out.

Beyond Wynberg we took the Constantia Road and a little way along it branched to our left to Groot Constantia.

It was not all beauty. Modern housing estates can be ugly and supermarkets blots. At the gates of Constantia, which should have been grace and history, a supermarket was doing a busy trade where Jacob Cloete—who here in his time had made the best wine in the world—had once hung a proud notice saying he never sacrificed quality of wine for quantity.

The Constantia Valley is naturally a beautiful place (much cut up now for housing estates), and Simon van der Stel had an eye for both beauty and soil when he built his house here—as Alys Trotter described it, among the wild geraniums, the gladioli and the lilies, and planted his vineyards, his fruit trees and oaks. His house was, it is certain, handsome for the day—organized beauty started with him— but it fell on bad times after his death in 1712, and it was only after 1778—when the wine farmer, Hendrik Cloete, bought it—that it began again to shine.

The house was rebuilt, probably by Thibault, who enlarged it, and it emerged at the end as unusually wide and high with tall gables, and with a new wine cellar built in 1791: the lively, beautifully executed 'Gannymede' pediment symbolic of wine-making was sculpted by Anreith, who also did the figure of 'Plenty' in the niche on the main gable. In 1925 the Cloete house was largely destroyed by fire, although the gables and Anreith's pediment escaped, and the house was rebuilt in the same form by the architect, F. K. Kendall, who did considerable detective work in the reconstruction. This is the house of today.

After Van der Stel's death, the land was split up, the various parts being known by different names. The section on which Van der Stel's house had stood was **Groot Constantia,** and it was this—in 1778 derelict and weed-infested—that Hendrik Cloete took over. Cloete care and husbandry were to make it one of the world's great names.

Van der Stel had made a good wine, but the Cloetes did better. Here they made the sweet, aromatic, liqueur wine that was the Constantia of the late 18th and 19th centuries, the glorious topaz-coloured red and the almost-as-famous white that for a century were rated among the world's outstanding wines. The Cloete account book read like Debrett —emperors, kings, princes, lords, dukes, figured here. Napoleon during his years of exile on St Helena preferred Constantia to his own French wines (the British complained bitterly about the cost), and even when he was dying it was Constantia he demanded. Visiting poets from Europe composed verses in honour of it, and even Jane Austen, who seldom ventured beyond her green hills, knew it: it mended the broken heart of one of her heroines.

Nobody today knows how the Cloetes made the wine, although some may guess. When the last Cloete died, so did the wine and its secrets of grapes and blending. Constantia Valley still produces red wines of quality but they are not the old wine, nor does today's 'Constantia' wine bear any resemblance to it. Cloete's wine had gone for good.

Yet even as we write this, we know it is not entirely so. In September 1977 Christies of London auctioned 14 half-bottles of Groot Constantia wines—the true, legendary old wines—from the cellar of the Duke of Wellington, who had lived from 1769 to 1852.

Four bottles were flown to the Cape. In *Wynboer* of January 1978 is a photograph of those who tasted the wine one epoch-making luncheon at the Volkskombuis in Stellenbosch—it was probably the first Constantia wine-tasting this century! It was, said Billy Hofmeyr, in his *Wynboer* article, more Frontignac than Muscadel: it was in perfect condition, 'perfectly balanced, beautiful on the palate, and of course, different to anything any of us had ever tasted'.

He could not be sure, he said, that Wellington had toasted his victory at Waterloo by raising a glass of Constantia wine. By implication, he knew it well!

Today Groot Constantia is a government experimental wine farm and the house a museum of old furniture, china and pictures. Hans Fransen and Dr Cook give it four stars, and call it the most monumental of all homesteads in the Cape.

The Wine Festival was in full swing the day we saw it, and this was a sharp lesson to us in choosing our times. Unless one is out for junketing, Groot Constantia has little to offer at such a time. It was filled with brashness; the officials were tired and surly; even the usually immaculate walls needed a new coat of white. Huge marquee tents hid Anreith's gay wine-making pediment from view, and there were rows of portable loos on the back lawns. Van der Stel must have turned smartly in his unmarked grave!

In contrast, we remembered the day when we had viewed the old house at our leisure. We had dawdled past the oak trees in front, admiring the outside of the house. Many of the Cape Dutch houses of today hide in their hearts the remains of an older building still, and this was true here too.

Ready money in the early days had often been used to change a rectangular cottage into a house, a new wing pushing out, sometimes at the back, making a design like a T upside down. Another wing made the T into an H on its side, and this is the plan of some famous country houses today. Not here, however—the Cloetes had used the U design, traditional in the Peninsula, so that now we walked through the big reception rooms into the courtyard, with rooms on either side of it: in the manner of Cape Dutch homes, room led into room without any passage. In tradition, too, everything was shining with good wood and polish.

The kitchen lay at the back and to one side, and was a big shining room with a tiled floor. Against the far wall was a generous hearth and chimney, and a projecting oven, and it was filled with the 'kitchen furniture' of centuries, big kettles, pots and churns, pestle and mortar, jars and spoons, copper and brass—this was how many kitchens had looked in the Cape, and sometimes, even in the days of electricity, still manage to do.

That morning we carried with us—as bird enthusiasts do their bird books—two light volumes, a small book by C. de Bosdari, *Cape Dutch Houses and Farms*, which fitted into a generous handbag, and was filled with fact and charming oddments, and Dr Mary Cook's *The Cape Kitchen*, which proved a treasure indeed: between them they illuminated, not only Groot Constantia, but the other homesteads in their lovely settings that we later saw.

Then we had walked out into the sun and along an avenue through the vineyards to a marble pool to which water was brought through a Triton's horn. The horn is said to be a ship's figure-head, and it was part of a quiet magic day smelling of grapes and sun.

This is the only historic Cape Dutch homestead in the valley, apart from Alphen Hotel, that is open to the public. It can be visited daily, including weekends, which is an advantage to many visitors; and it is a national monument. Yet that day of the festival there was nothing to hold us, and we turned away as soon as possible, finding our way southward to the Tokai Road along which we drove until, from the distance and through a closed gate, we saw an old house that restored our good humour.

It was **Tokai,** a Cape Dutch homestead built in 1795 on land that had been part of Van der Stel's grazing grounds and is now the home of the principal of the Porter Reformatory, and a national monument as well. We never got any closer to the house, for it is private, but this was as good a way as any to see its symmetry and grace, the high stoep, columns and twin flights of curving steps, all probably Thibault's work, backed by forest and mountain. Fransen and Cook, we were happy to see, gave it four stars.

In the 1880s this was the home to which Joseph Storr Lister—later the first Chief Conservator of Forests of the Union of South Africa—brought his bride, Georgina, the Georgina whom we had met before bumping through the forest in a wagon and later at Westbrooke with her grandparents.

It was before the old Cape houses had returned to fashion, and the young couple found a dilapidated home. Even the walls of the *voorhuis* or entrance hall—the great hall Georgina called it—were covered with layers of paper which they stripped off to find below the sixth a delicious green with a frieze of proteas beautifully painted. One wonders who that far-off flower artist was. Georgina loved it all, and many years later recalled the view of oaks, mountains and sea, the white marble stoep with its trellis of Crystal grapes, the small Batavian bricks that made the curving steps, and the entrance door, half stable, half sash with small glass panes. In her day, a tame crowned crane used to sleep on top of the chimney, balancing—crane-like—on one leg, with the other stretched out behind it!

The house is said to be haunted by the ghosts of a rider and horse—of a young man who, flushed with wine, rode his horse up the steps, round the dining-room table, and down, where on the high steps the horse fell, killing himself and rider. Georgina saw the hoof mark on the floor!

Before we left the valley, we slipped into the **Alphen** grounds in Alphen Drive to see the fine old house, now a first-rate hotel, with its oak trees outside and its cellar—flood-lit at night—and above all, its famous front stoep.

This is said to have been the site of a duel between the extraordinary Dr James Barry, physician at the Cape in the time of Lord Charles Somerset, and a Cloete, over the daughter of the house.

Barry was a woman, reputed variously to be daughter of an earl or of the prince Regent, who masqueraded successfully for a lifetime as a man. History knows her as a highly efficient army doctor reaching the rank of Inspector General of Army Hospitals: she worked all over the world, as well as at the Cape, and died in London in 1865, when the secret of her sex was said to have been revealed.

Five feet high and a dandy, vain, quarrelsome, arrogant, she was also brilliant, courageous and tender—the stories about her linger at the Cape: and so, it is said, does her ghost, roaming the mountain slopes above Camps Bay over the mountain from Alphen. Today she is little remembered, but as children we knew her name well. General Hertzog was our Prime Minister and he bore her name, James *Barry* Munnik Hertzog. His godfather was James Barry Munnik, who had been delivered—it is said by Caesarean—by Dr Barry, who had saved mother and child. It was an odd link with our conservative Prime Minister, and it delighted us.

We remembered Alphen, too, for another reason. The Swedish traveller, Andrew Sparrman, stayed here in the 1770s, and on a gentle stroll met a hippopotamus.

We spent a day at **Kirstenbosch,** and it was, of course, too little.

Kirstenbosch is the National Botanical Garden in Newlands on the southern side of Table Mountain, stretching up the slopes of the mountain to Maclear's Beacon on the summit, a place world-famous both for its scientific work and for its beauty.

It is a garden of indigenous plants, concentrating on the 16 000 wild—and most often beautiful or curious—plants that stretch across South Africa, with a special emphasis on those of the South-West itself, where plant life is perhaps the richest in the world.

The Cape Floral Kingdom, the great botanist, Marloth, called it, and the name has stuck, for a kingdom it is with Cape Town a more or less central spot in this plant-and-flower-famous land that stretches up the coast towards Namaqualand, and eastwards towards Humansdorp. In the Cape Peninsula alone more than 2 600 species of wild plants are known. South Africans tend to think of Britain as a country of wild flowers, yet in this little tongue of Cape land there are more different plants than in the whole of Britain, many of them bearing flowers of outstanding beauty.

There are, first and foremost, the proteas with the famous handsome flower heads which are exported now in quantities so that the world knows them, plants that link South Africa in a strange and exciting way with other southern lands that some scientists now see, with Africa, as one vast ancient continent.

Their flower heads—with the glowing bracts that people think are petals but are not, and the little true flowers in a cushion in the heart—are what people look for first in the Cape. They always have. Three hundred and seventy years ago—well before Van Riebeeck's time—some visitor, a sailor surely, saw a protea blooming and picked it and took it back to Europe: and in 1605 Clusius published a description and drawing of it. It was probably the first drawing of any Cape flower. It was the blue sugargush, *Protea neriifolia*, which we saw this day on Table Mountain, and which Clusius had thought was a thistle!

Then there are the ericas, or heaths to many, with their tough tiny leaves and their little massed fragile flowers borne in such abundance that they can colour the land. More than 600 different species are known in South Africa, most of them in the Caledon-Paarl-Worcester-Ceres area, and they colour Table Mountain nearer at

The goal of explorers for two millenia—the Cape of Good Hope

Tokai

One of Arthur Elliott's masterpieces, a photograph of the dovecote at Meerlust

A classic Cape vineyard, Nancy, set against the mountains

hand as well. There are the plants of the lily and the iris families with dazzling flowers, daisies of scores of kinds, wild geraniums, mesembryanthemums (split up now into groups bearing other names but still 'mesems' or 'mums' to most), nemesias, orchids, and many others.

It was spring time and we walked among the 'daisies', orange, yellow, pink, blue, white, and pink watsonias and other bulbous beauties, past the new protea and erica gardens, stunned by the prodigality and colour. There were pools, as well, and running water, and all the things associated with these.

When we walked up the mountain slopes we admired in particular the silver tree. This is *the* tree of the Cape Peninsula, growing naturally here and here only—although in cultivation it has crossed the world—perhaps the most famous 'protea' tree of all with its elegance and incomparable soft silky foliage, mouse grey or silver, depending on the weather.

Then there were special things to see. It is always moving to find a living thing that has outlasted bricks and stone, and Van Riebeeck's hedge which, like his pear tree, has outlived the other things of his day, has special appeal.

He had planted it in 1661—it was then the boundary of the settlement—a line of 'wild bitter almonds', which would, he wrote, in a few years become a fine, thick and high hedge. It was planned as a barrier to prevent the Hottentots stealing cattle, and he had used the wild shrub of the South-West that still grows along streams, the sturdy, wide-spreading *Brabeium stellatifolium*, of the protea family, with the velvety-gold poisonous fruit. We found the remains of the hedge on high ground to the left of the south gate.

We went, too, to see the cycad collection, and to Lady Anne Barnard's Bath—where she almost certainly never bathed—and finally to the grave of Professor Harold Pearson, who was the first director of the garden.

Kirstenbosch is said to be named after the Kirsten who was an official of the Dutch East India Company in the early days, and who had lived near here. But although it bears his name, others made it. There was Cecil Rhodes again, who bought the land, for Kirstenbosch is part of the Groote Schuur Estate, and Pearson, who was professor of botany at the South African College, who visited the site in 1911 and dreamed what it might become. Two years later Sir Lionel Phillips persuaded Parliament to have the ground proclaimed a national botanic garden—a motion unanimously approved—and Professor Pearson was put in charge. He gave it his imagination, work, and in the end his life, and here was his grave and epitaph. That it had been taken from

353

London's St Paul's Cathedral made it none the less apposite. It reads 'All ye who seek his monument look around.'

Professor R. H. Compton was the second director—the Compton Herbarium in the grounds was named after him—and the present director is Professor H. B. Rycroft. To his drive are due the other botanic gardens scattered through the country specializing in their own local flora.

We had tea and scones on the stoep of the tea house, a favourite Cape Town amusement, and later Sunday lunch, in company, it seemed, with half the city and the city's wasps. Nothing stung us, and it remains a friendly memory.

We set aside another day to drive around the Peninsula on the famous **Marine Drive,** starting from Cape Town and running through Sea Point and Hout Bay southwards to Cape Point, then northwards again along False Bay to Muizenberg. It is a route of unparalleled beauty, sea, rocks, cliffs, inlets, white sand, little bays, mountain peaks, white-washed houses, on a fine day filled with light and brilliant colour.

For most of the way it is a sea road, with the ocean on one hand, and at the most southern points, on two. So it was that at the start, we looked—not at the city—but at Table Bay.

It would take not one but many books to write its history, of the passing mariners, those who lived and those who died here, of its ships and sea creatures, its storms and treasure. It is not only a harbour but an ocean graveyard. One hundred and nineteen wrecks are known to lie in Table Bay, while the actual total could be more than double that. Round the Peninsula, and eastwards from Table Bay to Cape Agulhas, there is scarcely a bay or inlet that has not claimed a ship or lives. Known wrecks on this strip total 60. A cairn of stones on the beach hiding skulls or bones is all that sometimes remains, and often even the bones have returned to the sea.

Wrecks mean treasure and for over a century men have treasure-hunted in the bay. It has yielded prizes as solid as cannon, as fragile as Chinese porcelain, as precious as silver and gold. A special sort of treasure was tossed up under the walls of the Castle in 1722. It was a sea-waif named Ignatius Ferreira, who was cabin boy aboard the east Indiaman *Chandos*, that was driven ashore here. Ferreira stayed ashore and 13 years later married Martha Terblanche, founding the famous Ferreira line.

Such stories run on without end, and so do those of the sea creatures. There were the whales Capetonians once saw regularly being hunted in the Bay—perhaps 50 in a year—and there was a whaling station at Robben Island, the lonely island ahead of us. That grim fortress—convict settlement, then leper settlement, now prison once again—with its snakes and winds and treacherous currents, is part of the Table Bay story too.

At **Sea Point** there were hotels, flats, homes and a promenade. We remembered it of old because of a fine old restaurant, Chez Froggi, where we had eaten fresh soles and drunk for the first time that pale dry beauty, La Residence Montpellier. Time had taken both: but there was instead the five-star President—the only hotel in which we have breakfasted with the seagulls, Al Gambero with its bouillabaisse, and further on, in the Glen above Camps Bay, the **Round House.** This was Lord Charles Somerset's shooting box, an historic building with a stupendous view across the sea, now a restaurant, 'under inspired management' according to John Muir, where Cape food can be had, and where Dr James Barry's ghost is said to linger on the mountain side near by.

We went on, with the beaches and holiday-makers to our right and the Twelve Apostles to our left, beautiful in new ways every time we saw them, past Llandudno into the **Hout Bay** valley. We stopped to look at the fishing harbour, then drove on, up the **Chapman's Peak Drive,** past the rock crowned with the bronze leopard looking out to sea that for us is the most evocative of Ivan Mitford-Barberton's works.

Pundits have always argued as to how Chapman's Peak, which appears on early maps, got its name. John Muir has no doubts. It was, he says, named after John Chapman, one of the crew of the British *Consent*, who in 1607 was sent ashore here to see if the bay was a harbour. Sir Frederick de Waal, the first Cape administrator, planned the drive around it, and this was opened in 1922. We drove along it, a narrow slice cut out of the mountain-side, with precipices one side and ocean the other, thinking of the surveyors who had been tied together as they worked.

Then we swung inland, back to the sea at Kommetjie (famous for its surfing), passed the lighthouse at Slangkop, and went on down the Peninsula into the **Cape of Good Hope Nature Reserve,** where all plants and animals are preserved.

We made for the Point itself with its two lighthouses and climbed up the steep slope (harassed by an angry, demanding baboon) towards the first, which is now disused. At the top, a view broke upon us, of not one but two points, **Cape Point** to the left and **False Bay** beyond, and Cape Maclear to the right, the whole complex loosely known as the Cape of Good Hope: a little further south than Cape Point, Cape

Maclear is the southern-most point in the Peninsula but not in Africa, for that is to the east at Cape Agulhas, which we had seen before. It was a view of cliffs and sea, wild and magnificent, the most fitting end possible to a peninsula of drama.

This was the setting for fine stories too. There was that of Bartolomeu Dias, who sailed into False Bay in 1488 calling it the Bay between the Ranges and the promontory the Cape of Good Hope—it was he, according to Axelson, who gave it this illustrious name and not (as is generally thought) his master, John II, back home in Portugal. It was somewhere here that on 6th June 1488, he erected a *padrão*, dedicated to St Philip, and it was here that 451 years later Eric Axelson came to search for it. He found nothing then, or 17 years later when, with his wife, Hilda, he returned to make a more extensive search—the name 'Cape of Good Hope', he noted, has always been applied to a considerable region around the Cape itself, so the search they made was wide. For Dias, this *padrão* must have had a special significance, marking the Cape he thought was the end of Africa, but it has apparently disappeared, the only cross that Dias set up that has vanished without trace.

Then there is the *Flying Dutchman*, one of the famous ghost ships of legend, which is traditionally seen off the Cape Peninsula. Most people today are unaware that Vanderdecken, the Dutch captain, was an historical figure whose ship put in to the Cape in 1641 when outward bound for Batavia. The story goes that it was in the teeth of one of the Cape's wild winter northwesters that Vanderdecken, on his return voyage from Batavia, swore a profane oath that he would not give up trying to weather the Cape even if he should have to wait until the Day of Judgment. So in the end he was condemned to beat eternally round the Cape of Storms.

Fact and legend merge almost inextricably: in 1889 there was still a man living whose great-grandfather had seen the real *Flying Dutchman* actually moored in Table Bay. He left a fine detailed description of her, mentioning a 'castle' aft where (according to later sightings) Vanderdecken takes up his stand with a ghostly hailing-trumpet. We even know her colour—pale yellow.

It is extraordinary how examination of sightings of the ghost ship (and there have been many, even in modern times) tally with this old-fashioned hull and rig. The most famous sighting was on a clear, calm dawn on 11th July 1881, recorded by Prince George, later King George V, in *HMS Bacchante* off the Cape. He noted in his log: 'A strange red light, as of a phantom ship all aglow, in the midst of which light the masts, spars and sails two hundred yards distant stood out in strong relief as she came up.' The phantom then vanished, but 13 men saw it plainly. The warship's consorts, *HMS Tourmaline* and *HMS Cleopatra*, both signalled to ask whether *Bacchante* had seen the red light. The inevitable tragedy following a *Flying Dutchman* sighting followed. A few hours later the lookout who had first spotted her crashed from the masthead to his death, and the admiral commanding the squadron was stricken down in the next port.

Part of the *Flying Dutchman* superstition is that Vanderdecken first hails a ship, then lowers a boat with letters for home which his men last saw three centuries ago. If a ship heaves to to receive the boat, it is doomed. A British warship, *HMS Leven*, under Captain Owen, saw this happen *twice* in April 1823, at an interval of more than a week. The first occasion was off Danger Point, and the second when he put to sea again after being in port at Simonstown. On the latter occasion Captain Owen clapped on all sail and fled.

There was nothing sinister about another famous ship and sailor, Francis Drake. When he sailed by in the *Golden Hind* the day must have been as bright as ours. This was to him 'the most stately thing and the fairest Cape we saw in the whole circumference of the earth'.

We took the road back past Miller's Point to **Simonstown.** This little sea town has a history almost as old as Cape Town's for Simon van der Stel named it after himself in 1687, and in the mid 1700s it became a winter harbourage for ships in place of Table Bay where losses were heavy at this time of the year. In 1814 it became a British naval base, and continued as this until 1957 when the South African Navy took over the dockyard. The British influence and the naval character still make its atmosphere.

We drove along the main street past the Eastern Dockyard, with the **Martello Tower**—built in 1796, it is now a splendid museum—and after that history enveloped us. There was the Naval Harbour and a mixture of historic buildings, like the Royal Navy Club; then the West Dockyard with its old wall and beyond it, the little **St George's Church** that grew out of the sea. The first Anglican church in South Africa had been a St George's, not in Cape Town but here at Simonstown, but it had dissolved in the rainy winter of 1819. The Royal Navy had then offered its Sail Loft in Simonstown for use as a church. The Loft was the top storey of the Mast House, and half of it was set apart for worship. This became in time H.M. Dockyard Church, and in 1945 was formally dedicated as St George's Church, and this was the little building in front of us. It was taken over by the South African Navy in 1957, and is still in use.

A little further on, on the right hand side of the road, was another church, important in ecclesiastical history, for this was **St Francis,** built in 1837—it is the earliest Anglican Church designed as a church that still stands. Originally known as St Frances, the spelling caused embarrassment in ecclesiastical circles for a long time, for there was no such saint—the name had been given in gratitude to Frances, wife of the Governor, Sir Lowry Cole, who had collected funds for the church. Only in 1959 were things 'put right' and the name changed to Francis, St Francis of Assisi.

Soon we were passing Admiralty Pier on the seaward side, and **Admiralty House** built in 1760, once the centre of much social whirl. Then we were out on the Marine Drive once more, passing through Fish Hoek: once famous for its many kinds of fish, it is still beloved of anglers. It is also 'dry', a prohibition that goes back 150 years.

Many visitors, clinging to the sea views, continue along this road past Kalk Bay and St James to Muizenberg, all holiday places with fine views, Kalk Bay with a fishing harbour and **Muizenberg** with its kilometres-long beach and famous surfing. The cottage Rhodes died in is here, a simple place, in his day with a tin roof, and with a tremendous view over False Bay. Rhodes, who loved great vistas, had as monumental a one here as at the Matopos in Rhodesia where he was buried.

We ourselves turned to our left past Fish Hoek and drove northwards. To our far right were **Rondevlei Bird Sanctuary,** with its flamingoes and pelicans, and Zeekoevlei—Hippopotamus Marsh—where there were now yachts and power boats in place of hippo. On our far left was Silvermine Nature Reserve, and the *Ou Kaapse Weg*, with more views, and almost before we knew it, we were urban once again, and running through Claremont into Rondebosch.

It had been a magnificent day done, we thought, in the best possible way. Someone else, however, had done it in a way he thought better still: he had that day flown over the Peninsula, and even further afield, by helicopter. He had taken our route, circling, at the start, gently round Table Mountain, hovered over False Bay admiring the seals, then floated eastwards over the wine lands, coming down on the outskirts of Stellenbosch on the lawn of Lanzerac Hotel, where he had lunched leisurely and like a king.

We were transfixed. Could anyone do it? Anyone could. Who 'did' it? Court Helicopters. And the price? R245 for two to four passengers. We worked it out. At just over R60 a head, it would be an expensive treat; but—floating over that incredible patchwork of sea and sand, mountain and cliff, vineyard and valley—it would be a magic, a never-to-be-forgotten thing, with, of course, Lanzerac to make the fitting end.

CHAPTER TWENTY-FOUR

Wine Country

❧

Next day to Lanzerac we went.

This is the old Cape Dutch homestead on the edge of Stellenbosch, now a modern hotel, that a good many people associate more closely with the town than any other building. We were not due there for some hours; so for a morning we explored the town.

Stellenbosch, inland to the east of Cape Town and about an hour's run away, is a sight every tourist wants to see, and rightly. It is the oldest town in South Africa after Cape Town, the village that Simon van der Stel settled in the green fertile valley backed by blue mountains that he found on a day in 1679, and where later he was to plant so many of his famous oaks. It is also the loveliest town of all, a mellow old place of long leafy streets, open furrows of clear running water, and big, white-washed homes, patterned with oak shadows—a dream of a town, or a village, should one say, for this, more than a town, it seems. 'I'm going into the village,' we heard people on the outskirts say, so that the name itself is traditional.

The main street is **Dorp Street,** once the wagon road to Cape Town. Dorp means 'village', and this village street is perhaps the most beautiful in Southern Africa. We walked down it, looking at the Cape Dutch, Georgian and Victorian houses, big houses and little ones, some with trellises and cast iron work, some still with arched entrances—the *poortjies*—to one side, along which carriages once drove.

There were also the big old oaks—national monuments now—that gave character to the street, no longer in their prime but picturesque nonetheless.

That we could see these things as our grandfathers did is due to the combined efforts of the town itself and organizations such as the Historical Monuments Commission and the Historical Homes of South Africa; and we thought how well it had all worked out.

Of special interest were the houses from No 102 to 122 Dorp Street, which in the 19th century housed the Gymnasium which developed in time into the **University of Stellenbosch**—three prime ministers at least, Smuts, Hertzog and Malan, we remembered, had studied here.

Opposite was a sturdy house with a neo-classical gable and especially fine, elaborate fanlight, its white walls generously dappled with oak shadows. Like every other tourist, we looked up at the great eye in bas-relief upon the gable, the best-known gable decoration in the country and one with a touching history.

The house was built in 1798 for the Rev Meendt Borcherds, of Jengum in East Friesland, who came to the Cape in 1795. This sickly and almost penniless 23-year-old was soon minister at Stellenbosch with a wife and growing family—and with a stipend of less than R200 a year: so to augment this he bought land to farm in his spare time. He prospered: so that when he built his house in 1798 he had 'the all-seeing and protecting Eye' that had watched over him placed upon the gable, and named his home **La Gratitude.** The house is still a private one, owned by Mrs S. V. Winshaw, whose husband was one of the famous personalities in the early wine industry. He named the well-known wine, La Gratitude, after this house.

We wanted, for sentimental reasons, to see the home of Sibella— 'Isie'—Krige, General Smuts's wife, and 'Ouma' of World War II. Once a farm, it is now part of the **Libertas Parva** or Klein Libertas complex, gloriously restored, which houses the Rembrandt van Rijn Art Centre, and beyond it, the Oude Meester Wine Museum. Isie's home, from which she was married in 1897, was a wonderful old place, we found, with four side gables, and a ladder leading up to the loft—the loft and the ladder that are traditionally part of the Cape.

Stellenbosch is the heart of a wine land, as the wine museum suggests. At the entrance we found a massive, much-photographed wine press of 1790. Within, we could smell the wine, no residue from all the exhibits but from wine itself in huge vats: in one alone were 30 000 litres. Wine, indeed, can now be bought here.

Round the corner in Ou Strandweg is the new restaurant, the **Volkskombuis,** and the recently opened Brandy Museum (of considerable charm). The Volkskombuis, specializing in traditional Cape food, is not licensed so that everybody takes their own bottle of wine to drink with the meal—many people go especially to taste the ribs of Karoo lamb laced with rosemary and other herbs, a dish already in the process of becoming legend.

Beyond the far end of Dorp Street and its junction with the Faure Road, is the **Oude Libertas Centre,** the new cultural, conference and entertainment centre of the Stellenbosch Farmers' Winery. We walked among the buildings for a while watching a group of young people rehearsing in the open-air amphitheatre, Boland with a classical twist that always intrigues visitors.

There were many other places to see in the town itself, an astonishing number considering the three major fires the town suffered in its history. There were, in particular, the Stellenbosch Museum in Drostdy Street, and all the historic buildings around the green open space in the centre of the town, the Braak.

Soon the centre of the town began to throng with young people. Stellenbosch is a university town and the students bring life to its otherwise quiet streets and houses (what these in turn bring them is intangible but—they often say in later life—as real.) They were strolling now up and down the side of the open water runnels under the trees, with books under their arms, and a good deal of badinage and chatter. A Coloured petrol attendant was beckoning a driver into his garage. 'Ag, sir, here sir, we only put *fresh* water into our petrol'. On a bridge across the stream a small brown girl was sitting: her hair, in plaits, stuck out like little sausages, and she was trailing her bare feet tranquilly in the water. It was a Stellenbosch idyll.

Now it was lunch-time and we passed through the white gates of **Lanzerac** on the Jonkershoek road with considerable anticipation. For those who want to sample the old Cape (with all the pleasures of the present), this is the place to visit. The land on which the hotel stands was domesticated—brought in from the wild—almost 300 years ago when in 1692 it was granted to a soldier of the Dutch East India Company by Simon van der Stel. As in so many cases, land and house changed hands many times after: this century the house has belonged to five different owners, and this century, too, the name was changed from the original Schoongezicht to Lanzerac. It is the newest owner, David Rawdon, who has brought it fame.

The present home was built in 1830, and is U-shaped, with a splendid neo-classical gable, a lawn in front with rooms—once outbuildings—on either side, and a white 'werf' wall. It is a particularly good example of the versatility of these old Cape houses for, although still retaining its essential character, it has stretched and changed and adapted—*agterkamer* (inner room) turning into lounge, stables and fowl house into bedrooms, wine cellar into dining-room and other rooms, distillery into kitchens.

Many people remember it for the beauty and simplicity of the house, the slave bell, the oaks, red geraniums, and exquisite food. We have a personal memory of warmth and welcome, a brick-floored bedroom that was once a stable; wide, shadowed courtyards, and a white statue—a dolphin and boy entwined—flanked by dark thin cypresses.

That day we had lunch in the wine cellar with Phyl Hands, who runs the cellar. A meal at Lanzerac is always an occasion. David Rawdon, who has created the modern hotel, was known to us because of his Matjiesfontein hotel on the Karoo road to the north and its splendid food. But Lanzerac is known to still more people because it is more accessible, close to Cape Town.

The food is famous for three things—simplicity, excellence, and atmosphere. Our lunch in the wine cellar was fitted to every student's pocket, and it consisted of fresh rolls and Lanzerac bread, a plate of cheeses and pickles, and with it we drank not only wine but good wine. This is the only hotel in the country to offer selections of good wine by the glass: there were 15 listed and we noted, among others, Muratie Stein, Lanzerac Riesling, Zonnebloem Riesling, Alphen Selected Dry Red, and Bertram's Cabernet. We sat there, eating our cheese and drinking our wine—if the weather had been fine we would have been in the courtyard under the oaks—a simple, friendly, civilized meal. Lanzerac food is essentially simple, yet the dining-room was always overflowing, we knew, while the Sunday night suppers were fully booked for at least six weeks ahead. People adore this candlelit, very reasonably priced meal, and holidaymakers from Johannesburg and Durban often build their trip around it.

Talking of Lanzerac (which has been internationally rated as one of the world's great hotels) reminds us of South Africa's other hotels—among the best in the world, say travellers. There are many good ones, including those with five stars: at the same time, let no visitor be deluded into thinking that in this country 'stars' are granted for what most people consider excellence. They are awarded for such things as edge-to-edge carpeting, telephones in bedrooms and hours of service provided, and never for *quality* of food, beds, service or for atmosphere: so that one can eat poorly at a five-star hotel, and at Lanzerac, with only three stars, like a prince.

Food was much to the fore that day, for it was at Lanzerac that we met Mrs Magda Pretorius, president of a Stellenbosch guild then unique in South Africa. It was a guild of connoisseurs, the *Fynproewersgilde*, with the ideal of serving the community, and Mrs Pretorius was the apostle of 'simple food, well cooked, well served'.

The aims of the Guild, as expounded by her, were simple yet ambitious—to make people aware of the things that were Stellenbosch's own, particularly the food and wine; to gather good recipes; to have the best incorporated in the menus of some hotels and restaurants in the town; and to keep check on the standard of these—in the end, perhaps, to have its own eating-house; to uphold a good, gracious life that was without humbug or showing off.

The Guild was established very much from within by the Stellenbosch Farmers' and Wine-Tasters' Association, and—having suffered the food in many hotels along our routes—we were tremendously interested.

If Stellenbosch has a new food project, it has already broken new ground with wine. It has the Wine Route, at the moment the only one in South Africa.

It was Phyl Hands, over a glass of 1965 Chateau Libertas, who filled in the details for us in a long, gay, gossipy wine talk interspersed with a taste of this and a taste of that. Phyl is one of the Cape's foremost wine-tasters—a runnner-up in a recent Argus Wine Taster of the Year competition, with a palate so delicate and a knowledge so sure that she can name any Cape wine at a sip, its composition, where grown, and on what type of soil.

As cellarmaster at Lanzerac she is very good; as a generous guide through the intricacies of South African wines she was a joy to us that day. Soon the bottles began to line up beside us, and two young strangers, enthusiastically eaves-dropping, were drawn into the circle.

Most people today know something of the background of our wines; how those first three-inch vine slips from the Rhineland travelled to the Cape, each in a packet of wet earth wrapped in a sailcloth—and perished; and how the next lot lived; and how four years later they had produced grapes from which wine was pressed, which Van Riebeeck noted lyrically in his diary on February 2nd, 1659, 'Today, God be praised . . .'

They know how Simon van der Stel made wine at Constantia and the Cloetes after him; how in 1885 the vine disease, Phylloxera, devastated the vineyards and how resistant rootstock from America saved the day; how farmers had then begun to produce too much wine and how the great organization, KWV, had arisen to protect their interests and to control supply and marketing.

The main wine area of South Africa is a narrow strip of the South West Cape more or less parallel with the coast, reaching like a rough triangle from the Olifants River in the north, south to Constantia and east to Robertson and the Little Karoo beyond, with Stellenbosch the heart.

All this corner of the South-West is true wine land, with its unique character given by soil and climate, soils that are 'moderately fertile', and the dry summers and wet winters that make good grapes and wines. Here the Cape's summer wind, the southeaster—the fierce, wild Cape Doctor—that can rip a vineyard or cool sun-heated grapes, brings drought. Heat is the great bugaboo (it is detrimental to white wines in particular), heat during the growing of the grapes, during fermentation and maturation, and although the last two are being dealt with successfully, it is the vineyards where the grapes have shorter hours of sun that are often the lucky ones.

It was to these hills and valleys, which have so much in common with the other notable wine lands of the world that there came the varieties, the vine cultivars, that make the famous wines of Europe. There are those which yield the white wines, Riesling from Germany, Steen (Chenin Blanc) from France, Clairette Blanche from Mediterranean France, Palomino, which was known as the French Grape and in Spain today is grown for sherry, and Colombar, which is popular in France for brandy-making.

Red wine cultivars are mainly Shiraz, originally from Persia and imported into South Africa by way of the Rhône Valley; Cinsaut (once known as Hermitage) originally from the South of France, and Pinotage, of true South African origin: it is a cross between the Pinot Noir of Burgundy and Cinsaut, made here in the Stellenbosch area in the 1920s by Professor A. Perold, one of the great names in wine pioneering. Finally there is, among the greats, Cabernet Sauvignon from the Bordeaux region of France, a noble grape in Africa as in Europe.

'But don't believe they make the same wines here as in Europe,' said Phyl. 'They don't.' We knew how wines from the same varieties differed even from district to district, from hill slope to hill slope in the Cape, and we listened to her expanding on this theme. Cabernet Sauvignon, she said, was the basis of great European clarets but here in the Cape the wines took on a new character, becoming more full-bodied, 'not quite as full as a Burgundy, but more so than most clarets.' This grape was the basis of the best red wines in South Africa, wines 'with a pronounced nose and typical flavour', astringent when young and needing two or three years' maturation in cask and some years in bottle before being drunk. They were often blended with Cinsaut or Shiraz to make wine more palatable at a younger age.

Cinsaut, she said, was the most popular red wine grape at the Cape, often—because it was so high-yielding—giving a rather thin characterless wine. Yet, where yields were lower, as here in Stellenbosch, it produced a wine of fine quality. Pinotage, 'with a pronounced flowery nose', was lighter-bodied in cool areas like Constantia than in inland places.

Steen, the most popular white wine variety in the Western Cape, produced wines that differed considerably from area to area, those from the coast giving lighter wines than from the hotter Little Karoo inland.

Which did she think was the best? No, she replied, that was not for her to say. 'The thing is to make up your own mind what you like. You've got to drink wine and taste, experiment and learn what you like and why, and have adventure and fun with it. That's it—adventure and fun.'

Most people who lived in South Africa before World War II remember how second-rate our wines seemed compared to the imported: and how at official South African banquets the wines served were all French. Then came the introduction of new technologies and a more general awareness of wine, and almost imperceptibly the old days drew to their end, and the wines of the Cape had arrived.

This decade, when an international wine festival was held in Budapest at which 34 countries provided 1 400 different wines, South Africa won five gold medals: four were Nederburg wines and the fifth KWV's Paarl Petillant Rosé. When the competition was held in London in 1974 the Stellenbosch-based Gilbey's group won more awards than any other producer on the show—15 gold, 11 silver, and five bronze medals. Twenty of our wines were rated as 'exceptional' by the panel of international judges, and another 11 were ranked as 'very good'.

In March 1977 a number of overseas experts came to South Africa to sample our wines on the spot. They were members of the exclusive Institute of Masters of Wine and KWV invited 52 of them to make a tour of the wine lands. It was to the visitors (in their own words) 'a trip of a lifetime' not only for the wines but for the warmth and welcome, and the Cape itself with its mountains, its homes and tranquillity.

Some of the experts stressed the need for blending wines at the Cape (a need of which many South Africans are aware). John Davies of Chateau Lascombes, Bordeaux, for instance, was bothered by the emphasis on single cultivar wines for he believed that almost any wine was improved by judicious blending. Some criticized the amount of alcohol in South African wines. Comments on bouquet and flavour varied. Michael Broadbent of Christie's of London likened the bouquet of Shiraz in South Africa to a sweaty saddle, almost leathery, which he liked! James John of Harvey's of Bristol thought our whites had a rather earthy mousey taste, while that of the reds was like rusty nails and 'interesting.' Patrick Grubb of Sotheby's felt the whites were 'too steely' and the Rieslings too dry and almost harsh, while the reds needed more delicacy. Some felt there were few really fine wines because there was no demand for them, and that the public should be educated to expect them.

There was plenty, too, on the credit side, talk of many good and solid wines, their cleanness and freshness and overall quality, and of top Rieslings made with sophisticated machinery and techniques. Michael Broadbent cited a Backsberg Cabernet as a specially fine wine, and the Zonnebloem Cabernet 1945 as outstanding. At Nederburg two Edelkeur wines had been excellent by any standard—both were 'the summit of the winemaker's art'. James John thought the KWV sherries he had tasted exceptional—'my goodness, they were very, very good'.

This was all valuable to winemakers, of great importance to the export market, fascinating to wine-drinkers. Would it influence wine-drinkers' taste? Who is ever sure what people will want and when? Certainly in the early 1970s, when South Africans suddenly switched from white wine, a traditional favourite, to red, the wine industry was caught flat-footed. Red wines became a status symbol almost over-night, merchants scrambled for them and prices soared. In the end, things became more normal; but the wine industry still remembers the unexpected volcano.

Phyl led us in and out of these intricacies. Then she explained some of the newer developments in the wine world. In 1973 the 'Wine of Origin' legislation—broadly speaking, to guarantee the identity and pedigree of fine wines—came into operation. Its token is a seal, awarded by the South African Wine and Spirits Board, placed on the neck of the bottle, and this may carry one, two or three stripes of a different colour, each colour with its own particular significance.

The blue band guarantees that the wine comes from the particular area named on the label of the bottle.

The red band guarantees the vintage year printed on the label either on the neck or the body of the bottle.

The green band shows that the wine is derived from the vine cultivar shown on the label, such as Riesling or Cabernet Sauvignon.

Estate indicates that the wine in the bottle is truly from this particular estate.

Superior upon the label guarantees that an estate wine or wine of origin is of a superior quality according to the standards laid down by the Wine and Spirits Board.

So that when we have upon our dinner-table a bottle bearing a seal with three stripes, a vintage label, a label indicating origin and cultivar, and the word 'Superior', this means we have a good pedigreed wine. It may be the best we can get but is not necessarily so. The scheme is a voluntary one and the wines involved represent a small percentage of all the wine produced.

'No,' said Phyl with spirit, 'never think the Wine of Origin seal says the last word. Wines that lack it are still among the best. That WOS seal guarantees a good wine: the lack of it does not make a poor one. *Never be a wine snob.*'

But Phyl knows her wines. For all those people who are feeling their way about, for all strangers to our wines, a Superior label is a first-rate guide, and the wine in the bottle something on which to depend.

Getting to know the wines, however delectable a task, is not always an easy one, and here Stellenbosch leads on two counts. The latest is the Lanzerac Cellars Club, organized by Phyl Hands herself, through which members get special kinds of help, including Phyl's own introduction to the subject, *Enjoy Wine*—it was a résumé of it she gave us in the wine cellar that morning. Club members can attend wine tastings at Lanzerac and Phyl visits the main cities to let members at a distance taste the wines. At the club itself there is a pulpit to house the cash register and a hip bath filled with sparkling wines!

Stellenbosch's other attraction—it is a major one—is its **Wine Route,** and here we are back to Phyl's adventure and fun. It is one of the gayest, most exciting things to explore in all South Africa and since its start seven years ago it has become one of the country's major attractions.

It started with two well-known wine farmers, Frans Malan and Niel Joubert, on a wine tour of France. It was so good that it gave them the idea for a Cape Wine Route similar to the French. With the enthusiasm and help of Mr Spatz Sperling of Driesprong (Delheim), the Route was born.

In April 1971 the Wine Route was officially opened and for the first time the general public could follow a route through a rough square of Stellenbosch countryside (with Stellenbosch the heart) in which they could visit the famous wine estates and wineries, sample and buy their wine on the spot, admire the old Cape-Dutch homes and splendid settings, and—of first importance—meet the wine-makers themselves and talk about their wine.

Today 12 estates and six co-operatives are on the Route, offering a great many different kinds of wine—in December 1976 numbering 122. An illustrated map, listing the names of the estates and briefly their histories, their wines, and the times when wines are sold and cellars may be visited, is obtainable from the Public Relations Officer of the Stellenbosch Wine Route Co-op—'You will find more farms and wineries per kilometre than in any other district of South Africa' it claims—while details are obtainable from major tourist offices everywhere.

The scheme has roared ahead. Visitors are increasing by 40 per cent every year, and it is reckoned that in the month of December alone 10 000 people follow the Route. Plane-loads of people fly down from the Transvaal for a weekend—big groups now have to book a year ahead for a single day's visit.

It is all easy and pleasant, including places to eat. There is Lanzerac at the start, and the other places in Stellenbosch like the Volkskombuis in an old Sir Herbert Baker cottage, or the Drostdy Herberg where, with a day's notice, simple traditional food is served, and this is often what people want to accompany Cape wines. Spier, one of the estates on the Route, has a restaurant which is deservedly popular, and Delheim now has a cheese meal. There is also the restaurant at Boschendal which is not far away, and Fransch Hoek's Le Gourmet.

With Phyl as our guide we began our first adventures on the Wine Route. We went north along the Klapmuts Road, and then west towards the Simonsberg, the mountains that lie southeast to northwest in the direction of the south-east wind: the lie of the land, the extra shade hours a day protecting the ripening grapes from too much heat, produce good wines in the vineyards that the mountains overshadow. The names speak for themselves—Muratie, Delheim (Driesprong), Uitkyk, Schoongezicht-Rustenburg. We went first to **Delheim** Winery on Driesprong, with a cellar that is streamlined, modern and businesslike, where we bought a case of Goldspatz Steen Superior, a delicate fruity wine with a famous bouquet.

Then we returned to **Muratie,** nearer Stellenbosch, with its old buildings under the oaks, and traditions going back nearly 300 years. This was an estate we had longed to see because, by contrast to many other estates which now make wine (and very well) by ultra-modern processes, Muratie's wines are craftsman-made by time-honoured methods. No cultivated yeast here—the natural yeast in the bloom of the grape starts spontaneous fermentation of the wine. Even the bottles are filled by hand, and we had heard of (and saw) the bottling and corking machine which could take only six bottles at a time in contrast to the mechanized wonders of many of the other estates. Like anything made by hand with dedication and skill, Muratie's wines have a reputation for quality and distinction.

The estate is owned by Miss Annemarie Canitz—Annemie to her friends. We knew a little of her story and that of her home, and now we were to hear it first-hand. Muratie means ruin, for the present lovely homestead, built in the 1830s, incorporated the ruins of a yet older house. The land had originally been granted to a German, Lorenz Kamfer, in 1685 and, after changing hands many times, was bought some fifty years ago by Miss Canitz's father, George Paul Canitz, the painter ('he had the biggest heart in all the Cape'.) One day the two of them rode on horseback past the house and longed for it with passion. Soon Canitz bought it, painting for the rest of his life to pay it off. What matter! He had it, and with the help of Professor A. Perold he was to make Muratie a wine name. He was one of the first to plant Pinot Noir grapes and wines from these have been a Muratie speciality ever since.

Professor Perold had thought Muratie one of the best red wine farms in the country. Miss Canitz took over the estate on her father's death and under her care the tradition of fine wines has flourished: she does make white, but her fame still rests upon the reds, made from Pinot Noir and Cabernet Sauvignon, and there is never enough of these to satisfy her customers.

Miss Canitz was waiting to show us her cellar, part of it perhaps as old as the more-than-200-year oak tree standing between cellar and house. The rear portion was half underground against a knoll, making it one of the few underground cellars in the wine lands. We admired the equipment, vintage too, the purple fermentation tanks smelling of grapes, the baskets of corks from Portugal, the best in the world, for Miss Canitz does not economize on them. We enjoyed Miss Canitz as well with her dim old house full of books and pictures, and her talk of how 'Daddy' found the farm and planted the grapes, gentle proud talk full of graces like her wine.

Nearby on the slopes of Simonsberg was another famous estate rich in history, **Schoongezicht,** once owned by Hendrik Cloete, son of the Cloete who first made Constantia wine, a beautiful home in a classic setting, owned today by the Barlow family. The vineyards on the mountain-side yield red wines—the famous Rustenburg—and whites sold under the label Schoongezicht. We remembered it especially because it had been the home of John X. Merriman, the Prime Minister of the Cape Colony, who helped shape Union. He was a great figure in his day, statesman and orator, and he was the son of that walking parson, Nathaniel James Merriman, who had been too poor to buy a horse. From that humble if vital home to Schoongezicht was a leap. We liked, too, to imagine him on his high stoep, built nearly a century before by Hendrik Cloete, who had sat here before him drinking coffee, with a speaking trumpet hooked to an iron railing, which he took down now and then and shouted through to the slaves in the vineyard below.

369

We drove westwards to **Montagne Estate** at Hartenberg off the Bottelary Road—also on the Wine Route—where Phyl introduced us to Walter Finlayson and his modern wine-making techniques, stainless steel vats and automatic bottling machine. In the old homestead (early 18th century) we tasted a Montagne Cabernet Sauvignon 1971, a dry fruity Semillon, a full-bodied Late Harvest, and a Premier Grand Crû that we had first met at Matjiesfontein at a superb meal. Montagne's Riesling, dry enough for South African palates, has won its 'Superior' rating.

We went to **Spier** in the Eerste River valley—owned by Mr Niel Joubert—for lunch. Everyone on the Route much enjoys the stop here, the wonderful old buildings which have been carefully restored, with their variety of gables, the outside staircase and slave bell. The original cellar dating from the early 18th century still stands—the Spier labels are based on its gable design—and the slave house is now the restaurant.

Here we had a meal that was memorable, not so much for the pleasant food as for the wine and wine list—the most comprehensive we had seen in South Africa—and for the Coloured wine steward, Campbell. There were 83 estate wines on the list, to be pushed up to 100, we learned: Campbell himself was a man with over a quarter of a century's personal experience of handling wine. He was studying and taking courses at KWV in his spare time; he cared for what we drank that day, and how. It was a Spier Colombar, a dry light white wine that to Phyl was 'as fresh as a spring morning,' and Campbell, serving it, made up for other wine-waiters we had known, as a class among the dreariest in South Africa.

Beyond Spier, on the other side of Lynedoch station on the Faure road, is **Meerlust,** one of the greats among estates, for its history and glamour, its beauty and its wine. It is not open to the public; however, it can be seen from the road, and it is part of the wine lands story. The land was an old grant of 1693, in the middle of the 18th century becoming Myburg property, which it has remained ever since, one of the old family farms that has been cared for meticulously generation after generation. Hans Fransen and Dr Cook give it four stars—'a very fine homestead almost unchanged for 200 years.' In addition there are a charming pigeon-house, which is a national monument, a bell-tower and old sundial.

The present belongs to wine. In 1976 Nico Myburg's Cabernet was the champion red wine at the Cape Show, and in November that year Billy Hofmeyr found, at a wine-tasting on the estate, a new wine that was 'epoch-making.' Billy Hofmeyr is a well-known wine personality, wine-taster supreme, and regular contributor to *Wynboer*, and he wrote in this journal of a Meerlust blend, created by Dr J. Laszlo, of 40 per cent each Cabernet Sauvignon and Cabernet franc and 20 per cent Merlot, that had excited him more than any other South African wine in eight years.

It was a Chateau Libertas that we had drunk with Phyl in the Lanzerac Wine Cellar, the bottle with a label bearing a Libertas gable design. Before we left Stellenbosch we went to see the gables as they were on **Libertas** estate, close to Stellenbosch—the grapes from here go to make that famous wine.

This is a private estate, open to the public, by appointment, yet one whose history everybody knows, for it was the home of Adam Tas, who fought a battle for liberty against Simon van der Stel's son Adriaan, and who kept a racy diary, parts of which still exist.

Libertas is owned now by Mr Robbie Blake and his wife Yvonne. When they bought it more than 30 years ago, the main house had been a storeroom for a long time, and they themselves restored it lovingly and painstakingly through the wet Cape winters. The interior is one of the most unusual in any Cape Dutch home, for almost 200 years ago Jan Adam Hartmann, the artist, covered the walls with murals, pictures of heavenly figures, garlands of flowers, fruit and birds. Some of them point a special virtue. There is Hospitality, Thrift over the pantry, Mother Love over the fireplace, symbolic of warmth and comfort! The fireplace, hidden behind teak doors, entranced us as it had done Alys Trotter three-quarters of a century before—she left a sketch of it.

We sat in front of the fireplace with the Blakes, and Willem and Magda Pretorius, and drank wine, a Mymering sherry, a 1968 KWV Pinotage, a 1969 KWV Roodeberg, a prince among wines, eating with our fingers slivers of hot mackerel that were being smoked outside over oak sawdust with vine logs below. They did not drink spirits, our companions told us, because it ruined the palate—'at most, a very occasional liqueur-glass of 10-year-old KWV brandy last thing at night.' They were all experts on wine, the growing, the savouring and the drinking, and it was for Transvaalers a liberal education.

Before we left the Stellenbosch area, we went south to view from a distance an estate that had given us a memorable wine. It was **Alto,** on the slopes of the Helderberg south of Stellenbosch, where the Malan family from the 1920s onwards produced a blended wine known as Alto Rouge. Made from Cabernet Sauvignon, Cinsaut and Shiraz grapes, it not only won many awards in South Africa but for years was marketed in London by Burgoyne's

Wine is a thing for a mood, an occasion, a memory. So Alto Rouge was with us. In September 1953, the day that our son was born, we put down a bottle of Alto Rouge in our house cellar, and there it rested for 21 years. In September, 1974, at the Lombardy restaurant in Pretoria, our friend and owner pulled the cork. It was 24 years since the wine had been made and experts had shaken their heads. 'Twenty-four years! A South African wine! Never!' But they were wrong. It was wonderful liquid garnet, full-bodied, smooth, with a fine bouquet. We remembered how Malan had matured his wine in large casks in a cellar shaded by trees for three years, and how there had always been a bed in his cellar, 'a sign of conscientious wine-making at the Cape,' Bosdari had written, which even the non-technical could recognize. Our bottle of wine was the fruit of work, love and discipline, and we remembered to drink a toast to the Malans who had made it.

Every farm and estate on the Wine Route, and many others besides, has its own story—there are estates like Middelvlei where once the famous Parrot Shoot was held on Simon van der Stel's birthday; Koelenhof with its historic Anglo-Boer War water trough; Blaauwklippen; or Devonvale Estate where Bertrams wines are produced. The discovery of their character and tales is part of the charm of the countryside.

We went eastwards from Stellenbosch on the road to Groot Drakenstein and Fransch Hoek. At the top of Helshoogte—a gentle way to bear so desperate a name—was the view of the **Drakenstein Valley,** a noble one with mountains on every hand.

This was the country where came the French religious refugees, the Huguenots, in 1688: it did not need the Huguenot Memorial or Museum in Fransch Hoek to remind us that this was once a corner of France, for the names—Rhône, La Cotte, La Motte, La Provence, and many others—did this at every turn. It was here, immediately before us, that deciduous fruit farming in South Africa was started—again, by Cecil Rhodes—who instructed Pickstone (H. E. V. Pickstone of deciduous fruit fame) to buy up farms in the area, giving preference to those with fine old homesteads. These, when necessary, he restored.

Over Helshoogte, we passed Rhône and Boschendal—Wood and Dale—both Rhodes Fruit Farms, which is now a company in the Anglo American Corporation group. **Boschendal,** the home of generations of the De Villiers family, magnificently restored under the eye of Gabriel and Gwen Fagan, is today a wine farm again and a social centre, with a gallery for art exhibitions, a taphuis for wine-tasting, and a restaurant which is a big draw, another of the famous estates with a fine old homestead that can be seen by the public. It has, as well, a period garden of old-fashioned roses, bordered with lavender, rosemary and catmint which—speaking personally—we would cross the country to see in spring.

Where the road forked beyond Boschendal, we turned left towards Paarl. Over on our left again was the farm **Plaisir de Merle** where the first Marais had farmed, and further on was **La Motte** where Daniel Nourtier had settled in 1690, starting the well-known Nortje family. We looked at the first Marais home with especial interest. People of this big family are somewhat different from ordinary mortals, sometimes scallywags, sometimes predikants, usually quicker on the uptake than anyone else, and often scintillating.

On our right was **Bien Donne** where Pierre Lombard had settled and founded the Lombard family, and when we turned back again towards Fransch Hoek, there was **Lekkerwyn** close to the road upon our left, bearing the perfect name—Delicious Wine—for a wine land but being in fact a transliteration of the first owner's name, Ary Lécrevent.

On our right, too, was **Bellingham,** marked by the low white enclosing walls. Nearly everyone knows the name because of the wines that Mr J. B. Podlashuk, the owner, has made popular since World War II. It is a beautiful home, with the splendid Great Drakenstein mountains as a backing—the gable of the wine cellar follows the outline of the peak behind it, a famous view.

Although this home, splendidly restored and furnished by Mr Podlashuk and his wife Fredagh, is not open to the public, their hospitality is large; and they have laid down that after their deaths the homestead is to be maintained as a place where overseas visitors can be entertained. It is to remain a home.

Further on, we turned left again along the Wemmershoek road until we came to the farm **De Hoop.** What we were seeking was the place whence South Africa's best-known family, the Van der Merwes, had come—it was liking finding the spot where the Smiths had originated, tracking one's race to the source, so to speak.

Paul Roux and his pretty wife and their children live on the farm now, but the original grant was to Schalk Willemsz van der Merwe, ancestor of the Van der Merwe family. We walked to the memorial erected on the spot where Schalk and his wife had set up home in 1692—the ground plan is still visible. The memorial stands in a grove of oaks next to a little stream, with the Wemmershoek mountains all round and the turtle doves calling.

Back on the main road through the long Drakenstein valley, we passed another La Motte, then La Provence from where the Joubert family had sprung, and almost in Fransch Hoek itself was the farm **La Cotte,** with its ancient oak. We had come specially to see this huge old tree, which had been planted in 1694 by the Huguenot, Jean Gardiol, to whom the farm was granted by Simon van der Stel, and who had brought the acorn with him from France. It grows beside the farm-house, flanking an old water-wheel of early days, and people visit it with nostalgia. Acorns from it, so the young Hugos who now live here told us, had been taken back to France, so that now La Cotte oaks grow on Paris boulevards.

South of Fransch Hoek we found farms like Champagne and Burgundy, whence came the De Villiers, and La Dauphine, which the first Nel (then Niel) had farmed. It was a valley rich both in people and in beauty. The wind was full of the smell of wine; indeed, the very landscape seemed to reek of the tang of it. The narrow roads between the vineyards were bustling with tractors pulling trailer-loads of grapes for the presses. There was activity and ferment on every hand, reaping, conveying, the age-old process of garnering-in, pressing. Yet our next stop was not a wine occasion.

If this was wine country now, it once had been elephant land, and Olifantshoek—Elephants' Corner—the name of the valley long before it had become French Corner: it was not mildew but elephants that had ravaged the first vineyards of the Huguenots.

Alys Fane Trotter, when she had sketched in the valley, had talked with an old man whose grandfather had watched the departure of the last elephant with her calf. 'Eastwards over the mountainside they went, and none were ever seen again.'

So what we went in search of now was the elephant trail, the road the elephants had used over the mountain—Middagkransberg—beyond the town. It was the first road of all over these heights and was called **Olifantspad,** Elephants' Road, and men on foot and on horseback used it for over a century after the Huguenots arrived.

Then in 1818 a farmer, S. J. Cats, a complete amateur, built a road over the mountain which was known as Cats-pad: the little wagon that used to take provisions to the men working on the road is said to be preserved on a farm in the valley, although we could not trace it. The third road was Holloway's, built by British troops in the 1820s, under Major Holloway of the Royal Engineers, which in places followed Cats-pad closely. It was South Africa's first professionally-built road and was opened in its entirety in 1825.

The road beyond Fransch Hoek over the mountain by **Fransch Hoek Pass** is a tourist route today, and we drove up it from the town looking for traces of the three old roads. The Elephants' Road had gone. José Burman, who wrote a classic book on the passes of the Western Cape, *So High the Road*, hunted for it and thought it lay south-west of the present road—how fitting if it were to be found and marked, this astonishing piece of history of our wine land. We did, however, find what we thought were remnants of Cats-pad, while parts of Holloway's Road were clear.

We crossed the remains of these towards the summit of the pass. Here, at the top, was a pull-out where coach-loads of tourists were gazing out over the Fransch Hoek valley with its vineyards and orchards and the road sweeping below. The drivers were giving them a loudspeaker talk: we hoped they were pointing out Holloway's Road, clearly defined on the left, banked with stone, and telling them about the Elephants' Way. Here, the legend goes, is the Great Divide and when rain falls upon it some drops splash to the west, finding their way in the end to the Atlantic, and others splash to the east, ending up in the Indian Ocean. It is a simple story that always pleases everyone out of all proportion.

The fine old town of **Paarl** is a wine name much as is Stellenbosch, and like it, it has charm, oak trees and old houses, and as well the Strooidak Church in High Street, the thatched, gabled Dutch Reformed Church that is now a national monument.

Paarl means Pearl, and took its name from the huge granite rocks near the town, christened in October 1657 Diamond and Pearl by one of Van Riebeeck's men, who saw the wet rocks glistening in the sun: they still glisten like this today. Paarl Mountain was once revered by naturalists for its plants and animals, scientists like Charles Darwin making pilgrimages to it; and these memories remain as one takes the beautiful Jan Phillips Mountain Drive, and in the wild flower garden.

All the same, it is the KWV cellars that claim most visitors. They are said to be the biggest in the world, and a tour through them is something of an eye-opener. The oldest vat in South Africa, which has been in use for 150 years, is here: it is called Big Bill and came from Groot Constantia. This is big business, all very efficient and impressive —and so is the wine-tasting at a tour's end.

The Paarl countryside also has its estates yielding fine wines. There are Fairview and Backsberg to the southwest with well-known red wines—Fairview where the first private estate auction was held, and Backsberg where visitors enjoy the fun of colour television showing how grapes are grown and wines are made; Landskroon, a De Villiers home for over a century; and to the northeast a name the world now knows, Nederburg, owned by the Stellenbosch Farmers' Winery.

Nederburg is a show place, open to the public, with a fine home-stead of the year 1800 standing in a rose garden, and noble cellars.

From here come famous red and white wines, some of the best known in the country, often associated with the name Johann Graue, the German wine-maker who bought Nederburg in 1936 and here made his well-known wines. Six years after he had planted his first vineyards he was, astonishingly, at the top!

At a recent Nederburg Wine Auction a banquet was held on the lawns that was fabulous, an Arabian Nights affair, with tables loaded with brilliant food, scarlet lobsters, whole fishes and springbok, suckling-pigs, gorgeous salads, fruit and cheese—'the most prodigal and brilliant buffet I have ever seen,' wrote English wine writer Katie Bourke. With it went wines like Nederburg Paarl Late Harvest 1974, Paarl Riesling 1975, and Nederburg Edelrood. The auction it introduced was a window on the world, wrote Katie, showing wines of quality properly priced and bringing wine people from all over the world to view them. The setting in itself was of world class.

When **Tulbagh** to the north gets its wine route three greats—which lie under the shadow of the Great Winterhoek Mountains—should be upon it, all known for their white wines. They are Montpellier, Twee Jongegezellen and Theuniskraal, west and north of Tulbagh, lying in a line north to south and close to one another, their soils, rainfall and wines different, yet all producing famous whites.

Montpellier is a Theron farm—Tulbagh is Theron country—although it was the Frenchman, Jean Joubert, the first owner who named it after his home in France. The homestead that followed his mud cottage grew—in the way of so many old houses—about it, but unlike them, it was largely destroyed in Tulbagh's devastating earthquake of 1969. The new house, however, is the old one carefully rebuilt.

Everybody knows the wines. There was the La Residence Montpellier we remembered, recommended once by a wine waiter who knew his job, to underwrite a special occasion—it retains its glamour still; the Montpellier Riesling and the Gewürtztraminer, both carrying the 'Superior' label, wines pale and clear and shining.

The wines from **Twee Jongegezellen** next door are also well-known, the best today being—according to the owner, Mr N. C. Krone—Twee Jongegezellen 39, not a Riesling but a blend of the best estate wines which Nicky, his son, talks of as being their 'flagship'.

This is another Theron family farm, taking its name from two young men, 'Two Young Companions', who farmed it in the early 1700s. Mr Krone senior is a descendant of that first Theron, who was possibly one of the young companions.

And **Theuniskraal?** The Krones have mountain vineyards, but at

Theuniskraal the Jordaan brothers grow their grapes on the flats on rich alluvial soil. A Riesling comes from here that is distinctive, a wine that we ourselves have drunk to mark many good meals and happy celebrations. When we think of it, we remember what W. A. de Klerk, in his *The White Wines of South Africa*, had said about his glass of Theuniskraal Riesling as he drank it over a Boland supper.

'I was reminded of open vistas from the mountain, with the delicate scent of erica or protea scrub, then suddenly of wet sandstone boulders in a crystal stream.' What surer description of a 'fresh, honest-to-God' dry Cape white wine could there hope to be!

CHAPTER TWENTY-FIVE

Boland

✦

The wine lands are a part—for many of supreme fascination—but still only a part of the South-West Cape. This is a countryside crammed with interest and with charm, offering a super-abundance of pleasures to visitors.

There is the coastline to the east and south, with places like Gordon's Bay (Colonel Gordon again), Betty's Bay and Hermanus further on, or the national road N2 to be explored at leisure, and the mountains with their roads and passes, the Cape mountains which are so soft and blue and beckoning in the distance and at hand so harsh and grand and desolate, with orchards and vineyards at their foot, and roads like ribbons winding along and over.

There are roads to the north along the bleak Atlantic coast with Atlantic winds, penguins, crayfish tails and dried fish flapping in the wind, and further on to the east, the wheatlands of the Swartland, and the flats and gentle curves over which they flow: Piketberg's Gothic church steeple, orange groves, and mountains again with valleys of wild flowers, and on the slopes *waboom* with blue leaves and red-brown wood that make the coals over which Bolanders traditionally braai their chops—its smoke is a true scent of the South-West along with the smell of the fynbos scrub.

In Cape Town, one of the things that had interested us was the white-walled tombs of the Muslim holy men on Signal Hill seen from the road at the top of Strand Street behind the Malay Quarter. One day we drove across the Cape Flats to see the most famous tomb of all, the karamat or kramat—the shrine—of **Saint Sheik Yusuf,** that first great Muslim in our southern land.

A prince of Macassar—he was brother to the King of Goa—warrior, priest and saint, he was exiled by the Dutch East India Company after he had led a war against them to uphold the independence of Bantam on the island of Java. In 1694 he sailed to the Cape in the *Voetboog*—performing on the way a miracle, it is said, for when fresh drinking water was finished, he touched the sea with his foot, the casks were hauled up on board, and the salt water found to be fresh.

He landed together with his two wives, sons and daughters, friends and servants—49 persons in all—and it is pleasant to know that the Van der Stels, father and son, gave him help and courtesy. For five years he lived on the farm Zandvliet on the edge of the Cape Flats near the Faure of today, practising and teaching his religion, and when he died in 1699 was buried here on the top of a sand dune within sound of the sea—those dunes around are still sometimes known as the Macassar Downs, and Macassar on False Bay is marked on every map. It is a lonely spot today; in the 1690's it must have been beyond men's knowledge.

It is sometimes said that his body does not lie there any longer but that it was taken back to Macassar when his family returned in 1704. Whether this is true or not makes no apparent difference to the Malays of the Cape—they still make their pilgrimage to his tomb, and it is still a moving one.

We followed their path. Along the N2 out of Cape Town, via the Settlers Way towards Somerset West, we turned along the road going to Macassar, and there—nearly at the sea—was the sandy track to the left through the bush, with the tomb on the small hill beyond.

This was not as the grave looked in 1699. The tomb is now enclosed in a small mosque—the whole known as the karamat of Saint Sheik Yusuf—sturdy, domed and arched, the slender crescent-capped minaret standing without.

The door was unlocked. We took off our shoes and went in. The grave was hidden by countless covers of bright silk and satin piled upon it, offerings by those whose prayers had been answered through the intercession of the saint. The little room was dim and cool and smelt of incense, and had the familiar feel of much use. Outside there were cannons mounted on the ramparts, and a plaque on the minaret which read, 'Sheik Yusuf Martyr and Hero of Bantam, 1626 to 1699', and the graves of four of his followers.

They lay towards the sea, side by side, the headstones bound with linen and silk, the graves shrouded in yellow, gold and turquoise silks emblazoned with the Islamic crescent and star. These, although weighted down with stones, were streaming in the gale, while the wind, plucking at the cloths about the headstones, gave them the momentary appearance of movement and life.

It was an unearthly scene, the moving headstones, the low sombre scrub and the line of the sand dunes stretching beyond. Had the Sheik in exile known anything here but melancholy? He had. He had left a faith. And surely his own ghost confers a benison upon the place: he is sometimes seen here in his long robe, green, the colour of Islam. It is said that once, in the olden days when his grave had been lost and forgotten, the green-clad figure led a shepherd boy to the spot, and so the grave was found again to the comfort and the glory of the Faithful.

The shrine set the tone for the day, nostalgic and romantic, which the next stop was to emphasize. Somerset West lay close ahead, with the historic farm, **Vergelegen,** a little to the east. This was where Willem Adriaan, son of Simon van der Stel, made a grand home for himself when he became governor, and from which he was igno-miniously recalled in 1707. His house no longer stands, and the homestead is relatively modern, although the huge old camphor trees outside may be his. This is a private home owned by the Barlow family and not open to the public, but we had permission to look at the trees, which are national monuments and monumental.

Hottentots Holland, the valley was called, where Somerset West stands today; and ahead of us, as we travelled eastwards from the town, were the **Hottentot Holland Mountains.**

They are the mountains nearest to Cape Town, part of the shallow half-circle of ranges cutting off the Cape Peninsula and the land immediately beyond it from the rest of South Africa.

Van Riebeeck knew them as the Mountains of Africa, and longed to find a crossing through them. The Hottentots could have told him there *was* a path already over them, a path made by animals again, but this time not by elephant but by eland. They had come this way since immemorial times, travelling over the mountains in the spring to graze in the Somerset West valley, and back again in the autumn to the highlands. The Hottentots used the path and called it the Gantouw or Elands' Road, and soon the settlers gave it the same name, **Elands-pad.** They used it as the only road to the east, and it was not until 1830 that a new road took its place, planned by the governor, Sir Lowry Cole, and named after him.

Men and oxen had cause to bless him. For well over 100 years ox teams had dragged wagons up and down the steep, rocky, cruel mountain side in the tracks of the eland, the oxen battered and streaming blood, or where the way was too steep for even their great strength, they had carried the pieces of the wagons which had been taken apart below and loaded on their backs. On the July day when the new pass was formally opened, ox-wagons travelled down the pass without, it is said, once using their brakes.

Now we were on our way to see the Elands' Path, not by Sir Lowry's old road but on one modernized and reconstructed, along which we zoomed up the mountain side. Unlike the Elephants' Road, the Elands' was still visible in patches, its way marked by a line of electric pylons, but it was only from the other side of the mountains that we could approach it. Past the summit, where a notice said Steenbras Dam, we turned left to the Steenbras railway siding and on foot made our way over the railway line, up the mountain, the pylons on our left. Here was a fenced-off area and a track—a notice board told us it was the old Gantouw, the elands' path.

We stood at the top among the grey needle rocks and watched the path drop down the mountain side towards the valley and the sea—perpendicular, one traveller had called it—over grey and orange rocks scored with the inches-deep ruts made by countless bygone wagon wheels. We stooped and touched them: in parts their surface had been worn satin-smooth. When it is fine, a great view of False Bay lies below, but that day the country was hidden by mist. We looked down the steep track, the burnt proteas on either side rustling in an extraordinarily eerie way, each dark branch with a dark burnt cap, and the mist swirled between. It is not often the past intrudes on the present with violence, but as we looked, our flesh crawled.

There were frail, magenta-pink gladiolus-like flowers poking up among the blackened bushes. They must have shared this trail with the eland and later with the oxen. Did any man, we wondered, who had brought a wagon up that face ever have eyes tranquil enough to see them; or was he too busy closing them and saying 'Amen'?

For all the fine new road close to us, and the mountains' proximity to Cape Town, we knew that parts were still as little known as in ox-wagon days, and as inaccessible and lonely as when the Marsh Rose, *Orothamus zeyheri*, of the protea family, was found here in the last century by the botanist, Carl Zeyher. Botanists still tell the story of how for 50 years it was thought to be extinct, until—in the way of such things—it turned up on the stand of a flower-seller in Adderley Street, its pomegranate-red rose-like blooms quickly drawing attention. We thought of it, as we picked our way back through the protea scrub, of how people had hunted it here, had found it, tried to grow it and lost it, and how—still battling to save it—they had begun to think of it as a symbol of the devastated disappearing beauty of the Cape.

We were to remember it again at Caledon and at Hermanus, and now as we took the road from Sir Lowry's Pass, past Elgin with its apple blossom—still the route to the east—we talked of it idly, and of its relatives, the Blushing Bride from Fransch Hoek Mountains that had been saved from extinction, and of the Golden Protea, *Mimetes stokoei*, that not long ago grew in the Paardeberg above Kleinmond south of us as we drove, and now had disappeared, probably for good.

We were in the mood for such talk, for we were going to **Caledon** to see the flowers. This little town—named, like so many others—after a governor, spells flowers today, for here every spring is staged the major wild flower show of the country, and at the same time its wild flower reserve is a spring sight almost without parallel.

It was bright sunshine when we walked through the reserve at the entrance to Venster Kloof, every daisy flower open, the gazanias like velvet leopards, so bright and fierce were they, and—we remember in particular—the keurbooms a mass of pink and blue and purple babianas flowering with abandon even in the pathways.

Caledon's first flower show was held in 1892. Since then it has become one of the South African tourist draws—together with the other seven or eight shows at centres like Darling, Clanwilliam and Tulbagh: to drive through the countryside at this time is to understand that this South-West is—if briefly—one of the astonishing flower sights of the world. It is at the shows that flower-lovers see the individual blooms in detail and learn about them (there is usually a labelled section): in the veld, they may look at them but never pick, for the Cape's flowers are now protected by stringent laws.

Flower seasons—roughly from the middle of August until October—depend on weather, and the dates of the shows are never settled far ahead: so that as winter progresses tourist offices, and Kirstenbosch itself, are bombarded by requests for dates. The Caledon show is usually in September.

This whole area is flower-rich and famous for heaths and proteas in particular, 'daisy' flowers of many species, and a wealth of bulbous flowers: the most sought-after is perhaps the Caledon bluebell, a gladiolus with a single mauve or purple bell, that people have hunted almost to extinction. At this show it is possible to find nearly 500 different flower species, perhaps 100 of them ericas, which makes it and its wild flowers unique.

In 1975 a Marsh Rose was on show, possibly for the last time. The *same* flower was exhibited at the Hermanus and Betty's Bay shows as well, and it was the rarest flower in the world.

Hermanus, less than an hour's drive to the south of Caledon, has a flower show every second year. Even more important is the Eddie Rubenstein Reserve near the village, for it is a Marsh Rose reserve where some of these strange beautiful flowers flourished until a little while ago. What happened here made a crime story of the century. One night a thief crept in and dug up and stole a plant. In a sense he took the lot. His boots were infected with the killer fungus disease that had destroyed others of the protea family, and he infected the whole community.

When we returned to Cape Town that evening across the **Cape Flats,** we drove through kilometres of small trees and scrub growing luxuriantly out of the white sand. The Flats are the tongue of land, once under the sea, lying between the Peninsula and its interior, a barrier to the early people almost as formidable as the mountains beyond it because wagons sank into the soft deep sand, making journeys into nightmares.

John Montagu brought the first hard road across the Flats in the 1840s, and farmers and travellers blessed him as they did Sir Lowry Cole.

Today we know that he unwittingly opened a Pandora's box, freeing evils of which he never dreamed, for the trees he introduced mostly from Australia to bind the blowing sand, the Port Jackson willow and the rooikrans and others, took over the sand and finally parts of the South-West, and because their vigour and vitality are greater than that of the wild plants—the incomparable, beautiful plants that grow in this corner of the world alone—they have become a major threat to the Cape flora, and a head- and heartache for all who love the Cape.

One of the routes that visitors to Cape Town are always urged to follow is the **Four Passes Drive** over Helshoogte, Fransch Hoek Pass to Villiersdorp, from here over Viljoen's Pass and back to Cape Town via Sir Lowry's Pass. It can easily be done in a day, although it is more fun to do stretches at a time, slowly and exploring on the way.

The **High Noon Wild Animal Kingdom** beyond Villiersdorp is worth a long look too. In 1973 two cheetah cubs were born here that created something of a furore because they were the first to be born in captivity, and High Noon was in the news. Cheetahs, perhaps the most beautiful of our wild animals, are one of the South African species in danger of extinction, so that a cheetah born in captivity is of particular interest. Mr John Spense, the keeper, found them almost by accident, for nobody had noticed their mother's pregnancy. He reared them in his bedroom and they were South Africa's most publicized twins. Photographs of them being fed by bottle showed cubs smiling gently as if they were drinking cream—and they were. People took one look at them and rushed off to send money to the Endangered Wild Life Fund.

We took our time, too, when we set out for the north. The route to Tulbagh is rich in many things, including history, for here came Pieter Potter, an explorer of Van Riebeeck's day, seeking a road through these mountains stretching northwards, and after him travellers who had cut through them by the Roodezand, the Red Sand, Pass near Tulbagh: Roodezand is a name familiar from the old journals.

We drove to Tulbagh through Paarl and Wellington. This had once been Wagonmakers' Valley, because a wagon builder had set up shop here in the 1700s, to be followed soon by others—it was the day when wagon-making was the biggest single industry in the country— and in 1840 it was named after the Duke of Wellington. The Governor, Sir George Napier, had been in a tizzy about it: it was a disgrace that no Cape town bore the duke's name, so Wellington this became.

Beyond it we went north, and then east through the mountains, alongside the Klein Berg River through the **Tulbagh Pass,** much the same route that Van Riebeeck's man had spied, only now we looked, not for Hottentots and leopards, but the Blue Train. Then we were at **Tulbagh** lying at the head of the long north-south valley between the parallel mountain ranges, the Land of Waveren, Willem Adriaan van der Stel had called it after Holland's Waveren family, and sometimes people use the name today, rolling around on their tongues the sonorous old words.

People came to Tulbagh now mainly for two reasons, wine and houses, the wine from the three estates to the west and north— Montpellier, Twee Jongegezellen and Theuniskraal—and the buildings that have arisen in the town in the last decade, for here is South Africa's greatest restoration project.

Until 28th September 1969, this was a tranquil little town of wide streets and old houses. On September 29th it was hit by the worst earthquake in South African history, and as the mountains blazed and the earth shook, the town disintegrated. Eleven people died, many more were injured, and 80 per cent of the houses were damaged or destroyed.

Overnight the town made headlines. South Africa had lost an historic centre and people who never before had heard of Church Street—the fine through street—were roused. Within days, private people, experts and organizations concerned with preservation—the Simon van der Stel Foundation, the Historical Homes of South Africa, and others—were banding together in a unique common action to rescue and restore. All Church Street was declared a national monument and restored in its entirety—and with authenticity—to its old beauty.

Fire has often laid bare the secrets of old houses in South Africa making their detailed reconstruction possible: the earthquake did the same. A hundred and fifty years before, the traveller, William Burchell, had made a sketch of Church Street, and this, too, showed the detail of what had once been. Out went the corrugated iron roofs, the verandahs, modern extensions and ornaments, and in their place arose

Fanlight, Stellenbosch

The slave bell, De Hoop, Fransch Hoek

Two splendid old winepresses on display at the Oude Meester Stellenryck Wine Museum in Stellenbosch

Cape gannets and cormorants on the west coast

The Karamat of Sheik Yusuf

Cape Dutch houses, white-washed, gabled, thatched, correct to the last detail—the elegant Ou Pastorie, the De Wet House designed by Thibault in 1812, the church—the oldest one surviving in its entirety in the Cape—now a museum, and many more.

To understand fully the excitement Tulbagh has caused, it is necessary to know of the new flowering of interest in old buildings, old furniture, and other Africana, and the reawakened enthusiasm these have roused. Tulbagh, in particular, concentrated interest. How many old Cape Dutch houses still existed, people began to ask after the earthquake, and how many old buildings?

In 1974 Hans Fransen, former curator of the Stellenbosch Museum, gave an answer. He estimated the number of thatched homesteads and village houses surviving at about 925, not including minor houses and the hundreds of small flat-roofed ones of the Cape: and in the *Simon van der Stel Bulletin* of September listed the towns richest in old architecture. Tulbagh was sixth on the list, surpassed by—in order of excellence—Cape Town, Stellenbosch, Paarl, Worcester and Graaff-Reinet, while the best preserved all-over towns were Elim, Wupperthal and McGregor, the little town north-east of Caledon.

The town today has a good restaurant, Die Paddagang, specializing in traditional Cape food. It was closed the day we were there, which taught us another lesson—always book ahead. North of the town lie the **Great Winterhoek Mountains,** immortalized by at least two famous South Africans. Marloth, the botanist, used to climb here, pronouncing the view from the top 'ecstatic': General Smuts, looking at the colour, line and majestry of the mountains, could not think, in his long experience of scenery, of anything more lovely.

From Tulbagh we went not north but south down the valley with the Witzenberg mountains on our left—they had given their name to one of our early white wines that most of us remember still—and on our right the Elandskloofberge. We drove through a bare hard landscape with the sun biting and the wind blowing. Along this route Alys Fane Trotter had gone in the 1890s, riding her bicycle, through the same heat and dust and exquisite colours, and as the wind tore past us, we wondered how her long skirts had fared.

A little past Wolseley, she had struck north-east through the mountains along Mitchell's Pass to the plateau beyond, and we followed her spoor. No-one can escape from mountains in this South-West, or their tales, and many stories had been made here. One of the early ones was that of Jan Mostert, the farmer, who built the first horrific road, Mostert's Hoek Pass, over the mountains between the Tulbagh valley and the country to the north-east, the Warm Bokkeveld. Then in 1848 came Mitchell's Pass, following the Breede River as it cut through the mountains, named after Charles Mitchell, Surveyor-General and engineer. The pass was built by Andrew Bain and was the first great outlet from the south-west to the north. For a while it was one of the best-known stretches of road in the country, for after diamonds were discovered, this was the diamond road from the south-west to Kimberley, tough, harsh and dusty, littered with skeletons, beer cans and dreams, carrying everything from wheel barrows to coaches.

It knew a good many of the world's adventurers and, in later days when the traffic had been diverted to the east, Alys Fane Trotter as well, who found a country beyond the pass once again deserted and lonely, sand and renosterbos and milk bush, an ostrich in the dust, a lone Jewish store-keeper observing the Passover in a room beside the road.

The route we followed, modernized and concreted now, was almost the same as Bain's and Alys Trotter's, and a little Mostert's too, for his track still cuts through the pass at the northern end, where a monument stands. Nobody with a feeling for past adventures can pass along this way, or indeed any of the other old roads of South Africa, without a quickening of the blood. The odds are that if they stop and walk quietly along them and in the veld about they will find a keepsake—a cartridge case, a button, a bullet, a buckle, an old-fashioned bottle under a milk bush half buried in sand; and these, on the wide desolate lonely uplands, can be as evocative as any treasure that comes out of the sea.

From **Ceres** village, charming and fruitful as its name, on the northern side of Mitchell's Pass, we drove back to join the main road again at the southern end of the Tulbagh valley. To cut through the mountains between us and Cape Town, we now took the road through one of the most famous of the passes of the Cape, **Bain's Kloof.**

This was named after Andrew Geddes Bain, and rightly so: it was his in a very real sense. Most of the other Cape roads had followed a path of some kind—animals' or men's—but not this one. Men had hunted for a way through these mountains, and never found one; and when Mitchell's Pass was planned through the far range, it became imperative to find a pass through the first range to connect Cape Town with it and the world beyond. Andrew Bain himself spotted a wild trackless kloof leading in the right direction: thrilling with excitement, he surveyed it, and so found his 'North-West Passage'.

Thomas, his son, worked on the road with him, leaving it every now and then to dash down to Cape Town to court his 17-year-old love, Johanna de Smidt: and in 1854 the pass was officially opened.

The present road is still almost exactly the same as Bain's road, and the scenery as wild as when he knew it. When Capetonians want to impress visitors with grand views close to the city, it is often here they take them, up the winding road on the southern—the Wellington—side, with its low walls and oak trees on the edges, and over the summit, from where the road runs through mountains as fierce as any in Africa, past Dacre's Pulpit, the great rock hanging low over the road, precipices, rock masses, and cuttings through them, with strange colours and stranger shapes, the Witte River in a chasm below, the white stones in its bed visible from far.

There are leopards still in the Cape mountains, and this is where we always hope to see one. The pass has its lesser pleasures, too, the ever-popular picnics, *the* most South African amusement of all.

We had a personal memory of one on the southern side, vineyards below us, and the first southwester, the rain-bringing winter wind, blowing, the advancing rain blotting out the wine towns—first Paarl, and next Wellington—and reaching Bain's Kloof itself: of throwing a macintosh over a bush, crouching under it, and drinking a vintage Chateau Libertas for morning tea. It was a Boland memory of rain, the smell of mountain bush and laughter: the Cape mountains, which draw people to them for their wildness, know plenty of these other memories too.

The most modern of the Cape's passes is **Du Toit's Kloof** to the south of Bain's Kloof, connecting Paarl with Worcester: the original cattle track over the mountains is a stone's throw from it at the summit of the pass. Italian prisoners of war worked on this splendid road during World War II, so that we, as well, can claim our Roman road. We went over it to Worcester, yet another town named by Lord Charles Somerset, this time after his brother, the Marquis of Worcester, now the centre of the wine and fruit-producing Breede River valley. It is a bustling place set against mountains, which are exquisite in the long lights of early morning and late afternoon, and the gateway to the Hex River Valley beyond.

On the koppies to the north of the town is the **Karoo National Botanic Garden,** eldest offspring of Kirstenbosch and a succulent enthusiast's dream, for here (the rainfall is usually no more than 25 cm a year) flourish the plants of the arid areas, some no bigger than a five cent piece, others true trees, some white as the quartz around them, others brown and speckled like the stones. In October it blazes with the flowers of, in particular, the mesembryanthemum family, succulents that burst into a frenzy of bloom, so dense that it is hardly possible to find a centimetre of bare space, so brilliant that visitors from softer countries sometimes here close their eyes to rest them.

It was flowers again that took us to **Darling.** Darling is the little town between Cape Town and Saldanha Bay, lying in the low coastal plain not far from the Atlantic and swept by the cold Atlantic winds. In spring time the monotonous-looking sandy veld around it bursts into a bloom with a highly individual frail beauty that enchants all who see it; and some time, usually in September, a wild flower show is held that is, if not the biggest, the loveliest of all.

We took the road through the Swartland, the Black Land, which Van Riebeeck himself is said to have named, leaving on our left Bloubergstrand where the restaurant, Ons Huisie, with its traditional Cape food, had made a name.

It was open, undulating country we drove through, wheatlands mostly, with patches of scrub, sheep and long unbroken horizons. We remember of it that spring arum lilies blooming in ditches beside the road, the soft burring speech—the Malmesbury burr we knew of old from Smuts's speeches—and button spiders. The Cape wheatlands, green and gold, are the home of this little dark spider, relative of America's 'Black Widow', which is our only truly venomous species: although we talked of it and longed to view it (at a distance), never one did we see.

Far over to our right was Riebeeck West where Smuts was born and caught his burr; and Tulbagh beyond. We left them behind us, turning left towards the sea.

We came to Darling through flowers, and in the village itself, crammed with people, it was a gala flower day. At the entrance to the hall where the show was held we were greeted by a courtly old gentleman with grandee manners, welcoming us and others as if we had been important, specially invited guests. He was, we found, a Duckitt, and the Duckitts—as everyone knows—are Darling kings. He set the tone, for everyone was happy and full of cheer, crowding about the thousands of wild flowers (all picked by permit), grouped in bowls about the room.

Presently old Mr Duckitt sent us out to a Duckitt farm to see the plants growing, and then we went on to the flower reserve a little beyond the village, a field starred with flowers, cropped low by the winds, monsonias, nemesias, and a host of delicate bulbous ones, including something new to us, a carpet of little wine-cups, *Geissorrhiza rochensis*, purple with claret hearts. There were many species we did not know, and here Hilda Mason's *Western Cape Sandveld Flowers* was not only help but keenest pleasure. Hilda is Eric Axelson's wife, and he wrote the introduction to her book, history and flowers mingling in a very proper way.

Most gardeners know **Bok Baai** a little way away on the coast at least by name, because the seed of the Bok Baai vygies, the brilliant low spring-flowering succulents they grow in their gardens, came originally from here. For us it meant the name Duckitt again, for Hildagonda Duckitt, who wrote the early cookery book *Hilda's Where Is It*, used to stay on this Duckitt property. The pretty custom of sending South African chincherinchees abroad was Hildagonda's inspiration. These long-stemmed, starry white flowers of the lily family are picked in bud and despatched from South Africa, arriving in Britain, the Continent and the United States in prime condition, the buds opening slowly and lasting in water for several weeks. Hildagonda about 1880 picked a bunch in the veld near Darling and sent a parcel to friends in London, causing a sensation, and so the trade in them was born.

Northwards we turned from flowers to fossils. Hopefield, a little north of Darling, is famous fossil-wise for the bones of ancient man discovered on a nearby farm and dubbed Saldanha Man. Beyond Hopefield is **Langebaanweg,** known today for the Air Force base there, for the phosphate that is now mined, and for the extraordinary and exciting fossil fauna that has been turned up in the mining operations during the last two decades—including the fossil bones of a bear, a relative of China's giant panda, the only bear record south of the Sahara. It lived perhaps four to five million years ago, in company with a great assembly of mammals, including Hipparion, the three-toed horse, and giant otters, birds, reptiles and fishes.

It is no use thinking one can fossil sight-see here, for the excavations are closed to the public.

Langebaan, 18 kilometres to the south-west, offers sights of a different kind, for here the long, peaceful, unspoilt stretch of water, Langebaan lagoon, the vast shallow flats, the salt marshes, with their reeds and rushes, make a bird place, a wet-land, that attracts in summer some 100 000 birds of various species—and the hundreds of ornithologists and bird-watchers who come to see them. There are the waders, like the eye-catching flamingoes, and all the smaller breeds—sandpipers, plovers, turnstones, knots and many more—water fowl, and the land birds like the swallows that roost in the reeds. More than half the birds are migratory. Professor W. R. Siegfried, director of the Percy Fitzpatrick Institute for African Ornithology, calls Langebaan 'probably the single most important wintering ground in Southern Africa for migratory shore birds from northern Europe'.

So for ornithologists this is a place of particular—of world—importance; and they have anxiously watched the development of

Saldanha Bay into which the lagoon leads, and of Saldanha itself into an important port to cater for the new Sishen iron ore project.

Saldanha, with all the new activities, is no beauty spot, but the bay is a fine natural harbour: indeed, if there had been a good supply of fresh water there, the Dutch might never have plumped for Table Bay. It has had its share of wrecks and treasure, treasure below the water and above, for the guano islands in and near it have yielded riches worth millions in rands.

Today Saldanha is the centre, not so much of the guano as the fishing industry on the west coast. Yet the islands remain of great interest ornithologically as well as commercially. Dassen Island, a little to the south, is a Jackass Penguin stronghold. It was named Dassen or Dassie Island after the huge numbers of dassies the early sailors found there—how they got there nobody ever knew for sure, although C. J. Skead suggests they could have rafted there. Malagas Island, lying in the entrance to the bay, was named after the gannets. Jutten and Marcus Islands also have their bird populations, and so do Meeuwen—named after the gulls' cry—and Skaapen or Sheep Island, which took its name from the sheep left to succour ship-wrecked sailors.

The name Jutten was based on the Dutch word for davit. Lawrence Green had two stories about it which we remembered—he said the penguins had been known to bring up coins from the wrecks below in their beaks and put them in their nests; and that years ago the island was invaded by button spiders, blown across from the mainland by a south-east wind. They lurked under every stone and bit 20 people.

An item of history here that has always fascinated us was the deliberate sinking of the Dutch ship *Middelburg* by the first officer, Abraham de Smidt, in 1781 in the bay to prevent her falling into British hands. He was the progenitor of the South African De Smidts; and if he had sailed away in an intact ship there would have been no De Smidts at Groote Schuur and Westbrooke, and no Georgina Bain to write her delicious memoirs.

From Saldanha the road goes north to **Velddrif** on the shallow half-moon of St Helena Bay. Vasco da Gama named the bay, and his men hunted whales and seals here, and filled their casks with the soft water of the Berg River. We remember the wind here, the dried fish rattling, the crayfish, the fishing boats, and how the locals called the place Vellerif. But even clearer to us now are the last reaches of the Berg River before it flowed into the bay. We had known the Great Berg—the Mountain—River where it rose in the wineland mountains above Fransch Hoek, followed its clear waters northwards to its junction with the Klein Berg, and so westwards until south of Velddrif it reached the sea. For the last 70 kilometres it is navigable, passing through low swampy flats, above which stand out the masts and upperworks of trawlers. On a rainy day the scene resembles Holland. A heron fishes for his dinner among the sedges; here and there are little white-walled graveyards where the sea-wind sighs.

We reached the main road again at Piketberg and went north through the citrus groves of the Olifants River valley—we drank fresh orange juice at Citrusdal, and continued to **Clanwilliam,** smelling the early orange blossom, rich and sweet. Clanwilliam, when we reached it, was bustling, full of flowers and bougainvillea blooming. We went through it and headed for the north-east, away from the national road, over the **Pakhuis Pass.**

Now we were back again in mountain country and climbing a road which was spectacular, even for the mountains of the Cape which are mostly grand, with rocks of marvellous shapes and cliffs of even more marvellous colour, with proteas in bloom and sand olives with narrow yellow-green leaves pressed against the rocks, and when we got out and walked, with the fynbos scent. On the top, to our left, was something we would take our time over on our return, the grave of Louis Leipoldt, the poet; but now we went on, over the other side.

The mountain, we found, was a barrier: behind us were the wheat-lands, orange groves and orchards, and ahead was desert. It lay there, shimmering quietly, bare and beckoning. But it was for another day, and some 40 kilometres from Clanwilliam we turned to our right on the road to Wupperthal. At the junction of the roads was **The Englishman's Grave,** with its broken gum tree beside it. We stopped to read the inscription. It ran:

BRAVE AND TRUE
IN SACRED AND LOVING
MEMORY OF
GRAHAM VINICOMBE WINCHESTER
CLOWES
LIEUTENANT 1ST BATTN
THE GORDON HIGHLANDERS
SON OF THE LATE
WINCHESTER CLOWES OF
HITCHIN, HERTS
KILLED IN ACTION NEAR
THIS SPOT
ON THE 20TH JANUARY
1901

It is a lonely grave and landmark, in autumn and winter days desolate, but that day it was ringed with wild flowers, mainly little lapeirousias the colour of violets. Surely nobody living remembers Graham Clowes of Hertfordshire. Yet somebody had thought of him that day, for a little bunch of the purple flowers, tied with a bit of string, had been placed upon his grave. They were still fresh.

Soon the road dropped sharply into the Bidouw Valley, that day jewelled with colour, and we followed the path to **Wupperthal,** the Rhenish Mission Station in a valley of the Cedarberg. It is an enchanting little Coloured village with clear running water, terraces of thatched cottages, with gardens and tumbles of bright flowers. It is busy as well with shoe-making and agriculture, and the drying of the rooibos tea, indigenous to the mountains, a strange living pocket on its own to find among the mountains, and one people travel far to see.

We did not wish to leave, but we had a time to keep on the **Pakhuis Pass,** and here at the top we stopped. Close to the road on the right hand side was a line of cliffs, all deep colour and piled rocks, and at one end a shallow Bushman shelter in which lay Louis Leipoldt's grave.

Leipoldt is most often thought of today as poet, but he was more, writer of elegant prose, naturalist, physician and surgeon, master of Cape wine and food, ardent lover of South Africa, and in particular of Clanwilliam mountains, and as well a 'human catalyst' as his friends called him. He was a great figure in his day, not very far distant, and he came from these mountains, for his grandfather had been Rhenish minister at Wupperthal, and his father Dutch Reformed minister at Clanwilliam. He had wanted to die among the mountains, but had not; so his ashes had been buried here instead in a grave piled with stones, backed by a sandstone wall with faded Bushman paintings.

We found a trickle of water nearby, where the artists had once surely drunk: there were *kliphout* growing out of the cliffs, and small trees with little dark cones and patches of bright leaves.

We had our lunch under one. It should, á la Leipoldt, perhaps have been zebra meat rubbed with *blinkblaar* leaves, fried in its own deep chrome yellow fat (a recipe pre-dating conservationists) or leguaan steaks, cooked in a three-legged stew pot with coriander seeds and parsley leaves. Or the fat hen, the inside of which Leipoldt used to rub with lemon and green ginger, braised in a pot with lard and red wine, and then stuffed with sweet Hanepoot grapes—we were sure he would have managed to cook it to perfection over a picnic fire. And there should have been, as well, a Chateau Libertas, his beloved wine, to go with the zebra.

As we ate, we remembered his poetry, so full of Boland joys; how as a doctor he had earned honours abroad and at home had coped with bilharzia and malaria; how the love and respect he brought to good food and wine had been homeric; how he had caused a furore by proclaiming that babies should drink wine instead of mother's milk; and how the old Coloured woman who had taught him cooking had hit him with a wooden spoon when he went wrong.

Splendid moment—the very bottle in our basket was beatified! We leaned against the rocks, where the Bushman before Leipoldt had passed, and soaked it all up. We were three hours away from Cape Town. Happy city to have the sea at its face and this at its back, to have for half a morning's motoring, the land that Leipoldt sang of. We knew that we should be turning back, but all the same it was a long time before we moved. We sat there instead talking of Cape things, friendliness, food, wine and old song, enjoying the sun and the wind, and for company the dassies in the rocks and the ghosts that stirred.

Glossary of South African words

✤

Biltong: *Dried meat*
Blinkblaar: *A wild tree with shiny leaves*
Braai: *Barbecue*
Cocopan: *Small ore truck*
Dorp: *Village*
Frikadelle: *Spiced mincemeat balls*
Fynbos: *Cape coastal scrub*
Kloof: *Ravine*
Konfyt: *Preserve of whole fruit*
Kraal: *African home/village/town*
Kranz: *Precipice*
Muti: *African medicine*
Naartjie: *Tangerine-like fruit*
Nek: *A narrow pass*
Outspan: *to unyoke oxen, or a place where they are unyoked*
Poort: *Narrow pass through mountains*
Trekboer: *Nomadic farmer*
Werf: *Yard*

Selected Bibliography

❧

ALLEN, Vivien: *Kruger's Pretoria*, Cape Town, 1971

AXELSON, Eric: *Congo to Cape*, London, 1973

BAIN, Andrew Geddes: *Journals* (Van Riebeeck Soc.), Cape Town, 1949

BARNARD, K. H.: *South African Shore-Life*, Cape Town, 1954

BARROW, Brian: *Song of a Dry River*, Cape Town, 1975

BECK, Hastings: *Meet the Cape Food*, Cape Town, 1956

BIERMANN, Barrie: *Red Wine in South Africa*, Cape Town, 1971

BOND, John: Men who helped to make South Africa: The English-speaking Contribution: Reprinted from *The Star*, Johannesburg

BOSHIER, Adrian and BEAUMONT, Peter: 'Mining in Southern Africa and the Emergence of Modern Man,' *Optima*, Vol. 22, No. 1. Johannesburg, March 1972

BRAIN, C. K. and L. H.: *How Life Arose in South Africa*, Johannesburg, 1974

BROSTER, Joan, A.: *Red Blanket Valley*, Johannesburg, 1967

BROWN, A. C. (edit): *A History of Scientific Endeavour in South Africa*, Cape Town, 1977

BULPIN, T. V.: *Discovering Southern Africa*, Cape Town, 1970

BURCHELL, William: *Travels in South Africa*, Vols. I, II, *reprint*, London, 1953

BURMAN, Jose: *So High the Road*, Cape Town, 1963
Guide to the Garden Route, Cape Town, 1973

CAMPBELL, G. G.: 'A Review of Scientific Investigations in the Tongaland Area of Northern Natal': *Trans. Roy. Soc. S. Afr.* 38, Part 4, Nov. 1969

CARTWRIGHT, A. P.: *Valley of Gold*, Cape Town, 1961
The Corner House, Cape Town and Johannesburg, 1965
The First South African, Cape Town, 1971
Gold, Cape Town, 1973

CHILD, Daphne: *Saga of the South African Horse*, Cape Town, 1967

CHILVERS, Hedley A.: *Out of the Crucible*, revised by Alexander Campbell, Cape Town, 1948

CLARK, J. Desmond: *The Prehistory of Southern Africa*, London, 1959
CLEMENT, A. J.: *The Kalahari and its Lost City*, Cape Town, 1967
COLLIER, Joy: *Portrait of Cape Town*, Cape Town, 1961
  The Purple and the Gold, Cape Town
CONOLLY, Denis: *The Tourist in South Africa*, Durban (undated)
COOK, Mary Alexander: *The Cape Kitchen*, Stellenbosch (undated)
CORNELL, Fred: *The Glamour of Prospecting*, London, 1920
COURTENAY-LATIMER, M., Smith, G. G., Bokelmann H. and Batten
  A.: *The Flowering Plants of the Tsitsikama Forest and Coastal
  National Park*, Pretoria, 1967
DART, Raymond A., with Craig, Dennis: *Adventures with the Missing
  Link*, London, 1959
DE BOSDARI, C.: *Wines of the Cape*, Cape Town, 1955
  Cape Dutch Houses and Farms, Cape Town, 1964
DE KLERK, W. A.: *The White Wines of South Africa*, Cape Town,
  1967
DESMOND, Judy: *Traditional Cookery in Southern Africa*, Cape Town,
  1962
DUCKITT, Hildagonda: *Hilda's Where is It*, Cape Town (1904 edition)
DU PLESSIS, I. D.: *The Cape Malays*, Cape Town, 1972
DIJKMAN Mrs: *Mrs Dijkman's Cookery and Recipe Book*, Paarl, 1905
ELIOVSON, Sima: *Namaqualand in Flower*, Johannesburg, 1972
ELLIOT, Aubrey: *The Magic World of the Xhosa*, London, 1970
FAIRBRIDGE, Dorothea: *Historic Houses of South Africa*, London, 1922
  Historic Farms of South Africa, London, 1931
FARINI, G. A.: *Through the Kalahari Desert*, reprint, Cape Town, 1973
FITZPATRICK, Percy: *Jock of the Bushveld*, London, 1907
FORBES, Vernon S.: *Pioneer Travellers in South Africa*, Cape Town,
  1965
FOUCHE, Leo (edit): *Mapungubwe*, Cambridge, 1937
FRANSEN, Hans and COOK, Mary: *The Old Houses of the Cape*, Cape
  Town, 1965
GARDNER, Captain Guy, A.: *Mapungubwe*, Pretoria, 1963
GERBER, Hilda: *Traditional Cookery of the Cape Malays*, Cape Town,
  1958
GILL, E. L.: *A First Guide to South African Birds*, Cape Town, 1936
GODFREY, Denis: *The Enchanted Door*, Cape Town, 1963
GREEN, Lawrence: *So Few are Free*, Cape Town, 1946
  In the Land of Afternoon, Cape Town, 1949
  Grow Lovely, Growing Old, Cape Town, 1951
  I Heard the Old Men Say, Cape Town, 1964
  A Taste of the South-Easter, Cape Town, 1971

GUTSCHE, Thelma: *No Ordinary Woman*, Cape Town, 1966
 The Bishop's Lady, Cape Town, 1970
HANDS, Phyllis, and *The Argus: Enjoy Wine*, Cape Town, 1976
HELLER, David: 'Cape Silver', *University Extra Mural Studies*, Cape
 Town
HENDEY, Q. B.: *Early Man*, Cape Town, 1973
 'Wildlife Paradise', *African Wildlife*, Vol. 29, No. 1.
 Johannesburg, Autumn, 1975
HEWITT, Alice: *Cape Cookery*, Cape Town, 1891
HOCKING, Anthony: *Diamonds*, Cape Town, 1973
 Old Kimberley, Cape Town, 1974
HOCKLY, Harold Edward: *The Story of the British Settlers of 1820 in
 South Africa*, 2nd edit., Cape Town, 1957
HOOK, D. B.: *Tis But Yesterday*, London, 1911
HOW, Marian Walsham: *The Mountain Bushmen of Basutoland*,
 Pretoria, 1962
HUGHES, Betty: *Walking Through History*, Cape Town, 1972
JAMES, Angela and Hills, Nina: *Mrs John Brown*, London, 1937
KENNEDY, R. F. (compiler): *Shipwrecks on and off the coasts of
 Southern Africa*, Johannesburg, 1955
 Africana Repository, Cape Town, 1965
KNOX, Graham: *Estate Wines of South Africa*, Cape Town, 1976
KNOX, Patricia and Gutsche, Thelma: *Do You Know Johannesburg*,
 Unie-Volkspers, 1947
LAWRENCE, R. F.: *A Conspectus of Spiders*, Pretoria, 1964
 'Insects, Arachnids and Peripatus,' *A History of Scientific
 Endeavour in South Africa*, Cape Town, 1977: Unpublished MS
LEIPOLDT, C. Louis: *300 Years of Cape Wines*, Cape Town, 1952
 Leipoldt's Cape Cookery, Cape Town, 1976
LE VAILLANT, F.: *Travels into the Interior Parts of Africa in the years
 1780-85*, translated from the French, Dublin, 1790
LEWCOCK, Ronald: *Early Nineteenth Century Architecture in South
 Africa*, Cape Town, 1963
LEWIS, Cecil and EDWARDS, G. E.: *Historical Records of the Church
 of the Province of South Africa*, London, 1934
LEYDS, G. A.: *A History of Johannesburg*, Cape Town, 1964
LIGHTON, Conrad: *Cape Floral Kingdom*, Cape Town, 1960
LISTER, Georgina: *Reminiscences*, Johannesburg, 1960
MARAIS, Eugene N.: *My Friends the Baboons*, London, 1956
MASON, Hilda: *Western Cape Sandveld Flowers*, Cape Town, 1972
MASON, Revil: *Prehistory of the Transvaal*, Johannesburg, 1962

MERRIMAN, N. J.: *Cape Journals*, Cape Town, 1957
METROWICH, F. C.: *Scotty Smith*, Cape Town, 1962
MOFFAT, Robert: *Missionary Labours in Southern Africa*, London, 1842
MORRIS, Donald, R.: *The Washing of the Spears*, London, 1966
MOSSOP, E.: *Old Cape Highways*, Cape Town (undated)
MOUNTAIN, Edgar D.: *Geology of Southern Africa*, Cape Town, 1968
MUIR, John: *Know Your Cape*, Cape Town, 1975
  Guide to Cape Town and the Western Cape, Cape Town, 1976
NATHAN, Manfred: *The Huguenots in South Africa*, Johannesburg, 1939
NEWMAN, Kenneth: *Roadside Birds of South Africa*, Cape Town and Johannesburg, 1969
OBERHOLSTER, J. J.: *The Historical Monuments of South Africa*, Cape Town, 1972
PALMER, Eve: *The Plains of Camdeboo*, London, 1966
PATON, Alan: *Cry, the Beloved Country*, London, 1948
PEARSE, R. O.: *Barrier of Spears*, Cape Town, 1973
PLUMSTEAD, Edna P.: 'The Influence of Plants and Environment on the Developing Animal Life of Karoo Times', *South African Journal of Science*, Vol. 59, Johannesburg May 1963
  'Three Thousand Million Years of Plant Life in Africa.'
  Annexure to Vol. LXXII, *The Geological So. of South Africa*, No. 11, 1969
PRELLER, Gustaf: *Old Pretoria*, Pretoria, 1938
PRINGLE, Thomas: *Narrative of a Residence in South Africa*, London, 1835
PROZESKY, O. P. M.: *A Field Guide to the Birds of Southern Africa*, London, 1970
REITZ, Deneys: *Commando*, London, 1929
REYNOLDS, G. W.: *The Aloes of South Africa*, Johannesburg, 1950
RIVETT-CARNAC, Dorothy: *Thus Came the English*, Cape Town, 1961
ROBERTS, Austin: *The Mammals of South Africa*, Johannesburg 1951
  Birds of South Africa, revised by McLachlan, G. R. and Liversidge, R.: Cape Town, 1957
ROSENTHAL, Eric: *Gold! Gold! Gold!* New York, 1970
ROWE, Muriel: *They Came from the Sea*, Cape Town, 1968
RYAN, Ray and VERTUE, Eric: *Cape Homesteads*, Cape Town, 1973
SCHOEMAN, S.: *Strike*, Cape Town, 1962
SCHOLTZ, Merwe (edit): *Wine Country*, Cape Town, 1970
SCHREINER, Olive: *The Story of an African Farm* (under nom-de-plume Ralph Iron), London, 1883

SEAGRIEF, S. C.: *The Seaweeds of the Tsitsikama Coastal National Park*, Pretoria, 1967

SKAIFE, S. H.: *African Insect Life*, Cape Town, 1953

SKEAD, C. J.: *Sunbirds of Southern Africa*, Cape Town, 1967

SMAIL, J. L.: *With Shield and Assegai*, Cape Town, 1969

SMITH, Anna H.: *Johannesburg Street Names*, Cape Town, 1971 (edit): *Africana Curiosities*, Johannesburg, 1973 (collector); *Johannesburg Firsts*, Johannesburg, 1976

SMITH, Sir Harry: *Autobiography*, 2 Vols., edit. and with notes by Moore Smith, G. C.: London, 1901

SMITH, J. L. B. and Margaret, M.: *Fish of the Tsitsikama Coastal National Park*, Pretoria, 1966

SMITH, J. L. B.: *High Tide*, Cape Town, 1968
Our Fishes, Johannesburg, 1968

STEENKAMP, Willem: *Land of the Thirst King*, Cape Town, 1975

STEVENSON-HAMILTON, J.: *Wild Life in South Africa*, London, 1947

TABLER, E. C.: *Far Interior*, Cape Town, 1955

TAPSON, Winifred: *Timber and Tides*, Johannesburg, 1961

TELFORD, A. A.: *Johannesburg*, Cape Town, 1969

TIETZ, R. M. and ROBINSON, G. A.: *Tsitsikama Shore*, Pretoria, 1974

TOBIAS, Phillip V.: 'African Cradle of Mankind,' *Optima*, Vol. 25, No. 1, Johannesburg, 1975

TROTTER, A. F.: 'Old Cape Homesteads and their Founders', *Cape Times*, Christmas number, 1898
Old Colonial Houses of the Cape of Good Hope, London, 1900
Old Cape Colony, London, 1903

TYLDON, G.: The Ox-Wagon, *Africana Notes and News*, Vol. 12, No. 2, Johannesburg, June 1956

TYRRELL, Barbara: *Tribal Peoples of Southern Africa*, Cape Town, 1968

ULLMANN, Ernest: *Designs on Life*, Cape Town 1970

VAN H. TULLEKEN, S.: *The Practical Cookery Book for South Africa*, (18th edition), Cape Town, 1943

WALKER, Eric. A.: *A History of Southern Africa*, London, 1968

WALTON, James: *African Village*, Pretoria, 1956
Homesteads and Villages of South Africa, Pretoria, 1963

WILLCOX, A. R.: *The Rock Art of South Africa*, Johannesburg, 1963

WILLIAMS, Alpheus, F.: *Some Dreams Come True*, Cape Town, 1948

WOLHUTER, Harry: *Memories of a Game Ranger*, Johannesburg, 1948

WOODHOUSE, H. C.: *Archaeology in Southern Africa*, Cape Town, 1971

Farming in South Africa, special Van Riebeeck number, Pretoria. March, 1952

The Cape Peninsula, by the staffs of the University of Cape Town and the South African Museum, Cape Town, 1952

Wynboer, Panorama, Lantern (in particular the special commemorative issue, Natal, Vol. XXIII, No. 3. March, 1974), *Africana Notes and News, Simon van der Stel Bulletins, Bantu, Veld and Flora, Journal of the Botanical Society of South Africa, African Wild Life, Koedoe, Custos, Eastern Province Naturalist, Fauna and Flora.*

Index of Persons

❧

Index of Places and Subjects

✤

413

419

TRANSVAAL

Vaal

Parys

N1

Vaal

Kroonstad

Odendaalsrus

Memel

WELKOM

Willem Pretorius
Game Reserve

Winburg

Bethlehem

Golden Gate
National Park

Harrismith

Brandfort

NATAL

BLOEMFONTEIN

Ladybrand

Fauresmith

Jagersfontein

Caledon

Orange

LESOTHO

N1

Verwoerd
Dam

CAPE

Orange Free State

0	80	160	320 Km
0	50	100	200 miles

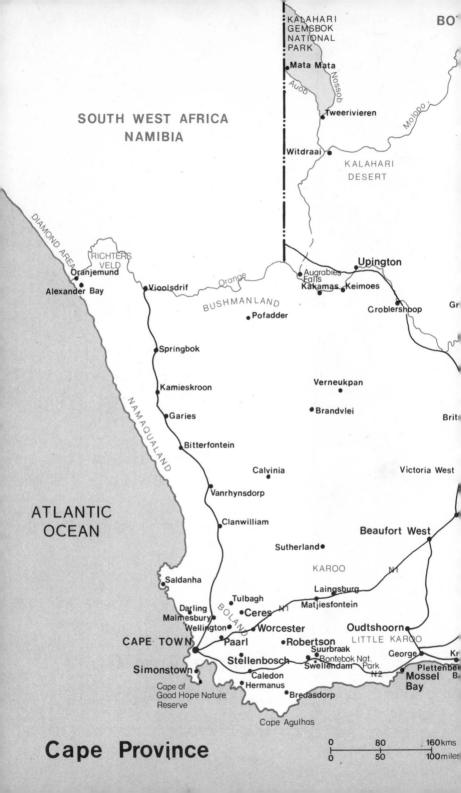